Abuse

Abuse

An Encyclopedia of Causes, Consequences, and Treatments

ROSEMARIE SKAINE, EDITOR

GREENWOOD™

An Imprint of ABC-CLIO, LLC
Santa Barbara, California • Denver, Colorado

Copyright © 2015 by ABC-CLIO, LLC

All rights reserved. No part of this publication may be reproduced, stored in a retrieval system, or transmitted, in any form or by any means, electronic, mechanical, photocopying, recording, or otherwise, except for the inclusion of brief quotations in a review, without prior permission in writing from the publisher.

Library of Congress Cataloging-in-Publication Data

Abuse : an encyclopedia of causes, consequences, and treatments / Rosemarie Skaine, editor.
     pages cm
  Includes bibliographical references.
  ISBN 978-1-61069-514-5 (hardback) — ISBN 978-1-61069-515-2 (e-book)
 1. Family violence—Encyclopedias.   2. Child abuse—Encyclopedias.   3. Sexual abuse—Encyclopedias.   4. Older people—Abuse of—Encyclopedias.   5. Psychological abuse—Encyclopedias.   6. Cyberbullying—Encyclopedias.   I. Skaine, Rosemarie.
  HV6625.A28 2015
  362.03—dc23   2014041222

ISBN: 978-1-61069-514-5
EISBN: 978-1-61069-515-2

19 18 17 16 15   1 2 3 4 5

This book is also available on the World Wide Web as an eBook.
Visit www.abc-clio.com for details.

Greenwood
An Imprint of ABC-CLIO, LLC

ABC-CLIO, LLC
130 Cremona Drive, P.O. Box 1911
Santa Barbara, California 93116-1911

This book is printed on acid-free paper ∞

Manufactured in the United States of America

To my husband, James C. Skaine,
my soul mate and best friend

२

Contents

Acknowledgments

I extend thanks to special people who made this encyclopedia a reality: my sincere appreciation to Maxine Taylor at ABC-CLIO, my editor and mentor; to Barbara Patterson, the project coordinator at ABC-CLIO; Erin Ryan, senior coordinator, editorial operations at ABC-CLIO; and Pete Feely, editorial project manager, Amnet Systems.

I am deeply grateful to my soul mate and lifelong companion, James C. Skaine, for his administrative and creative skill. His love and support helped bring this book to its successful conclusion.

Special thanks to the contributing writers who, with their special skills, expanded the encyclopedia's horizon.

I thank family members Richard L. and Nancy L. Craft Kuehner and William V. and Carolyn E. Guenther Kuehner for their unwavering support.

I remember my friend Cass Paley, of yesteryear, for the dream and the courage to face the morning.

Introduction

Abuse: An Encyclopedia of Causes, Consequences, and Treatments examines what abuse is, who is abused and who or what is the abuser, what harm the abuse causes, and what it takes to treat or prevent abuse.

Abuse is any behavior that intentionally or unintentionally harms or injures. The harm can be physical, mental, emotional, and psychological, and the abused may be an individual, a group, or a society. The abuse may occur over an extended period or it may result from a single incident. If abuse is to be treated and prevented, both voluntary and involuntary behaviors that cause harm must be considered.

Abuse is pervasive in American society. It impacts individuals, groups, and the whole society. Abuse affects people of all ages, in all walks of life, and at all levels of society. Abuse causes negative changes in the behavior and well-being of the abused and impacts the abuser. Death all too often results from abuse.

Causes of Abuse

The causes of abuse are many. A family member may strike another family member in anger, and a cycle of domestic abuse is initiated. One classmate may threaten or intimidate another classmate, and a pattern of bullying begins. A caretaker for an elder person has financial difficulty and fails to provide for that person and the elder person is abandoned. A driver becomes frustrated with traffic and does damage to other drivers and vehicles in anger, beginning a pattern of road rage. A woman becomes the object of attention from a stranger, and the stranger may rape and kill her. A person may have negative beliefs about persons of color and acts on those beliefs by discriminating against those persons. A parent believes in disciplining a child by spanking, but when the spankings become more severe, the abuse increases. These examples reveal a few of the causes of abuse in the United States.

What happens in society, what society affirms as positive, and what society accepts and uses, all contribute to the causes of abuse. Behaviors that society accepts, and even rewards, may produce abuse. Traditionally, it has been acceptable to discipline a child by spanking or hitting. A parent may believe that spanking will instill in the child the desire to do what is right. But the spanking may turn into a beating, and the beating may cause injury or even death. Spanking often produces emotional and psychological wounds that take a lifetime to heal. People believe in spanking because they believe the biblical phrase, "Spare the rod, and spoil the child," justifies it. The rod was not used by the shepherd to punish the sheep. The rod was used to guide the sheep along the right path, and as Psalm 23 states, "Your rod and your staff comfort me." In American society, spanking as a means of imposing discipline often leads to abuse.

Society understands fear and that a person's reaction to fear is usually fight or flight. When the fear is great, even the most timid of individuals will lash out. A bullied child will attack the bully. However, when the fear is great, the bullied child may flee from the bully, and the pain and humiliation may result in suicide, an outcome that has happened in an alarming number of cases.

Some in society exploit fear and increase its harm. "Stand your ground" laws say that an individual armed with a gun can defend herself or himself if she or he reasonably believes that such force is necessary to prevent imminent death or great bodily harm to herself or himself or to another or to prevent the imminent commission of a forcible felony. Traditionally, justifiable self-defense was limited to a person's home. Stand your ground laws permit a person, who can be anywhere in public and feels threatened by another person, to not have to retreat and be justified in using deadly force. These laws and the expansion of who can be permitted to carry a gun have increased gun violence in the United States.

Abuse does not happen in a vacuum; it happens within a context. In the context of American society, the acceptance of violence is a major contributor to abuse. American society has seen an increase in the acceptance of violence as part of everyday life. In sports, when a player violently hits another player, it is considered part of the game, even when the player is seriously injured or dies. Many Americans believe that they have a constitutional right to carry a gun on their person in public, even though the Second Amendment of the Bill of Rights was written to prevent the people from being unarmed if the country was invaded. This belief has increased gun violence. The tragedies in the movie theater in Aurora, Colorado; in the elementary school in Newtown, Connecticut; and at Congresswoman Gabby Gifford's Congress on Your Corner in Tucson, Arizona, are the most well-known recent cases of gun violence, but they are but the tip of the iceberg. Many of those who die from gun violence are unarmed, and some of the unarmed are killed by police.

The violence in the United States and the abuse that results from it are not only produced by guns. The acceptance of violence is a major factor in the abuse that takes place in athletics. At all levels, from children's sports to professional leagues, violence overshadows sportsmanship and teamwork. Aggressive competition accompanies a winning-at-any-cost approach. Rewards are given to the outstanding players who are expected to deliver victories and championships. These players become targets, and, as a result, there has been an alarming increase in injuries and injury-related deaths. It has also produced extensive emotional and psychological abuse. Child athletes are among those who are abused physically, psychologically, and emotionally by coaches, parents, and spectators. When injuries and deaths occur in sports, the officials often defend themselves by saying a game is a "contact" sport and, until recently, have resisted making any changes. But the climate is changing, and some types of violent behavior are being addressed in an effort to reduce injuries. However, violent contact, the hard hits, remain part of the sports.

The acceptance of violent behavior has been seen on the nation's playgrounds. Children take violent action against other children because, in their play, they imitate the violent acts they see on television. Some children have toy guns to use in their play. Some find loaded guns and, thinking they are toys, fire them and injure or kill their playmates, family members, or themselves.

The violent behavior that our society condones is not only physical, it is also verbal. Angry words and gestures directed by fans of one team against the opponents are justified as part of our society's belief in spirited competition. Condoning verbal behavior that attacks another contributes to abusive behaviors, including hate speech and prejudice. Scolding and berating individuals in a family setting are often considered to be justified and acceptable, but they often lead the targeted individuals to develop psychological disorders, even to commit suicide.

Sometimes violent behavior is caused by society's acceptance of a person's or a society's right to be outraged and to "get even" when a perceived wrong has happened. Some justify the get-even philosophy by quoting the passage in the Old Testament of the Bible that says, "An eye for an eye and a tooth for a tooth." States act on this principle when they use capital punishment: the taking of a life when a life has been taken. Individuals act on it when they kill and injure coworkers in their workplaces.

Sometimes society blames the abused person or group for creating the situation in which abuse occurs. They blame the victim. Female rape victims have been accused of inviting the rapist's attack because of the way they were dressed. Individuals and groups are accused of inviting abusive attacks because of the color of their skin. Homosexual women and men have been abused because of their sexual orientation.

One cause of abuse in America is society's ignoring the real cause of what has happened. Until recently, children who were missing from their homes were considered to be runaways who were unhappy at home. Often, these cases were not immediately investigated by authorities. However, when children were abducted and, soon after, found murdered, as happened to Adam Walsh and Polly Klaas, the public noticed, and the climate changed. Authorities were instructed to investigate all cases of missing persons and to notify the public as soon as a missing person's case was reported. Laws such as AMBER Alert have been enacted to ensure that all cases are immediately investigated. Such action groups as the National Center for Missing and Exploited Children were established and have had success in resolving missing person cases.

The immediate causes of most instances of abuse are relational and interpersonal. Most cases of abuse involve persons who know each other, as happens in domestic, child, and elder abuse, rape, and abduction. However, many instances of abuse involve individuals who are psychopaths or sociopaths who engage in serial rapes or serial killing.

Sometimes an abuse occurs when society does not believe that it exists. Such is the case with slavery. Slavery in many forms exists in the United States. Modern-day slavery exists in the forms of human trafficking, child trafficking, sex trafficking, child pornography, and in abduction cases in which an individual is captured and imprisoned. Slavery is one of the most negative forms of abuse.

Consequences of Abuse

The harm inflicted by abusers is not just physical; it is psychological, emotional, and mental as well. Harm is done to the child who withdraws and develops low self-esteem and to the elderly person who develops a fear of being left alone. Harm is seen in the abusive relationship that repeats the cycle of abuse. A father verbally abuses his child and thinks he is challenging his son to stick up for himself in the face of being bullied, and the child may become the abuser, may become a bully, as an adult. Of domestic abusers, 30 percent were abused as children.

Domestic abuse is widespread in the United States and in the world. The U.S. Department of Justice's National Crime Victimization Survey evidence of abuse includes: every nine seconds in the United States a woman is assaulted or beaten. Around the world, at least one in every three women has been beaten, coerced into sex, or otherwise abused during her lifetime. Most often, the abuser is a member of her own family. Domestic violence is the leading cause of injury to women, more than car accidents, muggings, and rapes combined. Studies suggest that up to 10 million children witness some form of domestic violence annually. Nearly one in five teenage girls who have been in a relationship said a boyfriend threatened violence or self-harm if presented with a breakup. Every day in the United States, more than three women are murdered by their husbands or boyfriends. Ninety-two percent of women surveyed listed reducing domestic violence and sexual assault as their top concern. Domestic violence victims lose nearly 8 million days of paid work per year in the United States alone, the equivalent of 32,000 full-time jobs. Based on reports from 10 countries, between 55 percent and 95 percent of women who had been physically abused by their partners had never contacted nongovernmental organizations, shelters, or the police for help.

Children suffer from a hidden epidemic of child abuse and neglect. Every year, 3.3 million reports of child abuse are made in the United States, involving nearly 6 million children (a report can include multiple children). The United States has the worst record of the industrialized nations. The country loses more than five children every day in abuse-related deaths. A report of child abuse is made every 10 seconds. Approximately 80 percent of children that die from abuse are under the age of four. It is estimated that between 50 percent and 60 percent of child fatalities from maltreatment are not recorded as such on death certificates.

More than 90 percent of juvenile sexual abuse victims know their perpetrator in some way. Child abuse occurs at every socioeconomic level, across ethnic and cultural lines, within all religions, and at all levels of education. About 30 percent of abused and neglected children will later abuse their own children, continuing the cycle of abuse. About 80 percent of 21-year-olds that were abused as children met criteria for at least one psychological disorder. The estimated annual cost of child abuse and neglect in the United States for 2008 was $124 billion.

Elderly abuse is increasing. The number of elderly abuse cases in 2010 was 5,961,568, or 9.5 percent of the elderly population. Of elder abuse victims, 67.3 percent were female.

Rape and sexual assaults are all too common in the United States. Each year, an average of 207,754 individuals, age 12 or older, are victims of rape and sexual assault.

Bullying is pervasive and affects all of society. It is a serious problem for children in schools and on the Internet. In one area of the areas where bullying occurs, statistics document the problem for school children:

- One out of four children is bullied.
- In schools, 77 percent of students are bullied mentally, verbally, and physically. Cyberbullying statistics are rapidly approaching similar numbers, with 43 percent of students experiencing cyberbullying.
- Of the 77 percent of students that said they had been bullied, 14 percent said they experienced severe (bad) reactions to the abuse.
- One in five students admits to being a bully or doing some "bullying."
- Each day, 160,000 students miss school for fear of being bullied.
- At school, 43 percent of kids fear harassment in the bathroom.
- Over 100,000 students carry a gun to school.
- Of youths who carry weapons, 28 percent have witnessed violence at home.
- In secondary schools, 282,000 students are physically attacked each month.
- More youth violence occurs on school grounds as opposed to on the way to school.
- On the school playground, a child is bullied every seven minutes.

Treatments for Abuse

Abuse in the United States must be treated by working with individual abusers and the abused. It also requires programs that are properly funded and staffed. Until laws and policies are changed, too many kinds of abuse will continue as they are and even get worse. Until violence and abusive behaviors become unacceptable in American society, the incidence of many kinds of abuse will not be materially reduced.

Abuse can be reduced if effective, coordinated action is taken.

- Abuse must be reported to be treated. Statistics show that the sexual abuse of children in the United States occurs frequently and often goes unreported. An estimated one in four girls and one in six boys will be sexually assaulted before age 18. Fewer than 10 percent of those victims will tell anyone what happened. According to the National Coalition against Domestic Violence, domestic violence is one of the most chronically underreported crimes. Only 25 percent of all physical assaults, 20 percent of all rapes, and 50 percent of all stalking perpetrated against females by their partners are reported to the police. For the small number of cases that do get reported, on average, a woman will be assaulted by her partner or ex-partner 35 times before reporting it to the police.

- To be treated, abuse must have agencies to which it is reported, and those agencies must be equipped to respond appropriately. In the past, authorities did not have the resources to respond to a missing child case when a child had been abducted, and they were hampered because the child was often considered a runaway. The situation has now changed for cases of abduction, and authorities have more resources and respond more quickly.
- To treat cases of abuse, there must be enough facilities, programs, and trained staff. Too often, these resources are not available or are underfunded. Ironically, the funding for these much-needed resources is often insufficient or has been reduced or eliminated from agency budgets. More facilities, such as those for battered women, are needed. Additional programs and trained staff are needed.

Abuse treatment must include the abused, the abuser, and the factors that led to the abuse. The focus needs to be on the abused as the victim of the abuse, but it must also realize that the abuser may also be a victim of forces that drove the abuser to abuse.

Treatment of abuse must have the backing of society and its laws. For the most serious abuses, society relies on laws to deal with the abusers. Rape, abduction, and abuse resulting in death are some of the abuses where the abuser may get a lengthy prison sentence or be sentenced to death. The laws also provide the support for programs that work to reduce abuse in our society.

Abuse will not be eliminated in our society in the near term, but it and its effects can be lessened with a united effort. Change is happening already. Bullying, once was accepted as normal growing-up behavior, is now considered a major societal problem. Nationwide programs have been developed and put into effect to make bullying unacceptable behavior and to take action when bullying occurs.

Abuse: An Encyclopedia of Causes, Consequences, and Treatments examines abuse through entries that identify the abuse, or an aspect of the abuse, and focuses on the causes, consequences, and treatment of abuse. When entries are related, they will be cross-referenced. For each entry, further reading is included.

Rosemarie Skaine

Further Reading

A4K Ambassadors 4 Kids Club. 2013. "Bullying Statistics." http://www.a4kclub.org/get-the-facts/bullying-statistics.

Bureau of Justice Statistics. 2012. "National Crime Victimization Survey (NCVS)." http://www.bjs.gov/index.cfm?ty=dcdetail&iid=245.

Chapter 776, Justifiable Use of Force. April 25, 2014. "The 2013 Florida Statutes." Online Sunshine. http://www.leg.state.fl.us/statutes/index.cfm?App_mode=Display_Statute&URL=0700-0799/0776/0776.html.

Child Help. 2013. "National Child Abuse Statistics." http://www.childhelp-usa.net/pages/statistics.

National Center on Elder Abuse. n.d. U.S. Department of Health and Human Services. http://www.ncea.aoa.gov.

National Domestic Abuse Hotline. n.d. "Abuse in America." http://www.thehotline.org/get-educated/abuse-in-america.

ABDUCTION, ADULT

Adult abduction occurs when a person is taken against her or his will and assaulted or held for personal gain. The abduction may result in the person's being injured or killed. The person may be abducted for ransom. Adults who come up missing have been called one of America's silent epidemics. Many adults go missing and are never reported. Missing adults, however, are being reported in increasing numbers.

Kidnapping and abduction can go together. In most states, statutes define kidnapping as an abduction carried out against the will of the person. The FBI's National Crime Information Center's (NCIC) Missing Person File, implemented in 1975, retains records indefinitely until the individual is located or the entering agency cancels the record. The Missing Person File contains the NCIC's Missing Person Circumstances (MPC) field, which is optional and has been available since July 1999. Of the 661,593 records entered in 2010, the MPC field was utilized in 322,936 cases (48.8%). At this time, 310,367 (96.1%) entries included a code for adult, with 9,752 (3.0%) as Adult.

In 2012, NCIC reported 164,266 missing persons who were 18 or older. Of that total, 37,745 were classified as endangered, 26,699 as disabled, and 13,774 as involuntary. Women numbered 67,687 and men 96,576. For missing persons 21 or older, 131,765 were reported. Of that total, 31,790 were endangered, 23,920 disabled, and 9,190 involuntary. Women numbered 51,379 and men 80,383.

In 1996, the Nation's Missing Children Organization added adult cases to its services. In 2000, the National Center for Missing Adults in Phoenix, Arizona, was created with the passage of Kristen's Law. This is the first national clearinghouse for missing adults and serves as a central place to store information available to the general public, advocacy groups, law enforcement officials, and medical examiners. It also provides support, technical assistance, and advocacy services to families dealing with the loss of a missing adult.

An AMBER Alert for adults was proposed in California. Connie Castaneda posted on Change.org a petition to the governor and California State legislature to pass a law for adult abduction alerts (Alex Alert). Alex Alert is very similar to the AMBER Alert for children. Castaneda reported that her friend Alex was abducted and brutally killed. His car was parked at a park around 6:00 a.m. the day he was abducted. Around 10:00 p.m., the killers returned and burned the car with his body in the backseat. If the alert had been in place, Alex could have possibly been found alive. Castaneda closed with the plea that adult and children abductions should be treated the same.

Interventions that teach safety skills are needed for all populations, but persons with intellectual disabilities are especially vulnerable to abuse and exploitation by unknown perpetrators. Disabled individuals are approximately twice as likely to experience crimes such as physical and sexual assault. Steps to ward off abduction include playing it safe by choosing and varying safe routes and being prepared to resist with mace or an object such as a set of keys. If the abductor attacks where other people are present, the person should fight or do anything possible to escape. If faced with more than one abductor and little or no chance of escape, the person should be cooperative.

Rosemarie Skaine

See also: Abduction, Capture and Imprisonment; National Center for Missing and Exploited Children; National Missing and Unidentified Persons System.

Further Reading

Castaneda, Connie. 2013. "State Legislature: Pass a Law for Adult Abduction Alerts (Alex Alert)." Change.org. http://www.change.org/petitions/state-legislature-pass-a-law-for-adult-abduction-alerts-alex-alert.

FBI. 2012. "NCIC Missing Person and Unidentified Person Statistics for 2012." National Crime Information Center. http://www.fbi.gov/about-us/cjis/ncic/ncic-missing-person-and-unidentified-person-statistics-for-2012.

Fisher, Marisa H., Meghan M. Burke, and Megan M. Griffin. 2013. "Teaching Young Adults with Disabilities to Respond Appropriately to Lures from Strangers." *Journal of Applied Behavior Analysis* 46 (2): 528–533.

Krajicek, David. n.d. "America's Missing." Crime Library. http://www.crimelibrary.com/criminal_mind/forensics/americas_missing/2.html.

ABDUCTION, CAPTURE AND IMPRISONMENT

Capture and imprisonment is a form of abduction in which an individual is abducted and held prisoner by the captor for an extended period of time, which may be for years. While the number of these incidents is difficult to determine, three cases demonstrate the kinds of capture and imprisonment that occur.

One case involved three women: Amanda Berry, Gina DeJesus, and Michele Knight. They had been held captive for years by Ariel Castro (52) in his home in Cleveland, Ohio. Knight was 21 when she went missing in 2002; Berry was nearly 17 in 2003, and DeJesus was 14 in 2004. During their captivity, Castro sexually assaulted each of them repeatedly. Police reported that Castro starved the women. He caused Michelle to have five pregnancies and then hit her in the stomach until she miscarried. Amanda gave birth to Ariel's daughter, Jocelyn, who was 6 years old at the time of the escape. They escaped on May 6, 2013, when Berry broke through the front door of Castro's home and called for help.

Castro was indicted on 329 charges, including 177 counts of kidnapping, 139 counts of rape, and two counts of aggravated murder for forcing abortions. Castro pleaded guilty to kidnapping and raping Berry, Knight, and DeJesus to avoid the death penalty. On August 1, 2013, Castro was sentenced to life in prison plus

1,000 years, without the possibility of parole. On September 3, 2013, Castro committed suicide by hanging.

A second case involved Josef Fritzl and his daughter, Elisabeth Fritzl. On August 29, 1984 in Amstetten, Austria, Fritzl lured Elisabeth (18) into the basement where she would be imprisoned for the next 24 years. During the first days of her imprisonment, Elisabeth pounded on the walls, scraped the ceiling, and screamed for help. Fritzl raped her repeatedly. He did not allow his wife in the basement. He later claimed that his wife knew nothing about the captivity. Fritzl told his wife, and later the police, that Elisabeth had joined a cult. Fritzl fathered seven children with Elisabeth. Three of the seven children he brought upstairs to live with him and his wife. He said Elisabeth had left them at their door for them to take care of. Three of the children lived their entire lives underground. One child died shortly after birth.

On April 27, 2008, when Elisabeth's oldest child, Kerstin (19), became ill and had to be hospitalized, the case became public. Fritzl (78) was found guilty of the murder of one of Elisabeth's babies, incest, sequestration, grievous assault, and 3,000 instances of rape. He was sentenced in 2009 to life with a minimum 15 years term. In 2013, Elisabeth (47) and her six surviving children, who had new identities, lived at an undisclosed location.

The third case involved Colleen Stan. In 1977, Colleen was 20 years old. As she hitchhiked in Red Bluff, California, she was picked up by a young couple. A child in the backseat made her feel safe. However, the husband, Cameron Hooker (24), a sexual sadist, raped Colleen after they arrived at the family's isolated trailer. The abuse became worse, including beatings with a whip, burning, and electroshock. Hooker renamed Colleen "K," saying she was his slave. He forced Colleen into a box the size of a coffin with holes and put the box under the couple's bed every night. Initially, he allowed her one hour in 24 outside the box. She was his slave for the next 7 years

In January 1978, Colleen was forced to sign a contract putting her into slavery for life. Because Hooker considered vaginal sex an act of infidelity to his wife, he orally raped Colleen and inserted objects vaginally and anally. Colleen felt she had no control, so she was willing to do whatever he asked, including not escaping when the opportunity presented itself in 1981. Hooker had taken her home for an overnight visit with her family. Because he had threatened to kill her family if she told them what was going on, she did not tell, and returned with him the next day to live in the box again for three more years.

Colleen's faith in God and her belief that someday she would be free helped her survive. She tried to be a good slave to avoid painful punishments. Consequently, she was allowed out to jog, do yard work, and care for the Hooker children alone. She did not try to escape.

In August 1984, with the assistance of Hooker's wife, Janice, Colleen walked away from Hooker. Hooker was tried and sentenced to 104 years in prison for sexual assault, kidnapping, and using a knife in the process. He will be eligible for parole in 2022. Janice Hooker was granted immunity for providing evidence and was never prosecuted. After her escape, Stan earned an accounting degree, married, had a daughter, and became a member of an organization to help abused women. She and Janice both changed their last names and live in California.

Rosemarie Skaine

See also: Abduction, Adult; Abduction, Child; National Center for Missing and Exploited Children; Slavery, Modern-day.

Further Reading

Keeler, Emily. 2013. "Amanda Berry, Gina DeJesus to Write Book on Abduction, Imprisonment." *Los Angeles Times*, October 22. http://www.latimes.com/books/jacketcopy/la-et-jc-ohio-kidnapping-victims-writing-a-book-20131022,0,5242517.story#axzz2iqsJU8Fg.

Take 25. n.d. "Child Safety: Child Abduction." http://www.missingkids.com/Take25.

Wissgott, Sim Sim. 2013. "5 Years Later: Raped for 24 Years in Her Father's Dungeon, Elisabeth Fritzl Surviving in Anonymity." InterAksyon, April 27. http://www.interaksyon.com/article/60417/5-years-later--raped-for-24-years-in-her-fathers-dungeon-elisabeth-fritzl-surviving-in-anonymity.

ABDUCTION, CHILD

Child abduction is defined as when a child is removed through means of force or violence, fraudulent means, coercion, held for ransom, held captive for a short or prolong period of time, wrongfully detained overnight, kept in isolation by force, or transported 50 miles or more. Child abduction is typically classified in three groups: family abduction, acquaintance abduction, and nonfamily abduction (stranger abduction).

According to the Federal Bureau of Investigation (FBI), over 58,000 children are abducted by family and approximately 115 children are abducted by complete strangers in the United States every year. Girls make up the largest percentage of abductions by strangers that occur each year. Accurate data on child abduction in the United States is often difficult to attain because most abduction reports filed each year with local authorities are false information and because the legal definition of *abduction* is often redefined as necessary and varies from state to state. If the situation presents itself to rescue the abducted child, negotiations take place between authorities and the abductor(s).

Family abduction is the most common and least harmful type of abduction. Children under the age of six are mostly victims; boys and girls are equally victimized. Family abduction is typically carried out by parents, usually the mother. In the United States, abduction laws pertaining to family abduction vary from state to state. For instance, in some states, authorities first determine whether a custody order is in effect and/or whether the parents are living together. It is family abduction when a custody order is violated by a failure to return the child with the intention of concealment to prevent any contact and/or transportation of a child across the state line. If it is determined that a custody order is not in effect and if both parents live separately, it is not considered a criminal act. To counter this problem, several states have made it illegal for perpetrators of family abduction to transport the child(ren) to another state.

There are various reasons why parents abduct their child(ren). The most common reason is during or after a divorce or when one of the parents has lost custody over the child(ren). According to the U.S. Department of Justice (DOJ), victims of family abduction are often told the other parent does not love them or has died. Also, children abducted by their parents live a life of deception, often times their identity is falsified, they are moved frequently to conceal their whereabouts or smuggled to another country, posing long-term emotional and psychological consequences to them.

Acquaintance abduction is carried out by a friend of the family; victims are usually lured with false hopes and promises. This type of abduction mostly affects teenage boys and girls, with the higher affected percentage being girls. Abduction by acquaintance is often motivated by sexual impulses; the victim is forced into sexual relations, resulting in a high percentage of victims being physically, emotionally, and sexually assaulted. Another motive for this type of abduction is the purpose of sexually exploiting the victim in the underage sex-trafficking trade across the United States. It is believed that this type of abduction occurs mostly from home and, similar to stranger abductions, has the highest percentage of injured victims.

Nonfamily or *stranger abduction* is the rarest, accounting for only a small fraction of abductions reported each year, posing the most harm to children who are victimized, making this type of abduction the most dangerous. According to the DOJ and FBI, although this type of abduction seldom occurs, the highest percentage of the victims are killed or never found. In rare occasions, victims are found or manage to escape their captor(s) in a short period of time or years later. Perpetrators mostly target school-age children, similar to acquaintance abduction; girls make up the higher percentage of the victims. Victims that are found or mange to escape suffer from long-term adverse psychological and emotional consequences. This type of abduction usually takes place outdoors in broad daylight, where the abductor(s) lure, intimidate, or force the victim into a getaway vehicle. Children who are abducted by strangers are done so through violent physical force for various reasons, including sexual gratification, possession, sexual exploitation through underage prostitution, and/or for financial extortion. Under rare circumstance, a child is abducted by perpetrator(s) during a home invasion.

Treatment is available for people who survive abduction: the victim, family, friends, and members of society in general. Victims and family may require privacy and therapy. Families often find healing in private projects such as Marc Klaas, father of Polly Klaas, who, after her abduction and murder, began his own organization, the KlaasKids Foundation for Children. Marc also advocated legal change in California that helped motivate the legislature to pass the "Three Strikes" law, designed to keep repeat felony offenders in prison for life. Legal change is also reflected in the adoption of the DOJ's AMBER Alert system that activates an urgent bulletin in the most serious child-abduction cases. In addition, John Walsh, the father of the abducted Adam Walsh, supported the passage of the Adam Walsh Child Protection and Safety Act that, in part, created a national sex-offender registry. John Walsh also founded the National Center for Missing and Exploited Children (NCMEC). These efforts, along with others, offer help and healing for survivors of abduction.

Juan Carlos Hernandez

See also: Adam Walsh Child Protection and Safety Act; AMBER Alert; Human Trafficking; Klaas, Polly; National Center for Missing and Exploited Children; Sex Offender; Sexual Slavery; Slavery, Modern-day; Walsh, John Edward.

Further Reading

Anderson, Vicki D. 2013. "FBI to Support National Children's Day." Federal Bureau of Investigation. http://www.fbi.gov/cleveland/press-releases/2013/fbi-to-support-national-childrens-day.

Bilich, Karin A. n.d. "Child Abduction Facts: Some Important Information about Kidnapping in the U.S." *Parents*. http://www.parents.com/kids/safety/stranger-safety/child-abduction-facts.

Finkelhor, David, Heather Hammer, and Andrea J. Sedlak. 2002. "Nonfamily Abducted Children: National Estimates and Characteristics." National Incidence Studies of Missing, Abducted, Runaway, and Thrownaway Children. Department of Justice. Office of Juvenile Justice and Delinquency Prevention. http://www.missingkids.com/en_US/documents/nismart2_nonfamily.pdf.

HG Legal Resources. n.d. "Child Abduction Law–Child Kidnapping Law." http://www.hg.org/child-abduction.html.

U.S. Department of Justice. n.d. "Children Exploitation and Obscenity Section." http://www.justice.gov/criminal/ceos/subjectareas/ipk.html.

U.S. Department of State. n.d. "Guarding against International Parental Child Abduction." http://travel.state.gov/abduction/prevention/prevention_560.html.

ACTION AGAINST ABUSE

Action Against Abuse (AAA) was founded in 2008. Its mission statement says, "We are ordinary people from around the world. We refuse to be silent whilst children suffer." It has 6,000 members that are committed to listening to and believing children. Its mission is three pronged: awareness, action, and change. The organization believes in prevention through self-education and by discussion with friends and family. The group's political action includes reporting concerns, contacting governmental representatives, general campaigning, signing petitions, and community outreach. It focuses on the United Kingdom, but it has a global outreach.

The Action Against Abuse Facebook page serves as an interactive site and gives directions to the organization's Web site. Campaigns developed on its Web site include six Change4Children campaigns that provide written messages to representatives and petitions to sign and share:

Campaign 1: Investigate Evidence of A Powerful Network of Pedophiles with Links to Parliament. During Prime Minister's Question Time on October 24, 2012, the evidence of a network of pedophiles was put forth. It came to light during the 1992 conviction of Peter Righton. The petition alleges evidence was covered up by the establishment and the police, who failed to investigate further. The petition demands an investigation.

Campaign 2: Who's Watching Your Children? Be Sure, Before Campaign. This effort asks the government to address the "stranger danger" myth and to make it more difficult for child abusers to abuse by tricking family members. Interventions include increasing awareness of parents and children. Information is distributed to parents. Information given to children is done through schools. Specific improvements to the child protection system are advocated. Research into child abuse and family dynamics is also conducted.

Campaign 3: Justice for the Children of Scotland Campaign. This campaign's purpose is to close the legal loophole that makes Scottish law inadequate.

Campaign 4: Ireland's Invisible Children Campaign. The Invisible Children is to reform Ireland's child protection system.

Campaign 5: Amazon Should Not Profit from Child Sex Exploitation. This campaign proposes that books that encourage sexual exploitation of children be removed and Amazon must review its safeguarding policy.

Campaign 6: Baby P—5 Years On: I Still Care Campaign. This campaign is a follow-up to Action Against Abuse's 2009 Master Letter campaign. After baby Peter Connelly was murdered, the government assured that the case had increased its awareness. In the U.K., 1 to 4 children die a week from abuse. This campaign monitors the government's commitment.

In addition to its campaigns, AAA provides information on child abuse, child abuse for parents and caregivers, and reporting abuse. It provides contacts, help and advice, and useful links and resources.

Rosemarie Skaine

See also: Abduction, Child; Child Abuse, Physical and Emotional; Child Abuse, Sexual; Pedophilia.

Further Reading

Action Against Abuse. n.d. "Campaigns." https://actionagainstabuse.wordpress.com.
Action Against Abuse. 2013. Facebook. https://www.facebook.com/ActionAgainstAbuseUK.

ADAM WALSH CHILD PROTECTION AND SAFETY ACT

On July 27, 2006, the Adam Walsh Child Protection and Safety Act was signed into law. Title I of the Adam Walsh Act established the Sex Offender Registration and Notification Act (SORNA), which aims to prevent and protect children against crimes such as child pornography, child abuse, sexual exploitation, and distribution of child pornography as well as to protect children against online predators. SORNA was passed to further strengthen existing laws aimed at sex offenders and child predators by establishing a new set of minimum requirements for sex offender registration and notification. The main objective of these requirements was to provide instructions to all 50 states, including Indian tribal governments and U.S. territories.

John Walsh, host of the television program *America's Most Wanted*, **talks at the Summer Television Critics Association Press Tour in Pasadena, California on July 25, 2006. Congress passed and sent to President Bush legislation establishing a national Internet database designed to let law enforcement and communities know where convicted sex offenders live and work. The act is named for Adam Walsh, Walsh's son who was abducted and murdered. (AP Photo/Reed Saxon)**

Under this provision, sex offenders must appear in person to register, get photographed, update, and provide comprehensive information that is made available to the public. In addition, the Adam Walsh Act authorizes under SORNA, the Office of Justice Programs (OJP), a branch of the U.S. Department of Justice, to establish the Office of Sex Offender Sentencing, Monitoring, Apprehending, Registering, and Tracking (SMART). SMART is responsible for administrating and safekeeping the standards of the Sex Offender Registration and Notification Program. Most importantly, when deemed as necessary, the SMART office is authorized to assist, work jointly, and provide access to law enforcement agencies and private organizations pertaining to the protection of children to the SMART database(s).

The Adam Walsh Act and SORNA were necessary to close possible discrepancies and loopholes that existed under former laws aimed at sex offenders and child predators. According to OJP, under SORNA, the nationwide system for sex offender registration and notification programs was strengthened by creating a three-tier classification system in which sex offenders are classified. For instance, Tier I includes sex offenders whose crimes are not punishable by more than one year in prison, and those who are required to appear and register every year for 15 years. Crimes pertaining to Tier I may include the receipt and/or possession of child pornography, sexual assault against an adult, which includes inappropriate contact but not a complete sexual act.

Tier II includes sex offenders whose crimes are punishable by more than one year in prison, and those who are required to appear and register every six months for 25 years. Crimes pertaining to Tier II may include the solicitation or attempted solicitation of a minor for prostitution, sex trafficking, any form of sexual contact with a minor, the production or distribution of child pornography, or if the crimes have been committed after previously having been classified a Tier I offender.

Tier III is the most serious as it includes sex offenders whose crimes are punishable by more than one year in prison, and those who must appear every three months and register for life. Crimes pertaining to Tier III may include kidnapping of minors (excludes parent(s) and/or guardians of the victim); sexual assault of a minor under the age of 13; aggravated sexual assault, including minors and adults; or if the crimes have been committed after previously having been classified a Tier II offender. However, it is important to note that Tier I, II, and III may also include other types of crimes in addition to the aforementioned examples.

Juan Carlos Hernandez

See also: Child Abuse, Sexual; Child Pornography; Child Trafficking; Sex Offender.

Further Reading

H.R.4472—Adam Walsh Child Protection and Safety Act of 2006: 109th Congress (2005–2006). 2006. Congress.gov. http://beta.congress.gov/bill/109th-congress/house-bill/4472.

Office of Justice Programs. n.d. "About SMART." http://www.ojp.usdoj.gov/smart/about.htm.

Office of Justice Programs. n.d. "SORNA." http://www.ojp.usdoj.gov/smart/sorna.htm.

Reinhart, Christopher. December 8, 2006. "Federal Assistance Programs; Legislation; Sex Crimes." http://www.cga.ct.gov/2006/rpt/2006-r-0765.htm.

ADINA'S DECK

Adina's Deck is a DVD series, curriculum, and Web site intended to educate 9- to 15-year-olds about the growing problem of cyber bullying. Cyber bullying is harassing someone using the Internet, cell phones, and any sort of digital technology.

The film is the story of four girls who form a club to help their peers with mysteries by using technology. The story was developed based upon first-hand research at three middle schools in Northern California for Debbie Heimowitz's master's thesis at the Stanford Graduate School of Education. Jason Azicri wrote and co-directed the film. In the film, Adina is a girl who got kicked out of school for cyber bullying, so her parents took away her computer and gave her a deck of playing cards. The deck symbolizes her transformation. The film is inspired by things Heimowitz saw happen, but all the characters are completely made up.

IMDb (Internet Movie Database) summarized the plot. Three tech savvy eighth grade girls try to help their friend who's been cyber bullied. When popular girl, Skye, receives threatening e-mails, text messages, and voice mails, her best friend, Melody, asks classmate Adina for help. When Adina says yes, her best friend, Clara, is confused. Skye is stuck up and has never been nice to them in the past, so why is Adina helping her? While solving the mystery, the girls learn more than just the bully's identity. They learn about friendship and growing up in the digital age of technology.

Adina's Deck won the award for Best Educational Film in the student category at the 2008 International Family Film Festival. It was an official selection at film festivals, including the Danville Children's Film Festival, 2008; the International Family Film Festival, 2008; the Sacramento Film Festival, 2008; the San Francisco Bay Area Children's Film Festival, 2008; the East Lansing Children's Film Festival, 2008; and the Kids First Film Festival, 2007.

Rosemarie Skaine

See also: Cyberbullying, Child and Adolescent; Sexual Harassment in Education; Telephone Harassment.

Further Reading

IMDb. 2007. "*Adina's Deck* (2007): Plot Summary." http://www.imdb.com/title/tt1103142/plotsummary?ref_=tt_ov_pl.

Whiting, Sam. 2007. "Debbie Heimowitz Brings Cyber Bullying to Light in a New Film." SFGate, September 14. http://www.sfgate.com/education/article/Debbie-Heimowitz-brings-cyber-bullying-to-light-3237872.php.

ADOPTED CHILDREN

Abuse of an adopted child by adoptive parents occurs when the child is harmed physically, psychologically, or sexually, or neglected or abandoned by the adoptive parents.

The abuse that a child who is adopted experiences is the same as the child who has birth parents. Hana Williams and her step brother were abused by their adoptive parents, Larry and Carri Williams of Sedro-Woolley, Washington. The Williams were found guilty of neglecting, abusing, and ultimately killing Hana. Hana's step brother testified that he and Hana were beaten with sticks, hosed down, forced to eat frozen food, and locked in closets as punishment.

Some of the abusive parents were foster parents of the children they adopted. Former foster parents, Janet and Dwight Solander of Las Vegas, Nevada, were arrested on charges of abuse and neglect of three children whom they had adopted. They faced multiple felony charges that included child abuse, neglect, or endangerment. The mother was also charged with sexual assault of a minor.

The adopted child has an increased likelihood of being abandoned. Adoptive parents solicit on the Internet for new families for their unwanted adopted children. They provided three reasons why they do. First, they don't believe they had received proper training going into their adoptions. Second, the children's emotional and behavioral problems hadn't been disclosed, and when the adoption didn't work out, the adoption agency wouldn't help them. Some didn't receive any assistance from the government. Third, they could face charges of abuse and neglect and put other children in their home in jeopardy. In short, the underground online network was their only option.

An underground market for adopted children operates on a loose Internet network where parents seek new homes for children who aren't working out. The children are advertised through Yahoo or Facebook and then given to strangers with little or no government scrutiny, sometimes illegally. No laws address it, and no government agency monitors the bulletin boards. The children are placed in great danger.

Certain risk factors may increase the likelihood of a child being abused including: intellectual disability, emotional disturbance, visual or hearing impairment, learning disability, physical disability, behavioral problems, or another medical problem. Thirteen percent (13.3%) of victims were reported as having a disability.

A Reuters study reports that part of the solution is to provide those services to help families succeed. Two big issues need to be rectified: the Internet and post-adoption services. In addition, the fact that no government oversight exists and that nobody here in the United States is trying to track these adoptions needs to be addressed. Re-homing is possible through a number of means:

- The families can seek a formal readoption. This requires court approval and affords the most protection for the child. The original adoptive family must terminate parental rights. The new family submits to a criminal background check and additional vetting by a social worker.
- The families can try to transfer guardianship in court. The original adoptive parents do not terminate parental rights. The new guardians may have to undergo a background check.
- The families decide to transfer custody of the child in a less formal way, with no court involvement. The original adoptive family signs a piece of paper granting the new family power of attorney over the child for a period of time. Once notarized, this document allows the new family to enroll the child in school and secure government benefits for the child. The document is not officially recorded anywhere. This is a preferred method for families seeking a temporary, out-of-home placement for the child, often called "respite." In other cases, it is used to transfer custody of a child for years at a time.

The child advocacy group Child Rights states that reform of the child welfare systems is needed to produce better results for the abused and neglected children in their care. The three actions they advocate are:

- Develop plans quickly for moving children in foster care into permanent homes through either safe reunification with their birth families or adoption, spelling out goals, tasks, and timeframes in detail.
- Work intensively to recruit adoptive families, including families willing and able to take in children with special needs and others regarded as difficult to place.
- Provide adequate postadoption services so children thrive with their new families, parents receive the support they need to enable them to adopt, and the adoptions remain stable.

The primary responsibility for child welfare services rests with the states, and each state has its own legal and administrative structures and programs that address the needs of children and families. However, states must comply with specific federal requirements and guidelines to be eligible for federal funding under certain programs.

Laws have been passed to protect adopted children from abuse and neglect. Beginning with the passage of the Child Abuse Prevention and Treatment Act (CAPTA) in 1974, the U.S. Congress has implemented a number of laws that have had a significant impact on state child protection and child welfare services. The largest federally funded programs that support state and tribal efforts for child welfare, foster care, and adoption activities are authorized under titles IV-B and IV-E of the Social Security Act (the Act). These programs are administered by the U.S. Department of Health and Human Services and include the title IV-B Child Welfare Services and Promoting Safe and Stable Families (formerly known as Family Preservation) programs, the title IV-E Foster Care Program, the title IV-E Adoption Assistance Program, and the title IV-E Chafee Foster Care Independence Program. The Social Services Block Grant (SSBG) is authorized under title XX of the Act and funds a wide range of programs that support various social policy goals.

Rosemarie Skaine

See also: Adopted Children, International; Adoption Agencies, Abuse in; Child Abandonment and Neglect; Child Abuse, Physical and Emotional; Child Abuse Prevention and Enforcement Acts; Foster Children; Intercountry Adoption Act.

Further Reading

Bartholet, Elizabeth. 1999. *Nobody's Children: Abuse and Neglect, Foster Drift, and the Adoption Alternative*. Boston: Beacon Press. http://www.law.harvard.edu/faculty/bartholet/pdfs/release1.pdf.

Belkin, Lisa. 2011. "Can Adoption Lead to Child Abuse?" *Huffington Post*, November 9. http://www.huffingtonpost.com/lisa-belkin/adoption-spanking-childabuse_b_1081617.html.

Child Welfare Information Gateway. 2013. "Parenting a Child Who Has Been Sexually Abused: A Guide for Foster and Adoptive Parents." *Factsheets for Families*. U.S. Department of Health and Human Services. https://www.childwelfare.gov/pubs/f_abused/f_abused.pdf.

Child Welfare Information Gateway. 2012. "Major Federal Legislation Concerned with Child Protection, Child Welfare, and Adoption." Administration for Children & Families, U.S. Department of Health and Human Services. https://www.childwelfare.gov/pubs/otherpubs/majorfedlegis.cfm.

Children's Rights. n.d. "Children's Rights Fights to Give Abused and Neglected Children a Better Chance of Growing Up in Safe, Loving, Permanent Homes." http://www.childrensrights.org/newsroom/fact-sheets/foster-care/.

IPTV. 2013. "Some Parents of Adopted Children Turn to Online Networks, Triggering Problems." *PBS News Hour*, September 11. http://www.pbs.org/newshour/bb/nation-july-dec13-adoption_09-11.

National Kids Count. 2013. "Safety & Risky Behaviors Indicators." Kids Count Data Center. http://datacenter.kidscount.org/data#USA/1/35/36,37,38,41.

Twohey, Megan. 2013. "Adopted Children Being Abandoned by Parents over Internet into Abuse, 'Nightmare' Homes." *Bangor Daily News*. Last modified September 11, 2013. https://bangordailynews.com/2013/09/09/news/nation/adopted-children-being-abandoned-by-parents-over-internet-into-abusive-nightmare-homes.

ADOPTED CHILDREN, INTERNATIONAL

Abuse occurs in international adoption when adoptive parents harm or abandon a child adopted from another country. The abuse in transnational adoptions is caused, in part, because the adoptive parents come to the realization that the reasons for the adoption may not, because of cultural differences, materialize in the ways they planned. When an adopted international child is abused, it has repercussions not only for the child and the abusive parents, but has implications for relations between the United States and the other country as well. Abuse of adopted children from Russia resulted in Russian President Vladimir Putin's signing a bill in December 2012 that banned all adoptions by U.S. residents.

Abuse cases involving children adopted from Russia include the following:

- In 2008, 21-month-old Dima Yakovlev died of heatstroke in Virginia when his adoptive father left him in a parked vehicle for nine hours.
- In 2010, an adoptive mother from Tennessee sent Artyom Solovyev, aged seven years, alone on a return flight to Russia with a note saying the boy was "violent and has severe psychopathic issues."
- In 2013, Russian officials accused a Gardendake, Texas, woman, Laura Shatto, of fatally beating a three-year-old boy, Maksim Kuzmin, that she and Alan Shatto had adopted from Russia in November 2012. The death was ruled an accident one week after Russian officials accused the adoptive parents of killing the child. U.S. authorities said that Max Shatto died of a self-inflicted wound on January 21, 2013. The autopsy report showed that he died from a lacerated artery in his abdomen from self-inflicted bruising because he had a mental disorder that caused him to harm himself.

The banning of adoptions from Russia impacted U.S. residents who had been approved for adoption but had not completed the process. The ban affected at least 1,000 families and Russian children, according to Jan Wondra, acting national chair of Families for Russian and Ukrainian Adoption, Including Neighboring Countries, a parent support and advocacy group.

The prospective parents were in varying stages in the lengthy adoption process, which involved multiple trips to Russia and cost about $50,000. Some families are fighting back with activism. They are participating in petition drives and lobbying government officials to change the law. Some have filed complaints in the European Court of Human Rights, protesting the ban.

A couple that was lucky because they made it home with their adopted child before the ban went into effect was Jim Thompson his wife, Sze Man Yau, who made it home from Russia with their two-year-old daughter, Elena, three weeks before Putin signed the law.

International adoptions do not escape the abuse that adoptive parents inflict on adopted children. In many ways, the cases involving children adopted from Russia are not unlike cases of domestic adopted children abuse.

Rosemarie Skaine

See also: Adopted Children; Adoption Agencies, Abuse in; Child Abandonment and Neglect; Child Abuse, Physical and Emotional; Foster Children; Intercountry Adoption Act.

Further Reading

Barry, Ellen. 2013. "After Adopted Boy Dies in U.S., Russian Officials Accuse Texas Woman." *New York Times*, February 19. http://www.nytimes.com/2013/02/20/world/europe/adopted-boys-death-in-us-stirs-outrage-in-russia.html.

Farberov, Snejana, and Daily Mail Reporter. 2013. "Adoptive Parents of Ethiopian Girl Who Died of Hypothermia and Starvation in Their Backyard Found Guilty of Manslaughter." *Mail Online*, September 10. http://www.dailymail.co.uk/news/article-2416514/Hana-Williams-Washington-adoptive-parents-Larry-Carri-Williams-GUILTY-manslaughter.html.

Herszenhorn, David M., and Erik Eckholm. 2012. "Putin Signs Bill that Bars U.S. Adoptions, Upending Families." *New York Times*, December 27. http://www.nytimes.com/2012/12/28/world/europe/putin-to-sign-ban-on-us-adoptions-of-russian-children.html?pagewanted=all&_r=0.

Holmes, Kristin E. 2014. "Russian Adoption Ban Still Affecting Prospective Parents." *Philadelphia Inquirer*, January 18. http://articles.philly.com/2014-01-18/news/46304667_1_russian-adoption-ban-russian-children-ukrainian-adoption.

Twohey, Megan. 2013. "Americans Use the Internet to Abandon Children Adopted from Overseas." The Child Exchange. Reuters, September 9. http://www.reuters.com/investigates/adoption/#article/part1.

ADOPTION AGENCIES, ABUSE IN

Child adoption abuse is abuse within the adoption process that causes abuse of the birth parents, the child, or the adopting family. It happens when the adoption agencies and people who assist and promote adoption do not fulfill their responsibility to all parties involved.

During the period from 1945 to 1972, unwed pregnant girls were encouraged to give their babies up for adoption by shaming them and persuading them that they could not care for their babies as well as an adoptive family could. Sometimes the birth mothers were not even allowed to hold their babies and were pressured into signing away their parental rights immediately after giving birth. This happened less, beginning in the 1970s, for two reasons. First, single motherhood became much more acceptable. Second, states began passing laws that mandated more time before a release of custody could be signed. In Iowa, for example, Chapter 600A.4(2)(d) of the Iowa Code says that a release of custody shall be signed not less than 72 hours after the birth of the child. This provision became law January 1, 1977.

These laws, however, have not always ended the pressure on birth mothers to give their babies up for adoption. They often are misinformed about their rights. For example, a girl called Reanne, pregnant at 19, was placed in a home for unwed mothers by her parents. It was a religious agency and stressed that she was doing a wonderful thing by having a baby for another family. She signed early to give up her baby. When, near the end of her pregnancy, she started having doubts about her decision, the agency pressured her by making her feel guilty about disappointing the adopting family.

When she gave birth, the baby was handed to the adopting couple first, and she was never allowed to hold the baby except when the couple was present. The lawyer, whom she thought was representing her as well as the family, told her that she had only 24 hours to change her mind about surrendering the baby. In Washington, the state where she lived, that was not true. She had at least 48 hours. While both she and her boyfriend agreed that they wanted to keep the baby, they believed it was too late. If birth mothers are not informed about the laws governing adoption, the laws provide no protection.

When fewer babies were available for adoption in the 1970s in the United States because women were keeping their babies and because abortion became legal, families began to seek international adoptions. International adoptions are generally expensive, so adoption agencies have the opportunity to make a good deal of money. Because of the high demand for adoptable children, adoption agencies took advantage of opportunities in underdeveloped countries where there was little government regulation.

In some countries, orphanages are essentially the child welfare infrastructure that families turn to in times of need. Sometimes, children have been fraudulently passed off as having no family. In others, children with intensive needs have ended up in homes that were unequipped to handle them. It is estimated that 6 to 11 percent of all U.S. adoptions fail, with that number climbing to nearly 25 percent for children adopted as adolescents.

In recent years, some evangelical churches have decided that it is their mission to have increased adoptions from the orphanages of the world. They have encouraged their members to adopt as many children as possible. Promotion of adoption of children from Liberia illustrates some of the problems that can develop. Nancy Campbell, editor of the magazine *Above Rubies*, urged readers to contact three Christian groups, Acres of Hope, Children Concerned, and West African Children Support Network, to arrange adoptions from Liberian orphanages. At the time, none of these groups were accredited in the United States as adoption agencies. Yet, they all placed children with American families for a fraction of the $20,000 to $35,000 that international adoptions usually cost. The response was huge. Families were going to Liberia and asking for as many children as their money could buy.

Patty Anglin, the cofounder of Acres of Hope, one of the groups promoted by "Above Rubies," found these adopting practices to be worrisome. Liberia had only recently emerged from a civil war and was in a state of near lawlessness. The prospect of a $6,000 adoption fee was enough to attract some shady operators. Adoptions that would take a year in other countries could take weeks or days in Liberia, and bribery was common. Not surprisingly, many of these adoptions ran into trouble. Many of the families were not equipped to handle children who had experienced the atrocities of war and displacement.

One act designed to curb international adoption abuse is the Intercountry Adoption Act of 2000. Its purpose is to protect the rights of children and families involved in intercountry adoption and to regulate the practices of adoption agencies in the best interests of children. To achieve this purpose, the act requires that the placement practices and records of an adoption agency be fully disclosed to prospective adoptive parents. Thus, adoption agencies and states are required to submit certain information on overseas adoptions that are unsuccessful.

Jane Teaford

See also: Adopted Children; Adopted Children, International; Intercountry Adoption Act.

Further Reading

Fessler, Ann. 2006. *"The Girls Who Went Away": The Hidden History of Women Who Surrendered Children for Adoption in the Decades before Roe v. Wade*. New York: Penguin Press.

Joyce, Kathryn. 2013. *The Child Catchers*. Jackson, TN: Public Affairs.

Moore, Mirah. 2007. *The Stork Market: America's Multi-Billion Dollar Unregulated Adoption Industry*. Dayton, NJ: Advocate Publications.

Smolin, David M. 2012. "Of Orphan and Adoption, Parents and the Poor, Exploitation and Rescue: A Scriptural and Theological Critique of the Evangelical Christian Adoption and Orphan Care Movement." *Regent Journal of International Law* 8 (2). http://works.bepress.com/david_smolin/10.

Wilson-Buterbaugh, Karen. n.d. "Systemic Abuses of Unmarried Mothers by the Adoption Industry: Evidence of Violation of Single Parent Rights." The Baby Scoop Era Research Initiatives. http://babyscoopera.com/adoption-abuse-of-mothers.

ADULT SEXUAL ATTRACTION TO ADOLESCENTS

When acted upon, adult sexual attraction to adolescents is an abuse because adult sexual contact with underage persons is traditionally seen as abusive to or exploitive of the person. Adult sexual attraction to adolescents has two forms. *Hebephilia* is adult sexual attraction to or preference for early adolescents between the ages of approximately 11 and 14, while *ephebophilia* is adult primary or exclusive sexual interest in adolescents who are 15 to 17 years old. Most adults having this propensity are males.

Hebephilia can be considered a form of abuse because adolescents cannot legally consent to sexual contact with an adult. Usually children dislike the contact and react distractedly, are frightened, and want to run away. However, empirical data also demonstrates that a minority (5% to 20%) experiences the contact as consensual and positive. One-third to one-half of 12- to 13-year-olds results in consensual partnership relations. How the genders perceive the sexual contact differs. More often, boys tend to view sexual contact with adults more positively than girls, labeling it an initiation. Girls see the sexual experiences as abuse. In some cases, neither gender views the contact the same as the adult. The adult is most likely caught up in orgasm, whereas the child, in the excitement.

Another reason hebephilia can be considered a form of abuse is that children can actually consent to sexual contact, but that consent is not a valid or true consent. Children may not have a mature understanding of the consequences but by consent are expressing willingness that it should take place. Although unplanned pregnancy may or may not be a consequence, transmittance of STDs or HIV/AIDS is a possible outcome, perpetuating the abuse. Even when children consent, the imbalance of power makes it difficult to decide whether a child truly consented or if the consent is a passive submission or a fear-based cooperation without inner willingness.

Abuse of the child can continue should criminal proceedings result. Interrogations and investigations are often repeated and intense, resulting in secondary harm that can be more severe than the harmful effects of the contact.

Although prevalence rates of sexual abuse in the general population are diffi-cult to analyze, studies demonstrate the incidence is about 4 percent. One study, confirmed by others, found that approximately 10,600 individuals alleged that a member of the Catholic clergy had sexually assaulted them. In 2004, the John Jay Report found that over 80 percent of adolescents who were abused by clergy were usually male. Cross-generational sexual contact is not limited to the Roman Catholic Church. Most likely, it occurs in other faiths and professions, such as the Boy Scouts or by coaches, teachers, and bus drivers, who have regular and private access to children. Because sexual contact with an adult has a significantly higher prevalence rate in the general population, it is not generally considered a mental disorder, though it has legal repercussions.

Controversy has surrounded a proposed change in diagnostic criteria and diagnostic labels. One issue is whether hebephilia is a sexual disorder. A pro-posed change was to increase the accuracy of diagnosis, not to increase the number of individuals diagnosed. But resistance surfaced. The opposi-tion included people who wanted paraphilia (a condition where a person's sexual arousal and gratification depend on fantasizing about and engaging in sex-ual behavior that is atypical and extreme, such as focusing on a particular object [children, animals, underwear]) removed from the *Diagnostic and Statistical Manual of Mental Disorders* (DSM). Opposition also included hebephiles who opposed list-ing hebephilia as a mental disorder and forensic psychologists and psychiatrists who saw all proposed changes in clinical diagnosis in terms of anticipated out-comes in the courtroom.

General principles resulting from the case law of the European Court on Human Rights suggest "that the basic right to privacy should be interpreted as providing comprehensive protection of the right of children and adolescents to sexual self-determination, namely both the right to effective protection from (unwanted) sex and abuse on the one hand and the right to (wanted) sex on the other."

Rosemarie Skaine

See also: Boy Scouts, Homosexual Policies of; Child Abuse, Sexual; Homosexuals; Pedophilia; Priests, Sexual Abuse by; Sex Offender; Transgender Individuals.

Further Reading

Blanchard, Ray. 2013. "A Dissenting Opinion on DSM-5 Pedophilic Disorder." *Archives of Sexual Behavior*, May. http://rd.springer.com/article/10.1007%2Fs10508-013-0117-x.

Bolcer, Julie. 2009. *Advocate*, October 13. http://www.advocate.com/news/daily-news/2009/10/13/vatican-ephebophilia-not-pedophilia.

Franklin, Karen. 2010. "Hebephilia: Quintessence of Diagnostic Pretextuality." *Behavioral Sciences & the Law* 28 (6): 751–768. doi:10.1002/bsl.934.

Graupner, Helmut. 1999. "Love versus Abuse: Crossgenerational Sexual Relations of Minors: A Gay Rights Issue?" *Journal of Homosexuality* 37 (4): 23–56.

Noonan-Karstens, Mary Ann. "Psychobiological Model of Personality and Ephebophilia within the Roman Catholic Priesthood." PhD diss. Fielding Graduate University, 2008. ProQuest (304825053).

Psychology Today. 2012. "Hebephilia: What Is Hebephilia?" http://www.psychologytoday.
    com/basics/hebephilia.

Ryan, Gregory P., Jeffrey P. Baerwald, and Gerard McGlone. 2008. "Cognitive Mediational
    Deficits and the Role of Coping Styles in Pedophile and Ephebophile Roman Catholic
    Clergy." *Journal of Clinical Psychology* 64 (1): 1–16.

Throckmorton, Warren. 2013. "Does the APA Consider Hebephilia to Be Normal?" *WordPress*,
    May 16. http://wthrockmorton.com/2013/05/does-the-apa-consider-hebephilia-to-be-
    normal.

AMBER ALERT

The AMBER Alert System was created as a legacy to Amber Hagerman, a nine-year-old that was kidnapped in Arlington, Texas, while riding her bicycle and then brutally murdered. The AMBER Alert Program is a voluntary partnership between law enforcement agencies, broadcasters, transportation agencies, and the wireless industry to set in motion an urgent bulletin in the most serious child abduction cases. The goal of an AMBER Alert is to immediately motivate the entire community to assist in the search for and the safe recovery of the child.

The America's Missing: Broadcast Emergency Response, or AMBER Alert System, began in 1996 in Dallas and Fort Worth, Texas. Broadcasters and local police developed the early warning system to help find abducted children. Other states and communities followed by setting up their own AMBER Alert plans, and the idea was adopted across the United States. In 2005, Hawaii became the 50th state to complete an AMBER Alert plan. In addition, by 2009, AMBER Alert plans were adopted by the District of Columbia, Puerto Rico, the U.S. Virgin Islands, Canadian provinces, and Mexican border states. Overall, AMBER Alert plans have had 656 successful recoveries, 120 total plans nationwide, 53 statewide, 29 regional, and 38 local.

As a result of the 2003 Prosecutorial Remedies and Other Tools to end the Exploitation of Children Today (PROTECT) Act, the Department of Justice suggested criteria for the issuance of AMBER Alerts: law enforcement confirmation that an abduction has taken place; the child must be 17 years old or younger and be at risk of serious injury or death; presence of sufficient descriptive information of the child, captor, or captor's vehicle to issue an alert; and the child's name and other critical data be entered immediately into the FBI's National Crime Information Center—information describing the circumstances of the abduction, and the case flagged as a child abduction.

The Department of Justice outlines how AMBER Alert works:

> Once law enforcement has determined that a child has been abducted and the abduction meets AMBER Alert criteria, law enforcement notifies broadcasters and state transportation officials. AMBER Alerts interrupt regular programming and are broadcast on radio and television and on highway signs. AMBER Alerts can also be issued on lottery tickets, to wireless devices such as mobile phones, and over the Internet.

Rosemarie Skaine

See also: Abduction, Child; Adam Walsh Child Protection and Safety Act; Walsh, John Edward.

Further Reading

National Center for Missing and Exploited Children. 2013. "AMBER Alert Success Stories." http://www.missingkids.com/amber/success.

U.S. Department of Justice. n.d. "AMBER Alert: America's Missing: Broadcast and Response." Office of Justice Programs. http://www.amberalert.gov.

U.S. Department of Justice. 2010. "AMBER Alert Chronology/Timeline." Office of Justice Programs. http://www.ojp.usdoj.gov/newsroom/pdfs/amberchronology.pdf.

AMERICANS WITH DISABILITIES ACT

The Americans with Disabilities Act (ADA) of 1990 was enacted by Congress in an effort to protect and provide needed services for children and adults with disabilities. Senator Tom Harkin (D–Iowa) authored and sponsored the bill. The ADA was signed into law on July 26, 1990, by President George H. W. Bush and later amended with a variety of changes that became effective January 1, 2009.

The ADA seeks to end discrimination and ensure equal opportunity in employment, public accommodations and building access, transportation, and government services for those with disabilities. It also made TDD telephone relay services for the deaf and hard of hearing mandatory. The current text of the ADA includes changes made by the ADA Amendments Act of 2008 (P.L. 110-325), which went into effect on January 1, 2009.

The ADA states that a *covered entity* shall not discriminate against *a qualified individual with a disability*. This applies to job application procedures, hiring, advancement and discharge of employees, workers' compensation, job training, and other terms, conditions, and privileges of employment. Covered entity can refer to an employment agency, labor organization, or joint labor-management committee and is generally an employer engaged in interstate commerce and having 15 or more workers. Discrimination may include, among other things, limiting or classifying a job applicant or employee in an adverse way, denying employment opportunities to people who truly qualify, not making reasonable accommodations to the known physical or mental limitations of disabled employees, not advancing employees with disabilities in the business, and/or not providing needed accommodations in training materials or policies, and the provision of qualified readers or interpreters.

If an individual has a disability, as defined by the ADA, the next step must be to determine whether that disability "substantially limits a major life activity." Such activities initially included caring for oneself, seeing, hearing, speaking, breathing, performing manual tasks, walking, learning, and working, and later grew to include such things as sitting, standing, bending, communicating, lifting, reaching, sleeping, eating, reading, and mental and emotional processes such as thinking, concentrating, and interacting with others. The definition of "major life activity" has also been expanded to include the operation of major bodily functions and systems, such as the circulatory, neurological, and digestive systems.

The expansion of this list has led to numerous lawsuits over the years, as employers and others contest what does or does not constitute an impairment of a major life activity. In some cases, courts have ruled in the plaintiffs' favor.

Defendants and those advocating for the disabled argue that such rulings may render the ADA less effective and, in some cases, may lead to inadequate accommodations or even abuse.

Four federal agencies enforce the ADA. The Equal Employment Opportunity Commission (EEOC) enforces regulations covering employment. The Department of Transportation enforces regulations governing transit. The Federal Communications Commission (FCC) enforces regulations covering telecommunication services. The Department of Justice enforces regulations governing public accommodations and state and local government services.

Rosemarie Skaine

See also: Disabled Adults; Disabled Children.

Further Reading

Civil Rights Division. n.d. "ADA Responsibilities: ADA Enforcement." U.S. Department of Justice. http://www.ada.gov/enforce_footer.htm.

Duston, Sheila D., and Beth Reiter. 2010. "Definition of Disability under the ADA: A Practical Overview and Update." Employment and Disability Institute. ILR School. Cornell University, Ithaca, NY. http://www.hrtips.org/article_1.cfm?b_id=27.

U.S. Department of Labor. n.d. "Americans with Disabilities Act." *Disability Resources*. http://www.dol.gov/dol/topic/disability/ada.htm.

ANGER

Anger is often a factor in abuse, including domestic abuse, and is often the cause of the abuse. Anger is an emotional response related to one's psychological interpretation of having been offended, wronged, or denied. Often it indicates when one's basic boundaries are violated. Some have a learned tendency to react to anger through retaliation. Anger may be used effectively when used to set boundaries or escape from dangerous situations. William DeFoore described anger as a pressure cooker in that we can only apply pressure against our anger for a certain amount of time until it explodes.

Anger is an emotion that involves a strong uncomfortable and emotional response to a perceived provocation. Anger has more negative dimensions than positive. If it gets out of control, it becomes destructive. Unrestrained anger can lead to problems at work, in personal relationships, and in the overall quality of life. Easily angered people have a low tolerance for frustration. Unable to accept situations, they believe that they should not have to be subjected to frustration, inconvenience, or annoyance. If the situation appears unjust, for example, being corrected for a minor mistake, anger will erupt. Unwarranted anger can cause problems for and harm to the angered person as well as for the object of the abuse. Increased blood pressure and other physical changes occur making clear thinking hard and harm physical and mental health.

Genetic or physiological causes may be at the root of uncontrolled anger. Signs can be detected in very early childhood, for example, irritability, touchy, and easily angered. Sociocultural causes play a role, anger is often regarded as negative and not to be expressed; thus, people fail to learn how to handle or channel it. Family background is also is a factor. People who are easily angered come from families that are disruptive, chaotic, and not skilled at emotional communications.

About two-thirds of adolescents have experienced an anger attack that involved threatening violence or violent behavior or destroying property. Nearly six million young people (one in 12) meet criteria for a diagnosis of intermittent explosive disorder (IED), a syndrome characterized by persistent uncontrollable anger attacks not accounted for by other mental disorders.

Raymond Novaco stratified anger into three modalities: cognitive (appraisals), somatic-affective (tension and agitations), and behavioral (withdrawal and antagonism). To manage anger, psychologists use basic strategies that combine these modalities to more effectively treat anger: relaxation; cognitive therapy, finding alternative ways of thinking about and reacting to anger; and skill development, learning new behaviors.

Behaviors that can help control anger include keeping a diary of anger outbursts, understanding how and why anger erupts, being assertive but cautious, letting go of what is beyond control, and learning techniques of conflict resolution and of nonconfrontational and positive self-expression.

Counselors or psychologists can assist in managing anger. Clinics that specialize in managing anger are available.

Rosemarie Skaine

See also: Anger Management; Intermittent Explosive Disorder.

Further Reading

American Psychological Association. 2014. "Anger." http://apa.org/topics/anger/index.aspx.

Harvard Medical School. 2012. "Uncontrollable Anger Prevalent among U.S. Youth: Almost Two-thirds Have History of Anger Attacks," *Science Daily*, July 2. http://www.sciencedaily.com/releases/2012/07/120702210048.htm.

Lohmann, Raychelle Cassada. 2012. "Uncontrollable Anger: The Path of Destruction." *Psychology Today*, August 3. http://www.psychologytoday.com/blog/teen-angst/201208/uncontrollable-anger.

Marano, Hara Estroff. 2003. "The Downside of Anger." *Psychology Today*, July 1. http://www.psychologytoday.com/articles/200308/the-downside-anger.

ANGER MANAGEMENT

Anger is normal and healthy, unless it gets out of control and becomes destructive. Because uncontrolled anger may lead to violence and abuse, it is important that it be managed effectively, either by the individual or through an organized anger management course or program.

When anger is not effectively managed, it can lead to explosive outbursts. It can also lead to repression of feelings of anger, which may eventually surface as even more violent outbursts. Anger explosions occur when individuals have very little control over their emotions, and these outbursts may lead to physical abuse or violence. Uncontrolled anger also negatively impacts the individual feeling it,

An angry child sits by himself in a corner. Anger and its management are concerns of an increasing number of people, including parents, teachers, and caregivers. (Atm2003/Dreamstime.com)

and he or she may suffer from anxiety, stress, depression, and low self-esteem as a result. It may also lead to physical problems such as high blood pressure and a weakened immune response.

About two-thirds of adolescents have experienced an anger attack that involved threatening violence, violent behavior, or destroying property. Nearly 6 million young people (1 in 12) meet criteria for a diagnosis of intermittent explosive disorder (IED), a syndrome characterized by persistent, uncontrollable anger attacks not accounted for by other mental disorders.

Genetic or physiological causes may be at the root of uncontrolled anger. Signs can be detected in very early childhood, for example, irritability, touchiness, and easily angered. Sociocultural causes play a role. Anger is often regarded as negative and not to be expressed; thus, people fail to learn how to handle or channel it. Family background is also a factor. People who are easily angered come from families that are disruptive, chaotic, and not skilled at emotional communications.

Unrestrained anger can lead to problems at work, in personal relationships, and in the overall quality of life. Easily angered people have a low tolerance for frustration. Unable to accept situations, they believe that they should not have to be subjected to frustration, inconvenience, or annoyance. If the situation appears unjust, for example, being corrected for a minor mistake, anger will erupt. Unwarranted anger can cause problems for and harm to the angered person as well as for the object of the abuse. Increased blood pressure and other physical changes occur making clear thinking hard and harm physical and mental health.

Anger is not something that can be cured, only managed. Even people who seem to keep an even keel are not free of the emotion—they've simply learned how to manage it effectively. Learning to control anger may take professional help. Group and individual anger or stress management training classes and counseling are available. The most effective approach typically involves cognitive behavior therapy (CBT), which combines cognitive restructuring and coping skills training and psychotherapy.

Anger management methods can produce benefits for the individual in communicating needs, maintaining better health, and preventing psychological and social problems linked to anger. Anger management classes or counseling for anger management can be done in a group or one-on-one with a partner, child, or someone else. The setting, length, and number of sessions vary, depending on the program or counselor and your needs. Anger management courses or counseling can be brief or last for weeks or months.

Rosemarie Skaine

See also: Anger; Intermittent Explosive Disorder; Road Rage.

Further Reading

American Psychological Association. 2014. "Anger." http://apa.org/topics/anger/index.aspx.

Harvard Medical School. 2012. "Uncontrollable Anger Prevalent among U.S. Youth: Almost Two-thirds Have History of Anger Attacks." *Science Daily*, July 2. http://www.sciencedaily.com/releases/2012/07/120702210048.htm.

Lohmann, Raychelle Cassada. 2012. "Uncontrollable Anger: The Path of Destruction." *Psychology Today*, August 3. http://www.psychologytoday.com/blog/teen-angst/201208/uncontrollable-anger.

Marano, Hara Estroff. 2003. "The Downside of Anger." *Psychology Today*, July 1. http://www.psychologytoday.com/articles/200308/the-downside-anger.

Mayo Clinic Staff. 2014. "Anger Management." Tests and Procedures. Mayo Clinic. http://www.mayoclinic.org/tests-procedures/anger-management/basics/definition/prc-20014603.

WebMD. 2014. "Mental Health and Anger Management." Accessed January 10, 2015. Anxiety & Panic Disorders Health Center. http://www.webmd.com/anxiety-panic/guide/mental-health-managing-anger.

ANIMAL ABUSE

Animal abuse is the harming of an animal. It includes neglect, beating, torturing, and killing of the animal. Animal abuse, while problematic in its own right, is also often seen as a precursor to abuse directed against humans.

In 2007, 1,880 animal abuse cases were reported. Of these cases, 1,212 involved dogs, 337 involved cats, and over 470 involved some other animal species. The types of abuse included, according to the Animal Abuse Registry Database Administration System (AARDAS) Project's March, 2012 report, neglect/abandonment (5319), hoarding (2036), shooting (1871), fighting (1471), beating (1153), mutilation/torture (915), throwing (411), stabbing (406), burning-fire or fireworks (351), vehicular (299), poisoning (308), kicking/stomping (235), choking/strangulation/suffocation (222), bestiality (219), unlawful trade/smuggling (203), theft (184), unlawful trapping/hunting (132), hanging (122), drowning (122), burning–caustic substance (97).

Animal abuse occurs by two kinds of abusers. The animal abuse is either active or passive. The active abusers purposefully inflict as much pain and damage as possible. They enjoy hurting things, and animals are easy targets. They hurt animals to be

Confinement in a very small cage is just one way that animals are abused. (Shutterstock)

in control of something, quite often due to a lack of control in their own life. People participate in dog fighting because it gives them the thrill of being powerful by having the dog capable of killing other peoples' dogs. These abusers are seeking power, by any means. They feel superior by controlling and inflicting pain on animals that are incapable of stopping the abuser's behavior. They abuse animals because the animals are unable to expose their abuser.

The active abuser frequently uses animals as a means of controlling others. A husband may abuse the family pet as a means of expressing what he would do to the wife should she fail to do his bidding. According to a report by the Humane Society of the United States, nearly 1 million animals a year are abused or killed in connection with domestic violence, and 71 percent of domestic violence victims report that their abuser also targeted their animal. This group is the most difficult to correct and are often unchangeable.

Children may be coerced by peers to tease animals that are unable to run away, or think animals running away in fear are funny. When children abuse their family pet, they may feel unable to fight with their parents.

People who passively abuse animals out of ignorance do not mean to cause the animal pain or discomfort. They may be trying to control the animal's behavior by tying it up or kenneling it. This becomes cruelty to animals when the animal is chained too shortly or the kennel prevents adequate exercise. People may acquire excessive animals when attempting to rescue animals seeming to be in need of assistance. Hoarders may fail to provide appropriate care to all their animals simply due to their inability to physically care for them. In some cases, busy families may forget to feed and water the animal on a regular basis.

Forms of discipline also vary with the family pet. There are many corrective training methods without striking the animal, yet most people will strike the animal as a means of punishment. Most of the time the punishment is so disconnected to the behavior the animal has no idea why it is being abused. Therefore, the corrective action is completely lost on the animal's cognition. This type of treatment eventually may lead to aggressiveness toward specific people, or the animal's complete withdrawal mentally from socialization.

Currently, 47 states have legislation that makes animal cruelty a felony. Before 1986, only four states had felony animal cruelty laws. Forty-two of the 47 state felony animal cruelty laws were enacted in the last three decades: 13 were enacted between 1986 and 1996, and 28 more were enacted between 1997 and 2011. The number of reported abusive incidents highlights the problem that most of the cases remain unreported. Many cases are never revealed or prosecuted. People may call local agencies or national hotlines to anonymously report abusive situations. The situation will be investigated and if necessary, the animal may be removed and the local police may be notified to process animal abuse charges. Most local agencies are aware of people in the district who will foster parent the abused animal and reintroduce it to society for adoption when the animal is emotionally prepared.

People who abuse animals out of ignorance, or children participating due to peer pressure, are in the group of abusers who can usually be helped through education and supervision. Once they understand the impact of their behavior, they are usually willing to cease their abusive actions. Animal abusers who were abused as children by adults are more difficult to rehabilitate. They have witnessed animal abuse most of their lives in addition to being abused themselves. They have been conditioned to express anger through striking out, most often at animals incapable of reporting the abuse to authorities. People who have been raised in abusive environments often participate in the cycle of abuse. Psychologists believe the people in this group suffer from serious psychological problems that often require the assistance of licensed professionals.

The key to stopping abuse is intervention by those cognizant of the situation. Too often people refrain from intervening because they know the people or they do not consider animal abuse a serious issue. Associations that people may contact when suspecting abuse include the American Society for the Prevention of Cruelty to Animals (ASPCA) and the Humane Society of the United States. In their communities, these organizations have local numbers to call to report the suspicious treatment of animals without revealing one's identity.

Connie Kerns-Grams

See also: Anger; Cycle of Abuse.

Further Reading

AARDAS Project. 2012. *U.S. Animal Abuse Classifications and Occurrences, Graphed: 2012.* http://www.intellectualtakeout.org/library/chart-graph/us-animal-abuse-classifications-and-occurences-graphed-2012.

Animal Cruelty Facts. 2011. "Facts about Animal Cruelty." http://animalcrueltyfacts.org.

Animal Cruelty Facts and Statistics. 2014. "Statistics on the Victims and Current Legislative Trends." http://www.humanesociety.org/issues/abuse_neglect/facts/animal_cruelty_facts_statistics.html.

ASPCA. n.d. "ASPCA Kids." http://www.aspca.org/aspcakids/real-issues/why-do-people-abuse-animals.aspx.

Batul, N. A. Buzzle. 2012. "Animal Abuse Statistics," March 14. http://www.buzzle.com/articles/animal-abuse-statistics.html.

Online Veterinary Technician Schools. 2012. "20 Startling Statistics about Animal Abuse and Neglect." *The Pet Gazette*, January 22. http://onlineveterinarytechnicianschools.com/2012/20-startling-statistics-about-animal-abuse-and-neglect.

Pet-Abuse.com. 2014. "Animal Abuse Database," 2001–2014. http://www.pet-abuse.com.

Simon, George. 2009. "Abusing Animals: Some Psychological Reasons behind Animal Abuse." Ask the Psychologist. http://askthepsych.com/atp/2009/06/05/psychological-reasons-behind-animal-abuse.

ANTIGAY LOBBY

Opposition to homosexuals, both male and female, has been active among groups in the United States. Groups that have organized to oppose what they call the "homosexual agenda" are included in the antigay lobby. The Family Research Council (FRC) and the American Family Association (AFA) are two of the most important in the antigay lobby in this country.

The FRC each year hosts the Values Voter Summit, a conference for social conservatives that attracts public figures. It has a $12 million budget and is politically powerful. Its spokespersons appear regularly on the national media. The FRC is powerful in the political realm and its lobbying efforts have produced support from legislators on Capitol Hill. The AFA has a $20 million budget and a network of about 200 radio stations. It is regularly quoted in the press and has worked to organize grassroots Christians to lobby for its goals.

The FRC and the AFA are certainly among the most powerful groups on the American religious right. Other groups that are active in their opposition to gays, especially same-sex marriage, include Abiding Truth Ministries, Springfield, Massachusetts; American Family Association; American Vision; Chalcedon Foundation, Vallecito, California; Concerned Women for America, Washington, D.C.; and Traditional Values Coalition, Anaheim, California.

Reasoning behind the antigay position are the positions taken by the Family Research Council and the American Family Association. The FRC has claimed that gay activists work to normalize sex with boys, seek to abolish all age of consent laws, and to eventually recognize pedophiles as the prophets of a new sexual order, and support antibullying programs solely to promote homosexuality. The AFA has declared that homosexuality gave us Adolph Hitler, the Nazi war machine, and 6 million dead Jews. It suggested that gay sex be punished like heroin use and said that the homosexual agenda endangers every fundamental right in the Constitution, including religious freedom. Both groups have enthusiastically promoted reparative therapy, which claims, against the bulk of the evidence, that it can cure gay men and lesbians and make them heterosexual.

After the Supreme Court struck down the Defense of Marriage Act and overturned California's Proposition 8 ban on same-sex marriage in June 2013, the antigay lobby continued their efforts against homosexuals and same-sex marriage, but the efforts shifted to the state level.

The Southern Poverty Law Center opposes the antigay lobby and has conducted research to examine the lobby's claims. One claim that the FRC and AFA make is that homosexuals are child molesters. The SPLC has found that such claims have produced violence against homosexuals. Based on an analysis of 14 years of FBI hate crime data, the evidence showed that homosexuals were by far the American minority most victimized by hate crimes. They were more than twice as likely to be attacked in a violent hate crime as Jews or black people and more than four times as likely as Muslims. And that doesn't include the antigay bullying that has resulted in so many teen suicides.

Rosemarie Skaine

See also: Hate Crimes; Homosexuals.

Further Reading

Beirich, Heidi, Evelyn Schlatter, and Robert Steinback. 2011. "The Anti-gay Lobby: The Family Research Council, the American Family Association & the Demonization of LGBT People." Southern Poverty Law Center. http://www.splcenter.org/get-informed/publications/the-anti-gay-lobby-the-family-research-council-the-american-family-association-the-demonization-of-l.

Huffington Post. 2013. "Anti-gay Groups," August 20. http://www.huffingtonpost.com/tag/anti-gay-groups.

Schlatter, Evelyn. 2010. "18 Anti-gay Groups and Their Propaganda." *Intelligence Report*, Winter (140). Southern Poverty Law Center. http://www.splcenter.org/get-informed/intelligence-report/browse-all-issues/2010/winter/the-hard-liners.

BATTERED PERSON SYNDROME

Battered person syndrome (BPS) is a series of common characteristics that appear in persons who are physically and psychologically abused over an extended period of time by their mate or dominant figure in their lives. Some states refer to BPS as battered woman syndrome, however, women and men develop the syndrome.

Battered person syndrome occurs when a person attacks or kills a partner as a result of having been physically and psychologically abused or beaten over an extended period of time. BPS is often paired with posttraumatic stress disorder (PTSD). When BPS manifests as PTSD, the following symptoms are apparent: reexperiencing the battering whether or not it is reoccurring; avoiding activities, people, and emotions to avoid the psychological impact of battering; overarousal or excessive vigilance; disrupted interpersonal relationships; distorted body image or other somatic concerns; and sexuality and intimacy issues. These symptoms may cause the victim to develop an irrational belief system to justify their situation, such as believing that the violence is their fault, always fearing for their life, and that the abuser is always present.

Battered women have killed their abusers. More are in confrontational situations than in nonconfrontational situations. Identifying this type of homicide is not easy. A study of appellate cases from 1902 to 1991 wherein female defendants claimed to have killed their abusive domestic partners in self-defense estimated that 20 percent of the killings (about 45 cases) were nonconfrontational, with 8 percent (about 18 cases) involved sleeping victims. These figures are consistent with a study of self-defense cases from 1979 to 1999 in which imminence was at issue. The study found that battered women committed approximately 9 percent of the killings in nonconfrontational settings.

A battered woman is characterized as a woman who is subject to any forceful physical or psychological behavior from a man in order to force her to do something without any concern for her rights. Battered women consist of wives or women in intimate relationships with men. Additionally, to be classified as a battered woman, the couple must have gone through the battering cycle at least two times. The reasoning is that any woman may find herself in an abusive relationship with a man one time, but when the abuse occurs a second time and she remains in the situation, she is defined as a battered woman.

The violence follows a pattern with three stages: tension building with small abusive incidents that intensify until the second stage erupts, the acute battering phase, with physical beatings, and psychological abuse. The third stage is a calm and loving period and the batterer seeks forgiveness and promises never to be abusive again. Usually in the third stage, the victim decides to continue the relationship with the hope that the abuse will cease. In time, the cycle repeats. The cycle also has four psychological stages: denial, guilt, enlightenment, and responsibility.

Battered person syndrome is important because it is considered an affirmative defense, for example, in Georgia, used in combination with a self-defense or justification defense. For example, a woman is charged with the murder of her husband who abused her over a long period of time. However, if the woman can convince a jury that she suffers from battered person syndrome and that "the circumstances were such that would excite the fears of a reasonable person possessing the same or similar psychological and physical characteristics of the defendant at the time that the deceased victim used force against the defendant, then she may be acquitted by a jury." Furthermore, battered person syndrome is important because, in addition to using BPS as a criminal defense, it may used to explain the conduct of a crime victim. For example, a woman's failure to report ongoing domestic abuse by her husband or intimate partner may be explained because she suffers from battered person syndrome.

When battered person syndrome is a complete defense, the battered defendant is basically free of blame, and he or she is acquitted of the criminal charge(s). However, this type of defense is challenging, and testimonial evidence has to be gathered and presented. A court may consider: expert witness testimony, usually a psychologist, concerning the defendant being a battered person; independent witness testimony relating a history of abuse; relationship closeness between the victim and the abuser; type of abuse, psychological abuse alone may not be adequate; and whether the defendant should reasonably fear forthcoming physical injury based on previous abuse.

When battered person syndrome is used as a defense when someone has been seriously hurt or killed due to the actions of another person, the fact that someone has been hurt or killed may result in a very serious criminal prosecution, so the best strategy to avoid this prosecution is to call the police and report what happened. Court intervention, drug and alcohol treatment, shelters, anger management training, and family counseling can help in avoiding the acts committed by the battered person.

Rosemarie Skaine

See also: Battered Women Shelters; Cycle of Abuse; Domestic Abuse; Domestic Abuse, Psychological Effects of; Posttraumatic Stress Disorder; Victim Empowerment Models.

Further Reading

Castillo, Jaime. July 11, 2011. "Battered Person Syndrome, PTSD, and Bullying." American Counseling Association Blog. http://www.counseling.org/news/blog/aca-blog/2011/07/11/battered-person-syndrome-ptsd-and-bullying#sthash.7r79Hwvl.dpuf.

Chester v. State. 471 S.E.2d 836, 837 (Ga. 1996).

Krause, Joan H. 2007 "Distorted Reflections of Battered Women Who Kill: A Response to Professor Dressler." *Ohio State Journal of Criminal Law* 4: 555–572. http://moritzlaw.osu.edu/students/groups/osjcl/files/2012/05/Krause-PDF-03-11-07.pdf.

Leshchinskiy, Pavel. 2013. "Battered Person Syndrome." *LegalMatch*, November 5. http://www.legalmatch.com/law-library/article/battered-person-syndrome.html.

Parker, K. Tiffany. 1999/2000. "Comment: Georgia Supreme Court Expands Battered Person Syndrome to Include Psychological Abuse." *Cumberland Law Review* 30: 545.

Smith v. State. 486 S.E.2d 819, 822 n.2 (Ga. 1997).

Swindle Law Group, P.C. 2012. "Battered Person Syndrome." http://www.swindlelaw.com/battered-person-syndrome.

BATTERED WOMEN SHELTERS

Battered women shelters are the major places women and children can go to escape the danger and violence of living with a batterer. Shelters are a refuge where women can feel safe. Domestic violence shelters are used in cases of emergency and are usually open 24 hours a day. After the emergency stage has passed, a woman may have the opportunity to move to a transition house. Transition houses are also temporary, but are environments available to help support a family while they stabilize their lives enough to become self-sufficient. There are 1,500 emergency battered women shelters in the United States.

The Domestic Violence Resource Center reported that each year between 600,000 and 6 million women are victims of domestic violence. Studies also show that access to shelter services leads to a 60 percent to 70 percent reduction in incidence and severity of repeated assault during the 3–12 months follow-up period compared to women who did not access shelter. Shelter services led to greater reduction in severe repeated assault than did seeking court or law enforcement protection or moving to a new location.

Historically, battered women shelters have provided safety, healing, and have saved lives.

The construction of a Domestic Abuse Intervention Services shelter in Madison, Wisconsin, in March 2014. Domestic abuse shelters, often tucked away in the protective privacy of obscure neighborhoods, are moving out of the shadows with more public profiles aimed at generating more community support and better access for victims. (AP Photo/Taylor W. Anderson)

Shelters developed in the 1970s in response to women who were isolated within their homes in an abusive relationship. Survivors recognized the dangers and began opening their homes. Groups of women purchased homes for shelter. The action of these survivors was revolutionary because at the time, laws against intimate partner abuse did not exist and men were viewed as the unquestioned head of the household. If a woman sought safety, she, not the abuser, was expected to leave the home. The initial onset of laws failed to correct this perception, and even if the abuser did leave, a woman's safety was uncertain and protection orders were ineffective.

In 2013, shelters offered many services designed to repair the effects of domestic abuse, such as the physical and psychological damage. The goal is to get the battered woman able to independently care for herself and her family. Battered women shelters are short-term solutions focusing their services on immediate needs and safety, repair of damage and preparation for moving forward with life with hope instead of fear and possibly a better life. Battered women's shelters may ask for, but do not require, personal information. Sometimes victims give a false name to protect against being found by the batterer. Battered women's shelters' addresses are kept confidential.

Services at a domestic violence shelter may include housing and meals, information, referrals, educational programs, a crisis line, support groups and counseling, housing assistance, employment assistance, personal and medical needs, child care, assistance with restraining orders and other legal activities, accompaniment to health care and legal appointments, transportation, addiction services, and outreach services to nonresidents. Local or toll-free numbers are available at most agencies, and some also have hotlines.

WomensLaw.org makes finding a domestic violence shelter easy by visiting their Web site and searching by state. Shelters are an excellent first stop for women who are considering leaving an abusive relationship, starting a legal action against an abuser, thinking through a plan to stay safe, or trying to sort out whether the partner's behavior is abusive.

Rosemarie Skaine

See also: Battered Person Syndrome; Domestic Abuse; Domestic Abuse, Psychological Effects of.

Further Reading

Domestic Violence Resource Center. 2013. "Domestic Violence Statistics." http://dvrc-or. org/domestic/violence/resources/C61.

Janovicek, Nancy. 2007. *No Place to Go: Local Histories of the Battered Women's Shelter Movement*. Vancouver, BC, CAN: UBC Press.

Olsen, Linda. 2007. "Battered Women's Shelters: Reflections." *Inside Scoop*, March. Washington State Coalition Against Domestic Violence. http://www.wscadv.org/docs/Mar_07_Inside_Scoop.pdf.

Tracy, Natasha. 2013. "Battered Women Shelters: What Are They? How to Find One?" *HealthyPlace.com*. http://www.healthyplace.com/abuse/domestic-violence/battered-women-shelters-what-are-they-how-to-find-one.

WomensLaw.org. 2009. "State and Local Programs (Shelters)." Where to Find Help. http://www.womenslaw.org/gethelp_type.php?type_name=State and Local Programs.

BOY SCOUTS, HOMOSEXUAL POLICIES OF

The Boy Scouts of America (BSA), one of the largest private youth organizations in the United States, has policies that prohibit open or avowed homosexuals from membership in its Scouting programs. The BSA contends that its policies are essential in its mission to instill in young people the values of the Scout Oath and Law. It believes that a known or avowed homosexual is not an appropriate role model of the Scout Oath and Law.

The Boy Scouts of America denied or revoked membership status or leadership positions for what it considered violations of these foundational principles. As early as 1980, the BSA denied membership to openly homosexual individuals who applied for adult leadership positions. In 1991, it issued a position statement that was the organization's official position: "We believe that homosexual conduct is inconsistent with the requirement in the Scout Oath that a Scout be morally straight and in the Scout Law that a Scout be clean in word and deed, and that homosexuals do not provide a desirable role model for Scouts."

The organization's legal right to have these policies was upheld repeatedly by both state and federal courts. In *Boy Scouts of America v. Dale*, the Supreme Court of the United States has affirmed that as a private organization, the BSA can set its own membership standards. Its policies were not found to constitute illegal discrimination because as a private organization in the United States, it had the right to freedom of association.

In recent years, the policy disputes intensified, including the terms under which the BSA can access governmental resources, including public lands. The BSA still maintained its policy on homosexuals. In July 2012, the BSA reached a unanimous consensus that recommended that its restrictive policy be retained. The pressure to change was increased when, in 2012, both President Barack Obama and Republican presidential candidate Mitt Romney stated that they opposed the ban on gay Scouts. Bowing to the pressure, in May 2013, the BSA's national council approved a resolution to remove the restriction denying membership to youth on the basis of sexual orientation alone, effective January 1, 2014. The ban on openly homosexual adult Scout leaders is to remain in effect.

The reaction to the policy was both for and against. Some wanted even further lessening of the restrictions to permit homosexual adult leaders to become members. Others who were opposed to allowing any avowed homosexual to be a Scout moved to disassociate their organizations, usually churches, from sponsoring Boy Scout troops. Other opponents moved to set up antihomosexual Scouting alternatives.

Rosemarie Skaine

See also: Antigay Lobby; Homosexuals; Homosexuals in the Military, Abuse of; Transgender Individuals.

Further Reading

Boy Scouts of America. 2013. "Membership Standards Review." http://www.scouting.org/
    sitecore/content/membershipstandards/resolution/resolution.aspx.
Hallowell, Billy. 2013. "Opponents of Boy Scouts' Gay Youths Policy to Launch New 'Godly'
    Alternative for Kids." *The Blaze*, July 10. http://www.theblaze.com/stories/2013/07/10/
    opponents-of-boy-scouts-new-policy-on-gay-youths-to-launch-new-alternative-
    organization.
Raby, John. 2013. "Boy Scouts Anti-gay Policy. *Huffington Post*, July 16. http://
    www.huffingtonpost.com/tag/boy-scouts-anti-gay-policy.

BRADY HANDGUN VIOLENCE PREVENTION ACT

The Brady Handgun Violence Prevention Act of 1993 was named after President
Ronald Reagan's press secretary, Jim Brady. Brady was seriously wounded in a 1981
assassination attempt on Reagan. As a result, Brady was confined to a wheelchair.
The gunman was a mentally unstable young man, John Hinckley.

The act imposes a mandatory five-day waiting period and, after 1998, a background check on all sales of firearms to unlicensed individuals. Included in the act
was a ban on assault weapons. The ban expired after 10 years.

The Brady law has blocked an estimated 2 million prohibited gun purchases and
decreased deaths from gun violence. From the law's passage until 2009, over 107
million Brady-mandated background checks were conducted. The Brady Act was
one of two laws passed in 1994 that became the center for the gun control debate.
The Violent Crime Control and Law Enforcement Act also passed, banning certain
types of assault weapons entirely.

James Brady, wounded during the 1981 assassination attempt on President Ronald Reagan,
attends a press conference with the president and first lady. The Brady Handgun Violence Prevention Act is named after James Brady. (Ronald Reagan Library)

The permanent provisions of the act, which went into effect on November 30, 1998, required the U.S. attorney general to create the National Instant Criminal Background Check System (NICS). According to the FBI, when a firearm licensee starts a NICS background check, a search is conducted for matching records in the National Crime Information Center (NCIC) (providing information about wanted individuals and protection orders); the Interstate Identification Index (III) (which houses criminal history records); and the NICS Index (which contains names of individuals predetermined to be prohibited from receiving firearms under federal or state law). For non-U.S. citizens, a search of the Department of Homeland Security's U.S. Immigration and Customs Enforcement (ICE) index is performed.

A match on one of these databases results in immediate disqualification of the firearms transfer. Record checks usually take only a few minutes. However, if the results of the match are unclear, the NICS must contact the relevant law enforcement or judicial authorities for further information and clarification. If a final decision is not made within three business days, the firearm may be legally transferred at the discretion of the owner.

In 1996, President Clinton awarded Brady the Presidential Medal of Freedom, the highest civilian award in the United States. On February 11, 2000, Clinton named the White House Press Briefing Room, the James S. Brady Press Briefing Room. The Brady Center to Prevent Gun Violence was also named after Jim Brady. The center is the largest grassroots organization promoting gun control legislation. Its positions include: certain classes of guns should not be legal for private ownership such as assault weapons and small, lightweight handguns; guns in the home are more often used in accidental shootings, suicides, or criminal activity than in acts of self-defense; and gun violence strains the economy and health system. The Brady Center advocates increased gun control legislation, better enforcement of current law, and public policy that addresses gun violence at the federal and state levels. Its Legal Action Project is a venue to represent victims of gun violence in cases against irresponsible gun sellers and owners.

Rosemarie Skaine

See also: Gun Violence; Stand Your Ground Law.

Further Reading

Brady Campaign to Prevent Gun Violence. 2013. "About Gun Violence." http://www.bradycampaign.org/about-gun-violence.

Brady Handgun Violence Prevention Act. November 30, 1993. (Pub. L. 103–159, 107 Stat. 1536). http://www.gpo.gov/fdsys/pkg/BILLS-103hr1025enr/pdf/BILLS-103hr1025enr.pdf.

FBI. 2013. "National Instant Criminal Background Check System." Brady Handgun Violence Prevention Act of 1993. http://www.fbi.gov/about-us/cjis/nics/general-information/nics-overview.

Fuller, Jaime. 2014. "It's Been 20 Years since the Brady Bill Passed: Here Are 11 Ways Gun Politics Have Changed." *Washington Post*, February 28. http://www.washingtonpost.com/blogs/the-fix/wp/2014/02/28/its-been-20-years-since-the-brady-law-passed-how-have-gun-politics-changed.

Stingl, Lee, and M. Alexander. 2013. "Gun Control Overview." *Salem Press Encyclopedia*. Database: Research Starters.

BRAINWASHING AND MIND CONTROL

Brainwashing and mind control are abuses because the free will of the individual is overridden. Coercive methods are used to achieve goals. Coercion takes away the element of choice from an individual and causes the person to act or think in a predetermined manner. It functions by dominating, restraining, or controlling and forces the person to perform the desired behavior. Coercive psychological systems bring behavioral change using psychological force in a way to cause the learning and acceptance of an ideology or selected set of beliefs, ideas, attitudes, or behaviors. The techniques of brainwashing usually involve isolation from former associates and sources of information; an exacting regimen calling for absolute obedience and humility; strong social pressures and rewards for cooperation; physical and psychological punishments for noncooperation, including social ostracism and criticism, deprivation of food, sleep, and social contacts, bondage, and torture; and constant reinforcement.

The amount of coercive brainwashing or mind control that exists is difficult to measure. It is used in cults, terror organizations, ritual abuse, abductions, prisoner of war settings, situations of unethical influence, and some religious groups. Coercion goes beyond persuasion because it deprives the individual of choice in thought and action. In an open society, persuasion is used to influence attitudes and modify behavior. Persuasion is used in every part of our society and provided for in the constitutional freedoms of speech, press, and religion. Coercive thought control is distinguished from other social influence efforts because it is a totalistic and sequenced nature and works to destabilize the victim's sense of self and reality and values. Programs called *thought reform* depend on organized peer pressure, the development of bonds between the leader or trainer and the followers, the control of communication, and the use of a variety of influence techniques. The goal is to promote conformity, compliance, and the adoption of specific attitudes and behaviors desired by the group.

The concepts and models of brainwashing, such as those used during the Korean War and the Iraq War, employed suggestibility-increasing drugs, physical pain, and torture. These methods are not necessary for a coercive persuasion program to be effective. With drugs, the effects are temporary. The steps employed in mind control are small, so the victims will not note the changes or recognize the coercive nature of the processes or will not understand the hidden organizational purpose until much later, if at all. Because the victim considers the group doing the manipulating to be a friend, normal ego defenses are down. The goal is to overcome the victim's critical-thinking abilities and free will. Gradually, victims are unable to make independent decisions and use informed consent.

Attempts to brainwash and use mind control are ever present in a society. In some cases, the best defense is communication among those who are the targets. Those who are targeted can inject reality into a world that those who would brainwash and exercise mind control are attempting to create.

Rosemarie Skaine

See also: Abduction, Capture and Imprisonment; Human Trafficking; Prisoner Abuse, Adult; Satanic Rituals, Abuse in; Torture.

Further Reading

Singer, Margaret. "Coercive Mind Control Tactics." *F.A.C.T.net*. http://www.factnet.org/node/357.

Singer, Margaret. "How Does Mind Control Work?: A Technical Overview of Mind Control Tactics." *F.A.C.T.net*. http://factnet.org/how-does-mind-control-work.

Singer, Margaret. "Mind Control/Brainwashing/Thought Reform Exists." *F.A.C.T.net*. http://www.factnet.org/node/1830/#content.

Taylor, Kathleen E. 2006. *Brainwashing: The Science of Thought Control*. Oxford, U.K.: Oxford University Press.

Wollersheim, Lawrence. "How I Healed the Psychological Injuries from My Abuse in a Cult." *F.A.C.T.net*. http://www.factnet.org/node/654.

BULLY PROJECT

In April 2012, the BULLY Project was announced as a national social action campaign inspired by the award-winning film *BULLY*. Its goal is to stop bullying and change the lives of children and alter a culture of bullying into one of empathy and action. Partners in this campaign, such as Facing History and Ourselves, work to create safe, caring, and respectful schools and communities. On June 6, 2013, the One Million Kids initiative reached 1 million kids, which represented about 11 percent of the kids in the nation. The goal now is to reach 10 million kids or more to end bullying in America.

The One Million Kids initiative has brought the film *BULLY* to young people and educators throughout the country along with a curriculum and training to help prepare educators to lead a discussion with their students that emphasizes developing empathy and taking action. The campaign has made possible screenings for over 250,000 students and 7,500 educators in approximately 120 cities.

BULLY is available on DVD, and in 2013, the campaign launched an Educators DVD Activation Toolkit. Partners who contributed to the kit include Facing History and Ourselves, The Harvard Graduate School of Education, Not In Our School, Love is Louder, the National Center for Learning Disabilities, and Common Sense Media. Facing History and Ourselves is the BULLY Project's leading educational partner and has developed a complete curriculum for educators. After participating in the online workshop, 98 percent of the teachers said they would recommend the workshop to colleagues, and 88 percent agreed that the film and training helped to make the classroom safe and reflective.

Along with a definition of bullying and the toolkit that the BULLY Project Web site offers to educators, tools for groups that can make a difference, for example, students, parents, and advocates. For students, two activation guides are offered, one for the Youth and the other for the School Community. As a youth, suggestions include: start your own bully project; express that love is louder through posting photos; make a video sharing your story or a community action project; and speak up to stop bullying. Resources for parents are comprehensive including: a Parent Action Toolkit; 10 Tips for Parents; Prevention and Intervention Tips for Families, Creating Just and Caring Communities for Parents,

10 Questions Parents Can Ask Elementary School Students, When the Advice is Ineffective, Sample Letter to School, Bullying Prevention Resources, and Advice for Parents on Cyberbullying. Resources for advocates include Advocacy Toolkit, Framing Bullying for Advocates, Bullying Prevention Resources, and 10 Ways to be an Upstander.

In 2013, the BULLY Project surpassed its initial goal of 1 million kids and has reached over 2.2 million kids in over 1,700 cities and 3 countries, and the number is continually rising. The 2.2 million represents 14 percent of all secondary students in the United States. As a result, the project increased its goal and is now working to reach 10 million kids.

Rosemarie Skaine

See also: Bullying, Child and Adolescent; Cyberbullying, Child and Adolescent; Cyberstalking; Disabled Children; Homosexuals; Internet Victimization, Child; Racism; Stalking.

Further Reading

cngrams65. 2013. "BULLY Reaches 1 Million, Students Receive Lesson in Religious Tolerance after Sikh Attack." *Not in Our Town* (blog), June 6. http://www.niot.org/blog/bully-reaches-1-million-students-receive-lesson-religious-tolerance-after-sikh-attack.

Herron, Kelsey. 2013. "The Bully Project Launches New Toolkit for Educators." *Common Classroom: The Common Sense Education Blog*, May 30. Common Sense Education. http://www.commonsensemedia.org/educators/blog/the-bully-project-launches-new-toolkit-for-educators.

Powers, Simeon. 2012. "Simeon Powers." The BULLY Project. http://www.thebullyproject.com/simeonpowers.

The BULLY Project. n.d. "About the BULLY Project." http://www.thebullyproject.com/about_the_bully_project.

The BULLY Project. 2012. "Bully Project: 1 Million Kids Initiative." http://b.3cdn.net/bullyproject/4858d97af6384d2812_mlbrgn8v4.pdf.

BULLYING, ADULT

Bullying is an unwanted, aggressive behavior that involves a real or perceived power imbalance. The behavior is repeated, or has the potential to be repeated, over time to a person considered vulnerable. Adult bullying can take place anywhere in our society; on the streets, on the Internet, in the workplace, the home, business, education, sports, government, churches, and the media. The person bullied can be any age and any place in society.

The Workplace Bullying Institute estimates that up to one-third of workers are victims of workplace bullying. Approximately 20 percent of workplace bullying becomes harassment. The *New York Times* found that about 60 percent of workplace bullies are men who usually bully male and female employees equally. Women who bully are more likely to bully women. In older adult environments, estimates indicate that 10 percent to 20 percent of residents or clients may be victims, but often acts of bullying go unreported.

Adults tend to bully people they dislike because of differences. Usually bullies select capable, dedicated, popular, intelligent, attractive, and nonconfrontational victims. Their objective is to gain control by making others feel angry or afraid through such verbal abuse as name calling, sarcasm, teasing, threatening, mocking, insulting, ignoring, or discrediting.

The workplace is a common place where adult bullying occurs. Workplace bullying is committed when one person or group single out another person for unreasonable, embarrassing, or intimidating treatment. Some forms include getting ignored, being put down in front of others, left out, talked about, or humiliated. Usually workplace bullying is subtle. Men bully more aggressively and are more physical than women.

Bullying behaviors form a pattern rather than occurring in isolation. Forms include: verbal abuse, exclusion from company activities or having work or contributions purposefully ignored, treated rudely or disrespectfully, ignoring contributions, interfering with or sabotaging work, mean pranks, lying, denied a raise or promotion without a valid reason, given bigger workloads or shorter deadlines than coworkers, accused of making a mistake on purpose, and/or coworker temper tantrums when disagreed with.

Workplace bullies are usually in a position of authority who are threatened by the victim, but the bully can also be an insecure or immature coworker. Workplace bullying can be the result of a single individual or of a company culture that allows or even encourages the negative behavior. Women who bully other women may do so because of more pressure to succeed in male-dominated workplaces and more competition between women for promotions.

Workplace bullying has negative effects on employees and employers. Employees suffer from stress, low self-esteem, depression, anxiety, medical problems, insomnia, troubled relationships, and posttraumatic stress disorder. Consequences for employers include high turnover, absenteeism, low productivity, lost innovations, and a negative company reputation.

Bullying of elder adults occurs in the home, care facility, or other elder living environments. The bully may be a family member, a care giver, a resident or staff member in a care or other facility. The resident may be mocked, taunted or tormented and may be ignored or excluded from social involvement. Obscene gestures, name calling, and threatening language and intimidation are some of the bullying behavior.

The place where elder bullying occurs provides insight into the cause. During meals, bingo games, and other community events where there is a need to share space, seats, and resources, cliquish behavior is demonstrated to lay claim to certain spaces or territories in the building to feel a sense of belonging at the expense of others.

Consequences of bullying for older adults in living environments range from subtle, such as spreading rumors, to actual physical assaults resulting in serious harm up to and including death. As a result of cliquish behavior, victims sometimes feel ignored, teased, or shunned. Because elder bullying is often unaddressed due to untrained and uncertain staff, it can lead to self esteem issues, depression, and injury.

State and federal laws exist to prevent some types of bullying. Harassment that is classified as bullying is one example. Federal civil rights laws define harassment as unwelcome conduct based on a protected class (race, national origin, color, sex, age, disability, religion) that is severe, pervasive, or persistent and creates a hostile environment. When harassment turns violent such as in the workplace, bullying becomes a crime and is subject to a variety of laws designed to address fatal and nonfatal violence.

The solutions for older adults can be, in part, applied to other formal organizations. Social workers can apply three strategies. The first strategy is to help change the organization's culture so that bullying is not tolerated. Second, utilize interventions aimed at changing the bullies' behavior and helping them develop other ways of interacting. Finally, intervening with the victims by helping them develop skills to take back the power that bullies take from them.

The victim who takes proactive measures becomes part of the solution, such as analyzing the relationship with the bully, considering his motivation and psychological state, remaining calm, documenting what is happening, deciding on a course of action such as a private conversation, removing oneself from the situation, and/or geting support.

Rosemarie Skaine

See also: Cyberbullying, Adult; Elder Abuse; Hate Speech; Hazing; Sexual Harassment in Employment; Stalking.

Further Reading

Bullying Statistics. 2013. "Adult Bullying." http://www.bullyingstatistics.org/content/adult-bullying.html.

Bullying Statistics. 2013. "Workplace Bullying." http://www.bullyingstatistics.org/content/workplace-bullying.html.

Corporation for Public Broadcasting and Public Television. 2009. "This Emotional Life." University of Phoenix. http://www.pbs.org/thisemotionallife/topic/bullying/adult-bullying.

Hooks, Kristen. 2011. "Bullying: When Adults Are the Victims." Achieve Solutions. https://www.achievesolutions.net/achievesolutions/en/Content.do?contentId=10627.

Jackson, Kate. 2014. "Older Adult Bullying—How Social Workers Can Help Establish Zero Tolerance." *Social Work Today*. http://www.socialworktoday.com/archive/exc_051513.shtml.

Meece, Mickey. 2009. "Backlash: Women Bullying Women at Work." *New York Times*, May 9. http://www.nytimes.com/2009/05/10/business/10women.html?pagewanted=all&_r=0.

StopBullying.gov. n.d. "Young Adults." U.S. Department of Health and Human Services. http://www.stopbullying.gov/what-is-bullying/related-topics/young-adults.

BULLYING, CHILD AND ADOLESCENT

Bullying is an unwanted, aggressive behavior that involves a real or perceived power imbalance. The behavior is repeated, or has the potential to be repeated, over time. A bully is a blustering, quarrelsome, overbearing person who habitually badgers and intimidates smaller or weaker people. The bullying of children and adolescents

Bullying of children and adolescents occurs frequently in the schools. This girl is being taunted in the hallway of her school. (michaeljung/Shutterstock.com)

is found everywhere in our society, but it is found extensively in the schools and on the Internet.

The key to the definition is "a real or perceived power imbalance." What creates the power imbalance in the child's world may be size. The bully is bigger and stronger than the child being bullied. What the bully gets out bullying could be the satisfaction of seeing the bullied child cry. It could be to exact a price, like lunch money, from the bullied. In the older adolescent's world, it may be the ability to exploit the power imbalance by having the person bullied to quit a job.

Bullying is usually repeated over time. Forms include physical, such as hitting or punching; verbal, teasing or name calling; nonverbal or emotional, intimidation through gestures or social exclusion; and cyberbullying, sending insulting messages by email or other electronic programs.

The American Psychiatric Association reported that half of all children are bullied at some time during their school years, and the National Education Association estimated that more than 160,000 stay home from school every day due to bullying. The A4K Ambassadors 4 Kids Club reported that 70 percent of students are bullied mentally, verbally, and physically. One in five students admits to being a bully, or doing some bullying. Secondary students that are physically attacked number 282,000 a month. On playgrounds, a child is bullied every seven minutes.

Factors that contribute to the cause of bullying include: the individual, the family, peers, school, and the community, according to the U.S. Department of Health and Human Services. Children who bully tend to have certain characteristics such as: impulsivity, temper, need to dominate, easily frustrated; lack empathy; difficulty following rules; and view violence in a positive way. Family risk factors include: parents who lack warmth and involvement; are overly permissive; are lacking in supervision; practice harsh, physical discipline; and exhibit bullying behavior and serve as bullying models. Peer risk factors include: children and youth who are more likely to have friends who bully and have positive attitudes toward violence.

Teenagers report that revenge is the strongest motivation (87%) for school shootings, with 86 percent reasoning that other kids picked on them, made fun or bullied them causing them to turn to lethal violence in the schools. Students recognize that being a victim (61%) of abuse at home or witnessing others (54%) being abused at home may cause violence in school, according the Bureau of Justice School Bullying and Cyberbullying statistics study.

Bullying affects the total well-being of children and adolescents. U.S. Department of Health and Human Services reported that possible changes include unexplained injuries, lost or destroyed clothing, books, electronics or jewelry, frequent headaches or stomachaches, feeling sick or faking illness, changes in eating habits, such as suddenly skipping meals or binge eating, difficulty sleeping or frequent nightmares, declining grades, loss of interest in schoolwork, not wanting to go to school, sudden loss of friends or avoidance of social situations, feelings of helplessness or decreased self esteem, and self destructive behaviors such as running away or talking about suicide. A very small number of bullied children might retaliate through extremely violent measures. In 12 of 15 school shooting cases in the 1990s, the shooters had a history of being bullied.

No federal law directly addresses bullying, but some cases are viewed as discriminatory harassment when it is based on race, national origin, color, sex, age, disability, or religion. In these cases, federally funded schools have an obligation to resolve the harassment. When the situation is not adequately resolved, the US Department of Education's Office for Civil Rights and the US Department of Justice's Civil Rights Division may be able to help. Additionally, bullying may, in some instances, be a violation of state criminal or tort law.

A Department of Education study found that between 1999 and 2010, 120 bills and amendments to existing bills were introduced by states. As of 2013, 49 states had passed antibullying legislation. Most of these laws instruct school districts to adopt anti-bullying policies.

Part of the solution to bullying may be the bystander's intelligent intervention such as reporting the incident. Reasons exist why bystanders do not intervene. They may think someone else may step in and defend the bullied. Sometimes, they fear that they may be the bully's next target. Other reasons include: loyalty to the bully because he or she may be a friend; lacks loyalty to the one being bullied; has a dislike for the attention from peers; and is ignorant as to how to make the bullying stop.

The National Education Association recommends that educators respond quickly and consistently to bullying behavior to send the message that it is not acceptable. They believe that consistant intervention procedures can stop bullying behavior over time. Not intervening will make the bullying worse. To stop bullying, educators must take appropriate action before, during, and after the incident.

Before the incident the intervener should know his or her rights and responsibilities including how and what to do, and how laws and policies support actions. During the incident separate the bully from the target, standing between them blocking eye contact, make sure everyone is safe by notifying authorities and acquiring medical assistance if needed, make it clear bullying is wrong and follow up will take place, support the person bullied, and encourage bystanders. After the incident, the intervener should conduct an investigation, document the results, impose immediate consequences, and be an advocate for the bullied student(s).

Rosemarie Skaine

See also: BULLY Project; Cyberbullying, Child and Adolescent; Cyberstalking; Hate Crimes; Hate Speech; Sexual Harassment in Education.

Further Reading

A4K Ambassadors 4 Kids Club. 2013. "Bullying Statistics." http://www.a4kclub.org/get-the-facts/bullying-statistics.

American Psychiatric Association. 2014. "Bullying." http://www.psychiatry.org/mental-health/bullying.

McCallion, Gail, and Jody Feder. 2013. "Student Bullying: Overview of Research, Federal Initiatives, and Legal Issues." *Congressional Research Service*, October 18. http://www.fas.org/sgp/crs/misc/R43254.pdf.

National Education Association. 2002. "How to Intervene in a Bullying Incident." http://www.nea.org/home/53358.htm.

U.S. Department of Health and Human Services. n.d. "Effects of Bullying." Stopbullying.gov. http://www.stopbullying.gov/at-risk/effects/index.html.

U.S. Department of Health and Human Services. n.d "Federal Laws." Stopbullying.gov. http://www.stopbullying.gov/laws/federal.

U.S. Department of Health and Human Services. n.d. "Warning Signs." Stopbullying.gov. http://www.stopbullying.gov/at-risk/warning-signs/index.html#top.

U.S. Department of Health and Human Services HRSA. 2010. "Stop Bullying Now!" Education.com. http://www.education.com/reference/article/Ref_Children_Who_Bully.

Whitson, Signe. 2013. "6 Reasons Why Bystanders Choose Not to Intervene to Stop Bullying." *Huffington Post*, November 19. http://www.huffingtonpost.com/signe-whitson/six-reasons-why-bystander_b_4295181.html.

BURNING BED, THE

The Burning Bed, a nonfiction book published by Faith McNulty in 1980, is about Francine Hughes, who in 1977 killed her abusive husband by setting fire to the bedroom in which he was sleeping. The book chronicles Hughes's life up to and through the murder and subsequent trial. It tells a tale of physical and emotional abuse over a period of 14 years, her many attempts to become independent and leave, and the loss of hope that drove her to end the abuse by killing her husband. The book was made into a television movie by the same name, which aired in 1987.

Francine started dating Mickey Hughes when she was in ninth grade. She quit school at the beginning of her sophomore year and married Mickey in November 1963, when she was 16 years old. Mickey and Francine had four children, and their life together was punctuated by many moves, Mickey's lost jobs, little money, and Mickey's violent beatings of Francine. Although Francine managed to leave Mickey several times, she was coerced by his family to move back so that she could give Mickey the physical care he needed during his rehabilitation following a serious automobile accident.

The beatings and terrorization of the family intensified after his accident. Finally, on a night when Francine had planned to escape with the children, Mickey came home early and beat her for the last time. When he passed out drunk in bed, Francine soaked his bedroom in gasoline and set it on fire. Hysterical, she drove with her children to the police station, where she was arrested and charged with first-degree murder. Her subsequent trial and acquittal became national news. She was found not guilty of murder by reason of temporary insanity.

Rosemarie Skaine

See also: Domestic Abuse; Domestic Abuse, Psychological Effects of; Rape, Marital.

Further Reading

Finley, Laura L., ed. 2013. *Encyclopedia of Domestic Violence*. Santa Barbara, CA: Greenwood.
McNulty, Faith. 1980. *The Burning Bed*. New York: Harcourt.

BYRD, JAMES, JR.

James Byrd, Jr., was living in Jasper, Texas, and 49 years old on June 7, 1998, when three men, Shawn Berry, 36, Lawrence Brewer, 44, and John King, 36, offered him a ride. The men brutally beat Byrd, chained his ankles to the back of the pickup truck, and dragged him three miles over asphalt and road that caused severe injuries. Byrd was believed to be conscious during most of the time until he was decapitated when his body hit a culvert in the road. The men were charged with capital murder and tried separately. King, the ringleader, and Brewer were part of a white supremacy group and sentenced to death. Berry was sentenced to life in prison. Brewer had been a member of "Exalted Cyclops," a racist prison gang affiliated with the Ku Klux Klan. He spent most of his adult life in prison for burglary, cocaine possession, and parole violations. He was executed in 2011, 13 years after the murder. In 2014, King's case was still in the appeal process.

Thomas Wicke and Roxane Cohen Silver, two university scholars. investigated how the community of Jasper changed on crime, economic, health, educational, and social capital measures collected at multiple pre- and postcrime times. Their analysis revealed significant postevent changes and a noteworthy degree of resilience and lack of negative consequence. Intervention of external organizations exacerbated the severity of the events. But local social institutions such as faith-based, law enforcement, media, business sector, and civic government organizations, elicited an effective response from the community to the initial threat and to the potential negative effects of external entities. The study also found that crime did not increase after the murder.

Byrd's death inspired the Texas James Byrd Jr. Hate Crimes Act, signed by Governor Rick Perry in 2001, and the Matthew Shepard and James Byrd, Jr., Hate Crimes Prevention Act, signed by President Barack Obama in 2009. The 2009 law expanded on the 1969 federal hate crime law to include acts motivated by racial, sexual, gender, religious, and ethnic bias.

Rosemarie Skaine

See also: Hate Crimes; Matthew Shepard and James Byrd, Jr., Hate Crimes Prevention Act; Racism; Shepard, Matthew.

Further Reading

Chandler, D. L. 2012. "Racist Murder of James Byrd Jr. Took Place on This Day in 1998." *Newsone*, June 7. http://newsone.com/2019388/james-byrd-jr-murdered.

CNN Wire Staff. 2011. "Man Executed for Dragging Death of James Byrd." CNN.com, September 22. http://www.cnn.com/2011/09/21/justice/texas-dragging-death-execution.

Nolan, Heather. 2012. "1 Killer in Byrd Murder Executed, 1 Still Awaiting Lethal Injection." *Beaumont Enterprise*, January 2. http://www.beaumontenterprise.com/default/article/1-killer-in-Byrd-murder-executed-1-still-2407420.php.

Wicke, Thomas, and Roxane Cohen Silver. 2009. "A Community Responds to Collective Trauma: An Ecological Analysis of the James Byrd Murder in Jasper, Texas." *American Journal of Community Psychology* 44: 233–248.

C

CAPITAL PUNISHMENT

Capital punishment is the legal imposition of death as a punishment for committing a felony. The word *capital* originates from the Latin *capitalis*, which means "concerning the head." Therefore, being subjected to capital punishment means (nonliterally) losing one's head. The term *death penalty* is also used interchangeably with *capital punishment*. It is arguably the most controversial penal practice in contemporary times, and in modern liberal democracies, the legitimacy and effectiveness of the death penalty have increasingly come into question. Some opponents of capital punishment argue that the death penalty constitutes abuse.

The death penalty has been practiced in the United States for more than 400 years. The first execution took place in the Jamestown colony of Virginia in 1608. The offender, Captain George Kendall, was executed for being a spy for Spain. During most of the 20th century, the vast majority of states allowed capital punishment for convicted criminals. Although the legal roots of capital punishment dates back to early English common law, the practice has always been much more widespread in the United States than in the United Kingdom, which abandoned the death penalty in 1973. At present, 32 states still practice the death penalty, and 18 states have abolished it. In 1794, Pennsylvania became the first state to restrict the death penalty to first-degree murder. In May 2013, Maryland became the last state to abolish the practice. To date, the highest number of executions have taken place in Texas.

Proponents of the death penalty argue that it works as a deterrent for potential criminals. They also point out that the death penalty is a just retribution for serious crimes and ensures that the offenders do not commit further crimes. Opponents, however, argue that the practice of capital punishment is brutal, inhuman, and abusive. They believe that killing someone through a legal mechanism is morally wrong. The Roman Catholic Church has consistently opposed the death penalty, and U.S. Catholic bishops have also urged to abolish the practice. The abolitionists claim, often with the help of social scientific studies, that the death penalty cannot deter serious crimes and, more importantly, even the most advanced criminal justice system cannot ensure efficiency and fairness while dealing with capital cases. As a consequence, innocent people may be caught up with the guilty.

The fundamental legality of the death penalty was challenged during the 1960s as abolitionists began to suggest that the death penalty was a "cruel and unusual"punishment and therefore unconstitutional under the Eighth Amendment. Before then, the Fifth, Eighth, and Fourteenth Amendments were construed as permitting capital punishment. Countrywide deferral of capital punishment officially began in 1972, when the U.S. Supreme Court held in *Furman v. Georgia*

The execution chamber at San Quentin prison, California. In 1996, William Bonin became the first person in the state to be executed by lethal injection for the rape and murder of 14 teenage boys. (California Department of Corrections)

that the death penalty was being administered in an indiscriminate and capricious manner that amounted to "cruel and unusual punishment."

Following the *Furman* judgment, states began to pass new death penalty legislation through which juries were given discretion to choose between prison and the death sentence. The new laws also delimited the categories of murder for which capital punishment could be enforced. Moreover, the new statutes specified directives on circumstances and components that judges and juries should take into consideration while deciding capital cases.

Later, in the 1976 case of *Gregg v. Georgia*, the Supreme Court opined that such systems of guided discretion did not infringe the constitutional prohibition against cruel and unusual punishment. As a result, the death penalty was reinstated in 1976, and the first execution under the new circumstances was that of Gary Gilmore by firing squad in Utah in 1977. The Supreme Court has also ruled that the execution of defendants with mental retardation, as well as those who, because of mental illness, are incapable of understanding the meaning of their impending execution, is forbidden under the Eight Amendment. In the 1988 case of *Thompson v. Oklahoma*, the Supreme Court held that the execution of an individual who was under the age of 16 at the time his crime was cruel and unusual punishment and prohibited by the Eighth Amendment to the Constitution. In the 2002 case of *Ring v. Arizona*, the court directed that only individuals convicted of crimes involving death are eligible for capital punishment.

Empirical evidence suggests that race, location, money, politics, and other arbitrary factors exert a powerful influence on determining who is sentenced to death.

A number of studies have also shown that the cost of executing a criminal far exceeds the cost associated with life imprisonment. Despite the fact that half of all murder victims in the United States are black, more than three-quarters of death penalty verdicts are for felonies involving white victims. Moreover, a black suspect accused of killing a white victim is three times more likely to receive the death sentence than a white person accused of murdering a white victim.

According to the latest Death Penalty Information Centers Innocence List, 142 death row inmates have been exonerated since 1971. To be included in this list, defendants must have been found guilty and sentenced to death and their convictions then overturned. The average number of years between being sentenced to death and exoneration is 9.8 years.

All these factors explain the widespread dissatisfaction with the system that governs the death penalty and executions in the United States. Polling data in the United States indicates that while support for the death penalty has dropped significantly in recent years, there still remains a stable level of such support. However, it has also been noticed that the level of support declines when citizens are given a choice between the death penalty and life imprisonment with no possibility of parole. The movement to abolish the death penalty has also been supported by Hollywood movies such as *Cell 2455 Death Row* (1955), *In Cold Blood* (1967), *Kill Me if You Can: The Caryl Chessman Story* (1977), *Dead Man Walking* (1995), *Monster* (2003), and *The Life of David Gale* (2003).

Mohammad Sajjadur Rahman

See also: Prisoner Abuse, Adult; Torture.

Further Reading

Banner, Stuart. 2002. *The Death Penalty: An American History*. Cambridge, MA: Harvard University Press.

Garland, David, Randall McGowen, and Michael Meranze. eds. 2011. *America's Death Penalty: Between Past and Present*. New York: New York University Press.

CENTER FOR ELDERS AND THE COURTS

The Center for Elders and the Courts (CEC) serves the courts of the nation on issues pertaining to aging, probate, and elder abuse. The CEC began in 2008 and is funded by a grant to the National Center for State Courts (NCSC) from the Retirement Research Foundation of Chicago.

The CEC's program on issues related to aging begins with providing information on the high number of senior individuals that has resulted because of the large population of baby boomers entering this period and the advent of longer life spans. In 2030, about one in five Americans will be 65 years or older. Society as a whole will consist of older individuals, and every major institution will be affected and of concern to the courts: the economy, health care, housing, transportation, and the justice system.

Other issues pertaining to aging are medical and social aspects, legal issues, and the role of the courts. Statistics related to physical impairments that tend to be associated with the aging process show that the elderly comprise a significant proportion of physiologically impaired Americans: about 30 percent of all visually impaired, about 37 percent of all hearing impaired, about 10 to 15 percent have severe memory problems, and about 88 percent have at least one chronic health condition. Also discussed are common mental health issues such as depression, dementia, and their relationship to the substance abuses of alcohol and prescription medication.

Three key legal concepts that often must be considered in addressing cases involving older persons are capacity, consent, and undue influence. Capacity may involve areas of functioning, for example, physical, mental, cognitive, emotional, and behavioral. Capacity is not a fixed or static condition, and capacity can vary depending on the activities and tasks, across time, situations, and location. Consent requires an individual to be able to understand the transaction or activity, make judgments about it, and decide if it is something they want to do and is often related to capacity. These decisions are most often related to health care, but can also be related to property issues.

The role of the courts includes practices and programs that courts can implement to improve access for older persons and to create multiagency coordinated responses. Courts can help make certain that older persons with a physical or mental limitation have full access and participation by making accommodations to the courtroom setting, the handling of court hearings, and case and calendar management. For example, the courtroom could provide hearing amplification, nonglare lighting, a magnifying glass, an oxygen cylinder, and a safe waiting area for older victims and their families. In handling hearings, examples include memorializing testimony through videotaped or conditional examinations, closing the courtroom to the public to reduce anxiety, or use of victim or witness advocates. Case and calendar management might include expediting guardianship and elder abuse cases and avoiding unnecessary continuances and delays, or when conducting a domestic violence restraining order calendar, first calling cases involving elder victims.

The CEC advocates that one of the promising practices is the use of technology and physical accommodations. Stetson Law's Eleazer Courtroom is an example of such a combination. For example, some of the features include carpeting with a border along the edge in a color different from the carpet with diamond insets marking each row to give a visual clue regarding seats; tables and desks with rounded corners; sturdy chairs with locking wheels and firm arms; a witness box at floor level with no steps; a ramp to the judge's bench inside his chambers; a podium that is electronically height adjustable with electronic side shelves or wings for those in a wheelchair and with limited upper body mobility; use of technology; and nonglare, nonbuzz lighting. Stetson's courtroom is the only courtroom in the country designed specifically for the needs of elderly. This courtroom provides maximum access to elders and people with disabilities.

Rosemarie Skaine

See also: Disabled Adults; Domestic Abuse, Psychological Effects of; Elder Abuse.

Further Reading

CEC Center for the Elders and the Courts. n.d. "Aging." http://www.eldersandcourts.org/Aging.aspx.

Stetson Law. n.d. "Eleazer Courtroom." http://www.stetson.edu/law/academics/elder/home/eleazer-courtroom.php.

CENTER OF EXCELLENCE ON ELDER ABUSE AND NEGLECT

The Center of Excellence on Elder Abuse and Neglect at the University of California, Irvine, School of Medicine is dedicated to eradicating abuse of the elderly. In 2005, the Archstone Foundation established the center through a grant as part of the School of Medicine's program in geriatrics. The center's program works to promote aging with dignity and eliminate aging with fear. The center serves local, state, and national clientele. Locally, it provides medical, forensic, and victim services to abused and neglected seniors who live in the community or in long-term care facilities. It also serves as a "living laboratory" of innovative approaches. On the state and national levels, the center offers technical assistance, multidisciplinary training, useful research, and relevant policy.

In 2011, the Center of Excellence was named by the U.S. Administration on Aging as the National Center on Elder Abuse. The National Center's mission states that "National, state, and local partners in the field will be fully prepared to ensure that older Americans will live with dignity, integrity, independence, and without abuse, neglect, and exploitation."

The National Center created resources that are free to download and distribute. These resources include a report of its work since 2011, a database of research studies and articles, and elder and adult abuse coalitions by state. Two other resources, community education and research briefs on adult abuse, are available. Sources of help in community education include "Red Flags of Elder Abuse"; "Protect Yourself from Abuse, Neglect, and Exploitation"; "Why Should I Care about Elder Abuse?"; "12 Things Anyone Can Do to Prevent Elder Abuse"; and "10 Things Administrations on Aging (AAAs) Can Do to Prevent Elder and Vulnerable Adult Abuse."

The second resource, research briefs on adult abuse, includes "Elder Abuse and Its Impact: What You Must Know"; "Adults with Dementia"; "Residents of Long Term Care Facilities"; "Adults with Disabilities"; "Asian and Pacific Islander (API) Elders"; and "Lesbian, Gay, Bisexual, Transgender (LGBT) Elders."

In 2012, on World Elder Abuse Awareness Day, the White House announced the Formation of Ageless Alliance (www.agelessalliance.org) and the U.S. Administration on Aging awarded the University of California, Irvine, a grant: Take AIM against Elder Abuse.

Rosemarie Skaine

See also: Elder Abuse; Homosexuals; Transgender Individuals.

Further Reading

Center of Excellence on Elder Abuse and Neglect. 2013. University of California, Irvine, School of Medicine. http://www.centeronelderabuse.org.

CHILD ABANDONMENT AND NEGLECT

A child is considered abandoned when the parent's identity or whereabouts are unknown, the child has been left alone or the parent has failed to maintain contact with the child or provide reasonable support for a specified period of time. The parent has left the child in circumstances where the child suffers serious harm.

Neglect is the failure of a parent, guardian, or other caregiver to provide for a child's basic needs. Neglect may be: physical such as not providing food, shelter, or supervision; medical, such as not providing necessary medical or mental health treatment; educational, for example, failure to educate a child; and emotional, such as inattention to emotional needs, failure to provide psychological care, or permitting use of alcohol or other drugs.

In 2012, national estimates of abuse and neglect victims numbered 686,000, resulting in a rate of 9.2 victims per 1,000 children. This is a 4.2 percent decrease from the 2008 estimate of 716,000 victims. The percentages of child victims were similar for boys (48.7%) and girls (50.9%). Over three-fourths, 78.3 percent, of victims were neglected, 18.3 percent were physically abused, and 9.3 percent were sexually abused. In addition, 10.6 percent of victims experienced such "other" types of maltreatment as "threatened abuse," "parent's drug/alcohol abuse," or "safe relinquishment of a newborn." Except for sexual abuse, who were less than 1 to 2 years, neglect had the largest percentages across all maltreatment types. Of the children who suffered medical neglect, one-third (33.2%) were under three years old, and the percentage was approximately twice as large as the next age group (three to five years old).

Causes of abandonment include poverty, lack of education, cultural values, and low levels of standard care for the community. Occasional causes include child or parent mental and physical illness, lack of information or the education to identify medical problems, and parental inability to care for themselves because of drug or alcohol abuse. In all cases, the common elements are the parent's personality and the lack of sound psychological and parenting development.

Causes of neglect are complex, but child or caregiver risk factors may increase the likelihood of child maltreatment. Child risk factors include having a disability; an intellectual, learning, or physical disability; emotional disturbance; visual or hearing impairment; behavioral problems; or another medical problem. Caregiver risk factors include alcohol abuse, drug abuse, and domestic violence, either as the perpetrator or the victim.

Child neglect is the result of a combination of personal deficits in parents, conflict-ridden and unsupportive family systems and informal support networks, highly stressful life circumstances, and absence of environmental supports for parenting. Parental history plays a role in the ability to parent. It is not so much the inadequate or abusive nurturing possibly experienced as children, but the unacknowledged deprivations and unresolved feelings from early experiences that leave the parents unable to develop secure psychological attachments. Thus, a cycle of neglect is operative.

The consequences of abandonment include a deep sense and fear of loss; having a mental injury, such as a borderline personality disorder; feelings of shame that affect self-worth; and problems with intimacy because of issues with trust. Consequences to children of neglect are a negative effect on their development: health and physical, intellectual and cognitive, emotional and psychological, and social and behavioral. These categories are related; for example, a delayed development of the brain may lead to cognitive delays or psychological problems, which may manifest as social and behavioral problems. Another illustration is that the failure to develop secure psychological attachments as infants seriously handicaps their subsequent development and is demonstrated in children's lack of readiness for learning, behavior problems, having less active interaction with peers, and performing poorly in school. Children under three are at high risk for child fatalities. Children with higher IQs or who live in less stressful, stable home environments suffer less serious effects of neglect.

Some states have enacted safe haven laws that in cases of abandonment provide safe places for parents to relinquish newborn infants. The purpose of these laws is to prevent babies from being abandoned at places that might bring them harm. Infant safe haven laws were enacted as an incentive for mothers in crisis to safely give up their babies at designated locations where the babies are protected and provided with medical care until a permanent home is found. The laws usually allow parents anonymity and a shield from prosecution. Providers who accept the infants have responsibility but are immune from liability for anything that might happen to the infant while in their care, unless evidence demonstrates major negligence on the part of the provider.

All states require that certain individuals are designated as mandatory reporters of child maltreatment. In their official capacity, they report when they either have knowledge of or suspect abuse or have reasons to believe that a child has been abused or neglected. These professionals usually have frequent contact with children and include social workers; teachers, principals, and other school personnel; physicians, nurses, and other health care workers; counselors, therapists, and other mental health professionals; child care providers; medical examiners and coroners; and law enforcement officers.

Rosemarie Skaine

See also: Child Abuse, Physical and Emotional; Child Abuse, Poverty and; Child Abuse, Verbal; Child Abuse Reporting Laws; Child Protective Services; Cycle of Abuse; Disabled Children.

Further Reading

Child Welfare Information Gateway. 2013. "Infant Safe Haven Laws." *State Statutes*. Washington, D.C.: U.S. Department of Health and Human Services, Children's Bureau. https://www.childwelfare.gov/systemwide/laws_policies/statutes/safehaven.cfm.

Child Welfare Information Gateway. 2013. "What Is Child Abuse and Neglect? Recognizing the Signs and Symptoms." Washington, D.C.: U.S. Department of Health and Human Services, Children's Bureau. https://www.childwelfare.gov/pubs/factsheets/whatiscan.cfm.

Child Welfare Information Gateway and J. M. Gaudin Jr. 1993. "Child Neglect: A Guide for Intervention." Washington, D.C.: U.S. Department of Health and Human Services, Children's Bureau. https://www.childwelfare.gov/pubs/usermanuals/neglect_93/index.cfm.

Ryan, David B. 2014. "What Is the Leading Cause of Child Abandonment?" Globalpost. http://everydaylife.globalpost.com/leading-cause-child-abandonment-19850.html.

Ryan, David B. 2013. "Psychological Effects of Child Abandonment." Livestrong.com. http://www.livestrong.com/article/246340-psychological-effects-of-child-abandonment.

U.S. Department of Health and Human Services. 2012. "Child Maltreatment." http://www.acf.hhs.gov/programs/cb/resource/child-maltreatment-2012.

CHILD ABUSE, PHYSICAL AND EMOTIONAL

Physical abuse of a child is nonaccidental trauma or physical injury caused by punching, beating, kicking, biting, burning, or otherwise harming. It is the most visible form of child maltreatment. Emotional abuse of a child is a pattern of behavior by parents or caregivers that can seriously interfere with a child's cognitive, emotional, psychological, or social development. Emotional child abuse takes many forms and can occur independent of or in conjunction with some forms of physical abuse. These acts include: ignoring, rejecting, isolating, exploiting, or corrupting, for example, encouraging or forcing the child to develop inappropriate or illegal behaviors, verbally assaulting, terrorizing, and/or neglecting the child.

In 2011, 686,000 children were victims of abuse and neglect, which means that there were 9.2 victims per 1,000 children in the population. Some children suffered more than one kind of abuse: 118,825 (17.6%) were physically abused; 531,413 (78.5%) were neglected; 15,074 (2.2%) were medically neglected; and 69,466 (10.3%) suffered other types of neglect.

In 2011, the National Institute of Justice reported that the Family Violence Services Study (FVSS) found that, of families involved in child welfare investigations for child maltreatment, 29 percent of the perpetrators had abused children within the past year. Approximately 45 percent of children in these families had experienced maltreatment over the course of their lifetime.

Risk factors or characteristics of a child or caregiver that may increase the likelihood of child maltreatment include: children with a disability (13.3%): intellectual disability, emotional disturbance (2.5%), visual or hearing impairment, learning disability, physical disability, behavioral problems (3.2%), or another medical problem (4.3%). Caregiver risk factors include: depression, alcohol and drug abuse, and domestic violence, with the caregiver being either the perpetrator or the victim. A caregiver may also have very high expectations of the child, a lack of knowledge and skills in bringing up children, low self-esteem and self-confidence, mental or physical ill health, work pressures, and/or were abused as a child. Other influencing factors may include: poverty, lack of education, frequent changes of addresses, lack of support from the extended family, loneliness and social isolation, unemployment, and inadequate housing.

Developmental difficulties are also a result of chronic child maltreatment leaving their brains in a state of hyperarousal or expectation of imminent danger that may interfere with learning and the ability to bond emotionally with others. The National Institute of Justice identifies symptoms as: inability to control emotions or frequent outbursts, unusually quiet or submissive behavior, difficulty learning in school, interpersonal difficulties with siblings or classmates, unusual eating or sleeping behaviors, aggressive or sexually provocative behavior, socially or emotionally inappropriate behavior for their age, and lack of response to affection.

Treatment for child abuse should be combined with treatment for caregivers and abusers of domestic violence. Because the cycle of abuse can occur hundreds of times in an abusive relationship and the total cycle can take anywhere from a few hours to a year or more to complete, the abuse exposes the intimate partner and any children in the home to abuse in unpredictable time frames.

One of the consequences of child abuse is its generational cyclical nature. Understanding the cycle of abuse toward intimate partners aids understanding of the nature of exposure to children in the home. When victims of child abuse become adults, they are twice as likely to abuse their own partners and children. Breaking the cycle of child abuse may depend on professional and/or legal intervention. Intervention processes include removal and placement and parenting programs. Prevention programs include in-home visitation programs and nurse–family partnership.

A child abuser can learn new ways to manage his or her emotions and break old patterns. Although talking about the abuse may be very difficult for the child, talking with the victim in a calm, reassuring manner and offering unconditional support is important. Taking early steps to stop the abuse will also help the child.

When it is necessary to report child abuse, the U.S. organization Justice for Children provides the following suggestions in reporting child abuse in your home or in a custody situation: stay calm and do not vent emotions onto the people who are assigned to investigate your case, for example, law enforcement officers; in an emergency, call 911 or local police; document everything from this point forward; keep all documents from all professionals; have your child evaluated; begin investigation; talk to Child Protective Services; get an attorney and start proceedings to gain full custody of your child and terminate the abuser's parental rights. Assistance can be also received through national hotlines such as Justice for Children (1-800-733-0059).

Rosemarie Skaine

See also: Child Abuse, Poverty and; Child Abuse, Sexual, Child Abuse, Verbal, Child Abuse Reporting Laws; Child Protective Services; Cycle of Abuse; Disabled Children.

Further Reading

American Humane Association. 2013. "Emotional Abuse." http://www.americanhumane. org/children/stop-child-abuse/fact-sheets/emotional-abuse.html.

Children's Bureau. n.d. *Child Maltreatment 2011*. Administration for Children and Families, U.S. Department of Health and Human Service. https://www.acf.hhs.gov/sites/default/files/cb/cm11.pdf#page=57.

Children's Bureau. n.d. *Child Maltreatment 2012*. Administration for Children and Families, U.S. Department of Health and Human Service. http://www.acf.hhs.gov/sites/default/files/cb/cm2012.pdf#page=31.

Department of Human Services. 2013. "What Are the Causes of Child Abuse?" Victoria. http://www.dhs.vic.gov.au/for-individuals/children,-families-and-young-people/child-protection/about-child-abuse/what-is-child-abuse/what-are-the-causes-of-child-abuse.

National Institute of Justice. 2011. "Child Abuse and Maltreatment." U.S. Department of Justice. http://nij.gov/topics/crime/child-abuse/Pages/welcome.aspx.

Ronan, Kevin R., Doreen F. Canoy, and Karena J. Burke. September 2009. "Child Maltreatment: Prevalence, Risk, Solutions, Obstacles." *Australian Psychologist* 44, no. 3: 195–213.

Smith, Melinda, and Jeanne Segal. 2013. "Child Abuse & Neglect." HelpGuide.org. http://www.helpguide.org/mental/child_abuse_physical_emotional_sexual_neglect.htm#reporting.

CHILD ABUSE, POVERTY AND

Poverty is a major cause of child neglect and abuse. According to the American Academy of Family Physicians, "Poverty is the most frequently and persistently noted risk factor for child abuse."

Although child abuse happens in families of all income levels, neglect and physical abuse occur disproportionally in poor families. Raising a child is stressful, and when poverty and unemployment are added to the mix, some parents simply find it too hard to cope, and they end up neglecting or taking out their anger and frustration on their children.

The connection between poverty and child abuse has been known among child welfare professionals for many decades. However, politicians who hoped to prevent child abuse have tended to downplay this connection. Senator Walter Mondale of Minnesota, who was supporting an anti-child abuse bill in Congress in the early 1970s, did not want to associate child abuse with poverty, because he feared that this would cause it to be seen as "just another welfare program." As a result, the Child Abuse Prevention and Treatment Act (CAPTA), which passed in 1974, and was the first major federal law on child abuse, does not place special emphasis on poor families.

By 1990, it had become more acceptable to acknowledge the tie between poverty and child neglect and abuse. In that year, the U.S. Advisory Board on Child Abuse and Neglect—a 15-member board appointed by the U.S. Department of Health and Human Services—wrote in their report that "data have shown that the higher the poverty rate is in a neighborhood, the higher the rate of maltreatment will be."

A 2003 report put out by the federal government's Office on Child Abuse and Neglect stated that "poverty and unemployment show strong associations with child maltreatment, particularly neglect," and went on to explain that, in 1993, children from families with annual incomes below $15,000 were 22 times more likely to be victims of child abuse and neglect than children from families with annual incomes above $30,000.

Nevertheless, most government laws and programs to prevent child abuse do not emphasize reducing poverty, but instead talk about multiple causes of child abuse. For example, CAPTA, which provides federal funding to states to deal with child abuse, rarely mentions poverty. Funds are not targeted to poor people. Instead, states can use the funds for research about child abuse, technical assistance for governments and nonprofit agencies, and training programs for people working in the fields of medicine, law, education, and social work. CAPTA funds also can be used to teach parenting skills and to provide comprehensive support for families, which could include help with finding a job or connecting with government services for the poor.

Some government aid programs for the poor have been found to reduce child abuse, including the federally funded Special Supplemental Nutrition Program for Women, Infants and Children (WIC) and home visitation programs, which are funded by state and local governments and private organizations.

Jyotsna Sreenivasan

See also: Child Abuse, Physical and Emotional; Child Abuse, Psychological and Behavioral Effects of; Child Abuse, Sexual; Child Abuse, Treatment for; Child Abuse, Verbal; Domestic Abuse, Poverty and.

Further Reading

Conte, Jon R., ed. 2014. *Child Abuse and Neglect Worldwide*. 3 vols. Santa Barbara, CA: Praeger.

Lyon, Eleanor. 2000. *Welfare, Poverty, and Abused Women: New Research and Its Implications*. Harrisburg, PA: National Resource Center on Domestic Violence.

CHILD ABUSE, PSYCHOLOGICAL AND BEHAVIORAL EFFECTS OF

Each year, hundreds of thousands of children experience some form of child abuse, whether physical, emotional, verbal, sexual, neglect, or abandonment. Child abuse and neglect have long-lasting effects, including psychological and behavioral issues. Although physical injuries may or may not be immediately visible, abuse and neglect can have consequences for children, families, and society that last lifetimes or for generations. The U.S. Surgeon General reported that severe and repeated trauma during youth may have enduring effects on both neurobiological and psychological development by altering stress responsiveness and adult behavior patterns. These children experience a greatly increased risk of mood, anxiety, and personality disorders throughout adult life.

Child abuse violates the trust that parents are the primary source of safety, security, love, understanding, nurturance, and support. This violation allows a negative set of beliefs to develop that affects an individual's ability to establish and keep significant attachments throughout life. Survivors often experience conflictive relationships, chaotic lifestyles, and difficulties forming adult intimate attachments. They display behaviors that threaten and disrupt close relationships. These difficulties are manifested in frequent crises, such as job disappointments, relocations, failed relationships, financial setbacks, and unresolved childhood abuse issues.

Many function in a crisis mode with temporary solutions that do not resolve the underlying issues. Functioning in a crisis mode can be exhausting, dispiriting, and contribute to feelings of helplessness and hopelessness.

In addition, early childhood development demonstrates that the brain develops in response to experiences with caregivers, family, and the community, and that its development is directly related to the quality and quantity of those experiences. Healthy brain development depends on meeting a child's needs during these early stages. Repeated exposure to stressful events can affect the brain's stress response, making it more unable to adjust in different conditions. With time, a child may react as if danger is always present, regardless of what the present situation actually is. Children exposed to unaddressed violence or abuse are at an increased risk for future emotional and behavioral problems. Children who are abused may not be able to express their feelings safely and, as a result, may develop difficulties regulating their emotions.

Childhood experiences of abuse contribute to the likelihood of depression, anxiety disorders, addictions, personality disorders, eating disorders, sexual disorders, and suicidal behavior. Survivors of child abuse tend to be depressed, have low self-esteem, and have problems with family functioning. Child sexual abuse has been found to be a key factor in the cause and continuation of youth homelessness. Between 50 percent and 70 percent of young people within the Supported Accommodation Assistance Programs experienced childhood sexual assault.

Long-term consequences of child abuse and neglect are physical, behavioral, and societal as well as psychological. The U.S. Department of Health and Human Services reported that the immediate emotional effects of abuse and neglect, isolation, fear, and the inability to trust, can result in lifelong psychological consequences, such as low self-esteem, depression, and relationship difficulties. An example of difficulties during infancy was found in 2010, when 19 percent of infants and young children entered out-of-home care due to abuse or neglect. The upset of a primary caregiver change harmfully affects attachments. Almost half of infants in foster care who have experienced maltreatment show some form of cognitive delay and have lower IQ scores, language difficulties, and neonatal challenges compared to children who have not been abused or neglected.

Poor mental and emotional health can result, for example when childhood trauma and adversity, such as physical or sexual abuse, occur. These experiences produce risk factors for borderline personality disorder, depression, anxiety, and other psychiatric disorders. One study found that approximately 54 percent of cases of depression and 58 percent of suicide attempts in women were related to adverse childhood experiences. Child maltreatment also negatively affects development of emotion regulation, which often continues into adolescence or adulthood.

Cognitive difficulties were substantiated in the U.S. Department of Health and Human Services National Survey of Child and Adolescent Well-Being (NSCAW) studies. Over 10 percent of school-aged children and youth showed some risk of cognitive problems or low academic achievement, 43 percent had emotional or behavioral problems, and 13 percent had both.

Social difficulties developed by children who experience neglect include the likelihood of developing antisocial traits. Parental neglect is connected with borderline personality disorders, attachment issues or affectionate behaviors with unknown or little-known people, inappropriate modeling of adult behavior, and aggression.

The San Francisco Child Abuse Prevention Center lists the percentage of elements that affect the long-term impact of child abuse: 22 percent of maltreated children have learning disorders requiring special education; 27 percent of children who are abused or neglected become delinquents, compared to 17 percent of children in the general population.

In a study of 17,000 adults, those abused as children were more likely to become suicidal; more likely to have heart disease, cancer, chronic lung disease, and liver disease; twice as likely to be smokers; twice as likely to be severely obese; twice as likely to become alcoholics; and three times as likely to develop a drug addiction.

In 2007, Stanford University researchers found that children suffering posttraumatic stress disorder and exposure to severe trauma actually have smaller brains. Severe trauma includes parental homicide, sexual assault, sexual abuse, school shootings, and ongoing community violence. Researchers found a nearly 9 percent reduction in the size of the hippocampus, a horseshoe-shaped sheet of neurons that controls memory and emotions.

A study conducted in 2009 showed an increased risk of sexually transmitted diseases (STDs) in childhood abuse or neglect survivors tracked over time. In addition to the known mental health impacts of child abuse, a 2009 control study found that childhood maltreatment reduces immune function, an effect that can linger long after the maltreatment has ended.

Rosemarie Skaine

See also: Child Abandonment and Neglect; Child Abuse, Physical and Emotional; Child Abuse, Sexual; Child Abuse, Verbal.

Further Reading

Adults Surviving Child Abuse. 2014. "Impact of Child Abuse." http://www.asca.org.au/about/resources/impact-of-child-abuse.aspx.

Joyful Heart Foundation. 2014. "Effects of Child Abuse and Neglect." http://www.joyfulheartfoundation.org/learn/child-abuse-neglect/effects-child-abuse-neglect.

Mayo Clinic. 2009. "Psychological Impact of Child Abuse." ScienceDaily, May 24. http://www.sciencedaily.com/releases/2009/05/090521112831.htm.

San Francisco Child Abuse Prevention Center. n.d. "Information about Child Abuse & Prevention." http://www.sfcapc.org/press_room/information_about_child_abuse_and_prevention?gclid=CPey7taT3r0CFexcMgodGg8AgA.

U.S. Department of Health and Human Services. 2013. "Long-term Consequences of Child Abuse and Neglect." Child Welfare Information Gateway. Children's Bureau. https://www.childwelfare.gov/pubs/factsheets/long_term_consequences.pdf.

CHILD ABUSE, SEXUAL

Child sexual abuse is perpetrated by a person with a dominant position that allows him or her to force or coerce a child into sexual activity. The abuser may be a family member, relative, friend, peer, acquaintance, or stranger. Most frequently children are sexually abused in the home, but they are also victims of pedophiles, sex offenders, child pornographers, women offenders, and persons in the professions such as clergy and coaches.

Abuse may include fondling a child's genitals, masturbation, oral-genital contact, digital penetration, and vaginal and anal intercourse. Child sexual abuse can include noncontact abuse, for example, exposure, voyeurism, and child pornography.

In 2001, the National Institute of Justice reported that about 30 percent to 60 percent of perpetrators of intimate partner violence also abuse children in the household. In 2011, 9.1 percent of child abuse victims had been sexually abused. One in three girls and one in six boys are sexually abused before the age of 18. Abuse typically occurs within a long-term, ongoing relationship, escalates over time, and continues for an average of four years. Many victims never disclose their abuse, and less than 10 percent is reported to the police. Ninety-three percent of juvenile sexual assault victims know their attacker, 34.2 percent of attackers were family members, 58.7 percent were acquaintances, and 7 percent of the perpetrators were strangers. Nearly 50 percent of all the victims of forcible sodomy, sexual assault with an object, and forcible fondling are children under the age of 12. An estimated 60 million survivors of childhood sexual abuse exist in the U.S.

The causes of sexual abuse are psychological, social psychological, and sociological. Psychological causes are operative when the abuser has an inborn characteristic that puts him or her at greater risk of abusing. Motivation is tied to biological or instinctive aspects of human behavior. Child abuse is the result of a caregiver's deprived learning experiences, which may lead to inadequately managing children's behavior. Social psychological causes are based on the abuser's ability to relate to their immediate environment, while sociological causes are rooted in social conditions and the political atmosphere.

The immediate effects of child sexual abuse are manifested physically and behaviorally, according to RAINN (Rape, Abuse & Incest National Network). Physical signs include: difficulty walking or sitting, bloody, torn, or stained underclothes, bleeding, bruises, swelling, pain, itching, or burning in the genital area, frequent urinary or yeast infections, and sexually transmitted infections and/or pregnancy, especially if under 14 years old. Behavioral signs include: reports sexual abuse, inappropriate sexual knowledge or behavior, nightmares or bed-wetting, large weight changes/major changes in appetite, suicide attempts or self-harming, especially in adolescents, shrinks from or seems threatened by physical contact, runs away, overly protective and concerned for siblings, assumes a caretaker role, and posttraumatic stress disorder (PTSD) or rape trauma syndrome symptoms.

In addition, a sexually abused child may exhibit the following reactions: withdrawal, depression, sleeping and eating disorders, self-mutilation, phobias, psychosomatic symptoms such as stomachaches or headaches, school problems such as absences, drops in grades, poor hygiene/excessive bathing, anxiety, guilt, and regressive behaviors such as thumb sucking.

In 2001, the National Institute of Justice reported that childhood victimization increased the risk of being arrested and being arrested for a violent crime, with almost half (49%) of the abused and neglected individuals having had an arrest for a nontraffic offense.

Child victims of sexual assault are three to five times more likely to suffer from PTSD compared with adolescents who were not victimized, according to a National Institute of Justice report. Girls who witnessed violence are nearly twice as likely as boys to experience PTSD later in life. Childhood abuse and neglect also increases the likelihood of arrest as a juvenile by 59 percent, as an adult by 28 percent, and for a violent crime by 30 percent.

Treatment for child sexual abuse cases within the family are best handled by a multidisciplinary team, according to Child Welfare Information Gateway. Prior to the implementation of the treatment plan, case management decisions to address include whether: the child should remain a part of the family, the courts have a role, and visitation is a consideration. In addition, it is important to understand why the sexual abuse occurs, in general and in the particular case under consideration.

Treatment for child sexual abuse has two basic approaches: family focused and offender focused. Two main objectives in sexual abuse treatment are dealing with the effects and decreasing risk for future abuse. Issues important to the victim include: trust, including patterns in relationships; emotional, behavioral, and cognitive reactions to sexual abuse; and protection from future victimization. Issues important for the mother or nonoffending parent are related to: the sexual abuse, the mother-victim relationship, the offender (spouse), and other personal issues. Issues related to the sexual abuse include: difficulty in understanding why an adult wants to be sexual with a child, not believing the victim's disclosure, lack of understanding on the part of the nonoffending parent of his or her role. The primary issue related to the mother-victim relationship is that treatment of sexual abuse within the family that results in successful reunification of the family rests upon the mother's relationship with the victim. Issues related to the offending spouse are that the mother must decide whether she wants to end the relationship or try to save the relationship and low self-esteem.

Treatment for the offender should address: issues related to his or her past and possible future sexual victimization of children, and other dysfunctional behaviors and problems. The offender may be reluctant to be forthcoming for fear of court charges. To prevent future abuse, it is important to understand why the offender sexually abuses children. The treatment involves understanding the offender's arousal pattern and why the acts increase arousal.

Rosemarie Skaine

See also: Adult Sexual Attraction to Adolescents; Child Pornography; Child Abuse Reporting Laws; Child Protective Services; Child Trafficking; Cycle of Abuse; Incest; Pedophilia; Priests, Sexual Abuse by; Sandusky, Jerry; Sex Offender; Sex Trafficking; Sexual Slavery; Sibling Violence and Abuse.

Further Reading

American Psychological Association. 2014. "Understanding Child Sexual Abuse: Education, Prevention, and Recovery." http://www.apa.org/pubs/info/brochures/sex-abuse.aspx?item=1.

Child Welfare Information Gateway. n.d. "Treatment of Child Sexual Abuse." Children's Bureau. Administration for Children and Families. U.S. Department of Health and Human Services. https://www.childwelfare.gov/pubs/usermanuals/sexabuse/sexabusef .cfm.

Childhelp. n.d. "National Child Abuse Statistics." http://www.childhelp-usa.com/pages/ statistics#gen-stats.

Miller, Laurence. 2013. "Sexual Offenses against Children: Patterns and Motives." *Aggression and Violent Behavior* 18: 506–519.

National Institute of Justice. 2011. "Child Abuse and Maltreatment." U.S. Department of Justice. http://nij.gov/topics/crime/child-abuse/Pages/welcome.aspx.

Parents for Megan's Law and the Crime Center. n.d. "Statistics Child Sexual Abuse." http://www.parentsformeganslaw.org/public/statistics_childSexualAbuse.html.

RAINN. 2009. "Child Sexual Abuse." http://www.rainn.org/get-information /types-of-sexual-assault/child-sexual-abuse.

Thurston, C. 2006. "Part 29e: Child Abuse: Recognition of Causes and Types of Abuse." *Practice Nurse* 26: 31 (10): 51–54, 56–57.

CHILD ABUSE, TREATMENT FOR

A broad range of methods are utilized for cases of child abuse including individual therapy, group therapy, art therapy, and family therapy. According to Anthony J. Urquiza and Cynthia Winn, abused children are first introduced to individual therapy as a form of treatment. During the first stage of the treatment process, the child is able to interact with a therapist on a one-on-one basis which allows the child to learn and mimic an appropriate child-adult relationship. A significant benefit of individual therapy, apart from the child interacting with a supportive and knowledgeable therapist, is the private and personal environment that enables the therapist to quickly assess and measure the child's existing communication skills. This enables the therapist to teach the child age-appropriate behaviors and communication skills that will assist the child to positively interact with others of similar age. Another benefit of individual therapy is that it helps the child cope with developmental problems, including trust and identity issues. The above-mentioned sessions also enhance the child's ability to deal with his or her traumatic experiences.

In group therapy, the child is placed in a safe and supportive environment with other abused children. This treatment setting enables the child to develop personal and communication skills over a period of time. The child benefits from being in a social setting with other children of similar age and similar traumatic experiences. Group therapy helps the victims realize that many of the symptoms they experience are common among abused children, and that enables the child to appropriately deal with his or her emotions and behavior reactions. Group therapy may also help abused children learn and identify new ways to effectively communicate their traumatic experiences with peers and therapists and to relate and appropriately assess relationships. Group therapy provides the child with the sense of hope and demonstrates that he or she is not alone in experiencing the symptoms associated with this type of abuse. This therapy helps lessen the child's feelings of isolation and/or the negative stigma associated with abuse through interaction with other victims.

Art therapy is a form of psychotherapy that enables the child to use his or her imagination to create art. The child is given an opportunity to explore and express the exact and intimate images that are at the foundation of his or her personality. Art therapy helps battered children express dreams, apprehensions, emotions, and sentiments. Childhelp, a nonprofit organization dedicated to helping victims of child abuse and neglect, states that art therapy has been used since the 1970s and is a powerful tool to treat children who are suffering from severe cases of child abuse. Art therapy provides abused children with a powerful way to express themselves in a nonthreatening manner. A key advantage of art therapy is that creating art provides the child with opportunities to permanently record their thoughts and emotions. As the child progresses in this type of environment, as with other types of therapy, the therapist is able to observe the child's progress and the areas in which the child has improved or where the child is lacking, and the therapist is able to make any adjustment(s) to the treatment as necessary.

Family therapy is a form of treatment involving the family of the abused child. In this treatment setting, the family of the child has to be willing to address and resolve the issues of abuse. This type of therapy is only ideal in less severe cases of child abuse. If a health care professional and/or therapist determines that the parents of the child pose a threat to the rehabilitation of the abused child, the child is placed with relatives who are willing to facilitate the rehabilitation process. Family therapy enables the abused child to improve and to develop problem-solving skills, communication skills, and to develop a sense of acceptance. These skills form an important part of the child's overall development as he or she transcends into adulthood. A benefit of this form of therapy is that it allows the family to address and solve many internal and/or external issues associated with child abuse and facilitates the family to improve communication among other family members involved in the process. Another benefit of family therapy is that the child is placed with individuals with whom he or she is familiar. This type of treatment is a less invasive way to rehabilitate an abused child because the child can be rehabilitated in his or her residence and be in a supportive environment with immediate relatives.

Juan Carlos Hernandez

See also: Child Abuse, Psychological and Behavioral Effects of.

Further Reading

Childhelp. 2013. "Residential Treatment Facilities." http://www.childhelp.org/programs/type/residential.

Dale, Peter, Tony Morrison, Murray Davies, Phillip Noyes, and Wilf Roberts. 2003. "A Family-therapy Approach to Child Abuse: Countering Resistance." *Journal of Family Therapy* 5: 121. doi:10.1046/j..1983.00611.x.

Lipovsky, Julie A., and Rochelle F. Hanson. 2013. "Treatment of Child Victims of Abuse and Neglect." Children's Law Center. http://childlaw.sc.edu/frmPublications/TreatmentforChildVictimsofAbuseandNeglect.pdf.

Urquiza, Anthony J., and Cynthia Winn. 2013. "Treatment for Abused and Neglected Children: Infancy to Age 18." U.S. Department of Health and Human Services, Child Welfare Information Gateway, HHS 105–89–1730 (1994): 61–62. https://www.childwelfare.gov/pubs/usermanuals/treatmen/treatmene.cfm.

CHILD ABUSE, VERBAL

The American Academy of Pediatrics defines psychological abuse as belittling, denigrating, exploiting, or terrorizing a child to the point where their well-being is at risk. Verbal abuse is considered a form of psychological or emotional abuse. Family members, caregivers as well as peers, teachers, and coaches are examples of perpetrators of verbal abuse. Current day bullying exemplifies verbal abuse.

Verbal abuse includes: name calling, belittling, swearing, insults, for example, saying "You are stupid"; indirect criticism, such as disapproving of a child to the spouse; rejecting or threatening with abandonment, such as commenting, "I wish you'd never been born"; threatening bodily harm; scapegoating or blaming; using sarcasm; and berating the spouse. Verbal assault by a parent involves exaggerating a child's flaws, making fun of the child, name calling, berating, screaming, threatening or criticizing, blaming for everything, and humiliating with sarcasm and endless insults.

Child Protective Services reported that 6 percent of all child abuse cases involved emotional maltreatment. Verbal abuse is the most common form. Verbal child abuse is more prevalent in homes with more than one source of stress, such as depression, mental health issues, physical violence, and substance abuse. In addition, it is more likely that the parents were victims of abuse at some point in their lives, or because they are bitter, angry, or resentful. The result is they vent their feelings on their children. Parents may be unaware or refuse to consider that they are abusive because they were brought up in the same way.

Some of the effects of verbal abuse include: low self-esteem, self-image, or perception or worldview; acting out the negative and aggressive behaviors received from parents; using substances, alcohol, and illegal narcotics; antisocial rooted behaviors; and self-mutilation. Like many forms of abuse, verbal abuse may continue the cycle into the child's adult life. Thus, verbal abuse causes long-term harm when as an adult, the child either becomes a victim of abuse later in life, becomes abusive, or depressed and self-destructive.

Therapy for verbally abused children is similar to that used for emotionally abused victims and includes individual, group, and family. Individual therapy focusing on rebuilding self-esteem and autonomy is helpful to victims of verbal abuse. Recognizing and understanding a healthy relationship, children can begin to appreciate the dysfunctional way they have been raised. When children have been traumatized by emotional abuse, they are often hesitant to share the details and may respond best to treatments that include creative play, such as art therapy and therapy of trauma relief.

Group therapy involves sharing experiences creating commonality and acceptance that results in rebuilding self-esteem and confidence. Psychotherapy, cognitive behavioral therapy, and somatic therapies are also forms of treatment. In addition, journal therapy provides some victims relief.

Family therapy works with offenders and victims to understand their role, responsibility, and rights. Offenders acquire skills to address what causes them to abuse, and victims learn ways to move past the abuse. All types of treatment attempt to foster learning how to develop emotional intelligence, set boundaries, and modify behavior.

Rosemarie Skaine

See also: Bullying, Child and Adolescent; Child Abuse, Physical and Emotional; Child Abuse, Poverty and; Child Abuse Reporting Laws; Cycle of Abuse; Sibling Violence and Abuse.

Further Reading

Brown, Asa Don. August 16, 2013. "What Are the Effects of Verbal Abuse on Children?" Counseling Connect/Connexion. Canadian Counseling and Psychotherapy Association. http://www.ccpa-accp.ca/blog/?p=867.

GoodTherapy.org. 2013. "Emotional Abuse." http://www.goodtherapy.org/therapy-for-emotional-abuse.html.

Harper, Michael. 2012. "Verbal Abuse from Parents Harmful to Children." RedOrbit. http://www.redorbit.com/news/health/1112666005/parents-verbal-abuse-harms-children/ or http://www.redorbit.com/news/health/1112666005/parents-verbal-abuse-harms-children/#rdFqYFUvKR7qcQk2.99 redOrbit.com.

Vardigan, Benj. 2015. "Yelling at Children (Verbal Abuse). HealthDay. http://consumer.healthday.com/encyclopedia/children-s-health-10/child-development-news-124/yelling-at-children-verbal-abuse-648565.html.

CHILD ABUSE PREVENTION AND ENFORCEMENT ACTS

The primary responsibility for child welfare services is placed with the states, but states must comply with specific federal requirements and guidelines to receive federal funding under certain programs. The first federal law that had a significant impact on state child protection and child welfare services was the Child Abuse Prevention and Treatment Act (CAPTA) of 1974. The act's purpose was to create a single federal focus for preventing and responding to child abuse and neglect. It established the National Center on Child Abuse and Neglect and approved funding for fiscal years 1974 through 1977 for demonstration projects on the prevention, identification, and treatment of child abuse and neglect.

This act was amended several times, including the CAPTA Amendments of 1996. It also reauthorized and amended the Family Violence Prevention and Services Act and the Abandoned Infants Assistance Act. The Child Abuse Prevention and Enforcement Act of 2000 sought to reduce the incidence of child abuse and neglect through law enforcement initiatives and prevention activities. The CAPTA Reauthorization Act of 2010 amended the Child Abuse Prevention and Treatment Act, the Family Violence Prevention and Services Act, the Child Abuse Prevention and Treatment and Adoption Reform Act of 1978, and the Abandoned Infants Assistance Act of 1988 to reauthorize the acts, and for other purposes.

To receive state grant funds, states are required to have procedures for receiving and responding to allegations of abuse or neglect and for ensuring children's safety. CAPTA's first procedure is that states are required to define child abuse and neglect in a way that is consistent with CAPTA, which defines the terms as "at a minimum, any recent act or failure to act on the part of a parent or caretaker, which results in death, serious physical or emotional harm, sexual abuse or exploitation, or an act or failure to act which presents an imminent risk of serious harm," according to the *Congressional Research Service.*

Usually, definitions elaborate on the meaning of different types of abuse: physical abuse, normally involves nonaccidental physical injury and, in some states, substantial threat of injury; neglect, includes withdrawal of necessary food, clothing, shelter, medical care, or supervision, and, typically, the reasons are other than economic failure; sexual abuse/exploitation; and emotional abuse or mental injury. Some states also define other forms of abuse and neglect, for example, abandonment or harming or exposing a child to harm due to substance abuse or the manufacture of a controlled substance. Another state effort to be consistent with the definition in CAPTA is to specify that the finding of child abuse or neglect may only occur if the perpetrator is a parent or caregiver of the child.

The second procedure requires that states have laws or programs for receiving, screening, and investigating referrals of individuals known or suspected of child abuse and neglect. Although any person can report abuse, some states require certain professionals such as health or teaching professionals report. Some states develop criteria as to when a referral should be disregarded.

The third procedure outlines what an investigation must include in a determination regarding the safety of the child and, in most states, the safety of other children on the scene. Other requirements include an assessment of service needs and, if needed, a recommendation for court intervention. Three-fourths of the states provided temporary services to the family as necessary. During the investigation, common practices include reviews of any prior records relevant to the family; visits to the family without making an appointment; and interviews with relevant individuals, such as family members other than the caregiver, professionals known to the family, witnesses, and/or the person who reported the abuse or neglect. Other investigation activities might include performing a criminal background check on the alleged perpetrator, managing family group conference meetings, and discussing the case with a multi-disciplinary team.

The fourth procedure addresses an alternate response of assessing family strengths and needs to ensure children's safety rather than an investigation. The fifth procedure examines who is the victim?

One addition was made to the CAPTA 2010 act's provisions on representation of children in court. In 2003, language was added to the mandate that every child's court-appointed representatives have "training appropriate to the role." Since then, no formal specification by the Children's Bureau of the U.S. Department of Health and Human Services (HHS) was stated as to what comprises "appropriate training." The 2010 act specifies that it is "training in early childhood, child, and adolescent development." The same language is added in a section on the acceptable areas of caseworker training that is conducted using CAPTA state grant funding.

According to the American Bar Association, other changes in 2010 include

- An added category for grant referral of "Newborns with Fetal Alcohol Spectrum Disorder"
- No reunification requirement if a parent sexually abused any child of the parent and if the parent must register with a sex offender registry under the 2006 Adam Walsh Child Protection and Safety Act

- Criminal record checks on other adults that live in the home of prospective foster or adoptive parents before a placement is made or federal kinship guardian assistance
- A requirement that every state have "systems of technology" that support CPS's ability to "track reports of child abuse and neglect from intake through final disposition"
- A requirement that states must submit additional agency data
- The promotion, but not requirement, of family participation, cooperation with programs such as child welfare agencies and domestic violence programs when applicable, and use of differential response
- The promotion of school attendance by homeless children
- System reform that includes former child abuse and neglect victims and homeless youth
- Support activities that build and share knowledge, or support training, on related issues, for example, improved medical diagnosis and the impact of child abuse on children with disabilities, and a requirement for two national studies on "shaken baby syndrome" and "immunity from prosecution"
- Support for greater protections for children made vulnerable by domestic or dating violence and new efforts designed to keep adoptions intact as extensions of these programs

Rosemarie Skaine

See also: Adam Walsh Child Protection and Safety Act; Child Protective Services; Foster Care Acts.

Further Reading

CAPTA Reauthorization Act of 2010: Public Law 111–320. 111 P.L. 320; 124 Stat. 3459. 2010. Enacted S. 3817; 111 Enacted S. 3817. http://library.childwelfare.gov/cwig/ws/library/docs/gateway/Blob/75315.pdf?w=+NATIVE%28%27sti+%3D%22Index+of+Federal+Child+Welfare+Laws%22%27%29&upp=0&rpp=-10&order=+NATIVE%28%27year+%2F+descend%27%29&r=1&m=8.

Child Abuse Prevention and Treatment Act: Public Law 93–247: S. 1191. 1974. http://www.gpo.gov/fdsys/pkg/STATUTE-88/pdf/STATUTE-88-Pg4.pdf.

Child Abuse Prevention and Treatment Act Amendments of 1996: Public Law 104–235: S. 919. http://library.childwelfare.gov/cwig/ws/library/docs/gateway/Blob/56414.pdf?w=+NATIVE%28%27sti+%3D%22Index+of+Federal+Child+Welfare+Laws%22%27%29&upp=0&rpp=-10&order=+NATIVE%28%27year+%2F+descend%27%29&r=1&m=37.

Child Abuse Prevention and Enforcement Act of 2000: Public Law 106–177: H.R. 764. http://library.childwelfare.gov/cwig/ws/library/docs/gateway/Blob/56365.pdf?w=+NATIVE%28%27sti+%3D%22Index+of+Federal+Child+Welfare+Laws%22%27%29&upp=0&rpp=-10&order=+NATIVE%28%27year+%2F+descend%27%29&r=1&m=25.

Child Welfare Information Gateway. 2012. "Major Federal Legislation Concerned with Child Protection, Child Welfare, and Adoption." *Factsheets*. Administration for Children and Families. Washington, D.C.: U.S. Department of Health and Human Services. https://www.childwelfare.gov/pubs/otherpubs/majorfedlegis.cfm.

Child Welfare Information Gateway. 2011. "About CAPTA: A Legislative History." Washington, D.C.: U.S. Department of Health and Human Services, Children's Bureau. https://www.childwelfare.gov/pubs/factsheets/about.pdf#page=1&view=Introduction.

Child Welfare Policy Manual. 2013. Iowa Judicial Branch. http://www.iowacourts.gov/wfdata/files/ChildrensJustice/ParentAttyRepresen/CWPM_CAPTA_fin2011.pdf.

Davidson, Howard. 2011. "The CAPTA Reauthorization Act of 2010: What Advocates Should Know." *Children's Rights Litigation*. American Bar Association. http://apps.americanbar.org/litigation/committees/childrights/content/articles/010311-capta-reauthorization.html.

Stoltzfus, Emilie. 2009. "The Child Abuse Prevention and Treatment Act (CAPTA): Background, Programs, and Funding." *Congressional Research Service*. http://www.napcwa.org/Legislative/docs/CAPTACongressionalResearchReport.pdf.

CHILD ABUSE PREVENTION ASSOCIATION

The mission of the Child Abuse Prevention Association (CAPA) is to prevent and treat all forms of child abuse by creating changes in individuals, families, and society that strengthen relationships and promote healing. Founded in 1975, as a crisis and information hotline, the Child Abuse Prevention Association (CAPA) staffed by members of the Junior Service League, became a United Way agency in 1978.

In the 1980s, CAPA partnered with Children's Place to develop day treatment programs for victims of child abuse. During this same period, CAPA became a Parent Anonymous support group sponsor. During the 1990s, CAPA's child sexual abuse treatment programs were expanded, and it began collaborating with Head Start in providing parenting education classes and support groups for high-risk families.

Since 2000, the organization has expanded its Healthy Family Connections program. This provides home-based case management and counseling services to high need families with newborns until age three. In June 2010, CAPA celebrated its 35th anniversary of service to the community. Its focus continues to be on preventing and treating all forms of child abuse by utilizing a continuum of services: prevention education, family support services, and counseling, which are available in English and Spanish.

To prevent child abuse and neglect, CAPA advocates a six-step approach:

1. Understand the causes of child abuse and learn all you can about abuse and neglect.
2. Learn to identify the warning signs that signal that a child is being abused.
3. Report any known or suspected case of child abuse immediately.
4. Seek help if you feel you are at risk of abusing a child.
5. Be a friend to a child or parent in need.
6. Alert others to the problem and help them to recognize and understand the effects of physical, sexual, and emotional abuse and neglect.

To break the cycle of abuse, CAPA provides counseling to children and their families after abuse has occurred. When a child is able to heal from abuse and learn how to keep safe, the chances of additional abuse are greatly reduced. CAPA also provides family support services and educational opportunities that help reduce the risk factors that cause abuse and neglect before they occur.

The Child Abuse Prevention Association is a 501(c)(3) not-for-profit organization that relies on donations and foundation grants to provide essential services.

Rosemarie Skaine

See also: Child Abuse Prevention and Enforcement Acts.

Further Reading

Child Abuse Prevention Association (CAPA). n.d. http://www.childabuseprevention.org.
Child Abuse Prevention Association (CAPA). n.d. "Preventing Abuse." *Abuse Information.* http://www.childabuseprevention.org/content/abuse-information.
San Francisco Child Abuse Center. n.d. "Our Mission, History, and Values." http://www .sfcapc.org/about_us/our_mission_history_and_values.

CHILD ABUSE REPORTING LAWS

Reporting laws require certain persons to report reasonable suspicions of child abuse to a state child welfare agency responsible for the investigation and prosecution of such acts. Reporting laws have been in existence only since the early 1960s, when national attention was focused on the problem of child abuse by the medical community's recognition of identifiable symptoms suffered by battered children. A groundswell of legislation in all 50 states, the District of Columbia, and American protectorates around the world attempted to bring the hitherto quietly ignored epidemic of child abuse into the open and eradicate it.

Reporting laws differ on the point of which persons are required to report. Generally, anyone who regularly sees children in a professional capacity is required to report suspected abuse. This includes physicians, dentists, psychologists, psychiatrists, and other medical personnel—such as nurses—who treat children. Many states also include guidance counselors, teachers, day care providers, social workers, residential care workers, and police officers. Other states also require attorneys and clergymen to report suspicions of child abuse. In some states, everyone is obligated to report suspected child abuse. In states that do not require everyone to report, anyone may report it.

In order to induce compliance, mandatory reporting laws usually immunize those persons who are required to report suspected child abuse from legal liability if their suspicions turn out to be wrong. So long as a reporter has a good faith belief that child abuse may be occurring, he or she is shielded from lawsuits for libel, slander, invasion of privacy, or breach of confidentiality for reporting suspicions to an appropriate agency. The duty of attorneys, physicians, and clergy not to disclose the confidences of their clients has been abolished in some states for the narrow purpose of reporting to an appropriate agency that child abuse may be occurring. If a person makes a knowingly false report, however, or if he or she spreads allegations of abuse to persons other than a state law enforcement or child welfare agency, immunity from legal responsibility for such statements may not be granted.

Persons who are required by a reporting law to inform authorities of suspected child abuse may be prosecuted under the criminal law if they fail to do so. However, there have been relatively few such prosecutions—probably because it is so difficult to prove that someone had knowledge of child abuse. In some states, a child welfare agency that receives a report of suspected child abuse may be sued for negligence if it fails to investigate properly and a child is injured as a result.

Lauren Krohn Arnest

See also: Child Abandonment and Neglect; Child Abuse, Physical and Emotional; Child Abuse, Psychological and Behavioral Effects of; Child Abuse, Sexual; Child Abuse, Treatment for; Child Abuse, Verbal.

Further Reading

Arnest, Lauren Krohn. 1998. *Children, Young Adults, and the Law: A Dictionary*. Santa Barbara, CA: ABC-CLIO.

Davis, Samuel M., and Mortimer D. Schwartz. 1987. *Children's Rights and the Law*. Lexington, MA: Lexington Books.

Kfoury, Paul R. 1991. *Children before the Court: Reflections on Legal Issues Affecting Minors*. 2nd ed. Salem, NH: Butterworth Legal Publishers.

CHILD AND FAMILY SERVICES IMPROVEMENT ACTS

The Child and Family Services Improvement Act of 2006 amends part B of title IV of the Social Security Act to reauthorize the Promoting Safe and Stable Families program and for other purposes. According to the Center for Law and Social Policy (CLASP), special benefits of the act are the addition of $40 million annually and the attention given to improving the workforce and to addressing substance abuse, specifically methamphetamine abuse. Other changes include amending the case review requirements so that courts conducting permanency hearings must consult with each child in an age-appropriate way regarding his or her permanency plan and requiring, in part, that states develop a disaster response plan that explains how the state would identify, locate, and continue to provide services for children under state care or supervision who are displaced. Some programs were reauthorized, including the Program for Mentoring Children of Prisoners. Changes were also made in reporting systems, such as how actively health care professionals are involved in the medical care of children in foster care and number of caseworker visits with children who are in foster care.

The Child and Family Services Improvement and Innovation Act of 2011 also extends the Child and Family Services Program through fiscal year 2016, reauthorizes two child welfare programs, and includes improvements to make certain that children can safely remain with their own parents or be supported by other caring adults. The law renews child welfare waiver authority to allow more states to invest in new ways of serving children at risk of abuse and neglect. The law also establishes a process to create child welfare data standards that can bring more improvement to foster care systems.

The child and family welfare programs affected include the Stephanie Tubbs Jones Child Welfare Services program, Promoting Safe and Stable Families program, Monthly Caseworker Visits and Regional Partnership grant programs, and the Court Improvement Program, and they reauthorize child welfare demonstration projects designed to test innovative strategies in the states.

Rosemarie Skaine

See also: Foster Care Acts.

Further Reading

Casey Family Programs. 2011. "Passage of Federal Foster Care Law Will Help Improve the Lives of More Vulnerable Children and Their Families across the Nation." *PR Newswire*, September 30. http://www.prnewswire.com/news-releases/passage-of-federal-foster-care-law-will-help-improve-the-lives-of-more-vulnerable-children-and-their-families-across-the-nation-130885418.html.

Child and Family Services Improvement Act of 2006. 2006. "Overview." P.L. 109-288. Child Welfare Information Gateway. U.S. Department of Health and Human Services. https://www.childwelfare.gov/systemwide/laws_policies/federal/index.cfm?event=federalLegislation.viewLegis&id=62.

Child and Family Services Improvement Act of 2006. 2006. P.L 109–288. 109th Congress. http://www.gpo.gov/fdsys/pkg/PLAW-109publ288/pdf/PLAW-109publ288.pdf.

Child and Family Services Improvement and Innovation Act. 2011. "Overview." P.L. 112-34. Child Welfare Information Gateway. U.S. Department of Health and Human Services. https://www.childwelfare.gov/systemwide/laws_policies/federal/index.cfm?event=federalLegislation.viewLegis&id=122.

Conway, Tiffany, and Rutledge Q. Hutson. 2007. "In-depth Summary of the Child and Family Services Improvement Act of 2006." Center for Law and Social Policy (CLASP). http://www.clasp.org/admin/site/publications/files/0337.pdf.

Office of the Press Secretary. 2011. "On Friday, September 30, 2011, the President Signed into Law." *Statement by the Press Secretary*, September 30. The White House. http://www.whitehouse.gov/the-press-office/2011/09/30/statement-press-secretary.

CHILD PORNOGRAPHY

Federal law states that child pornography is any visual depiction of sexually explicit conduct involving a minor, defined as a person less than 18 years of age. Child pornography images are also referred to as child sexual abuse images. Child pornography differs from conventional pornography in that it is a form of child sexual exploitation wherein each image graphically memorializes the sexual abuse of that child. Each child involved in the production of an image is a victim of sexual abuse. The law prohibits the production, distribution, importation, reception, or possession of any image of child pornography. Violating the federal child pornography law is a serious crime, and convicted offenders face severe statutory penalties.

In the mid-1980s, the trafficking of child pornography was almost completely eliminated, but with the arrival of the Internet and advanced digital technology, the market for it increased dramatically. Producing and reproducing child sexual abuse images is no longer difficult and expensive. More than 1 million pornographic images of children are on the Internet, with 200 new images posted daily. It is difficult to estimate the number of sites because many survive only a brief period before they are shut down, and much of the trade occurs at hidden levels of the Internet. Pedophiles involved in organized pornography rings are estimated to be between 50,000 and 100,000 globally with one-third of them operating from the United States.

Females are more likely to be victims of child pornography production, but all ages are victimized including infants and toddlers. About half of the victims are 12 years or younger. The National Center for Missing & Exploited Children (NCMEC) reported 24 percent of victims were pubescent, and 76 percent were prepubescent. Ten percent of the prepubescent victims were infants or toddlers. Child pornography producers may target young victims because they do not yet communicate well and are unable to report their abuse. They are also less likely to recognize inappropriate touching.

Most victims are abused by a family member or acquaintance who may pressure the victims through parental authority, threats, or payment with drugs, alcohol, or money. Other abusers manipulate one child to recruit others, including her/his siblings. Peer pressure is used to encourage multiple children to participate.

Images of child pornography often present a distorted picture of what actually occurred. Some images portray forcible rape, forced penetration, and other violent sexual assaults. Most images do not depict a child crying, but show a compliant, willing, and sexually involved child. Most images are created with the victim's knowledge, but about one-quarter have been produced without the victim's knowledge through use of hidden cameras, creating images transformed into different ones, or by photographing or filming sleeping or drugged victims.

Child pornography is so plentiful, in part, because of its effects on the abusers Among the effects are: pornography sexually stimulates the user in preparation for offending; attraction to images of increasing severity and becoming desensitized to the harm victims experience; and is a substitute for, or even helps the individual resist, engaging in hands-on offending. When these reasons are combined with lucrative financial benefits, child pornography flourishes.

Another reason child pornography is so plentiful, in addition to the advent of the Internet and effects on abusers, is the skill of pimps and traffickers in targeting and luring children. The child is also vulnerable to a person who promises to meet his or her emotional and physical needs. The relationship is highly manipulative because it may appear to be loving and caring, but, in reality, it is designed to make sure the youth will remain loyal to the exploiter even in the face of severe victimization.

Child pornography producers use different methods: some groom their victims before engaging in sexual abuse; since children cannot give legal consent, manipulation is used to make them agree to participate; or convincing or coercing a child to take images of himself or herself. Although the majority of children are not abducted or physically forced to take part, the experience can have destructive physical, social, and psychological effects on them. They are first victimized when their abuse is perpetrated and recorded. They are again victimized each time that record is accessed. Effects can be apparent at the time it occurred and in later years. At the time, victims reported physical pain, for example, around the genitals, bone fractures, sexually transmitted disease; accompanying somatic symptoms including headaches, loss of appetite, and sleeplessness; and feelings of psychological distress such as emotional isolation, anxiety, and fear. Most cooperate with the offender and agree not to disclose the offense out of fear, loyalty, and/or a sense of shame. In later years, the victims reported that initial feelings of shame and anxiety intensified to feelings of deep despair, worthlessness, and hopelessness. They developed a distorted model of sexuality, and many had trouble establishing and maintaining healthy emotional and sexual relationships.

Laws to protect children from pornography are relatively recent. The first federal law passed in 1978, and the first laws that specifically referred to computers and child pornography were passed in 1988. Since that time, a steady tightening of child pornography laws has occurred. The Victims of Trafficking and Violence Protection Act of 2000 combats trafficking in persons, especially in the sex trade, slavery, and involuntary servitude.

Rosemarie Skaine

See also: Child Abuse, Sexual; Identity Theft; Internet Victimization, Child; Pedophilia.

Further Reading

18 U.S.C. § 2251; 18 U.S.C. § 2252; 18 U.S.C. § 2252A, Federal Law.

National Center for Missing and Exploited Children (NCMEC). 2013. "Commercial Sexual Exploitation of Children: A Fact Sheet." http://www.missingkids.com/en_US/documents/CCSE_Fact_Sheet.pdf.

United States Sentencing Commission. 2013. "Chapter 5: Victims of Child Pornography." *Report to Congress: Federal Child Pornography Offenses*. http://www.ussc.gov/Legislative_and_Public_Affairs/Congressional_Testimony_and_Reports/Sex_Offense_Topics/201212_Federal_Child_Pornography_Offenses/Chapter_05.pdf.

U.S. Department of Justice. n.d. "Child Pornography." Child Exploitation and Obscenity Section. http://www.justice.gov/criminal/ceos/subjectareas/childporn.html.

U.S. Department of Justice. n.d. "Citizen's Guide to U.S. Federal Law on Child Pornography." Child Exploitation and Obscenity Section. http://www.justice.gov/criminal/ceos/citizensguide/citizensguide_porn.html.

Victims of Trafficking and Violence Protection Act of 2000. 2000. Public Law 106-386 [H.R. 3244].

Wortley, Richard, and Stephen Smallbone. May 2012. "Child Pornography on the Internet." *Problem-oriented Guides for Police Problem-specific Guides Series* 41. U.S. Department of Justice. Office of Community Oriented Policing Services (COPS Office). http://www.cops.usdoj.gov/Publications/e04062000.pdf.

CHILD PROTECTIVE SERVICES

In most states, the governmental agency that must respond to allegations of child abuse and neglect is called Child Protective Services (CPS). State CPS agencies provide annual data on all forms of maltreatment to the federally sponsored National Child Abuse and Neglect Data System (NCANDS). At the federal level, the U.S. Department of Health and Human Services is responsible for oversight of state CPS agencies as well as NCANDS data collection.

Professionals such as social workers, doctors and other medical personnel, day care providers, and teachers are required by law to report suspected cases of child maltreatment to authorities. These individuals are referred to as *mandated reporters* because of their legal obligation to report abuse they encounter in the course of their professional activities. According to the U.S. Department of Health and Human Services, in 2009, 60 percent of CPS referrals resulted from mandated reporters. Concerned individuals may also report suspected child abuse to CPS authorities following the same procedures as professionals, but they are not legally required to do so.

State CPS agencies investigate allegations of all child abuse. Allegations are handled in a two-stage process. First, allegations are screened. During screening, an initial notification—called a *referral*—alleging child maltreatment is received by CPS. Agency hotline or intake units conduct the screening process to determine whether the referral is appropriate for further action. Approximately 38 percent of initial referrals are screened out, usually because they do not meet the state's standard for investigation or there is insufficient information to allow for a response to occur.

Second, CPS must respond to all abuse allegations that are screened in for further investigation. The decision regarding how soon CPS officials must initiate an investigation is determined by the nature of the allegation and the degree of immediate threat to the child. Cases that meet the highest safety threshold require an immediate response by authorities. High-priority cases include those in which the abuse is ongoing and presents an immediate, significant, and clearly observable threat to a child.

In extreme cases, where the parent or guardian is unable to present adequate safeguards to protect the child from ongoing abuse, the child may be removed from the home and placed in out-of-home care. CPS caseworkers may refer families and children to other postresponse services that are not directly provided by CPS caseworkers.

Shawna Lee

See also: Child Abuse, Physical and Emotional; Child Abuse, Psychological and Behavioral Effects of; Child Abuse, Sexual; Child Abuse, Treatment for; Child Abuse, Verbal; Child Abuse Reporting Laws

Further Reading

Arnest, Lauren Krohn. 1998. *Children, Young Adults, and the Law: A Dictionary*. Santa Barbara, CA: ABC-CLIO.

Davis, Samuel M., and Mortimer D. Schwartz. 1987. *Children's Rights and the Law*. Lexington, MA: Lexington Books.

CHILD TRAFFICKING

Child trafficking occurs when a person(s) is involved in the recruitment, harboring, transportation, provision, or obtaining of a person who has not attained 18 years of age for labor or services, including sex. Coercion is evident in child trafficking.

Under federal law, child trafficking is a serious offense, with penalties for the trafficker of up to life imprisonment. The types of child labor associated with trafficking include: forced labor, sexual exploitation, children in the armed forces, drug trade, and begging. Activities that the child is forced to do include: commercial sex, stripping, pornography, forced begging, agricultural work, and drug sales.

According to the National Center for Missing and Exploited Children, one in seven endangered runaways who reported to them in 2013 was a likely sex trafficking victim. The International Labor Organization reported that about1.2 million children are trafficked each year.

Risk factors for children that contribute to the cause of child trafficking include: school-age youth who are vulnerable because of challenging family situations and minors as young as 9 years old who make use of social media Web sites, telephone chat lines, after-school programs, are at shopping malls and bus depots, or through friends or acquaintances who recruit students on school campuses.

Trafficking can result in the death or permanent injury of the trafficked child. Denial of access to health care increases the child's chances of serious injury and death. A child may be beaten or starved to ensure obedience or given drugs to have him or her become addicted and thus dependent on the trafficker(s). The trauma is often prolonged and repeated, leading to severe psychological impact. According to UN.Gift, children suffer from depression, anxiety, and posttraumatic stress disorder.

Families also suffer. They believed the child is working to bring in additional income, but they may never see their trafficked child again. In some cultures, sexual exploitation of girls brings shame to families.

The Office of Safe and Healthy Students in the U.S. Department of Education indicates the following signs that a child is a victim of trafficking:

- Inability to attend school regularly and/or has unexplained absences
- Frequently runs away from home
- Refers to frequent travel to other cities
- Exhibits bruises or other signs of physical trauma, withdrawn behavior, depression, anxiety, or fear
- Lacks control over his or her schedule and/or identification or travel documents
- Is hungry, malnourished, deprived of sleep, or inappropriately dressed
- Shows signs of drug addiction
- Has coached/rehearsed responses to questions
- Has a sudden change in attire, personal hygiene, relationships, or material possessions
- Is uncharacteristically promiscuous and/or makes references to sexual situations or terminology that are beyond age-specific norms
- Has a boyfriend or girlfriend who is noticeably older
- Attempts to conceal recent scars

Signs that may indicate labor trafficking include:

- Expresses need to pay off a debt
- Expresses concern for family members' safety if he or she shares too much information
- Works long hours and receives little or no payment
- Cares for children not from his or her own family

The Department of Homeland Security offers a victim-centered approach. It encourages victims to come forward and citizens to take a proactive approach. Citizens can call their tip line at 1-866-347-2423 or submit a tip online at www. ice.gov/tips. They can get to know the Human Trafficking Task Forces by visiting www.bja and learn about T or U visas (available relief to trafficking victims) by watching a video. They can download helpful law enforcement certification guides or get in touch with U.S. Citizenship and Immigration Services (USCIS) with questions or visit www.uscis.gov/humantrafficking. Also, they can contact USCIS at 802-527-4888 or e-mail to LawEnforcement_UTVAWA.vsc@uscis.dhs.gov.

The key international documents dealing with the trafficking of children are the 1989 U.N. Convention on the Rights of the Child, the 1999 I.L.O. Worst Forms of Child Labor Convention, and the 2000 U.N. Protocol to Prevent, Suppress and Punish Trafficking in Persons, especially Women and Children.

U.S. federal law for severe forms of trafficking in persons includes both sex trafficking and labor trafficking. The federal antitrafficking laws include the Trafficking Victims Protection Act (TVPA) of 2000, the first comprehensive federal law to address trafficking in persons. The TVPA provides a three-pronged approach that includes prevention, protection, and prosecution. The TVPA was reauthorized through the Trafficking Victims Protection Reauthorization Acts (TVPRA) of 2003, 2005, 2008, and 2013. In addition, states have antitrafficking laws.

In general, trafficking prevails not only because individuals are vulnerable but also because it is a market-driven criminal industry based on the principles of supply and demand for cheap labor or services or for commercial sex acts. Traffickers are people who victimize others to profit from the existing demand. To ultimately solve the problem of human trafficking, it is vital to concentrate on the demand-driven factors as well as to alter the overall market incentives of high profit and low risk.

Rosemarie Skaine

See also: Abduction, Child; Human Rights; Human Trafficking; Sexual Slavery; Slavery, Modern-day.

Further Reading

Federal Bureau of Investigation (FBI). n.d. "Innocence Lost." *Violent Crimes against Children*. http://www.fbi.gov/about-us/investigate/vc_majorthefts/cac/innocencelost.

Human Trafficking Federal Law. [U.S.C. §7102(8)].

National Center for Missing and Exploited Children. 2014. "Child Sex Trafficking." http://www.missingkids.com/CSTT.

National Center for Missing and Exploited Children. 2010. *Commercial Sexual Exploitation of Children: A Fact Sheet*. http://www.missingkids.com/en_US/documents/CCSE_Fact_Sheet.pdf.

Polaris Project. 2014. "Human Trafficking." http://www.polarisproject.org/human-trafficking/overview.

UN.Gift. 2008. "Human Trafficking: The Facts." https://www.unglobalcompact.org/docs/issues_doc/labour/Forced_labour/HUMAN_TRAFFICKING_-_THE_FACTS_-_final.pdf.

U.S. Department of Education. 2013. "Human Trafficking of Children in the United States." Office of Safe and Healthy Students. http://www2.ed.gov/about/offices/list/oese/oshs/factsheet.html.

U.S. Department of Homeland Security. n.d. "Learn about Human Trafficking." http://www.dhs.gov/blue-campaign/learn-about-human-trafficking.

U.S. Department of Homeland Security. n.d. "Victims of Human Trafficking & Other Crimes." U.S. Citizenship and Immigration Services (USCIS).

COMMUNITY ACTION STOPS ABUSE

The Tampa Bay Community Action Stops Abuse (CASA) has been in existence since 1977 with a Free Clinic Spouse Abuse Shelter that had a capacity to serve eight victims. Because it takes courage to disclose abuse, CASA works with the community to build a network of support for survivors of domestic abuse and their children. It provides refuge, crisis intervention, advocacy, professional training, and community outreach to break the silence that isolates victims and prevents them from a life of hope, independence, and peace.

Community Action Stops Abuse grew following its founding. Highlights include receiving funding in 1997 for 14 units of transitional housing, called CASA Gateway, and for providing low-cost housing and advocacy services to families as they get ready for independent living. In 1998, CASA began an in-school Peacemakers Program for preschool and middle school students. In 1999, the organization began the Keys to Peace Capital Campaign to raise funds to complete the second phase of CASA Gateway transitional housing and to expand outreach services. It purchased a building for their CASA Community Center.

In 2013, the Gateway Transitional Housing Program included two apartment complexes, each with six three-bedroom apartments and one two-bedroom apartment. Advantages for residents include: reduced rent and utilities, participation in safety planning, support groups, and empowerment to enhance employment skills, life skills, and personal development. From July 2012 to July 2013, 91 percent of participants moved from a Gateway apartment into permanent housing. Eighty-two percent of participants who left the program increased their income. Eleven out of 12 participants obtained vehicles to travel to school or work.

Education accomplishments in 2013 included three prospective graduates, two registered nurses (RN), and one licensed practical nurse (LPN). The Gateway Program on Temporary Assistance for Needy Families helped support one RN. Others are still in school, one at St. Pete College to become a sign language interpreter and another at the University of South Florida's master's degree program. All students have won Women's Independence Scholarship Program grants.

Younger students are also accomplished. Five out of the eight to ten children that attend the CASA Youth Program after school are on the principal's honor roll at their schools, and two will attend the Pinellas County Summer Bridge Program to strengthen areas of academic weakness. Older youth meet monthly to participate in groups that address sex education, self-awareness, and self-sufficiency. They also take part in social activities with other young people who have been exposed to domestic violence at an early age.

In addition, CASA's shelter provision through Gateway Housing and Youth Center provides refuge, crisis intervention, and advocacy for up to 45 days when home is not a safe place. The shelter is always open, and the location is confidential. CASA maintains a 24-hour access line: (800) 799-SAFE (7233). Shelter residents receive emergency clothing, food, personal care items, child care, ongoing individual and group support, and mental health, substance abuse, and justice advocacy.

As part of its community-based advocacy, CASA provides in-home services, including information and referrals, relocation assistance, justice advocacy, and crisis intervention to families identified through the Pinellas County Child Protection Investigation Department. Also, part of its advocacy is providing a domestic violence advocacy team. The team develops treatment, safety, and case plans for families. The plans are identified through the child welfare system, which may benefit from intense to moderate in-home services to keep the family safe and intact.

Rosemarie Skaine

See also: Domestic Abuse; Safe House.

Further Reading

Community Action Stops Abuse (CASA). 2013. http://www.casa-stpete.org.

CORPORAL PUNISHMENT

Corporal punishment is any use of physical punishment against a child in response to misbehavior. Spanking and smacking are the most common forms, but it also includes slapping, pinching, pulling hair, twisting ears, or hitting with an object. Out of 24 countries with legislative bans on corporal punishment, 19 are in Europe, 3 in Central or South America, 1 in the Middle East, and 1 in Oceania. No bans exist in Asia or North America. Opponents of corporal punishment argue that it constitutes child abuse, while proponents believe that, when used correctly, corporal punishment is an effective discipline option. The United States is one of the few developed countries that still allows corporal punishment in a school setting.

The Ending Corporal Punishment in Schools Act of 2011 defines corporal punishment in schools as "paddling, spanking, or other forms of physical punishment, however light, imposed upon a student." This definition does not include the use of physical restraints intended to protect children or others from imminent injury. According to attorney Nicole Mortorano, no federal law exists in the United States banning this type of violence against children, and 19 states currently employ this tactic. During the 2005–2006 school year, out of one-quarter million students subjected to corporal punishment, 5 states, Texas, Mississippi, Arkansas, Alabama, and Georgia, accounted for almost three-quarters of the incidences.

In *Ingraham v. Wright* (1977), the Supreme Court upheld the constitutionality of corporal punishment in schools, finding it does not infringe on children's Eighth Amendment rights. Unanswered questions of whether corporal punishment in schools infringes on a student's substantive due process rights and Fourth

Amendment rights remain. The WorldSAFE studies included 6 national or multicity representative samples and found that spanking by a mother or her partner on a specific child in the last year varied from 16 percent of children in nonslum New Delhi to 76 percent of children in the Philippines. Spanking on the buttocks was most common in the United States (44%), Philippines (76%), Chile (53%), and Brazil (55%). Different forms of punishment were common in Egypt, such as slapping on the face (42%), shaking (68%), pinching (45%), and ear twisting (29%).

One of the causes of corporal punishment is that considerable societal support for child corporal punishment exists even though much research demonstrates its ineffectiveness and likely harm. In addition, parenting styles might contribute to the level of punitiveness. People who were subjected to parental physical punishment or abuse are more punitive than nonvictims of parental violence. Save the Children's campaign, Educate Don't Punish, provides reasons that parents resort to corporal punishment:

- It is appropriate to children's education.
- It relieves tension.
- They lack sufficient resources to tackle a situation or do not have needed strategies.
- They are not skilled at interpreting the social situations.
- They cannot control their emotions.

Parental corporal punishment perpetuates the cycle of abuse. Its effects on children include:

- It lowers self-esteem.
- They become victims.
- It interferes with intellectual, sensory, and emotional development.
- It discourages the use of reasoning.
- It hampers the capacity to understand the relationship between behavior and its consequences.
- It promotes feelings of loneliness, sadness, abandonment, and negative views of other people and of society as a threatening place.
- It creates barriers in parent-child communication and damages their emotional links.
- It stimulates anger and a desire to run away from home.

Corporal punishment in schools harms the physical, emotional, and intellectual well-being of students. In addition, corporal punishment violates students' civil rights. Civil rights data from the U.S. Department of Education indicates that corporal punishment is used disproportionately against students of color. African American students represent 17.1 percent of the national school population, but 35.6 percent of students who were paddled were African American schoolchildren. Students with disabilities are also subjected to corporal punishment. During the 2006–2007 school year, 41,972 special education students were subjected to corporal punishment. Students with disabilities represent 19 percent of those who receive corporal punishment but 14 percent of the nationwide student population. Increasing trends toward banning corporal punishment indicate that society's norms and understandings of children's dignity have evolved since the 1977 *Ingraham* decision. Shifts in public opinion, changing practices at the state and local levels, national movements, the overturning of some Supreme Court cases, and international law indicate physical punishment in schools is an outdated practice that attacks contemporary ideas of children's rights. Public opinion has shifted, no longer viewing corporal punishment as an acceptable means of discipline in schools.

Legislative strategies include: amending the Individuals with Disabilities Education Act (IDEA), creating incentive grants to encourage state actions, and enacting categorical bans against corporal punishment. These strategies are ways to protect children from physical punishment in schools. Mortorano recommends, in part: overturning *Ingraham* and lobbying Congress to enact legislation to ban corporal punishment in schools.

Save the Children's campaign, Educate Don't Punish, presents the following agenda for discontinuing parental corporal punishment:

- Raising public awareness, especially among parents, about the consequences of corporal punishment
- Encouraging positive and nonviolent methods of child education and care in families
- Informing children about their rights and involving them in their own defense through direct participation in actions undertaken

Their campaign involves actions in schools, universities, different childhood associations, and the media and provides training while distributing the Convention on the Rights of the Child of different ages. The campaign organizes public debates, conferences, and seminars.

Rosemarie Skaine

See also: Child Abuse, Physical and Emotional; Cycle of Abuse; Disabled Children; Racism; Torture.

Further Reading

Ending Corporal Punishment in Schools Act of 2011, H.R. 3027, 112th Cong. § 12(1) (2011).

Kemme, Stefanie, Michael Hanslmaier, and Christian Pfeiffer. 2014. "Experience of Parental Corporal Punishment in Childhood and Adolescence and Its Effect on Punitiveness." *Journal of Family Violence* 29: 129–142. doi:10.1007/s10896-013-9564-3.

Mortorano, Nicole. 2014. "NOTE: Protecting Children's Rights Inside of the Schoolhouse Gates: Ending Corporal Punishment in Schools." *Georgetown Law Journal* 102: 481.

Romano, Elisa, Tessa Bell, and Rick Norian. 2013. "Corporal Punishment: Examining Attitudes toward the Law and Factors Influencing Attitude Change." *Journal of Family Violence* 28: 265–275. doi:10.1007/s10896-013-9494-0.

UNICEF, CEAPA, and CONCAPA. n.d. "Educate Don't Punish." Save the Children. http://www.unicef.org/lac/spbarbados/Implementation/CP/Global/Educate_donthit_SaveManual.pdf.

Zolotor, Adam J., and Megan E. Puzia. 2010. "Bans against Corporal Punishment: A Systematic Review the Laws, Changes in Attitudes and Behaviours." *Child Abuse Review* 19: 229–247 (www.interscience.wiley.com). doi:10.1002/car.1131.

CYBERBULLYING, ADULT

Digital technology creates a new dimension to the problem of bullying. Cyberbullying is an intentional act with the purpose of harming someone that uses technology. Young adults interact online frequently and that may include aggressive behaviors. This aggression may take place through a variety of information and communication technologies, such as the Internet, gaming consoles, and mobile phones. Aggressive behaviors can include threats, insults, and spreading rumors.

Cyberbullying includes behaviors that usually do not occur in a face-to-face setting, such as sending harassing text messages or logging into another person's online accounts without permission. Using a masked identity allows anonymity and makes it possible to reach more potential victims and can take place at any moment. The ease and speed of accessing victims sets cyberbullying apart from face-to-face bullying.

Cyberbullying at work takes many forms, but in the workplace is expressed through e-mails and may involve video sharing. It includes: public humiliation through e-mail sharing of negative and humiliating comments with work colleagues and managers; inappropriate jokes or images that refer to race, religion, or sexual preferences; sharing embarrassing, offensive, or manipulated pictures or video of an individual; use of group e-mails or work forums to encourage people to post negative comments about an individual; supervisor attacks with work- and performance-related e-mails and unrealistic workloads, while other workers are left alone; and spreading rumors and gossip through social networks to provide a wider audience.

Ninety percent of young adults spend time online and over one-fifth act aggressively online at least once. Whether men or women engage more in cyberbullying is not clear, but women favor relational aggression. Not as much is known about adult bullying, but the Cyberbullying Research Center reported to have received on their blog more inquiries from adults than teens.

One of the causes of cyberbullying is the belief that aggression is acceptable and appropriate in face-to-face and online settings. People who lack the physical power to traditionally bully others may use available technologies. Cyberbullying can follow victims everywhere there is a cell phone or computer.

Social and economic reasons may factor into adult harassment and cyberbullying. Researchers from the Project for Wellness and Work-Life contend workplace bullying is not explicitly connected to demographic markers such as sex and ethnicity. In other words, all ages, races, ethnicities, and genders are perpetrators and victims of cyberbullying.

Anonymous cyber aggression allows the perpetrator to not necessarily witness any reactions, which may promote more impulsivity and aggressive behaviors. In addition, cyberbullying may happen more than once, cause psychological and emotional harm, may be intentional, victims may experience depression, loneliness, and anxiety, and become at risk for a young adult to become a school dropout and failure. Suicides of some cyberbully victims occur. In 2010, an 18-year-old college freshman, Tyler Clementi, jumped off the George Washington Bridge after his roommate broadcast Tyler's interactions with another man over the Internet.

No federal law exists against cyberbullying, but federal cyberstalking laws provide for the prosecution of people for using electronic means to repeatedly harass or threaten an individual online. Other laws pertaining to protection of civil rights can apply to harassment: Title IV and Title VI of the Civil Rights Act of 1964, Title IX of the Education Amendments of 1972, Section 504 of the Rehabilitation Act of 1973, Titles II and III of the Americans with Disabilities Act, and the Individuals with Disabilities Education Act.

In 2010, 38 states had laws against cyberbullying and 34 states against cyber-stalking. People look at what others are doing online, such as a victim's parent considering a lawsuit, a school considering expulsion, law enforcement planning to force a change in behavior, or a sexual predator or fraudster looking for an easy victim. Awareness that there are consequences to choices made online is necessary. It is best to assume that no digital communication is ever private. A person's words can be used in unintended ways.

Rosemarie Skaine

See also: Bullying, Adult; Cyberstalking; Hate Crimes; Hate Speech; Hazing; Identity Theft; Internet Abuse; Internet Fraud; Sexual Harassment; Telephone Harassment.

Further Reading

Corbett, Patrick E. Winter. 2010. "Cyberharassment, Sexting and Other High-tech Offenses Involving Michigan Residents—Are We Victims or Criminals?" *University of Detroit Mercy Law Review* 88: 237.

Cybersmile Foundation. 2013. "Cyberbullying at Work." http://www.cybersmile.org/advice-help/category/cyberbullying-at-work.

National Council of State Legislatures. n.d. "Cyberbullying Enacted Legislation: 2006–2010." http://www.ncsl.org/research/education/cyberbullying.aspx.

Schenk, Allison M., William J. Fremouw, and Colleen M. Keelan. 2013. "Characteristics of College Cyberbullies." *Computers in Human Behavior* 29: 2320–2327.

Workplace Bullying Institute. 2010. "Results of the 2010 WBI U.S. Workplace Bullying Survey." http://www.workplacebullying.org/wbiresearch/2010-wbi-national-survey.

Wright, Michelle F., and Yan Li. 2013. "Normative Beliefs about Aggression and Cyber Aggression among Young Adults: A Longitudinal Investigation." *Aggressive Behavior* 39: 161–170.

CYBERBULLYING, CHILD AND ADOLESCENT

Cyberbullying is unwanted, aggressive behavior that involves a real or perceived power imbalance. Cyberbullying involves using technology, such as cell phones and the Internet, to bully or harass another person. The behavior is repeated, or has the potential to be repeated, over time. It can include verbal harassment, physical assault, or coercion and may be directed repeatedly toward particular victims, perhaps on grounds of race, religion, gender, sexuality, or ability. The "imbalance of power" may be social power and/or physical power. The victim of bullying is sometimes referred to as a "target."

Cyberbullying can take many forms:

- Sending mean messages or threats to a person's e-mail account or cell phone
- Spreading rumors online or through texts
- Posting hurtful or threatening messages on social networking sites or Web pages

John Halligan shows the Web site devoted to his son, Ryan Patrick Halligan, in Underhill, Vermont, on February 7, 2007. Ryan committed suicide in 2003 at age 13, a death his father is certain was caused in part by vicious online bullying. John Halligan is now a proponent for tough laws to curb cyberbullying. Many states have laws that address cyberbullying. (AP Photo)

- Stealing a person's account information to break into their account and send damaging messages
- Pretending to be someone else online to hurt another person
- Taking unflattering pictures of a person and spreading them through cell phones or the Internet
- Sexting or circulating sexually suggestive pictures or messages about a person

Cyberbullying of children and adolescents is extensive. The Bureau of Justice Statistics, Cyberbullying Research Center reports that

- 52% of students reported being cyberbullied
- 33% of teens have experienced cyber threats online
- 25% of teens have been bullied repeatedly through their cell phones or the Internet
- 52% of teens do not tell their parents when cyberbullying occurs
- 11% of teens have had embarrassing or damaging pictures taken of themselves without their permission, often using cell phone cameras

Cyberbullying can be damaging to adolescents and teens. It can lead to anxiety, depression, and even suicide. Also, once messages are circulated on the Internet, they may never disappear, resurfacing at later times to renew the pain of cyberbullying.

A 2007 survey on cyberbullying of 2,000 middle school students from a large school district found that over 17 percent said they had been "cyberbullied" in their lives, 17.6 percent admitted to cyberbullying others, and 12 percent reported being both a victim and a bully. Of those who admitted being involved in cyberbullying, 42.9 percent had experienced at least one of the following within the last 30 days:

- Received an e-mail that made them upset (not spam)
- Received an instant message (IM) that made them upset
- Had something posted on MySpace that made them upset
- Had been made fun of in a chat room
- Had something posted on a Web site that made them upset
- Had something posted online they did not want others to see
- Had been afraid to go on the computer

The most serious effect of cyberbullying is suicide. Twenty percent of children and adolescents who are cyberbullied think about suicide, one in 10 attempts it, and they are part of the 4500 kids that commit suicide each year. One who did was 12-year-old Rebecca Ann Sedwick, who committed suicide after she was bullied online by more than a dozen girls in Lakeland, Florida. She jumped to her death on September 9, 2013, at an old cement business in Lakeland. Investigators say the girl was despondent after others had posted hate messages about her online.

Cyberbullying happens for many of the same reasons as any other type of bullying, but it may be even more appealing because it can be done anonymously. Stopbullying.gov describes two kinds of people who are likely to bully: those who are popular and those who are on the social fringes. Popular kids or teens may bully because they see it as a way to stay popular and hurting others makes them feel powerful. Less socially successful kids or teens may bully because it helps them cope with their own low self-esteem, they think it will help them fit in with their peers, or they have trouble empathizing with those they hurt.

Bullying online happens for the additional reasons of anonymity, ignorance of the consequences, and social pressure. Because cyberbullies do not have to face their victims, it requires less courage and provides the illusion that they will not get caught. Cyberbullies do not see their victims' reactions in person, so they may not realize how much damage they are doing. Social pressure includes the belief that those who cyberbully do it because they think what they are doing is funny. Some cyberbullies may think their behavior is normal and socially acceptable, especially when friends egg them on.

Actions to combat cyberbullying have included programs in the schools, focus on Internet sites, and state laws and proposed federal and state laws. All schools are required to have prevention and training programs. The i-SAFE Foundation is one of the programs that has worldwide distribution. Researchers Sameer Hinduja and Justin W. Patchin at the Cyberbullying Research Center have produced much that increases the understanding of cyberbullying.

Cyberbullying is a phenomenon that becomes abuse out of societal acceptance of certain behaviors. When cyberbullies do it because they think what they are doing is funny and that their behavior is normal and socially acceptable, it is because our society accepts teasing and the practical joker. These behaviors taken a step further become cyberbullying. Humor is good, but it can and does lead to hurt feelings and worse. Booing the opponent at a sporting event is considered fun, but it can produce deadly results. It provides the model for what children and adolescents do when they cyberbully.

Rosemarie Skaine

See also: BULLY Project; Bullying, Child and Adolescent; Cyberstalking; Hate Crimes; Hate Speech; Hazing; Identity Theft; Internet Abuse; Internet Fraud; Sexual Harassment; Telephone Harassment.

Further Reading

A4K Ambassadors 4 Kids Club. 2013. "Bullying Statistics." http://www.a4kclub.org/get-the-facts/bullying-statistics.

Bullying Statistics. 2011. "Cyberbullying Statistics." http://www.bullyingstatistics.org/content/adult-bullying.html.

CyberBully Hotline. 2012. "Cyberbullying Rampant on the Internet." http://www.cyberbullyhotline.com/07-10-12-scourge.html.

Delete Cyberbullying. n.d. "Why Do People Cyberbully?" http://www.deletecyberbullying.org/why-do-people-cyberbully.

Hinduja, Sameer, and Justin W. Patchin. 2013. "State Cyberbullying Laws: A Brief Review of State Cyberbullying Laws and Policies." Cyberbullying Research Center. http://www.cyberbullying.us/Bullying_and_Cyberbullying_Laws.pdf.

Hinduja, Sameer, and Justin W. Patchin. 2010. "Cyberbullying and Suicide." Cyberbullying Research Center. http://www.cyberbullying.us/cyberbullying_and_suicide_research_fact_sheet.pdf.

Hinduja, Sameer, and Justin W. Patchin. 2009. "What You Need to Know about Online Aggression." Cyberbullying Research Center. http://www.cyberbullying.us/cyberbullying_fact_sheet.pdf.

i-SAFE Foundation. n.d. "Cyberbullying: Statistics and Tips." http://www.isafe.org/outreach/media/media_cyber_bullying.

Leibowitz, Barry. 2013. "Rebecca Ann Sedwick Update: Fla. Police Confirm Suicide of Girl, 12, after Cyber-bullying, Probe Possible Charges." *CBS News Crimesider*, September 12. http://www.cbsnews.com/8301-504083_162-57602723-504083/rebecca-ann-sedwick-update-fla-police-confirm-suicide-of-girl-12-after-cyber-bullying-probe-possible-charges.

Statistic Brain. 2013. "Cyber / Bullying Statistics." http://www.statisticbrain.com/cyber-bullying-statistics.

CYBERSTALKING

Cyberstalking is a form of stalking that includes the use of the Internet, e-mail, and other electronic communication devices to stalk another person. It includes: threatening or obscene e-mail, spamming, harassing in chat rooms, tracing another person's computer and Internet activity, posting threatening or harassing messages on blogs or through social media, instant messaging, monitoring with GPS, and digital surveillance.

Aily Shimizu of the George Washington University Law School believes, "the Internet has provided a new vehicle by which individuals can commit the traditional act of stalking." Advantages include a low cost and effortless way to be in the same geographical area hidden in anonymity. Andrew King-Ries of the University of Montana School of Law adds that digital dependence enables electronic transactions in banking, travel, and legal activity. Personal information such as tax and medical records are electronically stored. And remotely monitoring keystrokes enables cyberstalkers to keep track of financial transactions, correspondence, and Web sites visited.

Twenty-six percent of stalking victims report being stalked through the use of some form of technology, reported King-Ries. Eleven percent report being monitored with GPS, 46 percent through video or digital cameras, and 42 percent through listening devices. The American Psychological Association reported that approximately 850,000 adults, mostly women, are targets of cyberstalking each year. Forty percent of women have experienced dating violence from using social media, had received harassing text messages and had disturbing information posted about them. Twenty percent of online stalkers use social networking. Thirty-four percent of female and 14 percent of male college students have broken into a romantic partner's e-mail.

Teens use technology, mainly cell phones and text messaging, in forming their sexual identities and the patterns of their intimate relationships, according to King-Ries. Since teens can use technology without adult supervision, a "boundarylessness" takes place that can lead to accepting more risk of abusive behaviors from their intimate partners. Teens are normalizing unhealthy relationship patterns while accepting technology as an effective way to establish power and control disparity in those relationships.

People who are cyberstalked experience higher levels of stress and trauma than people who are stalked or harassed in person. The reasons include: the 24/7 presence of online communication, the inability to escape to a safe place, and the global access to information. Responses to the stress and trauma include high levels of ongoing stress, anxiety, fear, nightmares, shock and disbelief, helplessness, hypervigilance, changes in eating, and sleeping difficulties.

Laws to prohibit cyberstalking on state and federal levels are evolving. On the state level, cyberstalking is not included in the traditional stalking statutes, which undermines the effectiveness of civil protection orders. For example, Shimizu states cyberstalking may not provide adequate grounds for a judge to issue a civil protection order. On the federal level, the protection is limited because the statutes do not criminalize specific acts that constitute cyberstalking. The new cyberstalking section in the Violence Against Women Act of 2013, however, does address cyberstalking specifically, within the context of domestic violence and gives victims more adequate protection. Other federal legislation that includes cyberstalking are: the Interstate Communications Act, 18 U.S.C. § 875(c), Federal Telephone Harassment Statute, 47 U.S.C. § 223, and the Federal Interstate Stalking Punishment and Prevention Act, 18 U.S.C. § 2261A.

Clinical management of stalking victims can be approached through the use of one or more of the following therapies: safe and confidential therapeutic setting, education and supportive counseling, cognitive-behavioral therapies for anxiety and avoidance, pharmacotherapy for psychiatric and physical morbidity, substance misuse counseling, family and partner counseling, support groups, and support organizations, according to Michele Pathé et al. Therapy should be adjusted to individual needs and, in some cases, needs to continue after the cyberstalking ceases.

Rosemarie Skaine

See also: Bullying, Adult; Domestic Abuse, Psychological Effects of; Internet Abuse; Sexting; Stalking; Telephone Harassment; Violence Against Women Act.

Further Reading

American Psychological Association. 2011. "Dealing with the Cyberworld's Dark Side." "*ScienceDaily*, August 8. http://www.sciencedaily.com/releases/2011/08/110806203525. htm.

Government Printing Office. 2013. *Violence Against Women Act*. Govtrack.us. http://www. govtrack.us/congress/bills/113/s47/text.

King-Ries. Andrew. 2011. "Teens, Technology, and Cyberstalking: The Domestic Violence Wave of the Future?" *Texas Journal of Women and the Law* 20 (Spring): 131.

Pathé, Michele, Paul E. Mullen, and Rosemary Purcell. 2001. "Management of Victims of Stalking." *Advances in Psychiatric Treatment* 7: 399–406. http://apt.rcpsych.org/content/7/6/399.full#sec-17.

Shimizu, Aily. 2013. "Recent Development: Domestic Violence in the Digital Age: Towards the Creation of a Comprehensive Cyberstalking Statute." *Berkeley Journal of Gender, Law and Justice* 28: 116.

Stalking Resource Center. n.d. The National Center for Victims of Crime. http://www. victimsofcrime.org/our-programs/stalking-resource-center.

CYCLE OF ABUSE

The term *cycle of abuse* was coined to refer to Lenore Walker's theory developed in the 1970s to explain predictable patterns of behavior and maltreatment in an abusive relationship. The theory is relevant to all kinds of abuse, emotional, physical, or psychological. Walker maintained that psychological abuse always preceded or accompanied physical abuse. In addition, prolonged periods in a cycle eventually led to helplessness and a battered person syndrome. The cycle of abuse has a common pattern in cases of domestic violence.

The four phases in Walker's cycle of abuse are

1. Tension-building phase. Occurring prior to an act of overt abuse, this phase is characterized by poor communication, escalating interpersonal tension, passive aggression, and fear of causing outbursts. During this stage, the survivor may attempt to modify his or her behavior to avoid triggering his or her partner's outburst.
2. Acting-out phase. This phase is characterized by overtly violent or abusive behavior, which may occur as a single outburst or as a series of incidents. During this phase, the abuser attempts to dominate his or her partner.
3. Reconciliation/Honeymoon phase. In the third phase, the abuser responds to the victim with affection, apology, or, alternatively, by ignoring the incident. It may appear that the violence has ended permanently, and the abuser often promises not

to engage in such behaviors in the future. The abuser may feel powerful remorse, sadness, or self-loathing. The abuser may engage in self-harm or even threaten suicide to gain the sympathy and forgiveness of the victim.

4. Calm phase. During this stage (which is often considered part of the reconciliation/honeymoon phase), the relationship between the abuser and victim is relatively calm and peaceful, and the past abuse and its aftermath may be temporarily forgotten. However, interpersonal difficulties will inevitably arise, leading to a return to the first phase.

Why does the cycle of abuse continue? According to the Women's Center, one reason is that few people identify themselves as either abusers or victims and thus do not see themselves as part of the cycle. Others may remain in the situation out of shame, fear, or ignorance about the nature of domestic abuse. Victims may feel that they have no other options, that they deserve the abuse, or that they could not do any better on their own. The pressures of poverty may also convince some individuals to stay in abusive relationships. When things are "going well," it can be easy for both the victim and the abuser to forget about previous instances of abuse. When abuse is not overtly physical, it may be difficult to recognize as abuse, and those involved may not even see a problem.

Breaking the cycle of abuse, whether by correcting the abusive behavior for good or by leaving the relationship, is very difficult and is rarely simple or quick. Those with a strong support system, however, generally have greater success.

Rosemarie Skaine

See also: Battered Person Syndrome; Domestic Abuse, Psychological Effects of; Victim Empowerment Models.

Further Reading

Domesticviolence.org. 2009. "Cycle of Violence." http://www.domesticviolence.org/cycle-of-violence.

National Coalition Against Domestic Violence (NCADV). 2007. "Did You Know?" http://www.ncadv.org/files/DomesticViolenceFactSheet(National).pdf.

Ramos, Patricia. 2013. "Dramatic Advocacy Campaign Depicts the Cycle of Abuse." *Exposure Guide* (blog) May 8. http://www.exposureguide.com/culture/dramatic-advocacy-campaign-depicts-the-cycle-of-abus.

Walker, Lenore. 1979. *The Battered Woman*. New York: Harper and Row.

Widom, Cathy S., and Michael G. Maxfield. 2001. "An Update on the 'Cycle of Violence.'" *National Institute of Justice Research in Brief*. U.S. Department of Justice. https://www.ncjrs.gov/pdffiles1/nij/184894.pdf.

The Women's Center. 2010. "Violence & Domestic Abuse—The Cycle of Abuse." http://www.thewomenscenter.org/content.asp?contentid=535.

D

DEBBIE SMITH ACT

The Debbie Smith Act of 2004 states that it is an act

> To protect crime victims' rights, to eliminate the substantial backlog of DNA samples collected from crime scenes and convicted offenders, to improve and expand the DNA testing capacity of Federal, State, and local crime laboratories, to increase research and development of new DNA testing technologies, to develop new training programs regarding the collection and use of DNA evidence, to provide post conviction testing of DNA evidence to exonerate the innocent, to improve the performance of counsel in State capital cases, and for other purposes.

In 1989, Debbie Smith was outside her home in Williamsburg, Virginia. Her husband, Rob, a police officer, was asleep upstairs after working a night shift. When Debbie returned indoors, she left the door unlocked. Shortly, a masked stranger grabbed her, dragging her outside to a wooded area where he robbed and repeatedly raped her. He continually said, "Remember, I know where you live. If you tell anyone, I will come back and kill you." After the rape, fear dominated Smith's life. Only with the support of her husband was she able to immediately report it and submit to a forensic exam. In 1995, the rapist was identified with the help of DNA, the only definitive evidence.

Debbie became an advocate for federal laws on DNA testing that led to the passing of the Debbie Smith Act in 2004. Then Rob and she organized the H-E-A-R-T (Hope Exists after Rape Trauma) foundation to support victims and affect positive change in laws that influence the lives of victims. H-E-A-R-T promotes the continued use of DNA and educates legislators, law enforcement professionals, and others.

For the first time, on August 4, 2011, H-E-A-R-T gave the Paul Ferrara Achievement Award to the Alabama Department of Forensic Sciences for its outstanding achievement and ongoing commitment to help victims of crime. The name of the award honors the memory of Dr. Paul Ferrara, as Director of the Virginia Crime Laboratory and a member of Attorney General Janet Reno's Commission on the Future of DNA Evidence, was responsible for Virginia being the first state to offer forensic DNA testing to law enforcement and was the first state to implement a DNA database system. Debbie Smith was among the first to benefit from his dedication to victims of crime.

Rosemarie Skaine

See also: Demi and Ashton Foundation; Rape.

Further Reading

Debbie Smith Act of 2004. 2004. 118 Stat. 2260. Public Law 108–405.108th Congress. U.S. Government Printing Office. www.gpo.gov/fdsys/pkg/STATUTE-118/.../STATUTE-118-Pg2260.pdf.

H-E-A-R-T. 2013. http://www.h-e-a-r-t.info.

National Center for Victims of Crime. n.d. "Profiles in DNA: Debbie Smith." U.S. Department of Justice. http://www.victimsofcrime.org/our-programs/dna-resource-center/profiles-in-dna/debbie-smith.

DEMI AND ASHTON FOUNDATION

Celebrities Demi Moore and Ashton Kutcher created the nonprofit Demi and Ashton Foundation (DNAF) in January 2009 to fight against organized sexual exploitation of girls. The foundation is committed to ending sex slavery of children globally and rehabilitating victims of human trafficking. Kutcher's idea to create a DNA foundation came while watching an episode of *Dateline* about six-year-old Cambodian girls who were being sold as sex slaves. He told his wife, Demi Moore, that living in a world where this was happening was not right. Together they formed DNA, which stands for Demi and Ashton.

Worldwide, human trafficking is a $32 billion industry. The average age of the girls is 13. Kutcher and Moore heard stories, such as a little girl who told them how she was raped by 30 men in a row. Their efforts have included working with legislators to change laws in states where human trafficking is not a felony.

The National Center for Missing and Exploited Children found that the number of child pornography files reported for victim identification had increased from 450,000 digital images and videos in 2004 to over 17 million in 2011. Three out of four victims are trafficked online. The Internet makes easier illegal transactions for johns, and helps create new opportunities for pimps to profit.

When technology began to have an increasingly substantial role in child slavery and in the sexual exploitation of children overall, in 2012, Moore and Kutcher renamed the DNA Foundation, THORN: Digital Defenders of Children, to reflect its refined mission. Technology's role includes the buying and selling of children for sex all over the world, soliciting sex with children, and the proliferation of child pornography across the Internet.

The focus of THORN includes: research, deterrence, innovation, and industry initiatives. It also works closely with law enforcement, other NGOs, the private sector, and its own Technology Task Force to alleviate illicit activities and protect children. Kutcher estimated that because 76 percent of sex slave transactions occur on the Web, partnering with major Internet companies to build a technology task force was necessary to help minimize online transactions. Moore and Kutcher's Real Men awareness campaign aims at the people who support the slave trade because, according to Kutcher, real men do not buy girls.

THORN Technology Task Force uses technology to protect children and deter predators. The Technology Task Force consists of approximately 25 tech companies that collaborate on technological initiatives to fight child sexual exploitation. Companies include Microsoft, Facebook, Google, Twitter, Symantec, SV Angel, Blekko, BlueCava, Connotate, Conversion Voodoo, DataXu, Hang, Irdeto, Mozilla, SalesForce Foundation, Digital Reasoning, and Palantir.

Rosemarie Skaine

See also: Human Trafficking; Internet Abuse; Internet Victimization, Child; Sexual Slavery; Slavery, Modern-day.

Further Reading

Giacobbe, Alyssa. 2010. "Shining Stars." *Instyle* 17 (13): 398.

National Center for Missing and Exploited Children. 2014. http://www.missingkids.com/home.

THORN. 2011. "THORN Launch Brings Technology Innovation to the Fight against Child Sexual Exploitation." *Business Wire (English)*.

THORN. n.d. "We Are the Digital Defenders of Children." http://demiandashton.com/aboutus/#boardExpanded.

DISABLED ADULTS

Abuse or mistreatment of a disabled person is any behavior that is unwanted, hurtful, inappropriate, neglectful, frightening, insulting, or demeaning. It includes physical, sexual, verbal, emotional, or financial mistreatment by anyone in a "helping" role.

In 2010, 56.7 million people with a disability lived in the United States. They represented 19 percent of the civilian noninstitutionalized population. The disabilities included: having difficulty seeing, hearing, having speech understood, walking, bathing, dressing, eating, preparing meals, going outside the home, or doing housework, having Alzheimer's, dementia, autism, cerebral palsy, or dyslexia, and being frequently depressed or anxious. By age, 8 percent were children under 15; 21 percent were 15 and older; 17 percent were 21 to 64; and 50 percent of adults 65 and older had disabilities. By gender, 20 percent of females had a disability and 17 percent of males.

Abuse of people with disabilities is prevalent and takes on many forms, including physical and emotional abuse and economic exploitation. Women with disabilities are also at serious risk for sexual abuse, with some studies citing rates as high as 80 percent having experienced such.

Many people with disabilities have no choice but to rely on friends, family, or other caregivers to survive. In 2010, 12.0 million people 15 and older required the assistance of others in order to perform one or more activities of daily living or instrumental activities of daily living, such as bathing, dressing, doing housework, and preparing meals. This need for assistance enables the disability to be used against the individual to perpetuate the abuse. When they are abused, it can create inescapable situations. There are numerous ways that they are at a higher risk of being exploited and abused, yet it is often far more difficult for them, beyond that which is directly related to the disability, to independently leave an abusive situation.

Abuse occurs within intimate relationships or at the hands of family, friends, or strangers. Abuse also comes from paid and unpaid caregivers in both private and institutional settings. When people with disabilities depend on others for support and assistance with daily life tasks, it can create an imbalance of power that is easily taken advantage of. Abuse is easily facilitated when a victim is dependent on his or her abuser for access to transportation, medical care, personal care, and other needs.

Additional barriers exist that can make achieving safety and justice for victims with disabilities a uniquely difficult and complex problem. People with disabilities often have very limited options when attempting to seek justice and safety. Whether due to physical limitations related to disability, lack of transportation, or due to the abuse itself, the disabled experiences isolation. Discrimination and stigma result in further isolation and present barriers to both seeking and receiving assistance. In cases where developmental disability or mental illness is involved, the victim may be perceived as unreliable, and their allegations may not be taken seriously.

People with disabilities also frequently do not have the level of access to economic and educational opportunity that people without disabilities may have, and may face poverty as a compounding factor. Only 33 percent of the civilian non-institutionalized population 18 to 64 with a disability were employed. With two-thirds of the people with disabilities not currently in the workforce and the social safety net programs that exist generally leave beneficiaries living below the poverty line, the problems of disabled individuals are compounded. The process to receive housing assistance can also be lengthy and complex. Accessible, affordable housing can be very difficult to find. Many who depend on these programs to survive may not have the resources to obtain better living arrangements or more suitable caregivers. For those who can work, they may be prevented from doing so by an abuser who wants to exploit them for their cash benefits, or if they do work, they may have their wages taken by abusive caregivers who feel entitled to an unfair share.

Some victims with disabilities can attempt to get help from domestic violence organizations; however, few (if any) disability-specific programs exist for victims of violence, and accessibility can be an issue in existing shelters. In institutional settings, there may be little or no recourse for patients who are abused by staff. Historically, institutions have tended to deal with abuse allegations internally rather than involving the police. This has led to many cases of abuse being overlooked and ignored and has resulted in the deaths of individuals whose lives were entrusted to the care of the state. In reaction to highly publicized instances of deaths due to abuse, New York has recently developed an office to investigate institutional abuse. Adult protective agencies do exist; however, limited resources and lack of training specific to disability-related issues create barriers to safety.

In most states, abuse of a person with a disability is a crime; however, disparity exists between the laws that exist and the rate at which abuse is reported and prosecuted. The Americans with Disabilities Act guarantees equal opportunity for people with disabilities in public accommodations, commercial facilities, employment, transportation, state and local government services, and telecommunications.

Rosemarie Skaine

See also: Americans with Disabilities Act; Domestic Abuse; Elder Abuse.

Further Reading

Emanuel, Ellie J. 2000. "Breaking the Power of Discrimination." *Impact* 13, 3. http://ici. umn.edu/products/impact/133/over4.html.

New York State Justice Center for the Protection of People with Special Needs. 2013. http:// www.justicecenter.ny.gov.

Sobsey, Dick. Fall 2000. "Faces of Violence against Women with Developmental Disabilities." *Impact* 13, 3. http://ici.umn.edu/products/impact/133/over2.html.

U.S. Census Bureau. 2013. "Facts & Statistics." http://www.disabled-world.com/disability/ statistics/info.php.

U.S. Census Bureau. n.d. "Americans with Disabilities: 2010." www.census.gov/ prod/2012pubs/p70-131.pdf.

U.S. Census Bureau. n.d. "2011 American Community Survey, Table B18120." http:// factfinder2.census.gov/bkmk/table/1.0/en/ACS/11_1YR/B18120.

West, Bernadette, and Sampada Gandhi. 2006. "Reporting Abuse: A Study of the Perceptions of People with Disabilities (PWD) Regarding Abuse Directed at PWD." *Disability Studies Quarterly* 26, 1. http://dsq-sds.org/article/view/650/827.

Wisseman, Kimberly Black. 2000. "You're My Pretty Bird in a Cage: Disability, Domestic Violence, and Survival." *Impact* 13, 3. http://ici.umn.edu/products/impact/133/over1. html.

DISABLED CHILDREN

Globally, at least 93 million children have disabilities. Children with disabilities are three to four times more likely to be the victims of neglect, violence, and physical, emotional, or sexual abuse. Prevalence estimates of violence and abuse against children with disabilities range from 26.6 percent for combined measures of violence to 20.4 percent for physical violence and 13.7 percent for sexual violence. Findings from a systematic meta-analysis and review of 17 international studies of prevalence of violence and abuse against children with disabilities indicated that children with disabilities are 3.7 times more likely than nondisabled children to be victims of any sort of violence, 3.6 times more likely to be victims of physical violence, and 2.9 times more likely to be victims of sexual violence.

Children with disabilities associated with mental illness or intellectual impairments appear to be among the most vulnerable, with 4.6 times the risk of sexual violence compared with their nondisabled peers. The type of disability, residential setting of the child, and treatment services available affect the prevalence and risk of abuse, although the evidence is often inconclusive. One cited example is children with intellectual disabilities were more than 4.6 times more likely to be abused sexually than their nondisabled peers. Results of extensive research found that 37.4 percent of abused children with disabilities had behavior disorders, 25.3 percent had mental retardation, 16.4 percent had learning disabilities, and 11.2 percent had health-related disabilities. Significant numbers of children with disabilities continue to be placed in residential settings, which is a major risk factor for sexual and physical abuse. Insufficient treatment and services to parents and caregivers seriously affect the prevalence of abuse.

Children with disabilities present a myriad of needs and challenges for their parents, teachers, and other caregivers. Although no single factor can usually be identified as the cause of abuse, neglect, and maltreatment, multiple factors appear to cause an increase of abuse and/or neglect of children with disabilities:

- Parents' or caregivers' unrealistic expectations for the child, poor impulse control, and low self-esteem
- Substance abuse or violence in the home
- Family isolation from and/or lack of support and knowledge about appropriate care
- Decreased parent-child attachment that may result from the child's disability
- The inability of children with disabilities to defend themselves, escape from harm, or communicate problems due to their disability

Consequences of child abuse and neglect include physical, psychological, behavioral, and societal effects. Physical effects range from bruising and broken bones to abusive head trauma, impaired brain development, and poor physical health. Psychological consequences of poor mental and emotional health, cognitive difficulties, and social skills difficulties may lead to behavioral consequences, including abuses of alcohol and other drugs. Children who have experienced abuse and neglect are nine times more likely to be involved in criminal activities. Without sufficient and appropriate treatment, interventions, and supports, these factors and consequences will exacerbate and escalate within a cycle of abuse and violence.

Policies have been enacted to protect children with disabilities from abuse, violence, and neglect. The Family Educational Rights and Privacy Act (FERPA) stipulates that educators supply information to appropriate officials in case of health and safety emergencies. The Child Abuse Prevention and Treatment Act (CAPTA) requires states to develop plans to ensure that children who are victims of substantiated abuse or neglect have access to developmental screenings and treatment.

Treatment to address the needs of children and families are becoming increasingly complex, as caregivers must develop, implement, and evaluate treatment options across disciplines to meet the many challenges. Many sources—including educators, child welfare personnel, social workers, mental health and health care providers, and child care agencies—can offer parent training and staff in-service programs as treatment and education supports. Within schools, positive behavior intervention systems provide proactive, comprehensive, and positive behavior management as one solution currently widely implemented. Caregivers and parents collaboratively identify and reinforce positive behaviors, skill development, and appropriate resources.

A multidisciplinary approach increases knowledge, expertise, and resources while sharing the responsibility for providing the services and interventions necessary for maltreated and abused children with disabilities. In addition, communication between service providers (e.g., educators, child welfare personnel, and law enforcement staff) sharing roles and expertise and coordination of treatment interventions decrease duplication of efforts. Coordination can prevent overburdening stressed families and caregivers and resource-depleted agencies and schools while treating the needs of children with disabilities.

Mary Little

See also: Child Abuse, Psychological and Behavioral Effects of; Domestic Abuse, Psychological Effects of.

Further Reading

Child Welfare Information Gateway. 2013. *Long-term Consequences of Child Abuse and Neglect*. Washington, D.C.: U.S. Department of Health and Human Services, Children's Bureau.

Eber, L., G. Sugai, C. R. Smith, and T. M. Scott. 2002. "Wraparound Positive Behavioral Interventions and Supports in the Schools." [Electronic version]. *Journal of Emotional and Behavioral Disorders* 10: 171–181.

Family Educational Rights and Privacy Act (FERPA). 1974. 20 U.S.C. § 1232g.

Jones, L., M. Bellis, S. Wood, K. Hughes, E. McCoy, L. Eckley, G. Bates, C. Mikton, T. Shakespeare, and A. Officer. 2012. "Prevalence and Risk of Violence against Children with Disabilities: A Systematic Review and Meta-analysis of Observational Studies." *The Lancet 380* (9845): 899–907. doi:10.1016/S0140-6736(12)60692-8.

Sullivan, P. M., and J. F. Knutson. 2000. "Maltreatment and Disability: A Population-based Epidemiological Study." *Child Abuse & Neglect* 24: 1257–1273.

Tarik, J. 2012. "Children with Disabilities Likely to Experience Violence." Geneva, Switzerland: World Health Organization.

UNICEF (United Nations Children's Fund). 2013. *The State of the World's Children with Disabilities*. New York: United Nations.

U.S. Department of Health and Human Services. 2012. *Child Maltreatment 2010: Reports from the States to the National Child Abuse and Neglect Data System*. Washington, D.C.: U.S. Department of Health and Human Services.

Web Sites with Helpful Information for Preventing Child Abuse and Neglect

Department of Health and Human Services, Children's Bureau: Child Welfare Information Gateway, http://www.childwelfare.gov. This site includes definitions, statistics, reporting, and intervention information and Web sites for each state's child welfare agency.

National Technical Assistance Center on Positive Behavioral Interventions and Supports (PBIS), http://www.pbis.org. Information and training is available on school-wide research-based interventions for preventing and addressing behavior problems, with information on including families in the process.

Prevent Child Abuse America, http://www.preventchildabuse.org. This agency promotes the prevention of child abuse and neglect. The Web site includes links to state prevention agencies and guidelines for preventing child maltreatment.

DOMESTIC ABUSE

Domestic abuse can take a variety of forms, from threats, verbal abuse, and stalking to sexual and physical abuse. When domestic abuse involves a physical component, it is called *domestic violence*, which is a crime. Domestic abuse is also referred to as *spousal abuse*, but a more accurate term would be *intimate abuse*. It is the abuse by one person of another in an intimate relationship. According to the Department of Justice, parties within these relationships are called "intimates." They can be married partners, ex-spouses, unmarried partners, dating and former boyfriends/girlfriends. The intent of domestic abuse is essentially the control one intimate exerts over another. The form of abuse is the tactics the intimate uses in gaining this control.

The accurate statistics on the prevalence of domestic abuse is difficult to establish. It is estimated that half of the incidents are not reported to police because of the victim's shame or fear of retaliation. Of those that are reported, the Centers for Disease Control and Prevention indicate that

- 1.5 million women and over 800,000 men are physically assaulted by an intimate partner each year in the United States.
- 76 percent of the women who were raped or physically assaulted since age 18 were assaulted by a former or current husband, cohabiting partner, or date.
- One in three women required medical care.
- Between 25 percent and 50 percent of women will be physically abused by their intimate at least once in their lives.

The victims of physical domestic abuse include both men and women; however, 8 out of 10 are women. The highest rates of intimate violence occur with women ages 16–24. More cases involve African American women than white. Victimization also occurs more frequently with women of lower income and among those living in the city. Almost three-quarters of the domestic violence occurs at or near home. Victims tend to sustain head or spinal injuries. Perpetrators tend to escalate the frequency and intensity of their violence from verbal criticism to slaps to inflicting physical injury, up to and including lethal violence. Seventy-five percent of victims eventually leave the relationship, but the offending intimate may still harass and stalk them. Approximately 9 percent of the murders in the United States involve intimate murder. Male intimates (70%) also tend to abuse children living in the home.

Ten risk factors are associated with domestic abuse. These factors are: abuse of illegal drugs, unemployment, the man having seen his father abuse his mother, the man being between the ages of 18 and 30, poverty level income, use of severe violence in disciplining children, the man not finishing high school, blue collar worker, couples with different religions, and unmarried couples cohabitating. The risk of violence increases the more risk factors are in the home. For example, if a home has seven or more factors, the risk of violence is 40 times greater.

Although no clear pattern to the personalities of those involved in abuse exists, a common behavioral pattern is the cycle of violence. In this cycle, the first stage involves escalation of control and aggressiveness that results in psychological duress for the victim. In the second stage, physical abuse erupts, which can extend to children or even to intervening police. In the third stage, the abuser calms down and becomes guilt ridden, remorseful, and seeks forgiveness. The abuser's behavior in this stage is a ploy to "normalize" the situation with excuses and to "turn on the charm" to get the victim back under control. Next, the abuser engages in fantasizing about the victim's supposed indiscretions and begins to plan how to punish those indiscretions. Finally, the abuser creates the "setup" or situation justifying another round of violence, and the cycle continues.

The Centers for Disease Control and Prevention classify three types of abusers. The first are abusers who follow with the cycle of violence. The second type is the episodic abuser who only on rare occasion loses control and becomes violent. The third is the most dangerous because this abuser commits violence outside the home (fights, sexual assault, etc.) The third type (20% of male abusers) is characterized as having an antisocial personality disorder and is least likely to benefit from therapy or intervention.

The societal response to domestic abuse has steadily evolved since the 1970s. Prior to that time, there were no shelters or social services for the victims of abuse. From a legal and law enforcement point of view, domestic abuse was considered a personal family matter. Eventually, the medical treatment data and improvements in the criminal tracking and reporting processes of the criminal justice system, including the FBI, have provided a clearer picture of the cost of domestic abuse.

Today, the problem is addressed through laws, medical care facilities that have improved their screening and standards of care for abuse, shelters that are established to aid victims and provide crisis hotlines, counseling, job training, drug treatment, housing assistance, medical and legal assistance, and programs for offenders. Public schools created programs aimed at family violence prevention, and universities and colleges began offering dating violence prevention programs. Significant progress has been and is being made, but much still needs to be done in understanding and preventing domestic abuse.

Randal W. Summers

See also: *Burning Bed, The*; Child Abuse, Physical and Emotional; Cycle of Abuse; Domestic Abuse, Immigrants and; Domestic Abuse, Poverty and; Domestic Abuse, Psychological Effects of: Mandatory Arrest Laws; Rape, Marital; Same-sex Relationships, Violence in; Stalking; Violence Against Women Act.

Further Reading

Berry, D. 1998. *The Domestic Violence Sourcebook*. Los Angeles: Lowell House.

Forward, S., and J. Torres. 1986. *Men Who Hate Women and the Women Who Love Them*. New York: Bantam.

Gelles, R. J., R. Lackner, and G. D. Wolfner. 1994. "Men Who Batter: The Risk Markers." *Violence Update*, 4 (12).

Murphy, P. A. 1993. *Making the Connections: Women, Work & Abuse*. Winter Park, FL: GR Press.

National Domestic Violence Hotline: 1-800-799-7233 (SAFE).

Smith, M., and J. Segal. 2013. "Domestic Violence and Abuse." *HelpGuide.org*.

Smith, M., and J. Segal. 2013. "Help for Abused and Battered Women." *HelpGuide.org*.

Summers, Randal W., and Allan M. Hoffman, eds. 2002. *Domestic Violence: A Global View*. Westport, CT: Greenwood Press.

Tjaden, P., and N. Thoennes. 1998. *Prevalence, Incidence, and Consequences of Violence against Women: Findings from the National Violence against Women Survey*. Washington, D.C.: U.S. Department of Justice, Office of Justice Programs, National Institute of Justice.

Walker, L. 1982. *The Battered Woman*. New York: Harper & Row.

DOMESTIC ABUSE, IMMIGRANTS AND

Many Americans know that domestic violence is a social problem, but they are not aware that it is an issue in immigrant communities that has necessitated the development of a range of legal protections to cover immigrants who do not have the rights of citizens. When immigrant women become naturalized citizens, they are guaranteed the same right to protection from violence as native-born women.

Protections for both citizens and authorized immigrant women were established by the Violence Against Women Act of 1994. Later, undocumented immigrant women subject to intimate partner violence, who were not given protection from deportation if they were discovered when they reported the abuse, were covered by the Violence Against Women Act of 2000 and the Victims of Trafficking and Violence Protection Act of 2000. Despite congressional legal actions, there are a lot of questions about whether the United States intends to safeguard the human rights of these women.

Because the expansion of both legal and undocumented immigration is a major issue among voters, there is little sympathy for women immigrants, especially those who are unauthorized entrants, even if they come to escape battering in their homeland. Domestic violence is a serious issue among immigrants because their cultural attitudes and fear of the police reduce reporting. In particular, undocumented women who are violently assaulted by citizens and temporary legal immigrant residents often lack information that could help them and may feel that they have nowhere to turn because they could be deported and/or lose their children.

Providing any type of social services for undocumented immigrants is controversial, but battered immigrant women have advocates. What should be considered is whether an immigrant woman, even if undocumented, has human rights. If so, should the United States follow its own laws and try to overcome barriers to helping provide protection from violence for her and any of her U.S.-born children? The failure of the United States to effectively carry out its own legal initiatives and continue to refine them to protect immigrant women is a controversial issue.

Domestic violence represents behavior used by an intimate to control the spouse or partner. The common elements of domestic violence include not just physical aggression but also emotional abuse, intimidation, threats, economic or other coercion, social isolation, destroying possessions including residency documents, and sexual abuse. A particularly damaging threat, or actuality, is harming or kidnapping children, sometimes by taking them to a foreign country. A circumstance specific to immigrant women is the stealing of her remittances, or money she was planning to send to support her children or family in her country of origin. In addition, violent men have used the immigration status of women as a means of controlling them in court cases or to turn the attention of civil authorities away from their violence.

An especially effective threat made by assailants of immigrant women is that if she contacts the police or the courts, the abuser will get custody of the children and/or she will be deported. Researchers have found that women's immigration status is a powerful tool of control by the abuser if the women are not aware of protective measures that can be applied to their situation. Abusive spouses or partners may threaten deportation, not file legalization papers, or withdraw papers as a power and control tactic. This keeps immigrant women in abusive relationships.

There are anti-immigration conservatives who see allowing undocumented or temporary resident women who are battered to remain in the United States as promoting more unauthorized immigration. Since the September 11, 2001, it has been hard to devise strategies for issuing special visas to protect victims of violence. Those who support immigration restriction and tougher enforcement are against the special visa system created by various congressional acts. They see it as a set of loopholes for the undocumented that foster more harm than benefit. Even some immigration policy critics who would support protection for battered immigrant women do not support special visas because they believe the entire immigration system needs to be changed. This has placed battered immigrant women in special jeopardy.

Judith Ann Warner

See also: Domestic Abuse; Domestic Abuse, Poverty and; Domestic Abuse, Psychological Effects of; Immigrants

Further Reading

Salcido, Olivia, and Adelman, Madeline. 2004. "'He Has Me Tied with the Blessed and Damned Papers': Undocumented Immigrant Battered Women in Phoenix, Arizona." *Human Organization* 63, 2: 162–163.

Thorton, Sharyne Shui, Kirsten Sentura, and Katherine Sullivan. 2005. "'Like a Bird in a Cage': Vietnamese Women Survivors Talk about Domestic Violence." *Journal of Interpersonal Violence* 20, 9: 959–976.

Warner, Judith Ann, ed. 2008. *Battleground: Immigration*. Westport, CT: Greenwood.

DOMESTIC ABUSE, POVERTY AND

Domestic violence and women's poverty are undeniably linked. Each year, approximately 1.5 million women in the United States are physically or sexually assaulted by an intimate partner. Domestic violence survivors face a pattern of psychological assault and physical and sexual coercion by their intimate partners. Although survivors face a number of barriers to escaping abuse, poverty is among the most formidable. This is true for survivors for whom leaving the abuser means giving up economic security and for those already trapped in poverty. As many as 60 percent of women on welfare report having been a victim of intimate violence at some point in their adult lives, and as many as 30 percent report having been the victim of abuse within the preceding year.

Abusers retain control over survivors by ensuring the survivors' economic dependency or instability. Although most domestic violence survivors report that they engage in wage work or that they want to work, some are prohibited from working by their abusers. Others are denied access to economic resources, including checking accounts or credit cards. Many abusers interfere with work, education, or training through phone calls, harassment, or threats of violence at the workplace. Among survivors, 25 percent to 50 percent report having lost a job due to abuse.

This economic insecurity is compounded for survivors who, because of race, ethnicity, disability, and the like, face discriminatory barriers to reemployment.

Despite the economic risks involved, most domestic violence survivors attempt to flee the abuse. Means of escape differ among women. Some go to family. Others go to domestic violence shelters, which provide only temporary accommodation. In addition, domestic violence is a primary cause of homelessness, a plight that poses significant barriers to survivors' workforce participation.

Assistance for survivors is often crafted to accommodate the model of a white woman survivor and fails to incorporate the experience or meet the needs of many immigrant women, women of color, lesbians, gay men, or disabled or drug- or alcohol-addicted survivors. Because these survivors fail to fit the model, they are more vulnerable to discriminatory state action, such as being perceived as violent and thus subject to mandatory arrest laws or not having an interpreter's assistance in response to 911 calls. These survivors are frequently unable to access formal channels of assistance.

Many domestic violence survivors depend on welfare to provide the economic support necessary to escape the violence. Certain requirements of the welfare law present potential problems for domestic violence survivors. These include the requirement that welfare recipients engage in a work activity within two years, the requirement that they establish paternity and cooperate with child support enforcement, and the five-year lifetime limit on welfare receipt. Access to benefits is available to battered immigrant women only on a limited basis, and eligibility requirements make it difficult for most immigrant survivors to qualify.

The work requirements of the welfare program established in 1996 (Temporary Assistance for Needy Families, or TANF) can expose survivors to more violence and can make it difficult to maintain eligibility for welfare. Recipients who are currently experiencing abuse report that their abuser sabotages work efforts by increasing the violence before a big event, such as an exam or interview, refusing to provide transportation or child care at the last minute, or inflicting guilt on the survivor for leaving the children. States need to adapt to the needs of survivors by waiving work requirements where necessary and by making work requirements more flexible to assist survivors in overcoming barriers to sustained employment and economic security.

Paternity establishment and child support enforcement requirements may also be dangerous. Studies of welfare recipients indicate that many survivors want child support regulations to be enforced against the abuser. Doing so can be dangerous either for the survivor or for the child. Court proceedings increase batterers' access to the mother and child and can be used by the abuser as a vehicle for continued harassment. Moreover, child support enforcement opens up the issue of visitation and custody, threatening the safety and security of the child. Although some survivors may need waivers from the entire process, others may need the state to institute policies and procedures (such as excusing her from court visits, protecting contact information, and ensuring that abusers are not granted unsafe visitation or custody) so that survivors can safely take advantage of pending child support reforms, which will aid welfare recipients in achieving economic security.

Domestic violence survivors are remarkably resilient. Nevertheless, survival can be a long, hard process. Survivors may take longer than five years to free themselves from the abuse and its effects. They may cycle between wage work and welfare, may need to overcome posttraumatic stress, and may need to deal with other violence-related problems. Moreover, domestic violence is linked to increased incidences of drug and alcohol abuse, which can create barriers to work, education, and training and can even threaten welfare eligibility. Hence, the five-year lifetime limit on welfare eligibility threatens survivors' physical, psychological, and economic security.

A Family Violence Option was put into the 1996 welfare law to provide states with the opportunity to waive welfare requirements that make escaping domestic violence more difficult or that unfairly penalize current or former survivors. The Family Violence Option is, however, just a state option, administered at a state's discretion. But even if the Family Violence Option was mandatory for states, survivors who are reluctant to expose intimate partners to the criminal justice system would not benefit. The challenge for survivors under the TANF welfare regime is to win implementation policies that provide full disclosure of available waivers and services while respecting survivors who do not wish to reveal their abuse to the government. Once informed, survivors must be free to choose what they decide will work best for them, and that choice must be honored and carried out in such a manner as to protect their safety and confidentiality. Only then will survivors be empowered to attain economic self-sufficiency and a life free from violence.

Jacqueline K. Payne

See also: Child Abuse, Poverty and; Domestic Abuse; Domestic Abuse, Immigrants and; Domestic Abuse, Psychological Effects of; Immigrants.

Further Reading

Lyon, Eleanor. 2000. *Welfare, Poverty, and Abused Women: New Research and Its Implications*. Harrisburg, PA: National Resource Center on Domestic Violence.

Tjaden, P., and N. Thoennes. "Full Report of the Prevalence, Incidence, and Consequences of Violence against Women." The National Violence against Women Survey. http://www.ncjrs.org/txtfiles1/nij/183781.txt.

Tolman, Richard M., and Jody Raphael. 2000. "A Review of Research on Welfare and Domestic Violence." *Journal of Social Issues* 56, 4: 655–682.

DOMESTIC ABUSE, PSYCHOLOGICAL EFFECTS OF

Domestic abuse is the abuse by one person of another in an intimate relationship. The intimate relationships can be among married partners, unmarried partners, ex-spouses, dating and former boyfriends/girlfriends. The abuse may be expressed in threats, verbal abuse, physical abuse, sexual abuse, and even stalking. The abuser does the abuse in order to gain control over another individual.

Domestic abuse produces profound and negative effects on the person abused. Initially there is love between the abuser and the abused, before the abuse begins.

Love may continue in the early stages of the abuse when the abused is hopeful that the abuser will change and stop the abusive behavior. Over time, the abuse that began with verbal acts escalates and includes physical acts. The abused experiences anxiety and clinical depression, with emotions ranging from anger, shame, and remorse to tremendous fear. The abused becomes quite cautious, "walking on egg shells" so as to not set the abuser off. After an instance of abuse, the abuser will often express remorse but continues the abuse.

The persons abused find themselves economically deprived, isolated from friends and family and, if children are present, they continually worry about the children being abused. In situations where men abuse their female partner, 70 percent physically abuse their children, and one-third sexually abuse the children. Children who are abused or witness abuse in the home display withdrawn, isolating behavior and have a higher risk of becoming an abuser in adulthood. They have low self-esteem, poor school performance, and often experience anxiety and depression. Sixty percent of males ages 15 to 20, in prison for homicide, had killed their mother's abuser.

Stockholm syndrome develops when an abused female believes the abuser's plea for forgiveness and promises to change. This syndrome was found when hostages in bank robberies began to identify with their captors and see them in a more positive light. The psychological intent of the syndrome is to feel safe in a dangerous situation. Battered women often believe that the abusers' motives for the abuse were positive or at least justified: "I must have messed up and deserve to be punished." This is reinforced when abusers, being insecure and very jealous, criticize and blame the abused for their own failures or shortcomings.

Seventy-five percent of those who are domestically abused leave the abusive relationship. Leaving, however, can add to the anxiety of the abused through the emotional "letting go" process and the fear of having to survive on their own. Leaving does not, however, always stop the abuse. The abuser may continue the abuse through threats and stalking.

Battered woman syndrome occurs when abused females experience symptoms long after they have left the abusive relationship. It is a subtype of post-traumatic stress disorder (PTSD). PTSD has been observed in war veterans and mistreated hostages. Women with this syndrome have anxiety attacks, phobias, sexual problems, sleep problems, anger, and hypervigilance (jumpy, easily startled).

Women who stay in abusive relationships have similar personalities and backgrounds. They have no "normal" perspective on what is a healthy relationship. Their family background is one in which they experienced physical or sexual abuse. They have low self-esteem and a high need for approval and affection. They tend to develop dependent personalities and often struggle with alcohol and drug abuse. Children who witness domestic abuse in the family also have an increased risk (50%) of engaging in substance abuse.

The psychological effects of domestic abuse are extensive and pervasive. Reduction and prevention of this societal issue requires the coordinated efforts of law enforcement, prosecution, social and medical services, and various private nonprofit organizations that provide shelter, counseling, therapy, and other direct services.

Randal W. Summers

See also: Battered Person Syndrome; *Burning Bed, The*; Child Abuse, Psychological and Behavioral Effects of; Domestic Abuse, Psychological Effects of; Stalking.

Further Reading

Berry, D. 1998. *The Domestic Violence Sourcebook*. Los Angeles: Lowell House.

Forward, S., and J. Torres. 1986. *Men Who Hate Women and the Women Who Love Them*. New York: Bantam.

National Domestic Violence Hotline: 1-800-799-7233 (SAFE).

Smith, M., and J. Segal. 2013. "Domestic Violence and Abuse." *HelpGuide.org*.

Smith, M., and J. Segal. 2013. "Help for Abused and Battered Women." *HelpGuide.org*.

Summers, Randal W., and Allan M. Hoffman, eds. 2002. *Domestic Violence: A Global View*. Westport, CT: Greenwood Press.

Tjaden, P., and N. Thoennes. 1998. *Prevalence, Incidence, and Consequences of Violence against Women: Findings from the National Violence against Women Survey*. Washington, D.C.: U.S. Department of Justice, Office of Justice Programs, National Institute of Justice.

Walker, L. 1982. *The Battered Woman*. New York: Harper & Row.

DULUTH MODEL

The Duluth Model, or the Domestic Abuse Intervention Project, was the first multi-disciplinary program designed to address the issue of domestic violence. It was developed in 1981 by the Minnesota Program Development, Inc., a nonprofit agency in Duluth, Minnesota. The program was largely founded by social activist Ellen Pence.

The Duluth Model was an experimental program that innovated ways to hold batterers accountable and keep victims safe. It is an ever-evolving way of thinking about how a community works together to end domestic violence. The Duluth Model was featured in the documentary *Power and Control: Domestic Violence in America*.

The Duluth Model maintains that women and children are vulnerable to violence because of their unequal social, economic, and political status in society and that violence is patriarchal. The model focuses solely on the men's use of violence in abusive relationships, rather than on the behavior of all parties concerned. It helps the men focus on changing their personal behavior in order to be nonviolent in any relationship.

The Duluth Model is successful because it is grounded in the experience of victims, helps offenders and society change, and pulls the whole community together to respond. What has been found that makes the model work includes:

1. Agencies work together to try new approaches. When agencies—from 911 to the courts—work together to create policies and procedures that interweave together, the whole system works in coordination to more effectively hold batterers accountable. Each agency has a part in identifying and rectifying gaps that hurt women. Each agency can do its job better.

2. Women are kept safe because it is developed from their own voices of experience. Sometimes policies or plans that are developed and thought to help women who are battered actually cause more harm than good. The Duluth Model's approach keeps the voices of victims central to any policies or plans that are made by including victims and the advocates who work closely with them in all decision making.

3. To keep women safe, we have to help abusive men change. When the Duluth Model first began, women told us that they wanted us to work with their partners—that helping their partners change is what would most keep them safe. So, we began nonviolence courses to help abusive men look more closely at their actions, intentions, and beliefs and the effect their actions had on their partners and others. Because it helps men get to the core of their actions and beliefs, the men's nonviolence program is the most replicated program for men who batter in the world.

4. Tests by research and replication has found that by applying all the components of the Duluth Model, 68 percent of offenders who move through Duluth's criminal justice system and men's nonviolence classes do not reappear in the system eight years out. Communities worldwide that have adopted components of the Duluth Model have also found significant reductions in reoffense rates.

The Duluth Model is community based. A community that uses the model approach:

- Has taken the blame off the victim and placed the accountability for abuse on the offender.
- Has shared policies and procedures for holding offenders accountable and keeping victims safe across all agencies in the criminal and civil justice systems, from 911 to the courts.
- Prioritizes the voices and experiences of women who experience battering in the creation of those policies and procedures.
- Believes that battering is a pattern of actions used to intentionally control or dominate an intimate partner and actively works to change societal conditions that support men's use of tactics of power and control over women.
- Offers change opportunities for offenders through court-ordered educational groups for batterers.
- Has ongoing discussions between criminal and civil justice agencies, community members, and victims to close gaps and improve the community's response to battering.

Programs based on the Duluth Model have been criticized because they may ignore research linking domestic violence to substance abuse and psychological problems, such as attachment disorders, traced to childhood abuse or neglect, or the absence of a history of adequate socialization and training. The Duluth Model is also criticized as being overly confrontational rather than therapeutic, focusing solely on changing the abuser's actions and attitudes rather than dealing with underlying emotional and psychological issues.

Rosemarie Skaine

See also: Battered Women Shelters; Safe House; Victim Blaming; Victim Empowerment Models.

Further Reading

Gondolf, Edward W. 2007. "Theoretical and Research Support for the Duluth Model: A Reply to Dutton and Corvo." *Aggression and Violent Behavior* 12: 644–657. http://www.biscmi.org/aquila/Gondolf_Reply_to_Dutton_on_Duluth_Model-1.pdf.

Home of the Duluth Model. 2011. "What Is the Duluth Model?" http://www.theduluthmodel.org/about/index.html.

E

EATING DISORDERS

Eating disorders are serious complex illnesses that can be life threatening. Eating disorders produce serious changes to a person's everyday diet, such as eating extremely small amounts of food, severely overeating or binge eating, and deliberately causing vomiting. The disorder may begin with small changes in the person's eating habits and then progress until the behavior is out of control and produces severe changes in body weight or shape. Although eating disorders may first appear to be only about food and weight preoccupations, individuals often use food to cope with emotions that seem overwhelming. Although not always the case, eating disorders may arise as the result of previous abuse or trauma.

Common eating disorders are anorexia nervosa, bulimia nervosa, and binge eating. Anorexia nervosa is characterized by self-starvation and produces excessive weight loss. Bulimia nervosa is recognizable by a cycle of bingeing and compensatory behaviors, such as self-induced vomiting, designed to undo or make up for the effects of binge eating. The disorder of binge eating includes disorders not otherwise specified and is characterized by recurrent binge eating without the regular use of measures to counter the binge eating.

In 2009, about 11 million Americans had an eating disorder. About 90 percent are adolescent and young women. Anorexia nervosa has the highest mortality rate of any mental illness, upward of 20 percent. Rates of recovery are 33 percent each for the following stages: after the initial episode, fluctuate with recovery and relapse, and suffer chronic deterioration.

The National Eating Disorders Association found that causes stem from a complex interaction of a variety of biological, psychological, and social factors. Biological factors include the belief that certain chemicals in the brain that control hunger, appetite, and digestion are unbalanced. In addition, since eating disorders often run in families, genetic contributions are significant.

Psychological factors that contribute to eating disorders include: low self-esteem, feelings of inadequacy or lack of control, and depression, anxiety, anger, stress, or loneliness. In addition, interpersonal issues include troubled personal relationships, difficulty expressing emotions, history of being teased or ridiculed based on size or weight, or a history of physical or sexual abuse.

Social issues that reflect societal norms can also contribute to eating disorders, such as: glorifying thinness or muscularity, valuing the perfect body, narrow definitions of beauty, valuing people on the basis of physical appearance and not inner qualities and strengths, and stress related to racial, ethnic, size/weight related, or other forms of discrimination or prejudice.

A young woman looks at her reflection in a mirror. Preoccupation with body image may lead to the greater likelihood of developing eating disorders. (George S. Zimbel/Getty Images)

The Mayo Clinic lists risk factors that may contribute to developing an eating disorder: being a teenage or young adult female, family history, having an emotional disorder, dieting, transitions, and sports, work, and artistic activities.

Consequences of eating disorders vary, and some are life threatening. Health complications, according to Mayo, include: death, heart problems, multiple organ failure, depression, suicidal thoughts or behavior, absence of menstruation, bone loss, stunted growth, digestive problems, kidney damage, severe tooth decay, and high or low blood pressure. The most common co-occurence with eating disorders is substance abuse.

Mental anguish is very great and persists beyond the medical consequences. The toll of inadequately treated illness is crippling for the patient, the family, and society. Treatment is available and recovery is possible. Sufferers should get professional help to receive an early diagnosis and intervention to improve recovery. Treatment involves some form of psychotherapy or counseling and attention to medical and nutritional needs. Medications are helpful. A multidisciplinary team is ideal, including a psychologist, psychiatrist, social worker, nutritionist, and/or primary care physician.

Treatment options include outpatient therapy, including individual, group, or family therapy, and medical management by the primary care provider. Inpatient care, such as hospitalization and/or residential care in an eating disorders specialty unit or facility, is necessary when physical problems that may be life threatening or severe psychological or behavioral problems exist. Inpatient stays usually require a period of outpatient follow-up and care. For minors, family-based treatment is an option.

Support groups, nutrition counseling, and psychiatric medications are also helpful. Information on support groups on the state and local levels is available on the Internet.

Rosemarie Skaine

See also: Anger; Substance Abuse.

Further Reading

Eating Disorders Coalition. 2009. "Facts about Eating Disorders: What the Research Shows." http://eatingdisorderscoalition.org/documents/TalkingpointsEatingDisordersFact SheetUpdated5-20-09.pdf.

Mayo Clinic Staff. 2013. "Eating Disorders." http://www.mayoclinic.org/diseases-conditions/eating-disorders/basics/definition/con-20033575.

National Association of Anorexia Nervosa and Associated Disorders (ANAD). 2014. "Eating Disorder Support Groups." http://www.anad.org/eating-disorders-get-help/eating-disorders-support-groups.

National Eating Disorders Association. n.d. "Learn." http://www.nationaleatingdisorders.org/learn.

National Institute of Mental Health (NMH). n.d. "Eating Disorders." http://www.nimh.nih.gov/health/topics/eating-disorders/index.shtml.

ELDER ABANDONMENT

Abandonment is the desertion of an elder without justifiable reasons committed by a caregiver or guardian, which endangers or impairs the elder physically or psychologically. Vulnerable elders may be those with Alzheimer's disease or other dementias, those with chronic health conditions, mental impairments or any other condition that prevents them from fully caring for themselves. Without someone assuming care of a vulnerable elder, the elder can be subjected to abuse by others. Abandonment is a form of neglect.

Signs that an elder has been abandoned can include: staying alone on streets, in parks or malls for a prolonged period and being dirty frequently. These behaviors or signs are not necessarily evidence of elder abuse; however, if these indicators appear, authorities should be alerted to pay more attention to these elders.

Abandonment of vulnerable elderly can lead to physical, financial, and emotional abuse from which the elder is unable to protect himself or herself. Vulnerable elders without a trustworthy caregiver's assistance can be taken advantage of by those who recognize the abandoned elder's situation.

Vulnerable elders are abandoned by their caregivers for a variety of reasons. In some situations, the elder is left behind because of the financial constraints of caring for that elder. Growing health care costs coupled with seniors living longer cause mounting bills and treatments that overextend caregivers who are not prepared to take on this role.

In nomadic cultures, the elderly have been abandoned to allow the success of the rest of the group, believing that the elderly would slow the group down and would need to be cared for by others in the group. Besides time, elders consume resources that younger tribal members might need to sustain life, such as food. During times of famine, elders have been abandoned or killed as to not use resources from which more viable members of the tribe might benefit.

In societies that value youth, elders can be abandoned with the thought that they no longer are of benefit to anyone. Those who would be charged with their care place no value on what the elderly can contribute to the society, so they abandon their loved one so as not to carry the stigma of the older adult and not have to assume the day-to-day care of an elder. Adult children may refuse to care for or stop caring for a parent with whom they have a strained relationship. Elders who were unable or unwilling to care for their children may not be able to expect that their children or other family members will be willing to care for them in later life.

In cases of abandonment and neglect, community agencies should be alerted and pay more attention to the elders and, where necessary, enlist the assistance of professionals (e.g., social workers, medical personnel) as soon as possible. Some cases can be resolved by placing the abandoned elders in care facilities or communities that serve their needs regardless of the presence of outside caregivers.

In other cases, the caregiver may be charged with criminal and civil offenses. While abandonment itself may not be punishable by law in all states, all states do have laws regarding abuse of elders that can occur when vulnerable elders are deserted by those charged with their care. Criminal statutes typically prohibit an elder's caregiver from knowingly or intentionally causing the elder to suffer harm that could result from actions or omissions. To determine whether a duty exists under these statutes, one must assess whether the alleged neglecter is actually a caregiver. Such an assessment is not necessarily a simple matter.

In states where there is no statutory definition of caregiver, the courts may be called on to determine whether an individual accused of neglect in a civil or criminal case is actually a caregiver. Even in states that have a statutory definition of caregiver, the courts may be asked to interpret the definition and decide whether the facts of the case before it meets that definition.

Carolyn Martin

See also: Disabled Adults; Elder Abuse.

Further Reading

Administration on Aging. n.d. "Elders and Families." U.S. Department of Health and Human Services. www.aoa.gov/AoaRoot/oa.goPressroom/Products Materials/fact/pdf/elder Rights.pdf.

National Center on Elder Abuse. n.d. "Types of Abuse: Abandonment." Administration on Aging, U.S. Department of Health and Human Services. http://www.ncea.aoa.gov/FAQ/Type_Abuse/index.aspx.

Social Welfare Department, the Government of the Hong Kong Special Administrative Region. 2004. "Protecting Elders against Neglect and Abandonment." http://www.swd.gov.hk/doc/family/elderly-NE&AB.pdf.

Stiegel, Lori, Ellen Klem, and Jenette Turner. 2007. "Neglect of Older Persons: An Introduction to Legal Issues Related to Caregiver Duty and Liability," National Center on Elder Abuse, Administration on Aging, U.S. Department of Health and Human Services. http://www.ncea.aoa.gov/Resources/Publication/docs/NeglectOfOlderPersons.pdf.

Turnquist, Carolyn. 2011. "Effects of Elderly Abandonment May Not Be Noticed by Observers." *The Post-Journal*, December 2. http://www.post-journal.com/page/content.detail/id/595288/Effects-Of-Elderly-Abandonment-May-Not-Be-Noticed-By-Observers.html?nav=5206.

ELDER ABUSE

The end of World War II gave rise to a huge population explosion. Returning service-men created the generation called the *baby boomers*. This huge population bulge is now reaching retirement age, and their surviving parents are in their 70s and 80s. The baby boomer parents may be living in their own home, living with family, residing in a senior retirement home or, in some cases, in a long-term care facility. Along with this natural aging process, or "graying of America," comes a serious problem: elder abuse. The term was first introduced in the 1970s, in congressional hearings that focused on the mistreatment of the elderly.

Elder abuse refers to physical abuse (physical battery and sexual abuse), psychological abuse (threats, intimidation, and verbal abuse), active and pas-sive neglect, financial abuse (including material exploitation), and overdosing or withholding of medications. Abuse of an elderly person has been considered criminal behavior since the 1990s. Elder abuse is a recurring pattern of behavior in a particular situation and a one-time robbery or scamming of an older person is not considered elder abuse.

It is estimated that there are 2 million cases of elder abuse each year. Only about one out of six cases of abuse are brought to the attention of the authorities. Most offenders of elder abuse are not institutional workers but rather the adult children of the abused.

Although most abuse occurs in the family's home, institutions are not beyond reproach. In 2000, 16 percent of all nursing homes in the United States were cited for abuse in their annual inspections. Federal standards for elder care facilities

An elderly woman, who has suffered abuse by a relative, is in her room at Cedar Village retire-ment community in Mason, Ohio. Cedar Village offers shelter and medical, psychological, and legal assistance to elderly abuse victims. (AP Photo/Al Behrman)

have been established, yet today, there is still one in three nursing homes that are violating these standards.

The causes of elder abuse can be explained through: psychopathology; cycle of violence; ageism; social exchange theory; family stress theory; financial difficulties; and institutional factors.

Psychopathology. Clinicians feel the cause lies in the sadistic personality traits of the abusers. They predict that where the caregivers have personality disorders, there is an increased likelihood of elder abuse. Some researchers have found that many abusers have been hospitalized and diagnosed with mental illness.

Cycle of violence. This cycle is where an abused child becomes a violent or abusive adult later in life. The problem is that not all abusers came from homes where there was violence present.

Ageism. This abuse refers to a bad attitude. Our society is very youth oriented. This attitude does not respect the elderly. Instead, it sees the elder person as stupid and weak. Attitudes can affect behavior and may account for the willingness or justification to abuse.

Social exchange theory. The more the abused elder is dependent on the caregiver, the greater the likelihood of abuse. An adult child may take in an elderly parent out of love and duty. Unfortunately, in some situations, a few things may ensue. This new life change may stress an already troubled marriage. Having to provide continual care can affect the caregiver's employment situation and social life. Resentment builds because of these sacrifices and may lead to abuse.

Family stress theory. Caring for an elderly person can put a lot of stress on the whole family. Family stress is considered a major factor in elder abuse. This is especially the case when the elder requires 24-hour care because of physical or psychological diseases (Alzheimer's or dementia).

Financial difficulties. Caring for an elder in the home can strain the family's economic resources. This can lead to the family caregiver engaging in financial abuse (taking their parent's assets or pension income). In situations where a woman with a modest income is both the breadwinner in the family and the caregiver, it can put her under tremendous strain/stress. This can lead to "short fuses" and along with other factors cause abusive behavior.

Institutional factors. In institutions, certain conditions seem to be present when abuse occurs. The facility may be short staffed, which places more strain on caregivers. In some cases, the abusive staff caregiver is suffering from burnout. Typically, there is the absence or poor training of staff. They may not know how to respond or handle situations when an elder person becomes belligerent or even violent, and the staff may respond in abusive ways.

Treatment of elder abuse varies, depending on the type of abuse and the background of the professionals involved (their causal theories). When professionals see a psychopathological cause, they tend to focus on "curing" the mental illness. If an elder has been physically abused and requires medical attention, the obvious approach of these professionals is to treat the physical trauma. Public health professionals, such as public health nurses and social workers, follow a certain approach/model: identify abuse, intervene to stop it, and monitor the ongoing situation. Legal and criminal justice professionals advocate for changes in public policy regarding elder abuse issues. Establishment of laws and institutional policies can provide a legal and ethical basis to intervene and prevent elder abuse.

In recent years, there has been a strong emphasis on prevention. Education and training become the significant tools of this approach. For example, training of medical professionals to not just treat trauma but utilize protocols to identify the symptoms and report cases of elder abuse. The public health professionals see the community as their patient and community health as their goal. They become very important elements in community education, providing support for families and individual victims. Various public agencies and not-for-profit private agencies see education (awareness of the problem) as a significant force in preventing elder abuse.

The AARP has created a guide titled *A Citizen's Guide to Preventing and Reporting Elder Abuse*. The guide includes warning signs of abuse and how to report it. Because abuse tends to occur at the hands of caregivers, it is recognized that as a group they need support. Creation of caregiver support groups has been a significant preventative measure.

Randal W. Summers

See also: Elder Abuse, Sexual; Elder Abuse, Verbal; Elder Neglect; Nursing Homes, Abuse in.

Further Reading

California Department of Justice. "A Citizen's Guide to Preventing and Reporting Elder Abuse." 2002. Bureau of Medi-Cal Fraud and Elder Abuse and Crime and Violence Prevention Center in conjunction with AARP. ag.ca.gov/bmfea/pdfs/citizens_guide.pdf.

National Center on Elder Abuse. n.d. U.S. Department of Health and Human Services. www.ncea.aoa.gov.

Summers, R. W., and A. M. Hoffman, eds. 2006. *Elder Abuse: A Public Health Perspective*. Washington, D.C.: American Public Health Association.

ELDER ABUSE, SEXUAL

Among the types of elder abuse, sexual abuse is usually studied as a form of physical abuse. The National Center on Elder Abuse defines sexual abuse of the elderly as any sexual behavior that is nonconsensual sexual contact of any kind with an elderly person. Sexual behavior can also include unwanted touching, rape, sodomy, coerced nudity, and sexually explicit photography.

Sexual abuse is one of the most understudied aspects of elder mistreatment. A National Institute of Justice–sponsored study that examined elder sexual abuse found that

- Elderly sexual assault victims were not routinely evaluated to assess the psychological effects of an assault.

- The older the victim, the less likelihood that the offender would be convicted of sexual abuse.
- Perpetrators were more likely to be charged with a crime if victims exhibited signs of physical trauma.
- Victims in assisted living situations faced a lower likelihood than those living independently that charges would be brought and the assailant found guilty.

Adult Protective Services has estimated that sexual abuse is less than 1 percent of all reported abuse cases. Of the reported sexual abuse cases, 95 percent involve women. Victims of sexual elder abuse can be found in all ethnic backgrounds and social statuses.

The victim's vulnerability to sexual abuse depends on factors such as the extent of social isolation, mental or physical impairment, their ability to communicate, and their constantly living with their caregiver. If the current victim at one time abused the caregiver, there is increased potential of abuse by the caregiver.

Elder abusers can be male or female and are more likely to be family members. Adult Protective Services reports that 62.5 percent of offenders of physical abuse are male. Research has also indicated that all sexual elder abuse is committed by males. Most sexual elder abusers are spouses or partners.

The physical and social-psychological signs that an elderly female may have been victimized include: frequent arguments between the caregiver and the elderly person and any changes in behavior and personality of the elder. Signs of sexual

Women protesting violence against women listen during a news conference at Central Park in New York on September 13, 2012. Investigators took a man in for questioning in the reported rape in broad daylight of a 73-year-old birdwatcher who was found battered and bloodied in a wooded area near one of Central Park's most popular spots. (AP Photo/Bebeto Matthews)

abuse include injuries in areas usually covered by clothes. The abused may have stained or bloody underclothing and show signs of pain, itching, bruising, bleeding in genital areas and unexplained venereal disease or genital infections. The social-psychological signs could include confusion, denial, withdrawal, depression, and fearfulness of caregivers or strangers. They may show signs of post-traumatic rape syndrome, which is common with most college-age sexual assault victims and is intensified with the elderly. Victims may exhibit the following:

- Reliving the trauma (dreams, hallucinations, flashbacks)
- Avoidance of thoughts and feelings and situations associated with the victimization
- Amnesia
- Reduced general responsiveness (lack of interest in significant activities and pessimism)
- Irritability, anger outbursts, lack of concentration, or exaggerated startle response

The first step in dealing with suspected sexual elder abuse is reporting it. All states have one or more toll-free helplines or elder abuse hotlines to report elder abuse. Facilities for the care of the elderly are required to post these numbers as well as contact information for an ombudsman. Suspected cases can also be reported to medical and public health professionals, who in turn are required to investigate and report. Adult Protective Services is the primary agency to receive, investigate, and intervene in reports of abuse.

What can be done to prevent elder sexual abuse? Listen to what the elderly person has to say, listen to concerned caregivers, intervene when abuse is suspected, and educate others on how to identify and report elder sexual abuse.

One approach to decreasing sexual abuse in the elderly is called the *intervention approach*. The intervention approach focuses on providing a variety of services to the elderly victims. Caretaker assistance is another way to prevent potential abuse. Educating caretakers about programs and services that are available to them in their community may defuse difficult situations and help meet their needs. Advocacy for changes in government and institutional policy and the laws that guide the criminal justice system are ways to help reduce elder sexual abuse. The Older Americans Act of 1965 and subsequent amendments were intended to provide the basis for financial aid by the federal government to assist states and local communities with meeting the needs of the elderly.

Randal W. Summers

See also: Elder Abuse; National Center on Elder Abuse

Further Reading

Administration on Aging. n.d. "Frequently Asked Questions." http://www.ncea.aoa.gov/faq/index.aspx. California Department of Justice. *A Citizen's Guide to Preventing and Reporting Elder Abuse*. 2002. Bureau of Medi-Cal Fraud and Elder Abuse and Crime and Violence Prevention Center in conjunction with AARP. ag.ca.gov/bmfea/pdfs/citizens_guide.pdf.

National Center on Elder Abuse. n.d. "Types of Abuse." http://ncea.aoa.gov/FAQ/Type_Abuse/.

National Center on Elder Abuse. n.d. "Prevention." http://www.ncea.aoa.gov/Stop_Abuse/ Prevention/index.aspx.

Summers, R. W., and A. M. Hoffman, eds. 2006. *Elder Abuse: A Public Health Perspective.* Washington, D.C.: American Public Health Association.

Teaster, Pamela B., Karen A. Roberto, Joy O. Duke, and Kim Myeonghwan. 2000. "Sexual Abuse of Older Adults: Preliminary Findings of Cases in Virginia." *Journal of Elder Abuse and Neglect* 12: 1–16.

ELDER ABUSE, VERBAL

Verbal abuse occurs when negative statements are said to a person or about the person that define the person. It also occurs when no response is given or a response is withheld from the person, which makes the person feel nonexistent. Verbal abuse creates emotional pain and mental anguish. The elderly are often subjected to verbal abuse. It occurs in the home, in care facilities, and in public. In nursing homes, verbal abuse is found four times more often than physical abuse.

Verbal abuse can be unintentional or intentional. It is unintentional when caregivers or health care professionals may discuss the condition of the elderly patient within hearing distance of them (referred to as *toxic talk*). Caregivers may innocently give their elderly charges "pet names" without first getting permission from them. Family members talking with each other and not maintaining eye contact with the elderly person can be an abusive behavior. Making jokes or playing practical jokes on an elder can easily be misinterpreted. These events may not seem serious, but they may still cause distress in the elderly person and when that happens, it is abuse.

Intentional verbal abuse is when threats and intimidation are used to control the elder person's behavior. Threats and intimidation are used to make the elderly person more compliant. Instead, it leaves them with a sense of helplessness, hopelessness, and resignation.

Communication neglect is a common form of verbal abuse. Caregivers and health care professionals withhold social contact from the elderly person. They may feel they have no time to stop and talk with that elderly person. They also want to avoid the frustration of trying to communicate with an elderly person who has difficulty communicating. Without family support and friends, communication neglect can result in feelings of loneliness. The signs of verbal abuse and communication neglect include: being withdrawn, nonresponsive, or noncommunicative; exhibiting biting or rocking behavior (as though they were suffering from dementia), and expressing emotional upset and agitation.

In some cases, elderly persons state that they are being verbally abused. One difficulty in identifying verbal abuse is that it is common for both the abused and the abuser to deny the abuse has happened. In addition, there could be underlying physical or psychological conditions that produce similar signs. Identifying abusive behavior is the responsibility of ethical, nonabusive family members, caregivers, and facility staff to observe the elder person's daily behavior and environment.

The causes of verbal abuse of the elderly include cultural differences (i.e., values and attitudes) and age disparity between younger generations and the elderly, which can pose barriers to communication. Another cause is physiological decline related to the aging process. Hearing degradation can begin in middle age and progress as the person ages. It is estimated that 28 million people are hearing impaired in the United States (75% of them are over age 55). Physical and psychological diseases, such as Alzheimer's, dementia, and strokes, may impair an elderly person's ability to communicate and leave the elderly person frustrated when trying to speak, hear, or understand communication with family members, friends, caregivers, and health care providers. One result is that the elderly person goes into self-imposed seclusion, self-pity, and anger.

Approaches to intervening in elder abuse include creating and using effective institutional policies, providing diligent oversight, and providing training for caregivers and family members. Some approaches also include the use of patient advocacy groups and the use of "volunteer buddies" who can provide social contact and monitoring of the elder person's environment. Verbal abuse can be treated also by changing the communication from negative to positive and affirming. Positive communication is associated with health and well-being.

Randal W. Summers

See also: Elder Abuse; Elder Neglect.

Further Reading

Pillemar, Karl, and David Finkelhor. 1988. "The Prevalence of Elder Abuse: A Random Sample Survey." *The Gerontologist* 28 (1): 51–57.

Reis, M., and D. Nahiash. 1988. "When Seniors Are Abused: An Intervention Model. *The Gerontologist* 29 (3): 321–327.

Ripich, D. N. 2003. "Communication and Aging: Moving toward a Unified, Systemic Approach." *The Gerontologist* 43 (1): 136–139.

Summers, R. W., and A. M. Hoffman, eds. 2006. *Elder Abuse: A Public Health Perspective*. Washington, D.C.: American Public Health Association.

Wolfe, R. 1997. "Elder Abuse and Neglect: Causes and Consequences." *Journal of Geriatric Psychiatry* 30 (1): 153–174.

ELDER ABUSE VICTIMS ACT

Elder Abuse Victims Act of 2011 creates within the Department of Justice (DOJ) an Office of Elder Justice to address issues of elder abuse. The act outlines the requirements of the office director as to (1) provide information, training, and technical assistance to assist states and local governments in preventing, investigating, prosecuting, and mitigating the impact of elder abuse, exploitation, and neglect and in addressing the physical and psychological trauma to victims of such abuse; (2) evaluate the efficacy of measures intended to prevent, detect, respond to, or redress elder abuse and the extent to which the needs of the victims in each state are met by crime victim services, programs, and sources of funding; (3) evaluate training models to determine best practices for investigating elder abuse, addressing evidentiary and legal issues, and interacting with victims; and (4) conduct, and regularly update, a study of state laws and practices relating to elder abuse, neglect, and exploitation.

The director is to provide grants and technical assistance to assist not more than 15 states in establishing and operating programs designed to improve (1) the response to elder abuse in a manner that limits additional trauma to victims and (2) the investigation and prosecution of cases of elder abuse. Eligible states are required to (1) have a qualified crime victims compensation program and (2) establish or designate a multidisciplinary task force on elder justice.

The act also directs the attorney general to perform annually the following: (1) collect from federal, state, and local law enforcement agencies and prosecutor offices statistical data relating to the incidence of elder abuse; (2) identify common data points among federal, state, and local law enforcement agencies and prosecutor offices that would allow for the collection of uniform national data; (3) publish a summary of the data collected; (4) identify the types of elder abuse data that should be collected and what entity is most capable of collecting it; and (5) develop recommendations for collecting additional data.

Rosemarie Skaine

See also: Elder Justice Act.

Further Reading

Blancato, Bob. 2011. "Elder Justice Act: Funding Status and Implementation." National Coordinator, Elder Justice Coalition. NASUAD HCBS Conference, September 11. http://www.nasuad.org/documentation/hcbs2011/Presentations/S3RegencyD.pdf.

Elder Abuse Victims Act of 2011. "Bill Summary & Status: 112th Congress." 2011–2012. S.462. THOMAS.gov (Library of Congress). http://thomas.loc.gov/cgi-bin/bdquery/z?d112:s462:.

S. 462—112th Congress: Elder Abuse Victims Act of 2011. 2011. http://www.govtrack.us/congress/bills/112/s462.

ELDER JUSTICE ACT

The Elder Justice Act was signed into law on March 23, 2010, as part of the Patient Protection and Affordable Care Act. It provides federal resources to "prevent, detect, treat, understand, intervene in and, where appropriate, prosecute elder abuse, neglect and exploitation."

The National Center on Elder Abuse defines elder abuse as any act that is knowing, intended, or careless and causes harm or serious risk of harm to an older person, physically, mentally, emotionally, or financially. A National Institute of Justice study reported that almost 11 percent of Americans 60 years of age and older were abused in the past 12 months. Frequently, the abusers are family or others close to them, either in home settings or in care facilities.

According to the Elder Justice Coalition, the major provisions of the act include, in part: the authorization of $777 million over four years and $72.5 million for the Long-Term Care Ombudsman program, data collection, forensic centers, a National Training Institute for Surveyors, background checks, Nurse Aide Registry study, and the immediate report of crimes in federally funded nursing homes and long-term care facilities.

To focus on education, research, leadership, and guidance in establishing programs to stop elder abuse, the Elder Justice Act requires the Department of Health and Human Services to oversee the development and management of the federal resources for protecting seniors, in part through the following: establishment of the Elder Justice Coordinating Council, an advisory board on elder abuse, and elder abuse, neglect, and exploitation forensic centers; enhancement of long-term care; funding to state and local adult protective service offices; grants for long-term care ombudsmen programs and for evaluation of programs; programs to provide training; and grants to state agencies to perform surveys of care and nursing facilities.

To improve the likelihood of the prosecution of abusers, the Elder Justice Act requires the Department of Justice to dedicate resources, study and evaluate existing laws, and provide grants to local and state agencies. Victims of financial exploitation, elder abuse, or neglect are three times more likely to die prematurely. Reported incidents of abuse in care facilities, long-term and day care, have dramatically increased in the past decade. The act establishes a nationwide database and program for background checks of employees of care facilities. It also requires that any elder abuse committed in a long-term care facility be reported immediately to law enforcement.

To combat financial crimes of elders, this act makes available grants to state and community agencies to create and promote awareness programs that focus on scams, online fraud, and abuse. Federal funding for programs and justice regulations was not available before the enactment of the Elder Justice Act. Now available are community education, awareness campaigns, training for law enforcement personnel, and Adult Protective Services.

Rosemarie Skaine

See also: Disabled Adults; Elder Abuse; Elder Abuse Victims Act; National Center on Elder Abuse; Nursing Homes, Abuse in.

Further Reading

American Psychological Association. 2013. "The Elder Justice Act (S. 1070 / H.R. 1783)." Fact Sheet. http://www.apa.org/about/gr/issues/aging/elder-justice-facts.aspx.
Blancato, Bob. 2011. "Elder Justice Act: Funding Status and Implementation." National Coordinator, Elder Justice Coalition. NASUAD HCBS Conference, September 11. http://www.nasuad.org/documentation/hcbs2011/Presentations/S3RegencyD.pdf.
Elder Justice Coalition. n.d. News Releases. http://www.elderjusticecoalition.com.
School of Gerontology. n.d. "What Is the Elder Justice Act?" University of Southern California, Davis. http://gerontology.usc.edu/news-resources/news/what-is-the-elder-justice-act.

ELDER NEGLECT

Elder neglect is the refusal or failure by those responsible to provide food, shelter, health care, or protection for a vulnerable elder. Neglect is the most frequently reported type of elderly abuse. In 2010, 5,961,568 elder abuse cases were reported. Of those, 58.5 percent, or 3,487,517, were neglect cases.

Elder neglect is extremely complex. A combination of psychological, social, and economic factors may lead to neglect and mistreatment. The risk factors related to elder abuse and neglect include dementia and cognitive impairment because such conditions may increase the caregiver's sense of burden and may make the victim less able to advocate for themselves. Another risk factor is domestic violence "grown old." A large percentage of those who abuse or neglect older adults are spouses, so patterns of domestic abuse established earlier in the relationship may continue into old age. Conversely, those who were abused earlier in their marriage may "turn" on their spouse in older age, precipitating neglect or other forms of abuse as a form of retribution. The personal problems of abusers, such as debt, drug abuse, and mental illness, also create a risk factor for elder abuse and neglect, especially among adult children caring for their elderly parent(s).

The response to elder neglect ranges from counseling and community involvement to civil and criminal laws. Steps in community involvement include learning: when and how to report abuse; about the agencies and organizations that respond to reports of abuse; what some communities and multidisciplinary teams are doing to prevent abuse from occurring; how to prevent abuse through volunteerism and raising awareness; and and exploring how the many fields and organizations that serve elders and adults with disabilities may play a role in abuse intervention and prevention.

Detection and prevention of elder neglect is a part of the Elder Justice Act of 2009 that was enacted in March 2010 as part of the Patient Protection and Affordable Care Act (H.R. 3590; P.L. 111-148). The Elder Justice Act coordinates federal programs aimed at preventing and detecting elder abuse. The act established an Elder Abuse Coordinating Council and an Advisory Board on Elder Abuse, Neglect, and Exploitation. The latter is made up of members of the public with expertise in elder abuse prevention, detection, treatment, and prosecution. However, to date, only limited funding has been provided to these groups.

The Older Americans Act (42 U.S.C. 3001 et seq.) contains definitions of elder abuse and authorizes federal funding for the National Center on Elder Abuse (NCEA), a program of the U.S. Administration on Aging.

All U.S. states have adult protective services (APS) or elder protective services (EPS) laws that authorize and regulate the services in cases of elder abuse and neglect. Such laws create systems for reporting and investigating suspected cases of elder abuse and for providing services to victims. Some states have both EPS and APS legislation, and others have more than one APS statute. Elder abuse is also addressed through criminal codes; probate, trust, and estate codes; and family law.

Elder neglect that occurs in long-term care facilities is addressed in the long-term care ombudsman program and institutional abuse laws. All states have statutes establishing a Long-term Care Ombudsman program. Such programs advocate for the rights and safety of all individuals in long-term care facilities.

Rosemarie Skaine

See also: Elder Abuse; Elder Abuse Victims Act; Elder Justice Act; National Center on Elder Abuse.

Further Reading

Center for Elders and the Courts. n.d. "Elder Abuse Laws." National Center for State Courts. http://www.eldersandcourts.org/Elder-Abuse/Elder-Abuse-Basics/Elder-Abuse-Laws.aspx.

National Center on Elder Abuse. 2013. "Elderly Abuse Statistics." Bureau of Justice Statistics. http://statisticbrain.com/elderly-abuse-statistics.

National Center on Elderly Abuse. n.d. "Stop Abuse." Administration on Aging. http://www.ncea.aoa.gov/stop_abuse/index.aspx.

Robinson, Lawrence, Joanna Saisan, and Jeanne Segal. 2013. "Elder Abuse and Neglect: Warning Signs, Risk Factors, Prevention, and Reporting Abuse." *Help Guide*. http://www.helpguide.org/mental/elder_abuse_physical_emotional_sexual_neglect.htm.

ELDER SELF-NEGLECT

Elder self-neglect is any failure of an adult to take care of himself or herself that causes, or is reasonably likely to cause within a short period of time, serious physical, mental, or emotional harm or substantial damage to or loss of assets.

A person may be self-neglecting as a result of a lifestyle choice or be depressed, have poor health, have cognitive (memory or decision-making) problems, or be physically unable to care for himself or herself. Signs that a person is engaged in self-neglect include living in grossly unsanitary conditions; suffering from an untreated illness, disease, or injury; suffering from malnutrition to such an extent that, without an intervention, the adult's physical or mental health is likely to be severely impaired; creating a hazardous situation that will likely cause serious physical harm to the adult or others or cause substantial damage to or loss of assets; and suffering from an illness, disease, or injury that results in the adult's dealing with his or her assets in a manner that is likely to cause substantial damage to or loss of the assets.

Self-neglect behaviors could include:

- Hoarding of objects (newspapers or magazines, mail or paperwork, etc.) and/or animal hoarding to the extent that the safety of the individual (and/or other household or community members) is threatened or compromised
- Failure to provide adequate food and nutrition for oneself
- Failure to take essential medications or refusal to seek medical treatment for serious illness
- Leaving a burning stove unattended
- Poor hygiene

- Not wearing suitable clothing for the weather
- Confusion
- Inability to attend to housekeeping
- Dehydration

In some cases, self-neglect leads to a higher risk of death. A study was conducted from 1993 to 2005 of residents living in a geographically defined community of three adjacent neighborhoods in Chicago, Illinois, who were participating in the Chicago Health and Aging Project (CHAP), a longitudinal, population-based study of residents aged 65 years or older. Some participants had suspected elder self-neglect or abuse reported to social services agencies. Of 9,318 CHAP participants, 1,544 participants were reported for elder self-neglect and 113 participants were reported for elder abuse. All CHAP participants were followed up for a median of 6.9 years, during which 4,306 deaths occurred. Elder self-neglect was associated with a significantly increased risk of one-year mortality. Mortality risk was lower but still elevated after one year.

Self-neglect is one of the most frequently reported concerns brought to Adult Protective Services. Oftentimes, the problem is paired with declining health, isolation, Alzheimer's disease or dementia, or drug and alcohol dependency. In some of these cases, elders will be connected to support in the community that can allow them to continue living on their own. Some conditions, such as depression and malnutrition, may be successfully treated through medical intervention. If the problems are severe enough, a guardian may be appointed.

Self-neglect is a form of elder abuse covered by federal law. Title XX of the Social Security Act, signed into law in 1975, mandates states to develop and maintain protective services agencies for vulnerable older adults. In 2004, the United States spent an estimated $500 million on these social services agencies. The Elder Justice Act was signed into law by President Obama on March 23, 2010, as part of the Patient Protection and Affordable Care Act. It provides federal resources to "prevent, detect, treat, understand, intervene in and, where appropriate, prosecute elder abuse, neglect and exploitation." The act requires that the Department of Health and Human Services oversee the development and management of the federal resources for protecting seniors from elder abuse.

Rosemarie Skaine

See also: Elder Abuse; Elder Neglect; Disabled Adults.

Further Reading

Dong, XinQi, Melissa Simon, Carlos Mendes de Leon, Terry Fulmer, Todd Beck, Liesi Hebert, Carmel Dyer, Gregory Paveza, and Denis Evans. 2009. "Elder Self-neglect and Abuse and Mortality Risk in a Community-dwelling Population." *Journal of the American Medical Association* 302 (5): 518–526. http://jama.jamanetwork.com.

Dong, XinQi, and Melissa A. Simon. 2011. "Enhancing National Policy and Programs to Address Elder Abuse." *Journal of the American Medical Association* 305 (23): 2460–2461. http://jama.jamanetwork.com/article.aspx?articleid=900852.

Gorbien, Martin J., and Amy R. Eisenstein. 2005. "Elder Abuse and Neglect: An Overview." http://www.ucdenver.edu/academics/colleges/medicalschool/departments/medicine/geriatrics/education/Documents/Elder%20abuse%20and%20neglect.pdf.

National Center on Elderly Abuse. n.d. "Stop Abuse." http://www.ncea.aoa.gov/stop_abuse/index.aspx.

School of Gerontology. n.d. "What Is the Elder Justice Act?" University of Southern California, Davis. http://gerontology.usc.edu/news-resources/news/what-is-the-elder-justice-act.

Vancouver Coastal Health. 2013. "VCH ReAct, about Adult Abuse and Neglect." http://www.vchreact.ca/read_selfneglect.htm.

FAMILY PRESERVATION AND SUPPORT SERVICES PROGRAM ACT

The Family Preservation and Support Services Program Act of 1993 (PSSF), H.R. 2264, was enacted August 10, 1993, as title XIII, chapter 2, subchapter C, part 1 of the Omnibus Budget Reconciliation Act of 1993. The act amended title IV-B of the Social Security Act.

Major provisions of the act included the requirement that states take part in a comprehensive planning process to develop more responsive family support and preservation strategies. It also encouraged states to use funds to create a continuum of family-focused services for at-risk children and families, to use funds to integrate preventive services into treatment-oriented child welfare systems, to improve service coordination within and across state service agencies, and to involve broad segments of the community in program planning at state and local levels.

The act initially provided states almost $1 billion over five years to establish preventive family support and family preservation services. Total funding was scheduled to grow. It expanded the definition of family to include people needing services regardless of family form: biological, adoptive, foster, extended, or self-defined. Family support services, usually community based, are designed to increase the strength and stability of families through activities such as parent support groups, home visits, drop-in family centers, and child care.

The Promoting Safe and Stable Families (PSSF) program defined services of the states to include preservation services that would assist families in crisis and support services and include preventive activities for families. Family preservation services include counseling, respite care, and intensive in-home assistance by parent aides to avert foster care placement or to help the family adjust when children are returned. PSSF tries to make state child welfare systems more responsive to the needs of families and better equipped to intervene with families before they go into crisis.

The act provided grants to the highest court of each state to conduct assessments of the roles, responsibilities, and effectiveness of state courts in child welfare cases and to implement changes.

Legislation since 1993 reauthorized PSSF, including the Child and Family Services Improvement and Innovation Act (P.L. 112-34), which reauthorized PSSF through fiscal year 2016. The reauthorization included: $345 million in mandatory funds and up to $200 million in discretionary funds; the added requirement that each state and tribe describe how it identifies which populations are at greatest risk of maltreatment and how it targets services to them; State Court Improvement

Programs (CIP), State Monthly Caseworker Formula Grants, and Research Progress Grants; and a new competitive Tribal Court Improvement Program.

Rosemarie Skaine

See also: Child and Family Services Improvement Acts; Foster Care Acts.

Further Reading

Ahsan, Nilofer. 1996. "The Family Preservation and Support Services Program." *The Future of Children: The Juvenile Court* 6 (3): 157–160. http://futureofchildren.org/futureofchildren/publications/docs/06_03_Revisiting.pdf.

Collins, Gail, Catherine Heath, and Eileen West. 2012. "Promoting Safe and Stable Families: History and Purpose." PSSF Pre-meeting Webinar, April 4. Children's Bureau, U.S. Department of Health and Human Services. http://nrcinhome.socialwork.uiowa.edu/events/documents/FinalPromotingSafeandStableFamiliesPresentation4-4-12_001.pdf.

Family Preservation and Support Services Program Act of 1993. 1993. "Overview." P.L. 103-66. Child Welfare Information Gateway. Administration for Children and Families. U.S. Department of Health and Human Services. https://www.childwelfare.gov/systemwide/laws_policies/federal/index.cfm?event=federalLegislation.viewLegis&id=23.

FERAL CHILDREN

A feral child is a child who since a very young age lived with no or little human contact, remained unaware of human social behavior, and unexposed to language. Even after they are discovered, feral children can continue the behavior of their early existence for the rest of their lives. The incidence of feral children is low. According to *Science Daily*, there are just over 100 known cases. *Unexplained Mysteries* reported over 40 well-documented cases in the last few hundred years.

What causes a child to become feral when kept restricted in the early years of life is the subject of controversy, but two elements are identified: the period for language acquisition and the effects of solitary confinement. Eric Lenneberg, a linguist and neurologist, first popularized the critical period (CP) hypothesis in the late 1960s. His research suggests that a specific window exists for learning language, either spoken or tactile. Outside of it, grasping the basics of communication becomes extremely difficult. Jay Shurley, an expert in solitary confinement, says solitary confinement is the most severe punishment. Significant symptoms can develop, even in a time frame as brief as an hour or a day, and will become severe if extended to a year or more.

Two cases in the United States provide support for the reason a child becomes feral. One case involved a girl from Los Angeles who was called Genie. The second case involved a girl from Florida, Danielle. Genie was 13 when she was found in November 1970. She was found tied to a potty chair. She had no language skills and could only babble like an infant. When she was released from the potty chair, she held her hands in front of her, hopped, and clawed the air. Genie had been abused by her father, who committed suicide shortly after Genie was discovered. Genie continued to live with her mother.

Susan Curtiss, a linguistics graduate student from UCLA, gave her the name "Genie" because a genie is a creature who emerges out of a bottle and into society past childhood. Genie was well studied for a number of years by researchers. One group, the Genie Research Team, worked with Genie. When the researchers ran diagnostic tests on Genie, sleep studies showed abnormal brain waves. Some researchers thought this suggested that she experienced brain damage at birth. Others, such as Curtiss, refused to accept that theory. Throughout Genie's testing, she showed improvement. Mentally challenged children and adults do not. Initially, Genie showed a lot of progress, but her language skills leveled, and word order and grammar were difficult. Even phrases were difficult, and her phraseology only got as far as "apple sauce buy store."

In 1975, Genie's mother no longer allowed contact with the Genie Research Team. Eventually, her mother became unable to care for her, and Genie lived in foster homes, some of which were abusive. Genie regressed after her experience in an abusive foster home. Twenty years later, she was found in a private facility for mentally underdeveloped adults.

The second U.S. case, Danielle, was discovered on July 13, 2005, by Plant City, Florida, police. She lived with her mother and two brothers. Law enforcement found her in an unclean diaper and curled up on a torn, moldy mattress on the floor. She was emaciated, and her hair was matted and full of lice. Her skin was covered with insect bites, rashes, and sores. Health professionals found that she did not make eye contact or react to heat, cold, or pain. She never cried. She could stand and walk sideways on her toes with assistance. She could not talk or nod yes or no, but did occasionally grunt. They diagnosed her with environmental autism because she had been deprived of interaction for so long that she had withdrawn into herself.

Danielle was abused by her mother. Danielle's mother did not want to give up custody of her, even though she had been charged with child abuse and faced 20 years in prison. She was offered a deal that if she waived parental rights, she would not do jail time. She agreed and received two years of house arrest, plus probation, and 100 hours of community service.

Danielle was placed in a group home. When Danielle started school, she was placed in a special education class. She avoided interaction and was agitated. In October 2007, Danielle was adopted, and her adoptive parents offered her treatment inside and outside the home. By 2008, Danielle was learning to listen, and understood simple commands. She used nonverbal signals because she did not have developed verbal ability.

The first step in treatment of feral children is intervention. Removal from home is usually the necessary first step. Health care administered by professionals and scientists is the next step. The treatment employed may not be fully successful. The psychologist in Danielle's case provided enlightenment as to why treatment may not be effective. Eighty-five percent of the brain is developed in the first five years of life. Early relationships help wire the brain and provide children with the experience to trust, to develop language, and to communicate—all needed to relate to the world.

Rosemarie Skaine

See also: Child Abandonment and Neglect; Child Abuse, Treatment for.

Further Reading

Curtiss, Susan. 1977. *"Genie" A Psycholinguistic Study of a Modern-day "Wild Child": Perspectives in Neurolinguistics and Psycholinguistics*. New York: Academic Press.

DeGregory, Lane. 2008. "The Girl in the Window." *Tampa Bay Times*, July 31. http://www.tampabay.com/features/humaninterest/the-girl-in-the-window/750838.

DeGregory, Lane. 2011. "Three Years Later, 'The Girl in the Window' Learns to Connect." *Tampa Bay Times*, August 19. http://www.tampabay.com/features/humaninterest/three-years-later-the-girl-in-the-window-learns-to-connect/1186860.

LaPointe, Leonard L. 2009. "Feral Children." *Journal of Medical Speech: Language Pathology Collective Essays*. Clifton Park, NY: Cengage Learning.

Sterbenz, Christina. 2013. "The Heartbreaking Story of Genie, a Feral Child Who Will Never Learn to Communicate." *Business Insider*, October 9. http://www.businessinsider.com/critical-period-for-language-acquisition-2013-10?op=1.

FOSTER CARE ACTS

The Foster Care Independence Act (also named the Chafee Act, after Senator John H. Chafee, who sponsored the bill) was passed by Congress in November 1999 and was signed into law by President Clinton in December 1999. The act expands the provisions for independent living programs by doubling the allotment for these programs as provided for under title IV-E. The federal allotment to states for independent living programs, called Chafee Foster Care Independence Programs, was doubled from $70 million to $140 million, with the states matching 20 percent of the cost. The act allows for more flexibility in providing independence-oriented services. The act also extends Medicaid to youth until the age of 21 and strengthens the focus on the accountability of states by allocating 1.5 percent of the total allotment (or $2.1 million) for the development and implementation of a national evaluation and provision of technical assistance to states in assisting youths.

The Fair Access Foster Care Act of 2005 amends part E of title IV of the Social Security Act. It provides for making foster care maintenance payments to private for-profit agencies. The act's main purpose is to amend section 472(b) of the Social Security Act (42 U.S.C. 672(b)) by striking the word "nonprofit" in each place it appears. This act allows foster care maintenance payments to be processed through private for-profit entities/agencies. It will assist with the distribution of financial payments to families providing foster service to children. The change in distribution of funds necessary to provide appropriate personal items for the foster children will ease the financial burden for providers associated with foster care.

Connie Kerns-Grams

See also: Foster Children.

Further Reading

English, A., and K. Grasso. July-August 2000. The Foster Care Independence Act of 1999. *Journal of Poverty Law and Policy*, July–August: 217–232. http://www.americanbar.org/content/dam/aba/migrated/child/PublicDocuments/englishgrasso.authcheckdam.pdf.

Graf, B. 2002. *Information Packet Foster Care Information Act 1999*. National Resource Center for Foster Care and Permanency Planning. Hunter College School of Social Work. http://www.hunter.cuny.edu/socwork/nrcfcpp/downloads/information_packets/foster_care_independence_act-pkt.pdf.

FOSTER CHILDREN

Foster care is frequently where children are placed when they have no other home. Children placed in foster care each year include over 76,800 who are removed from their parents' care. Infants and toddlers are the largest group of children that enter foster care. Each year, almost 200,000 children ranging in age from birth to three years old come into contact with the child welfare system.

Children of all ages who are in foster care suffer from abuse, but infants and toddlers are the most vulnerable to child abuse and neglect. Children ages birth to three constitute more than one-quarter of all children who are abused or neglected. Of the estimated 1,740 children who died from abuse and neglect in 2008, more than three-quarters (79.8%) were three years old or younger. During this age, when their brains are undergoing dramatic development, maltreatment can lead to permanent brain damage.

A New York University School of Social Work survey, in conjunction with a Baltimore lawsuit, found that over 28 percent of the children in foster care had been abused while in the system. Cases reviewed at the trial revealed children had suffered continuous sexual and physical abuse or neglect in foster homes. Cases included sexual abuse of young girls by their foster fathers and of a young girl who contracted gonorrhea of the throat as a result of sexual abuse in an unlicensed foster home.

A Louisiana study reported that 21 percent of abuse and neglect cases involved foster homes. Stephen Berzon of the Children's Defense Fund reported the findings of the court before a congressional subcommittee. The physical abuse of children included: handcuffs, beatings, chains, tying up, kept in cages, and over drugging with psychotropic medication. These forms of abuse were committed for institutional convenience.

Over the last decade, the U.S. foster care population has experienced a reduction in size and a shift in its racial and ethnic composition, according to the 2012 Adoption and Foster Care Analysis and Reporting System (AFCARS) report. The number declined by about a quarter (23.7%) between 2002 and 2012, from 523,616 to 399,546. Numbers declined among all major non-Hispanic race groups, but reductions among African American children were the most dramatic, declining by 47.1 percent between 2002 and 2012 and accounting for nearly three-quarters (74%) of the overall decline.

At any one time, the number of children in the foster care system depends on the number of children entering foster care and the amount of time each child spends in it. The average length of stay has declined by more than one-quarter overall between 2002 and 2012, from 31.3 months to 22.4 months. Declines in average length of stay occurred among all races and ethnic groups. The number of children entering the foster care system between 2002 and 2012 also declined. In addition, the number of children entering care declined for all major non-Hispanic race groups.

Children are placed out of the home for protection from further violence or maltreatment, but child maltreatment in residential and foster care by adult staff is not uncommon. Although less risk for abuse exists in foster care than residential, the risk increases due to frequent transitions, the nonbiological relationship between child and caregiver, and earlier maltreatment experiences of children. Physical abuse is primarily due to family factors rather than child characteristics, but difficult and coercive child behavior can provoke corporal punishment.

Two influences, placement disruptions and prenatal exposure to drugs and alcohol, contribute to negative psychological outcomes. Placement disruptions affect emotional and behavioral development. Each change in a foster home brings repeated discontinuity in caregiving experiences and social instability, such as in school and peer changes.

A primary vulnerability among foster children occurs in their mental health, marked by disruptions in emotional and behavioral development. Other areas that are harmed include: brain and neurobiological development, and the capacity to develop adaptive social relationships with caregivers and peers. High levels of behavioral problems predict increased stress among caregivers. Difficulties with peer relationships are reflected, for example, with girls in foster care having poorer peer relations at school entry than non-foster care girls. Foster children tend to be indiscriminately friendly toward others. About one-third of children in foster care eventually become homeless, and 35 percent of adolescents in foster care are arrested.

Children's Rights Project attorney Marcia Robinson Lowry reported that the most significant injury inflicted is the psychological death of so many children. Children who are being destroyed every day by a government-funded system designed to help them. Each state must look hard at the outcomes it wants to achieve. Recent studies show that 80 percent of children who have left foster care because they are older than the age for, that is, who have aged out of, foster care, are leading dysfunctional lives.

Compared to their counterparts in the general population, adults who had received foster care attain fewer years of education. They are more likely to be poor, less likely to be employed, and more likely to live in poverty. They are more likely to have experienced homelessness, to experience mental health problems, to use drugs, to be involved with the criminal justice system, and to have children young as teens and before marriage.

The Children's Defense Fund, with ZERO to THREE and other early childhood and child welfare organizations, released *A Call to Action on Behalf of Maltreated Infants and Toddlers*. The call gives recommendations for policies, programs, and practices to better address the developmental needs of infants and toddlers who come to the attention of the child welfare system that protect the development of infants and toddlers and their safety.

Rosemarie Skaine

See also: Adopted Children; Foster Care Acts.

Further Reading

Administration on Children, Youth and Families. 2013. "Data Brief 2013-1: Recent Demographic Trends in Foster Care." U.S. Department of Health and Human Services. http://www.acf.hhs.gov/programs/cb/resource/data-brief-trends-in-foster-care-1.

Children's Bureau. 2012. *Child Maltreatment: 2012*. Washington, D.C.: U.S. Department of Health and Human Services. http://www.acf.hhs.gov/programs/cb/resource/child-maltreatment-2012.

Children's Defense Fund. 2012. "Child Abuse and Neglect." *Policy Priorities*. http://www.childrensdefense.org/policy-priorities/child-welfare/child-abuse-neglect.

Cohen, Julie, Patricia Cole, and Jaclyn Szrom. 2011. *A Call to Action on Behalf of Maltreated Infants and Toddlers*. Washington, D.C.: American Humane Association, Center for the Study of Social Policy, Child Welfare League of America, Children's Defense Fund, and ZERO TO THREE. http://www.childrensdefense.org/child-research-data-publications/data/a-call-to-action-on-behalf-of.html.

Conway, Tiffany, and Rutledge Q. Hutson. 2008. *Healthy Marriage and the Legacy of Child Maltreatment: A Child Welfare Perspective*. Washington D.C.: Center for Law and Social Policy. www.clasp.org.

Euser, Saskia, Lenneke R. A. Alink, Anne Tharner, Marinus H. van IJzendoorn, and Marian J. Bakermans-Kranenburg. 2013. "The Prevalence of Child Sexual Abuse in Out-of-home Care: A Comparison between Abuse in Residential and in Foster Care." *Child Maltreatment* 18 (4): 221–231.

Helping Hand Home for Children Development Department. 2012. "Facts about Child Abuse and Foster Care." http://www.helpinghandhome.org/IMAGES/Facts%20about%20Child%20Abuse%20and%20Foster%20Care.pdf.

Leve, Leslie D., Gordon T. Harold, Patricia Chamberlain, John A. Landsverk, Philip A. Fisher, and Panos Vostanis. 2012. "Practitioner Review: Children in Foster Care—Vulnerabilities and Evidence-based Interventions That Promote Resilience Processes." *Journal of Child Psychology and Psychiatry* 53 (12): 1197–1211.

National Kids Count. 2014. "Safety & Risky Behaviors Indicators." Kids Count Data Center. http://datacenter.kidscount.org/data#USA/1/35/36,37,38,41.

Tikkanen, Mike. 2010. "A Very Critical Look at Foster Care." *Invisible Children, Public Policy*. http://www.invisiblechildren.org/2010/02/28/a-very-critical-look-at-foster-care.

G

GUN VIOLENCE

Most gun owners are responsible and law abiding, and they use their guns safely. However, a small minority of gun-owning individuals use guns to perpetrate abuse in a variety of forms.

Every day, on average, 32 Americans are murdered with guns, 140 are treated for gunshot wounds in an emergency room, 51 kill themselves with a gun, and 45 are shot or killed in an accident with a gun. A gun in the home is 22 times more likely to be used to kill or injure in a domestic homicide, suicide, or unintentional shooting than to be used in self-defense.

Guns are used to commit a crime about 10 times as often as they are used for self-defense. According to the FBI, homicides by firearms in 2011 numbered 8,583 out of 12,664 homicides. Over two-thirds of homicides involve a firearm. 6,220 of those killed by firearms (72%) are known to have involved a handgun.

About 310 million guns exist in the country. Guns are present in about 40 percent, or 45,904,544, of the 114,761,359 households in the United States. Households that own guns have an average of 15 guns.

Mass shootings and attempted assassinations demonstrate a significant form of gun abuse. From 1982 to 2012, 513 individuals died from mass shootings:

- On April 20, 1999, the Columbine High School massacre in Littleton, Colorado killed 15.
- On April 16, 2007, the shootings at Virginia Tech in Blacksburg, Virginia, killed 32.
- On January 8, 2011, in Tucson, Arizona, an assassination attempt on Congresswoman Gabrielle Giffords killed 6.
- On July 20, 2012, a shooting in an Aurora, Colorado, theater killed 12.
- On August 5, 2012, the shooting at the Sikh temple in Oak Creek, Wisconsin, killed 12.
- On December 14, 2012, the shooting in the Sandy Hook Elementary School in Newtown, Connecticut, killed 20 first grade students and 6 teachers. The gunman also killed his mother before the shooting.

Deaths resulting from other forms of abuse of firearms far outnumber those resulting from mass shootings. In 2010 alone, guns were involved in 31,328 deaths, 606 accidents, and 19,392 suicides. Many gun deaths, particularly in large cities, never make the national news.

High-risk groups include individuals age 15 to 24 are most likely to be the targets of attacks by guns. From 1976 to 2005, 77 percent of homicide victims ages 15 to 17 were gun related. Most violent gun crime, especially homicide, occurs in cities and urban communities.

Protesters marching in Washington, DC. The social activist group CREDO along with other concerned citizens descend on the offices of the NRA's (National Rifle Association) Capitol Hill lobbyist's office demanding the pro-gun lobby stand down in reaction to the shooting at Sandy Hook Elementary School in Newtown, Connecticut, on December 14, 2012. (PAUL J. RICHARDS/AFP/Getty Images)

The causes of gun violence vary depending on situational and cultural dynamics that make it likely an offender will use a gun and a victim will be injured in a particular situation. Differences in the nature of violence in communities depend on the types of victims, and the offenders involved in the violence, in part, are the result of a distinct culture that emphasizes and rewards toughness, status, and interpersonal violence.

A January 2013 CNN-Time poll of the American public found 37 percent believed that ways parents raise their children contribute to the cause of gun violence. Other causes included: influences of popular culture (37%) and availability of guns (23%). A police survey reported the following causes: decline in parenting and family values, pop culture, video games, violent movies, short sentencing, mental illness, or a combination of reasons.

Gun violence affects more than its victims. In areas where it is widespread, the threat of violence alone makes neighborhoods poorer. An attempt to avoid the threat is estimated to cost American society $100 billion.

From 1994 to 2004, the Federal Assault Weapons Ban prohibited the sale and manufacture of semiautomatic weapons (each pull of the trigger fires one shot) with military features such as large capacity magazines and pistol grips. Previously owned weapons were legal. The law expired in 2004 due to a built-in sunset clause.

Two major federal laws regulate firearm ownership and sales. The 1934 National Firearms Act restricts civilians from owning automatic weapons, short-barreled shotguns, hand grenades, and other powerful arms. The 1968 Gun Control Act concentrates on commerce prohibiting mail-order sales of weapons, and requires anyone in the business of selling guns to be federally licensed and keep permanent sales records. A gun cannot be knowingly sold to people with prior criminal records, minors, and individuals with mental health problems, for example.

The Brady Handgun Violence Prevention Act, signed into law in 1993, required licensed gun dealers to perform background checks, except for private gun sales. To guarantee privacy, section 103(i) of the act prevents the federal government from keeping the names submitted for background checks or from using this information to create any sort of registry of gun owners.

Limiting availability of guns alone may not solve abuse of gun usage. Community-based programs have been effective in addressing the abuse of guns. Project Exile transferred all gun possession offenses in Richmond, Virginia, to federal courts instead of state courts, where minimum sentences are longer. Programs to reduce gun abuse include public safety education and gun buy-back campaigns. White House proposals address gun access and gun use and include new laws and enhanced enforcement of existing laws.

Rosemarie Skaine

See also: Brady Handgun Violence Prevention Act.

Further Reading

American Bar Association. 2014. "Standing Committee on Gun Violence." http://www.americanbar.org/groups/committees/gun_violence.html.

Brady Campaign to Prevent Gun Violence. 2013. "About Gun Violence." http://www.bradycampaign.org/about-gun-violence.

Burgason, Kyle A., Shaun A. Thomas, and Emily R. Berthelot. 2014. "The Nature of Violence: Multilevel Analysis of Gun Use and Victim Injury in Violent Interpersonal Encounters." *Journal of Interpersonal Violence* 29 (3): 371–393.

Follman, Mark, Gavin Aronsen, Deanna Pan, and Maggie Caldwell. 2013. "US Mass Shootings, 1982–2012: Data from Mother Jones' Investigation." *Mother Jones*. http://www.motherjones.com/politics/2012/12/mass-shootings-mother-jones-full-data.

National Institute of Justice. 2013. "Gun Violence." Office of Justice Programs. http://www.nij.gov/topics/crime/gun-violence/Pages/welcome.aspx.

Obama, Barack. 2013. "Now Is the Time to Do Something about Gun Violence." The White House, January 16. http://www.whitehouse.gov/issues/preventing-gun-violence and http://www.whitehouse.gov/sites/default/files/docs/wh_now_is_the_time_full.pdf.

PoliceOne.com. 2013. "P1 Gun Control Survey: Top 10 Reasons for Gun Violence." http://www.policeone.com/Gun-Legislation-Law-Enforcement/articles/6253478-P1-Gun-Control-Survey-Top-10-reasons-for-gun-violence.

Stray, Jonathan. 2013. "Gun Violence in America: The 13 Key Questions (with 13 Concise Answers)." *Atlantic*, February 4. http://www.theatlantic.com/national/archive/2013/02/gun-violence-in-america-the-13-key-questions-with-13-concise-answers/272727.

H

HATE CRIMES

Hate crimes are crimes motivated by the victim's race, color, ethnicity, religion, national origin, or other group-related hatred. The National Crime Victimization Survey's definition of a hate crime requires that specific corroborating proof of hate motivation must be depicted at the scene of the crime. This evidence may include derogatory speech used by the perpetrator, physical evidence of hate images, or confirmation by legal authorities that such an incident has taken place.

Perpetrators committed 6,222 single-bias hate crimes in 2011, of which 46.9 percent were racially motivated, 20.8 percent resulted from sexual orientation bias, 19.8 percent were against specific religions, 11.6 percent focused on ethnicity, and 0.9 percent were related to a victim's disability.

In 2011, there were 7,713 victims of hate crimes. Victims are identified as individuals, businesses, institutions, or society as whole. Sixty percent of these 7,713 were victims of crimes against persons, while 39.8 percent were victims of crimes against property.

In 2012, Philadelphia experienced an increase in racially motivated hate crimes. The city had experienced 23 major violent crimes in the past 26 months (from February 2012), of which racial hatred appeared to be the primary motivation. Many of the crimes were major acts of street terrorism involving multiple victims.

In 2012, in Oak Creek, Wisconsin, seven people were shot and killed at a Sikh temple. The Bureau of Tobacco and Firearms is investigating this as a hate crime associated with possible skinheads or white supremacist groups.

Consequences of hate crimes may involve personal emotional distress causing fear of public places, certain groups of people, and fear for one's life. Hate crimes can separate communities, cause family strife, and numerous legal problems.

Approaches to combat hate crimes involve charging the person with criminal trespass and possibly malicious mischief or vandalism. In *Wisconsin v. Mitchell* (1993), the U.S. Supreme Court upheld a Wisconsin statute that increased the severity of punishment if a crime victim is chosen based on race or other designated characteristics.

Various regulations have been created and implemented. Federal civil rights statutes enacted during the Reconstruction era made it a crime to violate anyone's civil rights. The Hate Crimes Statistics Act was created in 1990. This act forced the attorney general to create a report about hate crimes based on race, religion, sexual orientation, or ethnicity. The Federal Bureau of Investigation reported in January 1993 that

Protestors demonstrate in Philadelphia, at John F. Kennedy Plaza, also known as Love Park, on September 25, 2014. The protestors were calling on Pennsylvania to add sexual orientation to its hate crime law. The renewed call for the legislation comes in response to the September 11 beating of a gay couple. (AP Photo/Matt Rourke)

4,558 bias-motivated offenses were committed in 1991, including 1,614 incidents of intimidation, 1,301 incidents of vandalism, 796 simple assaults, 773 aggravated assaults, and 12 murders. An amendment in 1994 changed the act to include crimes motivated by bias against disabled persons and, in late 2009, to include crimes of prejudice based on gender or gender identity. This act was created to assist with studying hate crime trends and establishing regulations to address the issues.

The Matthew Shepard and James Byrd, Jr., Hate Crimes Prevention Act, known as the Matthew Shepard Act of 2009, was written to expand laws against hate crimes due to a victim's actual or perceived race, color, religion, national origin, or other personal identifying factors.

Connie Kerns-Grams

See also: Homosexuals; Matthew Shepard and James Byrd, Jr., Hate Crimes Prevention Act; Racism; Transgender Individuals.

Further Reading

Curry, Colleen, Michael S. James, Richard Esposito, and Jack Date. 2012. "7 Dead at Sikh Temple in Oak Creek, Wis.: Officials Believe 'White Supremacist' behind 'Domestic Terrorism'." *ABC News*, August 5. http://abcnews.go.com/US/sikh-temple-shooting-oak-creek-wisconsin-domestic-terrorism/story?id=16933779.

Epstein, Lee, and Thomas G. Walker. 2010. *Constitutional Law for a Changing America*. Washington, D.C.: CQ Press.

Federal Bureau of Investigation, Civil Rights Unit. n.d. "Matthew Shepard/James Byrd, Jr., Hate Crimes Prevention Act of 2009." http://www.fbi.gov/about-us/investigate/civilrights/hate_crimes/shepard-byrd-act-brochure.

Federal Bureau of Investigation, Criminal Justice Information Services Division. 2012. "FBI Releases 2011 Hate Crime Statistics." National Press Office. http://www.fbi.gov/news/pressrel/press-releases/fbi-releases-2011-hate-crime-statistics.

Langton, Lynn, and Michael Planty. 2011. *Hate Crime, 2003–2009* (NCJ234085). U.S. Department of Justice, Office of Justice Programs, Bureau of Justice Statistics. http://permanent.access.gpo.gov/gpo21306/hc0309.pdf.

Rogers, Kyle. 2012. "Philadelphia Seen as Major Hotspot of Violent Hate Crimes." Examiner.com, February 26. http://www.examiner.com/article/philadelphia-seen-as-major-hotspot-of-violent-hate-crimes.

Stephens, Otis H., Jr., and John M. Scheb II. 2003. *American Constitutional Law*. Belmont, CA: Wadsworth/Thomson Learning.

United States Census Bureau. n.d. *Hate Crimes—Number of Incidents, Offenses, Victims, and Known Offenders by Bias Motivation*. U.S. Department of Commerce. http://www.census.gov/compendia/statab/cats/law_enforcement_courts_prisons/crimes_and_crime_rates.html.

Wolf Harlow, Caroline. 2005. "Hate Crime Reported by Victims and Police" (NCJ209911). *Bureau of Justice Statistics Special Report*. U.S. Department of Justice, Office of Justice Programs. http://bjsdata.ojp.usdoj.gov/content/pub/pdf/hcrvp.pdf.

HATE SPEECH

Hate speech is defined as speech that attacks a person or group on the basis of race, religion, gender, or sexual orientation. Hate speech abuse must be directed at members of targeted groups, such as women and minorities. It must also be identified with fighting words, defamation, or imminent lawless action. It arises from hostile, discriminatory, and prejudicial attitudes toward another person's innate characteristics, such as his or her sex, race, ethnicity, religion, or sexual orientation. Its goal is to be demeaning and generate hostility toward that group or individual. It may occur via telephone, mail, or electronic devices.

Hate speech enables the courts to issue increased penalties for crimes involving hateful attitudes and behaviors. The ideas or attitudes verbalized during the attack determine a hate speech status. Hate speech laws support hate crimes laws. Hate speech violations often accompany hate crime actions.

There is a parallel between intolerant or hateful rhetoric and its inevitable consequence. Key issues in our national discourse in 2010 correlate to the rise in anti-Muslim hate crimes. For example, the controversy surrounding the Park 51 Muslim community center in lower Manhattan, the building of "mega-mosques" around the country, and the threat by a Florida pastor to burn the Quran on the anniversary of 9/11—all of these instances contributed to a rising anti-Muslim sentiment in America.

Consequences of hate speech assaults have caused victims to move from their home or purchase a firearm. Emotions expressed by victims were similar to victims of physical assaults. Anger, fear, and sadness were the emotional responses most frequently reported by victims. About one-third of the victims reported behavioral responses, such as moving from the neighborhood or purchasing a gun. The responses of hate violence victims were similar to those of victims of other types of personal crime.

Under Title VII of the Civil Rights Act of 1964, employers may be prosecuted for tolerating hate speech by their employees, if that speech contributes to a broader pattern of harassment, resulting in a "hostile or offensive working environment" for other employees.

A federal court ruled that hate speech on the Internet is a criminal violation. The case involved Richard Machado, a University of California's Irvine campus student. After being expelled from the college, he e-mailed approximately 60 Asian students and threatened to kill them. He was charged under a 1968 Act making it a crime to interfere with federally protected activities, such as voting or attending a public school.

In *Wisconsin v. Mitchell* (1992), it was determined that it did not violate the person's First Amendment right when the Court enhanced penalties for assault when the victim was chosen due to their race.

After an increase of incidences in the late 1990s, state and local governments, as well as colleges and universities, passed ordinances making hate speech punishable. The regulations must not violate people's constitutional right to free speech. People concerned with protecting minority groups and the termination of bigotry believe hate speech must not be tolerated.

Connie Kerns-Grams

See also: Hate Crimes; Internet Abuse; Matthew Shepard and James Byrd, Jr., Hate Crimes Prevention Act.

Further Reading

Barnes, Arnold, and Paul H. Ephross. 1994. "The Impact of Hate Violence on Victims." National Association of Social Workers. http://www.socialworkers.org/pressroom/events/911/barnes.asp.

Duke, Selwyn. 2006. "Hate Crime to Hate Speech: The Road to Perdition." *American Thinker* (blog), December 6. http://www.americanthinker.com/2006/12/hate_crime_to_hate_speech_the_1.html.

Judgments of the Supreme Court of Canada. 1990. "Decisions-Supreme Court Judgments R. v. Keegstra." http://scc.lexum.org/decisia-scc-csc/scc-csc/scc-csc/en/item/695/index.do.

Schmidt, Steffen W., Mack C. Shelley, and Barbara A. Bardes. 1999. *American Government and Politics Today*. Belmont, CA: Wadsworth Publishing Company.

Singh, Hansdeep, and Simran Jeet Singh. 2012. "The Rise of Hate Crimes Can Be Tied Directly to Hateful Speech." *Daily Beast*, September 6. http://www.thedailybeast.com/articles/2012/09/06/the-rise-of-hate-crimes-can-be-tied-directly-to-hateful-speech.html.

Singh, Rupinder Mohan. 2013. "A Compendium of the Sikh American Experience." *American Turban* (blog), March 26. http://americanturban.com/2013/03/26/according-to-us-department-of-justice-most-hate-crimes-not-reported.

Stephens, Otis H., Jr., and John M. Scheb II. 2003. *American Constitutional Law*. Belmont, CA: Wadsworth/Thomson Learning.

Wisconsin V. Mitchell. 1993. Oyez Project at IIT Chicago-Kent College of Law. http://www.oyez.org/cases/1990-1999/1992/1992_92_515.

HAZING

Abuse by hazing involves initiating or disciplining (fellow students/peers) by means of horseplay, practical jokes, and tricks often in the nature of humiliating or painful ordeals. Hazing is a subtype of bullying that involves someone forcing someone else to submit to humiliating treatment in order to gain admittance/membership to a group, organization, or club. Hazing may be considered a rite of passage into a group or level of a group. Hazing occurs at all levels, including some military branches.

Methods of abuse by hazing vary often due to whether the initiation follows written or unwritten rules. Initiation usually follows unwritten rules. The most abusive hazing frequently occurs by athletic members. This may include sexual and scatological assaults to the potential member. A study of high school students resulted in statistics showing 48 percent of students who belonged to groups reported being subjected to hazing activities, 43 percent reported being subjected to humiliating activities, and 30 percent reported performing potentially illegal acts as part of their initiation.

Male students have the highest risk for dangerous hazing activities. A national hazing expert notes there has been a hazing death every year from 1970 to 2013, with some years having six or more deaths. Hazing incidents in military branches have been documented to include digging foxholes, performing excessive exercises, and physical assaults.

Consequences associated with hazing experiences involve emotional and physical disorders. Over 70 percent of the participants in the study reported negative experiences, including becoming involved in fights, poor academic records, and emotional problems involving sleep and eating disorders, and anxiety issues. Suicide is a common reaction due to their emotional distress from a hazing incident. Treatments for people guilty of hazing may involve verbal reprimands, restriction/removal of various privileges, and suspension or removal from the group, or legal sanctions.

Matt's Law originated through the California State University in an effort to allow for felony prosecutions when serious injuries or deaths result from hazing rites. The California Legislature amended the Penal Code to include a definition of hazing. This law was created in memory of Matthew William Carrington, who died as a result of hazing at college.

Legislation such as the Harry Lew Military Hazing Accountability and Prevention Act of 2012 was created to eradicate hazing in the military. Harry Lew was stationed in Afghanistan. After an intensive hazing incident by his peers, he committed suicide. Judy Chu introduced the bill to eradicate hazing in the military in honor of her nephew. It assisted with defining and tracking hazing incidents and their consequences. Military branches have implemented personal codes of ethical behavior to combat hazing.

Connie Kerns-Grams

See also: Bullying, Adult; Bullying, Child and Adolescent.

Further Reading

Blanco, Jodee. 2008. *Please Stop Laughing at Us*. Dallas: BenBella Book, Inc.

Chu, J. 2012. "Military Hazing." U.S. Congress. http://chu.house.gov/issue/military-hazing.

Marshall, Tyrone C., Jr. 2012. "Senior Enlisted Leaders Condemn Hazing in Military." *DOD News*. U.S. Department of Defense, American Forces Press Service. http://www.defense.gov/news/newsarticle.aspx?id=67657.

Nuwer, H. 2013. "Editorial: Anti-hazing Legislation a Good Start." *Daily Herald*, April 29. http://www.dailyherald.com/article/20130429/discuss/704299918.

Thomas, Murray R. 2006. *Violence in America's Schools*. Westport, CT: Praeger Publishers.

University of California. 2007. "Hazing Laws." http://www.hazing.ucla.edu/Hazing%20Laws.html.

HIRSCH, LEE

Bullying is one of the social problems on which Lee Hirsch has produced prize-winning films. Hirsch is a producer, writer, and cinematographer. He is an award-winning documentary filmmaker and an established director of music videos. Among his documentary films are: *Amandla! A Revolution in Four-part Harmony*, *Act of Honor*, *Bully*, and *The Last and Only Survivor of Flora*.

Lee Hirsch (1972) was born and raised on Long Island, New York. He attended the Putney School in Vermont, Hampshire College, and the New York Film Academy.

The 2011 documentary, *Bully*, written, directed, and produced by Hirsch, is about the misery that some children inflict upon others. It focuses on bullying when it is no longer tolerated as a fact of life and is being redefined as a social problem. *Bully*, initially called *The Bully Project*, was filmed for the over 13 million American kids who are bullied each year at school, online, on the bus, at home, through their cell phones, and on the streets of their towns. Bullying is the most common form of violence that young people experience in this country.

Bully documents the misery some children inflict upon others and arrives at a moment when bullying is being redefined from accepting "just kids being kids" into being considered a social problem. "Just kids being kids" can no longer be an acceptable response to the kind of sustained physical and emotional abuse that damages the lives of young people whose only sin is appearing weak or weird to their peers.

The film focuses on the specific struggles of five families in four states, but it is also about the emergence of a movement. It documents a shift in consciousness of the kind that occurs when isolated, oppressed individuals discover that they are not alone and begin the difficult work of altering intolerable conditions widely regarded as normal.

The feeling of aloneness is one of the most painful consequences of bullying. It is also, in some ways, a cause of it because it is almost always socially isolated children (the new kid, the fat kid, the gay kid, the strange kid) who are singled out for mistreatment. Too often, adults fail to protect their vulnerable charges.

The film was written by Hirsch and Cynthia Lowen and directed by Hirsch. It has won awards, including the Sundance Film Festival Audience Award, Freedom of Expression Award, Emmy, Fipresci Prize at the Sydney Film Festival, Best Film at the Telluride Mountain Film Festival, Reed Awards, and Pollie Awards.

Rosemarie Skaine

See also: BULLY Project; Bullying, Child and Adolescent; Cyberbullying, Child and Adolescent.

Further Reading

IMDb. 2011. "Bully." http://www.imdb.com/title/tt1682181/?ref_=nm_flmg_prd_1.

IMDb. n.d. "Lee Hirsch." http://www.imdb.com/name/nm1097276.

Lee Hirsch: Director. .n.d. http://www.leehirsch.net/1./awards.html.

Murphy, Mekado. 2011. "Tribeca Video Interview: Lee Hirsch." *New York Times*, April 23. http://artsbeat.blogs.nytimes.com/2011/04/23/tribeca-video-interview-lee-hirsch/?_php=true&_type=blogs&ref=movies&_r=0.

Scott, A. O. 2012. "Behind Every Harassed Child? A Whole Lot of Clueless Adults." *New York Times*, March 29. http://www.nytimes.com/2012/03/30/movies/bully-a-documentary-by-lee-hirsch.html?_r=0.

HOMOSEXUALS

A homosexual is a person who is sexually attracted to people of his or her own sex. Male homosexuals are referred to as *gays*, and female homosexuals are referred to as *lesbians*. Homosexual individuals have had a long history of not being accepted on the basis of their sexual orientation or being marginalized in situations where they are accepted.

Homosexual individuals can be subjected to a variety of kinds of abuse by a variety of people for a variety of reasons. The abuse takes on many different forms and occurs in many different situations in which homosexual persons find themselves on a regular basis. Jokes, innuendo, verbal harassment, discrimination, assault, and serious assault leading to injury or death are all forms of abuse that have been suffered by homosexual persons.

According to the FBI, gay men and lesbians have consistently been the third most targeted group for hate crimes. Fear of abuse or discrimination is one factor that leads homosexual individuals to hide their relationships and life choices from family, friends, and coworkers. Abuse of individuals identifying themselves as homosexual occurs not just among the individual's peers, but at the hand of those charged with protecting them.

According to Amnesty International, across the globe a person's sexuality may lead to regular subjection to verbal abuse, denial of employment, house or health services, or execution by the state. Often these abuses are carried out at the hand of state authorities and governments, with or without the legal right to do so. In these situations, it is often difficult for homosexual individuals who are the victims of crime to receive the assistance they need from authorities and then may become the victim of abuse, torture, or exploitation themselves.

The workplace is often the arena that homosexual individuals experience the most discrimination and abuse. Coworkers and supervisors alike may feel having a gay employee in the office to be bad for company morale and business. Studies have indicated that up to 43 percent of gay people have experienced some form of discrimination and harassment in the workplace. As many as 41 percent of the employees surveyed indicated they had been physically or verbally abused or had their work areas vandalized.

The religious life of gay individuals is not immune from abuse. It is a generally held belief that one's faith is the place to turn when looking for guidance and support. Religious abuse occurs when the tenets of a religion are used to condemn, reject, or shame the individual. The resulting confusion, incongruence, and hopelessness can create psychological distress among gay individuals. Such abuse by a religious organization or clergy can create feelings of lessened self-worth and other cognitive and emotional development.

Abuse can also happen between homosexual individuals as seen in same-sex relationships. Though the term *domestic violence* is most often used to describe violence in male-female relationships, the concept of partner against partner violence is not absent in gay relationships. Physical, sexual, and emotional abuse all occur in gay relationships, with the added dimension of specific abuse behaviors that play on some of the common threats felt by homosexual individuals, such as the threat to "out" one to coworkers, employers, family members, or friends. The fear of losing custody of one's children's because of gender orientation or sexuality can be used as a controlling or manipulative behavior by the abuser.

The magnitude of such abuse is difficult to ascertain due to low reporting rates. Those involved in such abuse have a multitude of reasons for not reporting the abuse to mainstream agencies that deal with such issues. It is a widely held belief that abuse in same-sex partnerships is the same as or slightly more prevalent than in male-female "traditional" partnerships.

In 2012, President Barack Obama declared that homosexuals are entitled to the constitutional right to marry, the same right as heterosexual couples have. He said that he would not have his administration defend the 1996 Defense of Marriage Act (DOMA). In June 2013, DOMA was declared unconstitutional by the U.S. Supreme Court. At the same time, by a 5–4 vote, the justices held in *Hollingsworth v. Perry* that the traditional marriage activists who put Proposition 8 on California ballots in 2008 did not have the constitutional authority or standing to defend the law in federal courts after the state refused to appeal its loss at trial. The ruling meant that homosexual couples could resume being married in California.

In February 2014, 17 states allow same-sex marriage, and the courts have ruled unconstitutional same-sex bans in every state in which the bans have been challenged. The opponents to homosexual rights and homosexual marriages are trying through legislation to enable discrimination to continue on the grounds of the religious liberty of store owners, but their efforts have not succeeded. The landscape has changed rapidly in favor of homosexual rights.

Carolyn Martin

See also: Hate Crimes; Men as Victims of Abuse; Priests, Sexual Abuse by; Same-sex Relationships, Violence in; Sexual Harassment in Employment; Transgender Individuals.

Further Reading

Amnesty International. 2013. "About LGBT Human Rights." http://www.amnestyusa.org/our-work/issues/lgbt-rights/about-lgbt-human-rights.

Burns, Crosby, and Jeff Krehely. 2011. "Gay and Transgender People Face High Rates of Workplace Discrimination and Harassment." Center for American Progress, June 2. http://www.americanprogress.org/issues/lgbt/news/2011/06/02/9872/gay-and-transgender-people-face-high-rates-of-workplace-discrimination-and-harassment.

Civilrights.org. 2013. "Hate Crimes against Lesbian, Gay, Bisexual, and Transgender Individuals." http://www.civilrights.org/publications/hatecrimes/lgbt.html.

Human Rights Watch. 2013. "Tanzania: Police Abuse, Torture, Impede HIV Services." June 18. http://www.hrw.org/news/2013/06/18/tanzania-police-abuse-torture-impede-hiv-services.

Pan American Health Organization and World Health Organization. 2013. "Stigma and Discrimination Jeopardize the Health of Lesbians, Gays, Bisexuals, and Transgender People." *Press Releases*, May 16. http://www.paho.org/hq/index.php?option=com_content&view=article&id=8670%3Astigma-and-discrimination-jeopardize-the-health-of-lesbians-gays-bisexuals-and-transgender-people&catid=740%3Anews-press-releases&Itemid=1926&lang=en.

ProCon. "13 States with Legal Gay Marriage and 35 States with Same-sex Marriage Bans." http://gaymarriage.procon.org/view.resource.php?resourceID=004857.

Sacks, Mike, Sabrina Siddiqui, and Ryan J. Reilly. 2013. "Supreme Court Rules on Prop 8, Lets Gay Marriage Resume in California" *Huffington Post*, June 26. http://www.huffingtonpost.com/2013/06/26/supreme-court-prop-8_n_3434854.html.

Super, John, and Almeria Jacobson. 2011. "Religious Abuse: Implications for Counseling Lesbian, Gay, Bisexual, and Transgender Individuals." *Journal of LGBT Issues in Counseling* 5 (3–4): 180–196.

HOMOSEXUALS IN THE MILITARY, ABUSE OF

Abuse of homosexuals in the military involves prohibiting them to serve, discharging them if their sexuality became known and subjecting them to sexual assault. Male and female homosexuals have been abused.

The discrimination against homosexuals in the military is rooted in the long-standing taboo that came to American society through the Judeo-Christian religion. Because society did not condone homosexuality, the U.S. military did not condone it. Discrimination against homosexuals in the U.S. military was evident during the Revolutionary War, when engaging in sodomy was grounds for discharge

Sexual orientation policies appeared in World War II. Homosexuality was seen as a form of psychopathology and was a disqualifying trait. When the army issued revised mobilization regulations in 1942, it distinguished "homosexual" recruits from "normal" recruits for the first time. Before the war, gay service members were court-martialed, imprisoned, and dishonorably discharged, but during wartime, commanding officers found it difficult to convene court-martial boards so they issued a blue discharge for handling gay and lesbian personnel. A blue discharge (also known as a "blue ticket") was a form of administrative military discharge formerly issued by the United States, beginning in 1916. It was neither honorable nor dishonorable.

In 1944, a policy decreed that homosexuals were to be committed to military hospitals, examined by psychiatrists, and discharged under Regulation 615-360, section 8. The term "Section 8" refers to a category of discharge from the U.S. military when judged mentally unfit for service. It also came to mean any service member given such a discharge or behaving as if deserving such a discharge.

In 1947, blue discharges were discontinued, and two new classifications were created: "general" and "undesirable." Under such a system, a serviceman or woman found to be gay but who had not committed any sexual acts while in service would tend to receive an undesirable discharge. Those found guilty of engaging in sexual conduct were usually dishonorably discharged. A 1957 U.S. Navy study known as the Crittenden Report dismissed the charge that homosexuals constitute a security risk but advocated stringent antihomosexual policies because "homosexuality is wrong, it is evil, and it is to be branded as such."

On December 21, 1993, Department of Defense Directive 1304.26, "Don't Ask, Don't Tell" (DADT), became the official U.S. policy on homosexuals serving in the military. The policy prohibited military personnel from discriminating against or harassing closeted homosexual or bisexual service members or applicants, while barring openly gay, lesbian, or bisexual persons from military service. These restrictions on homosexuality in the armed forces were mandated by a federal law signed on November 30, 1993, that prohibited people who demonstrate a propensity or intent to engage in homosexual acts from serving in the armed forces of the United States because their presence would create an unacceptable risk to the high standards of morale, good order and discipline, and unit cohesion that are the essence of military capability. The act prohibited any homosexual or bisexual person from disclosing his or her sexual orientation or from speaking about any homosexual relationships, including marriages or other familial attributes, while serving in the U.S. armed forces. The act specified that service members who disclose that they are homosexual or engage in homosexual conduct should be separated (discharged), except when a service member's conduct was for the purpose of avoiding or terminating military service or when it would not be in the best interest of the armed forces.

"Don't Ask, Don't Tell" did not prevent homosexuals from being discharged. From 1993 until it was repealed, over 14,500 service members were discharged under DADT. The number of discharges per fiscal year under DADT dropped sharply after the September 11 attacks and remained comparatively low through to the repeal. Discharges exceeded 600 every year until 2009.

DADT was repealed in 2011, and gays and lesbians can now serve openly, but the repeal has not decreased abuse through sexual assaults. A November 6, 2013, report released by the Center for American Progress (CAP) found that, in 2012, an estimated 26,000 military personnel experienced sexual assault: 14,000 were men, and 12,000 were women. CAP's analysts are concerned that the estimate may be too low.

Solutions to the abuse of homosexuals in the military began with the repeal of DADT. When the repeal provided that services could no longer separate a member because of sexual orientation, statements about sexual orientation in recruiting and accession were no longer permitted, service members who had been discharged could reenter, conduct standards became sexual orientation neutral, equal opportunity for advancement would prevail, gathering information was prohibited, and providing separate facilities was not allowed.

Petty Officer Autumn Sandeen, Lt. Dan Choi, Cpl. Evelyn Thomas, Capt. Jim Pietrangelo II, Cadet Mara Boyd and Petty Officer Larry Whitt (from left to right), handcuffed themselves to the fence outside the White House during a protest for gay rights in Washington, D.C., in April 2010. The group demanded that President Barack Obama keep his promise to repeal "don't ask, don't tell" within the year. Congress repealed and President Obama signed the repeal on September 20, 2010 and the repeal took effect on September 20, 2011. (AP Photo)

After the Supreme Court overturned the Defense of Marriage Act on June 26, 2013, the Department of Defense began giving the same benefits to same-sex married couples as it does to heterosexual married couples, from including the spouse for housing allowance to burial at Arlington National Cemetery.

Dissatisfaction with the way sexual assault cases are being handled by the chain of command has led to proposed reforms of the process. One reform advocated by Sen. Kirsten Gilibrand (D-NY) is to remove military sexual assault cases from the chain of command, stripping commanding officers of their ability to try cases in their units.

Rosemarie Skaine

See also: Homosexuals; Transgender Individuals; Women in the Military, Abuse of.

Further Reading

Brown, Hayes. 2013. "Number of Military Sexual Assault Victims May Be Higher Than Estimated, New Report Fears." *ThinkProgress*, November 6. http://thinkprogress.org/security/2013/11/06/2898711/report-sexual-assault-military.

Daniel, Lisa. 2012. "Nine Months after Repeal, Gay Troops Slowly Come Out." *American Forces Press Service*, June 20. U.S. Department of Defense. http://www.defense.gov/news/newsarticle.aspx?id=116825.

Ellison, Jesse. 2011. "The Military's Secret Shame." *Newsweek*, April 3. http://mag.newsweek.com/2011/04/03/the-military-s-secret-shame.html.

Jordan, Bryant. 2013. "DoD to Move Quickly on Same-sex Benefits." Military.com, June 27. http://www.military.com/daily-news/2013/06/27/dod-to-move-quickly-on-same-sex-benefits.html.

OutServe-SLDN. 2013. "About 'Don't Ask Don't Tell.'" http://www.sldn.org/blog/archives/dont-ask-dont-tell-fuels-the-burden-of-ptsd-for-gay-service-members.

Policy Concerning Homosexuality in the Armed Forces: Federal Law. Pub.L. 103-160 (10 U.S.C. § 654). Repealed May 27, 2010, to take Effect December 1, 2010. http://www.gpo.gov/fdsys/pkg/USCODE-2010-title10/pdf/USCODE-2010-title10-subtitleA-partII-chap37-sec654.pdf.

Rosenthal, Lindsay and Lawrence Korb. 2013. "Twice Betrayed: Bringing Justice to the U.S. Military's Sexual Assault Problem." Center for American Progress. http://www.americanprogress.org/issues/military/report/2013/11/06/78909/twice-betrayed/.

Rostker, Bernard D., Susan D. Hosek, and Mary E. Vaiana. 2011. "Gays in the Military." *RAND Review* (Spring). http://www.rand.org/pubs/periodicals/rand-review/issues/2011/spring/gays.html.

Skaine, Rosemarie. 2011. *Women in Combat: A Reference Handbook*. Santa Barbara, CA: ABC-CLIO.

Slater, Hannah. 2013. "5 Myths about Military Sexual Assault in the Military." *ThinkProgress*, June 7. http://thinkprogress.org/security/2013/06/07/2123511/5-myths-about-sexual-assault.

U.S. Department of Defense. 2011. "Repeal of 'Don't Ask, Don't Tell' (DADT): Quick Reference Guide." USD (P&R) Memorandum for Secretaries of the Military Departments. *Repeal of DADT and Future Impact on Policy*. January 28, 2011. http://www.defense.gov/home/features/2010/0610_dadt/Quick_Reference_Guide_Repeal_of_DADT_APPROVED.pdf.

U.S. Secretary of Defense. 2011. "Repeal of Don't Ask Don't Tell and Impact on Future Policy." Memorandum for Secretaries of Military Departments, January 29. http://www.defense.gov/home/features/2010/0610_dadt/USD-PR-DADT_28Jan11.pdf.

HUMAN RIGHTS

The human rights philosophy is simple. It holds that individuals have rights because it is morally right to protect humanity. International human rights laws protect individuals from many forms of abuse, especially in crisis situations, by requiring that nations follow certain procedures. International treaties protect individuals from abuse and persecution by governments as well as nonstate actors, such as religious or political groups.

Human rights protections are especially important in regions undergoing economic and political development. They establish the grounds for responsibility and accountability among those carrying out the changes. The legal basis for human rights is easy to define. But it is up to the political and legal framework of each country to define the content, scope, and enforcement of human rights. In many cases, human rights can point a nation toward democracy. Democratic government, with its focus on political equality, is very compatible with a culture of human rights.

The notion of human rights has always existed. Most world religions incorporate at least some of the ideas into their principles. But human rights as an end in themselves were not widely discussed until the 18th century, when philosophers such as John Locke explored them in their writings. The United States Declaration of Independence (1776) and the French Declaration of the Rights of Man (1789) incorporated the idea of human rights into politics and government.

Originally, human rights were regarded as an internal matter of individual states. However, they became a matter of international concern in the early 20th century. This concept was written into a document produced by the United Nations in 1948: the Universal Declaration of Human Rights. Gradually, most states have accepted the idea that individuals have certain rights simply by virtue of being human. This principle has been worked into a series of international laws over time. Usually, the basic human rights recognized by such laws include the right to life, the right to earn a living, and the right to be free from abuse.

Human rights abuses can take many forms and occur for many reasons. At their most extreme, abuses can take the form of torture, murder, or genocide. There are also subtler forms of economic, cultural, legal, political, and social suffering imposed on individuals by governments or groups. Some topics of concern in the human rights community today include issues as diverse as capital punishment, sweatshops and wages, discrimination against women and children, police brutality, slavery, and immigration. Any activity that deprives people of their lives, their freedom, or their ability to support themselves can be regarded as an abuse of their human rights.

The chief international human rights organization is the United Nations (UN). Smaller and more specific human rights safeguard institutions have been derived from UN-based treaties and the UN Charter. However, despite its strong stand on international human rights, UN bodies were not active in human rights condemnations until the 1980s. Some nations were able to get away with gross violations even after the United Nations began its campaign against human rights abuses. For example, France long denied using torture during a war in Algeria in the late 1950s and early 1960s. However, it is now known that torture was used widely, thanks to recent admissions by French general Jacques Massu.

Recognizing that human rights cannot be protected if there were no legally binding provisions, the United Nations established the International Covenant on Civil and Political Rights and the International Covenant on Economic, Social and Cultural Rights. These laws became effective in 1976. Several committees are in charge of making sure these laws are implemented and enforced.

However, a large amount of information about human rights abuses does not come from governments or the United Nations. It comes from nongovernmental organizations (NGOs). These include watchdog groups such as Amnesty International and Human Rights Watch. NGOs and independent experts provide crucial information to contradict government denials concerning violations. These organizations and others gather information on alleged human rights violations, publicizing abuses so that international public opinion will force offenders to change their behavior.

The modern human rights protection system works in the following way. The United Nations' expert committees review each nation's compliance with the standards established in each human rights treaty in reports and committee meetings. The UN groups tend to rely on NGO information in evaluating national performance because they are apolitical; their only interest is serving the world's people. The UN committees also review specific complaints ("cases").

Over the years, the human rights bodies have become much more direct in their criticism of country compliance. Various additional protocols have enhanced the powers of independent bodies in stopping abuses and bringing violators to justice. For example, the International Criminal Court (ICC) at The Hague prosecutes war crimes as well as genocide and crimes against humanity. At the moment, the ICC is investigating charges against suspected criminals from the war-torn nations of Africa: Uganda, the Democratic Republic of the Congo, and the Central African Republic. In another example, the 2003 Optional Protocol on the Involvement of Children in Armed Conflict allows the Committee on Children to review complaints against parties who exploit children by using them as soldiers in armed conflicts.

After 60 years of development, the challenge for the 21st century is not the creation of more human rights laws. The challenge is ensuring that existing laws are implemented and followed. This many be accomplished either through international or domestic institutions. Significant steps have been taken in the protection of human rights, but ultimate success remains to be seen.

Henry Frank Carey

See also: Child Trafficking; Human Trafficking; Sex Trafficking; Sexual Slavery; Slavery, Modern-day.

Further Reading

Amnesty International USA. n.d. http://www.amnestyusa.org.

Buergenthal, Thomas, et al. 2002. *International Human Rights in a Nutshell*. St. Paul, MN: West Group.

Donnelly, Jack. 2002. *Universal Human Rights in Theory and Practice*. 2nd ed. Ithaca, NY: Cornell University Press.

Human Rights Watch. n.d. http://www.hrw.org.

HUMAN TRAFFICKING

Human trafficking is a federal offense that violates the Thirteenth Amendment of the United States Constitution, which passed the Congress and was ratified in 1865 to formally abolish slavery in the United States. Human trafficking is a widespread form of modern-day slavery where an individual is denied his or her basic human rights and that individual's life and liberty are under the absolute control of another individual. The United Nations defines human trafficking as the recruitment, transportation, transfer, harboring, or receipt of persons by improper means (such as force, abduction, fraud, or coercion) for an improper purpose, including forced labor or sexual exploitation. Human trafficking is a serious from of abuse and a crime against humanity, and it is a criminal industry that enslaves individuals for involuntary servitude and forced labor. It is a highly complex, multidimensional problem that impacts socioeconomic, educational, health, religious, and political sectors in the United States.

Human trafficking does not only apply to the trafficking of women and young girls for sexual purposes, rather it varies, from trafficking of both men and women of all ages for numerous types of forced labor to trafficking of individuals for commercial sexual exploitation. Forced labor, sex trafficking, involuntary domestic servitude, bonded labor, forced child labor, child sex trafficking, and debt bondage among migrant laborers are considered forms of enslavement. Human trafficking has been connected with undocumented immigration into the United States. Human trafficking has an impact that extends beyond individual victims; it endangers the public health, safety, and security of a country.

A broad range of methods is used by traffickers, including threats of violence, manipulation, psychological abuse, and physical abuse to force individuals into forced labor, services, or commercial sex acts. Victims often experience direct physical abuse, such as rape, starvation, and beatings, and indirect forms, such as psychological trauma. Victims may come from a variety of cultural backgrounds, age groups, nationalities, genders, educational, religious, and socioeconomic statuses, but vulnerability is the characteristic they all share in common.

The United States is considered a transit and destination country for individuals who are subjected to human trafficking. Countless individuals among various populations, such as runaway and homeless youth, undocumented migrants, marginalized, and improvised groups, are targeted by traffickers. California, a state with a significant immigrant population, international borders, and a growing economy, is one of the country's main destinations and hot spots for human trafficking. Trafficking has occurred extensively along the U.S. and Mexican border. According to the State of California Department of Justice, between July 2010 to June 2012, California task forces initiated 2,552 investigations, identified 1,277 victims of human trafficking, and arrested 1,798 individuals who were suspected to be involved in this horrific trade.

The victims of human trafficking within the United States come from a range of backgrounds. In May 2006, two husband-and-wife doctors from Brookfield, Milwaukee, were convicted of keeping a Filipina domestic servant under conditions of servitude for almost 20 years. A Milwaukee federal jury convicted the couple of using threats of serious harm and physical restraint against their victim to obtain her services, a violation of the federal law. They were each sentenced to six years in federal prison, ordered to pay over $900,000 in restitution, and, in June 2012, they were deported by U.S. Immigration and Customs Enforcement. In June 2012, a MS-13 gang leader was sentenced to 50 years in prison for sex trafficking girls as young as 14 years from schools and homeless shelters within

Northern Virginia, and for forcing them to engage in commercial sex acts on behalf of MS-13. According to the *New York Times*, Backpage.com, a premier Web site for human trafficking in the United States, is responsible for posting approximately 70 percent of prostitution advertising in the United States, earning more than $22 million annually.

The Trafficking Victims Protection Act (TVPA) was adopted in October 2000 and is a legislative framework that has been strongly committed to combat trafficking in persons, to prosecute all types of traffickers, both in the United States and abroad. According to the U.S. Department of State, the Trafficking in Persons (TIP) Report is the U.S. government's principal diplomatic tool to engage foreign governments on human trafficking. Freeing victims, preventing trafficking, and bringing traffickers to justice are the ultimate goals of the report and of the U.S government's anti-human trafficking policy. The Human Trafficking Reporting System (HTRS) collects data on human trafficking investigations conducted and reported by both state and local law enforcement task forces.

Human trafficking is a form of human rights abuse that hurts men, women, and children. It takes a deep personal and psychological toll on our nation, which was founded on the principle that all people are born with an absolute right to freedom. According to a January 2010 presidential proclamation, we must join together as a nation and global community to provide that safe haven by protecting victims and prosecuting traffickers. Every human trafficking prosecution demonstrates the commitment of our nation's law enforcement and the judicial system to combat this inhuman crime.

Karunya Jayasena

See also: Abduction, Adult; Child Trafficking; Human Rights; Rape; Sexual Slavery; Slavery, Modern-day.

Further Reading

California Department of Social Services. n.d. "Human Trafficking Victims." http://www.cdss.ca.gov/refugeeprogram/PG1268.htm.

Goldman, Russell. 2007. "Modern-day Slavery in America." *ABC News*, March 26. http://abcnews.go.com/US/story?id=2981327&page=1#.UZ539tjWNvZ.

Henrehan, John. 2012. "MS-13 Gang Leader Rances Amaya Gets 50 Years for Sex Trafficking." MyFoxdc.com, June 15. http://www.myfoxdc.com/story/18680758/ms-13-gang-leader-rances-amaya-gets-50-years-for-sex-trafficking.

Kaufmann, Greg. 2010. "The Nation: Human Trafficking, a US Problem Too." National Public Radio, June 17. http://www.npr.org/templates/story/story.php?storyId=127900407.

Kristof, Nicholas D. 2012. "Where Pimps Peddle Their Goods." *New York Times*, March 17. http://www.nytimes.com/2012/03/18/opinion/sunday/kristof-where-pimps-peddle-their-goods.html?_r=0.

Office of Justice Programs. 2012. "Human Trafficking." http://www.nij.gov/topics/crime/human-trafficking.

Office of Justice Programs. n.d. "Bureau of Justice Statistics." http://www.bjs.gov/index.cfm?ty=pbdetail&iid=2372.

U.S. Department of Homeland Security. "Wisconsin Couple Who Kept Modern-day Slave for 19 Years Deported to the Philippines." http://www.ice.gov/news/releases/1206/120615milwaukee.htm.

U.S. Department of State. 2012. "What Is Trafficking in Persons?" http://www.state.gov/j/tip/rls/fs/2012/194732.htm.

U.S. Department of State. 2000. "Victims of Trafficking and Violence Protection Act of 2000." http://www.state.gov/j/tip/laws/61124.htm.

U.S. Department of State. n.d. "Trafficking in Persons Report." http://www.state.gov/j/tip/rls/tiprpt.

Vote YES on 35: Stop Human Trafficking in California. 2012. "What Is Human Trafficking?" http://www.caseact.org/learn/humantrafficking.

White House. 2010. "Presidential Proclamation—National Slavery and Human Trafficking Prevention Month." January 4. http://www.whitehouse.gov/the-press-office/presidential-proclamation-national-slavery-and-human-trafficking-prevention-month.

WITI-TV. 2012 "Update: Couple That Kept Modern-day Slave for 19 Years Deported." WMTV, June 15. http://www.nbc15.com/news/headlines/30109444.html.

IDENTITY THEFT

Identity theft is misusing a person's identity by a person who assumes the other person's identity in order to access resources, to obtain financial advantage, and to commit fraud. Identity theft also occurs when a person uses another's identifying information without permission with the intent to impersonate the other individual.

Identity theft may occur through lost and stolen documents that are taken from the person. It also occurs through online methods. Many people keep personal information stored in their computer system to enable them to use online resources, including bill payment methods. Personal information includes Social Security numbers, personal birth date statistics, and financial account PINs. When computer hackers illegally enter a computer and obtain this information, they are able to assume that person's identity. This enables the thief to drain financial accounts, access credit cards, and spend the victim's money, causing the victim excessive financial damages and even bankruptcy.

In 2008, almost 10 million people in the United States were victims of this crime. The U.S. Department of Justice states that, in 2010, 7 percent of all U.S. households had at least one member of the family, 12 years or older, who had been a victim of some sort of identity theft. In the years 2005 to 2010, 64.1 percent of the fraud cases involved credit cards.

The adverse consequences that victims of identity theft suffer include monetary damage, impaired credit, and even accusations of committing a crime. To recover from the effects of identity theft takes time. A victim takes between 55 to 130 hours to resolve the damage done. Most work with police to resolve the problem, but approximately 30 percent of the victims fail to notify the police.

In 2012, identity fraud incidents increased by more than 1 million victims over 2011 to 12.6 million and with a cost of more than $21 billion, the highest amount since 2009. The 12.6 million victims mean one victim every three seconds. Nearly one in four data breach letter recipients became a victim of identity fraud, with breaches involving Social Security numbers the most damaging.

Common targets of identity theft are deceased people, whose identities are stolen on average of 2,000 identities a day. Social media site studies exposed that people are revealing too much personal information in their social pages. Medical identity theft is also rising, but records were not kept prior to 1992. The crime involving medical records is most often committed by health care officials.

State laws on identity theft vary in financial penalties and prison sentences. A conviction for identity theft in Florida can result in 5 to 10 years in prison, depending on the amount of money and victims involved in the crime. The crime in Illinois is typically categorized as a Class 2 felony and is punishable by 3 to 7 years in prison and up to a $25,000 fine.

Federal courts are hearing cases on setting limits on identity theft charges. A case pertaining to illegal immigrants in Iowa who used fake Social Security numbers was overturned by the U.S. Supreme Court. The explanation was that no one can be charged with identity theft if he or she does not knowingly use the stolen identity. This ruling may have large-scale consequences for identity theft rings, which often use runners to cash fake checks because the runners may be able to say they were unaware of the falseness of the documents.

As a result of the increasing number of identity theft cases, the Identity Theft and Assumption Act was amended in 2004 with the Identity Theft Penalty Enhancement Act. This act makes the unauthorized transfer, possession, or use of a means of identifying another person a violation of federal law.

Courts are increasing penalties by adding other crimes to the identity theft crime: crimes involving the use of the mail service, terrorism activities, or physical assault in robbery cases. Companies are responding more quickly when identity theft is discovered, which means a consumer's information is being misused for fewer days than ever before, and the mean cost per victim has been flattening.

Victims must be proactive about stopping identity thieves. A theft should be reported to the police immediately, and assistance should be provided to law enforcement as they prosecute the crime. To prevent identity theft, people must be aware of their surroundings when they provide private information at ATMs and over the phone. In a restaurant that has the customer pay at the table, caution must be observed. Permitting the staff to leave the table with a bank card can result in excess charges if the wait staff is so inclined.

Connie Kerns-Grams

See also: Internet Abuse; Internet Fraud.

Further Reading

Brown, G. W., and P. A. Sukys. 2009. *Business Law*. New York: McGraw-Hill/Irwin.

Culina, Matt. 2012. "9 Alarming Statistics about Identity Theft." *Identity Theft* (blog), May 10. http://www.idt911blog.com/2012/05/9-alarming-statistics-about-identity-theft.

Jorgensen, A. n.d. "What Are the Consequences for Identity Theft?" eHow. http://www.ehow.com/about_5068247_consequences-identity-theft.html.

IMMIGRANTS

Immigrant abuse occurs when a person is harmed physically, psychologically, emotionally, financially, or dies as a result of coming to the United States. The abuse occurs to individuals who do not have legal status to remain in the United States. Immigrants who currently are not legally in the United States are those who are undocumented, have expired visas, are asylum seekers, and are children who came with the undocumented.

The abuse of unauthorized immigrants occurs

- In the process of coming to the United States
- In employment
- In domestic relationships
- In arrest and deportation

The process of coming to the United States is difficult and, for some, deadly. The undocumented person encounters dangers when traveling from his or her home country to the United States and after entering the United States. Crossing the border into the United States is dangerous and even deadly for immigrants. In fiscal year 2013 year that ended on September 30, there were 463 deaths, the equivalent of about five migrants dying every four days, according to the Washington Office on Latin America, a human rights group. In the time federal statistics have been compiled, only 2005 had more deaths, and in that year, there were more than three times as many apprehensions. In 2012, the U.S. Border Patrol found the remains of 463 migrants, of which 177 were discovered along the section of the border near Tucson, Arizona, and 150 migrant remains were found in the Rio Grande Valley of South Texas.

The financial cost of coming to the United States is high if the entry is assisted by human traffickers. Persons who smuggle people illegally across borders are called *coyotes*. Coyote fees range from $4,000 to $75,000, depending on the country of origin and mode of travel. Unauthorized Mexican immigrants usually pay $4,000 to cross the border on foot or $9,000 by boat, and there are an estimated 6.6 million of them living in the United States as of 2010. The smuggling fee for unauthorized Central American immigrants is currently between $7,000 and $10,000. The smuggling fee for an unauthorized Chinese immigrant is about $75,000.

Reasons that immigrants come to the United States include to join relatives who are already here, to escape danger in their home country, and to seek employment.

The recent surge in children immigrants has put pressure on the immigration system. In fiscal year 2013, 38,833 unaccompanied minors were apprehended by the border patrol. Until, or if, they are to be deported, the law mandates that the children be physically cared for, health care provided, and a deportation hearing scheduled. Many of these children are coming to help a family back home living in poverty or are trying to reunite with a parent or relative who left years ago. Still others leave their home as a result of child abuse, domestic violence, or gangs. According to a report from the United Nations High Commissioner for Refugees, 58 percent of the 400 youth the agency interviewed had suffered, been threatened, or feared serious harm.

Adult immigrants come to seek employment. For undocumented workers, the situation is particularly oppressive. Theoretically, they have the same legal protections in the workplace as documented workers. Yet unscrupulous employers use their immigration status against them, threatening to have them deported if they object to wage theft or working conditions. The situation facing Latino immigrants is reflected in the Southern Poverty Law Center (SPLC) survey responses:

- Forty-one percent of those surveyed had experienced wage theft, where they were not paid for work performed. In New Orleans, 80 percent reported wage theft.
- Most people surveyed (about 80%) had no idea how to contact government enforcement agencies, such as the Department of Labor. Many respondents did not know such agencies even exist.
- Thirty-two percent of Latinos surveyed reported on-the-job injuries.
- Among those injured on the job, only 37 percent reported that they received appropriate treatment.
- The remainder of the Latinos who said they suffered on-the-job injuries reported that they were not paid for their lost wages, they did not receive medical care, and/or they were fired because they were injured.
- In domestic relationships, a person's immigrant status may be used by abusive partners. Futures Without Violence and Casa de Esperanza report that abusive partners use tactics to abuse immigrant victims, including:
- Isolation. The victim is prevented from learning English or communicating with friends, family, or others from their home countries.
- Threats. Deportation or withdrawal of petitions for legal status is threatened.
- Intimidation. Legal documents or papers needed in this country, such as passports, resident cards, health insurance, or driver's licenses is destroyed.
- Manipulation Regarding Citizenship or Residency. Papers for residency are withdrawn or not filed. Telling untruthfully the victims they will lose their citizenship or residency if they report the violence.
- Economic Abuse Getting the victim fired from their job or calling employers and falsely reporting that the victim is undocumented.
- Children Threatening to hurt children or take them away if the police are contacted.

The federal agencies responsible for enforcing immigration laws are in the Department of Homeland Security (DHS). The agencies are

- Customs and Border Protection (CBP) oversees the entry of all people and goods at all ports of entry and enforces laws against illegal entry between the ports.
- Immigration and Customs Enforcement (ICE) is responsible for enforcement of immigration and customs requirements in the interior of the United States, including employer requirements, detention, and removals.
- U.S. Citizenship and Immigration Services (USCIS) adjudicates immigrant benefit applications, such as visa petitions, naturalization applications, and asylum and refugee requests, and administers the E-Verify program.
- An additional new post-9/11 immigration entity has been US-VISIT, which is housed in the National Protection and Programs Directorate (NPPD) of DHS. It manages the IDENT biometric fingerprint information system used by all immigration agencies—including consulates abroad in visa screening—to confirm the identity of noncitizens entering the country.

Arrest and deportation are two events that have the unauthorized immigrant most concerned. ICE's role in the immigration enforcement system is focused on two primary missions: (1) the identification and apprehension of criminal aliens and other removable individuals located in the United States and (2) the detention and removal of those individuals apprehended in the interior of the United States as well as those apprehended by CBP officers and agents patrolling our nation's borders.

In executing these responsibilities, ICE has prioritized its limited resources on the identification and removal of criminal aliens and those apprehended at the border while attempting to unlawfully enter the United States. This report provides an overview of ICE's fiscal year 2013 civil immigration enforcement and removal operations:

- ICE conducted a total of 368,644 removals.
- ICE conducted 133,551 removals of individuals apprehended in the interior of the United States; 82 percent of all interior removals had been previously convicted of a crime.
- ICE conducted 235,093 removals of individuals apprehended along our borders while attempting to unlawfully enter the United States.
- Of all ICE removals, 59 percent, a total of 216,810, had been previously convicted of a crime. ICE apprehended and removed 110,115 criminals from the interior of the United States. ICE removed 106,695 criminals apprehended at the border while attempting to unlawfully enter the United States.
- Of all ICE removals, 98 percent, a total of 360,313, met one or more of ICE's stated civil immigration enforcement priorities.
- Of the 151,834 removals of individuals without a criminal conviction, 84 percent, or 128,398, were apprehended at the border while attempting to unlawfully enter the United States, and 95 percent fell within one of ICE's stated immigration enforcement priorities.
- The leading countries of origin for those removed were Mexico, Guatemala, Honduras, and El Salvador.

The unauthorized immigrant, whether child or adult, has obstacles to face when coming to, and being in, the United States. One solution is to enact the bipartisan immigration reform bill that has passed the U.S. Senate but has not been voted on by the U.S. House of Representatives. Until then, the current laws must be enforced in a manner that is fair to the immigrants and upholds the values of American society.

Rosemarie Skaine

See also: Domestic Abuse, Immigrants and; Domestic Abuse, Poverty and; Human Trafficking; Sex Trafficking; Slavery, Modern-day.

Further Reading

Gordon, Ian. 2014. "70,000 Kids Will Show Up Alone at Our Border This Year. What Happens to Them?" *Mother Jones*, July–August. http://www.motherjones.com/politics/2014/06/child-migrants-surge-unaccompanied-central-america.

Hipsman, Faye, and Doris Meissner. 2013. "Immigration in the United States: New Economic, Social, Political Landscapes with Legislative Reform on the Horizon." Migration Policy Institute. http://www.migrationpolicy.org/article/immigration-united-states-new-economic-social-political-landscapes-legislative-reform.

The National Domestic Violence Hotline. n.d. "Immigrants in the US Have the Right to Live Life Free of Abuse." http://www.thehotline.org/is-this-abuse/abuse-and-immigrants.

Open Borders. n.d. "Coyote Fees." http://openborders.info/coyote-fees.

Santos, Fernanda, and Rebekah Zemansky. 2013. "Arizona Desert Swallows Migrants on Riskier Paths." *New York Times*, May 20. http://www.nytimes.com/2013/05/21/us/immigrant-death-rate-rises-on-illegal-crossings.html?pagewanted=all.

Southern Poverty Law Center. 2014. "Worker Abuse: Latino Workers in South Face Rampant Abuse." *Publications*. http://www.splcenter.org/publications/under-siege-life-low-income-latinos-south/1-worker-abuse.

U.S. Committee for Refugees and Immigrants. n.d. "Immigrant Children." http://www.refugees.org/our-work/child-migrants.

U.S. Immigration and Customs Enforcement. n.d. "Overview." *FY 2013 ICE Immigration Removals*. U.S. Department of Homeland Security. https://www.ice.gov/removal-statistics.

Workplace Fairness. 2014. "Hidden America: Undocumented Workers." http://www.workplacefairness.org/sc/undocumentedworkers.php.

INCEST

Incest is sexual intercourse between persons who are so closely related that they are forbidden by law to marry. It is also a statutory crime of such a relationship. Incestuous relationships include parents (and stepparents, in some cases) with their children, siblings with siblings, and uncles and aunts with nieces and nephews. Incest also includes the following behaviors: oral-genital contact, genital or anal penetration, genital touching, any other touching of private body parts, sexual kissing and hugging; staring sexually, accidental or disguised touching of the victim's body, verbal invitations to engage in sexual activity, verbal ridicule of body parts, pornographic photography, reading of sexually explicit material, and exposure to inappropriate sexual activity.

Estimates of the number of incestuous relationships vary because the taboos that surround incest make the number difficult to determine. In 2010, Health and Human Services reported that about one in three to one in four girls, and one in five to one in seven boys, are sexually abused by age 18, with an overwhelming number of incidences occurring within the family. The New York City Alliance against Sexual Assault reported that over 10 million Americans have been victims of incest and that 43 percent of the children who are abused are abused by family members, 33 percent are abused by someone they know, and 24 percent are sexually abused by strangers.

Families may attempt to hide the relationship, and physicians may not acknowledge evidence that the sexual acts had occurred. Children usually do not report their abuser because of their loyalty to the abuser or out of fear of reprisal for themselves or for family members. In addition, sexual behavior between siblings may be considered normal experimentation. Most cases that are reported to police involve incest between a father (or stepfather) and his daughter. Of cases not reported to the police, brother-sister incest is the most common. Incestuous activity usually occurs in the child's home. The child is usually enticed rather than forced. Most reported cases involve teenagers, but the age of children abused ranges from several months to adulthood.

Role confusion is a product of incest. A daughter having sex with her father holds power because of the secret she controls. Other siblings may be jealous of their father's preferential treatment of her. The mother may become her rival. The father sometimes behaves as a father and at other times as a lover, causing role confusion for the daughter. When the daughter is older, she may report the abuse, run away, or the incest may be discovered through an unwanted pregnancy. The mother may choose to remain silent because, if she reports the case, the entire family is affected. The daughter may feel that she is being blamed or if legal procedures are instituted, she may be embarrassed or humiliated. In the long run, the daughter may experience, low self-esteem, guilt, depression, or fear. She may develop eating disorders or PTSD, which includes amnesia, nightmares, and flashbacks. When she is older, she may have difficulty trusting. If she runs away, she may adopt self-destructive behaviors that include suicide, substance abuse, sexual promiscuity, and prostitution.

Incestuous families are characterized by secrecy, deception, isolation, and worthlessness. As a result, developing openness, honesty, support, and worthiness needs to be part of the healing process. At first, abusers, and sometimes other family members, deny the abuse. They may claim that society and the criminal justice system is overreacting to the abuse. They may maintain that the child liked the behavior, never objected, was already sexually active, and therefore, was not harmed.

Initial treatment should protect society from the offender and the offender from abusing again. Often this involves criminal charges and prison sentences. The criminal offense varies from state to state. In addition, the perpetrator and family members are evaluated for other problems, such as substance abuse, domestic violence, and psychiatric disorders.

Treatment should include careful assessments and detailed treatment plans that are directive, cautious, and comprehensive, with measurable and attainable goals and objectives. Treatment should work to change harmful behaviors while preserving the family and without risking the child's safety. Treatment methods include individual, family, or group therapy for all involved: for the offender, the victim, and the other family members. Family therapy should promote the recovery of all family members, with the focus on family safety.

Rosemarie Skaine

See also: Child Abuse, Sexual; Rape; Sexual Slavery.

Further Reading

Fontaine, Mia. 2013. "America Has an Incest Problem." *Atlantic*, January 24. http://www.theatlantic.com/national/archive/2013/01/america-has-an-incest-problem/272459.

Gilgun, Jane F. 2011. "Family Incest Treatment." *Child Sexual Abuse: From Harsh Realities to Hope*. Bukisa. http://www.bukisa.com/articles/45826_family-incest-treatment.

NetIndustries. n.d. "Incest—Treatment." http://family.jrank.org/pages/849/Incest-Treatment.html.

New York City Alliance against Sexual Assault. 1997. "Factsheets: Incest." http://www.svfreenyc.org/survivors_factsheet_37.html.

U.S. Health and Human Services. n.d. "Data Source CM2010 Table 5–5 Perpetrators by Relationship to Victims, 2010." http://www.acf.hhs.gov/sites/default/files/cb/data_source_cm2010_table5_5.xlsx.

Zastr, Charles. 2009. *Introduction to Social Work and Social Welfare: Empowering People*. Stamford, CT: Cengage Learning.

INDIAN CHILD WELFARE ACT

The Indian Child Welfare Act of 1978 (ICWA), Public Law 95-608, mandates that state courts act to preserve the unity of Native American families by granting preference for out-of-home placements first to extended families, then to foster families in the child's own tribe, and finally to foster families of another tribe. The law regulates how states handle child abuse and neglect and adoption cases involving Native American children. ICWA permits tribal courts to request that a child's case be transferred from the state court to the tribal court.

The Indian Child Welfare Act of 1978 was passed in response to concerns about the large number of Indian children who were being removed from their families and tribes and the failure of states to recognize the culture and tribal relations of Indian people. ICWA establishes procedural protections and imposes standards on the removal, placement, termination of parental rights, and consent to adoption of children who are members of or are eligible for membership in an Indian tribe.

The requirement in section 475 (5)(E) of the act applies to Indian tribal children as it applies to any other child under the placement and care responsibility of a state or tribal agency receiving title IV-B or IV-E funds. If an Indian tribe that receives title IV-B or IV-E funds has placement and care responsibility for an Indian child, the Indian tribe must file a petition to terminate parental rights (TPR) or, if appropriate, document the reason for an exception to the requirement in the case plan, on a case-by-case basis.

Rosemarie Skaine

See also: Adopted Children; Adopted Children, International; Child Abuse, Physical and Emotional; Child and Family Services Improvement Acts; Intercountry Adoption Act; Racism.

Further Reading

Administration for Children and Families. 2013. "9. Tribes/Indian Tribal Organizations." *Child Welfare Policy Manual*, September 15. U.S. Department of Health and Human Services. www.acf.hhs.gov/cwpm/programs/cb/laws_policies/laws/cwpm/policy_dsp_pf.jsp?id=9.

Administration for Children and Families. 1995. "Program Instruction." U.S. Department of Health and Human Services, Administration for Children, Youth and Families. www.acf.hhs.gov/sites/default/files/cb/pi9512.pdf.

Administration for Native Americans. 2012. "Social Development Resources." Administration for Children and Families, U.S. Department of Health and Human Services. www.acf.hhs.gov/programs/ana/resource/social-development-resources.

James Bell Associates, Inc. 2004. "Analysis of Funding Resources and Strategies among American Indian Tribes: Findings from the Study of the Implementation of the Promoting Safe and Stable Families (PSSF) Program by American Indian Tribes." Arlington, VA: James Bell Associates, Inc. www.acf.hhs.gov/sites/default/files/opre/fund_res.pdf.

McCarthy, Jan, Anita Marshall, Julie Collins, Girlyn Arganza, Kathy Deserly, and Juanita Milon. 2003. "Relevant Federal Laws/Policies." *A Family's Guide to the Child Welfare System*, 111–116. http://www.nicwa.org/indian_child_welfare_act/familyguide.pdf.

INTERCOUNTRY ADOPTION ACT

The Intercountry Adoption Act of 2000 amends title IV-B, section 422(b)(12). The act's purpose is to protect the rights of children and families involved in intercountry adoption and to regulate the practices of adoption agencies in the best interests of children. To achieve this purpose, the act requires that the placement practices and records of an adoption agency be fully disclosed to prospective adoptive parents. Thus, adoption agencies and states are required to submit certain information on overseas adoptions that are unsuccessful.

Specifically, section 422(b)(12) requires that states collect and report certain information on children who enter foster care because the adoption placement disrupted or the adoption dissolved. The state must report certain aspects, including: the specific agency that handled the placement, reasons for the disruption or dissolution, and plans for the child in its Annual Progress and Services Report.

States must also report a child who came to the United States for the purpose of adoption but entered foster care prior to the finalization of the adoption, regardless of the reason for the foster care placement as a disruption. These disruptions usually happen after a child enters the United States under the guardianship of the prospective adoptive parents or an adoption agency with an IR-4 visa to complete the adoption process domestically. States must report disruptions, even if the child's plan is reunification with the prospective adoptive parents and the stay in foster care is brief.

States must report a child who was formerly adopted from overseas, whether the full and final adoption took place in the foreign country or domestically, but entered foster care as a result of a court's terminating the parents' rights or the parents' relinquishing their rights to the child as a dissolution.

States must also report to the Administration on Children and Families children adopted from overseas who are already in foster care at the time that the adoption is dissolved because a child's legal relationship with his or her parents may not be severed until after the child enters foster care. A state is not required to report a child who enters foster care after a finalized adoption if the parents' legal rights to the child remain unharmed. In conclusion, the state is required to report only those children who enter foster care as defined in 45 CFR 1355.20 as a result of a disruption or dissolution.

Rosemarie Skaine

See also: Adopted Children; Adopted Children, International; Adoption Agencies, Abuse in; Racism.

Further Reading

Intercountry Adoption Act of 2000. 2000. (P. L. 106-279)—Section 205; 45 CFR 1355.20. http://www.gpo.gov/fdsys/pkg/PLAW-106publ279/pdf/PLAW-106publ279.pdf.

Intercountry Adoption Act of 2000. 2000. (P. L. 106-279). "Overview." Children's Bureau, Administration for Children and Families, U.S. Department of Health and Human Services. https://www.childwelfare.gov/systemwide/laws_policies/federal/index. cfm?event=federalLegislation.viewLegis&id=51.

7.3 TITLE IV-B, Programmatic Requirements. 2004. "4. Can You Clarify Which Children Must Be Included in the State's Report to ACF on Overseas Adoption Disruptions and Dissolutions under Section 422(B)(12) of the Social Security Act?" *Child Welfare Policy Manual*. Children's Bureau, Administration for Children and Families, U.S. Department of Health and Human Services. http://www.acf.hhs.gov/cwpm/programs/cb/laws_policies/laws/cwpm/questDetail.jsp?QAId=1200.

INTERETHNIC PROVISIONS OF 1996

The Interethnic Provisions of 1996 amends the Multiethnic Placement Act (MEPA). Major provisions include: the creation of the Title IV-E State Plan requirement that states and other entities that receive funds from the federal government and are involved in foster care or adoption placements may not deny any person the chance to become a foster or adoptive parent based upon the race, color, or national origin of the parent or the child or delay or deny a child's foster care or adoptive placement based upon the race, color, or national origin of the parent or the child. It also established a system of financial penalties for states that do not comply with the Title IV-E State Plan.

The provisions strengthened the Multiethnic Placement Act's recruitment requirement by making it a Title IV-B State Plan requirement and repealed language in MEPA that allowed states and other entities to consider the cultural, ethnic, or racial background of a child in addition to the capability of the prospective parent to meet the needs of the child.

Examples of activities not allowed under MEPA include: establishing time periods when only a same race or ethnicity search will take place; establishing orders of placement preferences based on race, culture, or ethnicity; requiring caseworkers to justify transracial placements; or otherwise have the effect of delaying placements, either before or after termination of parental rights, in order to find a family of a particular race, culture, or ethnicity. In addition, any other rule, policy, or practice that is unconstitutional.

The underlying philosophy of MEPA is that delayed placements harm children. The act focuses on the possibility that policies of matching children with families of the same race, culture, or ethnicity may result in delaying, or even preventing, the adoption of children by qualified families. It also ensures that every effort is made to develop a large and diverse pool of potential foster and adoptive families so that all children can be quickly placed.

Since the U.S. Constitution and Title VI of the Civil Rights Act of 1964 prohibit decision making on the basis of race or ethnicity unless the consideration advances a compelling governmental interest, which is, in this context, protecting the best interests of the child, an adoption agency may consider race only if it determines that the consideration of race in order to advance the best interests of a specific child.

Rosemarie Skaine

See also: Adopted Children; Child Abandonment and Neglect; Child Abuse, Treatment for; Child and Family Services Improvement Acts.

Further Reading

Children's Bureau. n.d. "What Are Examples of Some Impermissible Activities under the Multiethnic Placement Act (MEPA)?" Administration for Children and Families, U.S. Department of Health and Human Services. http://www.acf.hhs.gov/cwpm/programs/cb/laws_policies/laws/cwpm/policy_dsp.jsp?citID=171#629.

Interethnic Provisions of 1996. 1996. P.L. 104-188. "Overview." H.R. 3448. Enacted as Title I, subtitle H, section 1808, *Removal of Barriers to Interethnic Adoption*, of the Small Business Job Protection Act of 1996. Children's Bureau, Administration for Children and Families, U.S. Department of Health and Human Services. https://www.childwelfare.gov/systemwide/laws_policies/federal/index.cfm?event=federalLegislation.viewLegis&id=47.

INTERMITTENT EXPLOSIVE DISORDER

Intermittent explosive disorder (IED) is a severe, chronic, commonly occurring disorder that begins early in life. IED entails repeated occurrences of impulsive, aggressive, violent, behavior, or angry verbal outbursts that are grossly out of proportion to the situation. Road rage, domestic abuse, throwing or breaking objects, or other temper tantrums are often instances of intermittent explosive disorder. IED is a severe, chronic, commonly occurring disorder that begins early in life.

People with IED may attack others and their possessions. They may label the episodes *spells* or *attacks* that are preceded by a sense of tension or arousal and followed by a sense of relief. Later, the individual may feel upset, remorseful, regretful, or embarrassed. IED is undertreated because those who have severe anger problems may not see it as a problem or seek help.

People who have three IED episodes within the space of one year were found to have a much more persistent and severe disorder, particularly if they attacked both people and property. They caused 3.5 times more property damage than other violent IED groups. The disorder affects nearly 4 percent of adults within any given year, 8.5–9 million Americans, and leads to a mean of 43 attacks over the course of a lifetime.

The National Institute of Health's National Institute of Mental Health has found intermittent explosive disorder affects 11.5–16 million (7.3%) Americans in their lifetimes. The study is based on data from the National Comorbidity Survey Replication, a nationally representative face-to-face household survey of 9,282 U.S. adults conducted in 2001–2003. The majority of cases occur between late adolescence and late twenties. Other findings include: 63.3 percent of adolescents reported lifetime anger attacks that involved destroying property, threatening others, or engaging in violence; 12 years was the mean age of IED onset; 6.5 percent of teens with 12-month IED were treated specifically for anger, although 37.8 percent received treatment for emotional problems in the year before the interview; and 52.5 out 100 IED-related injuries require medical attention.

The consequences of IED are reflected in Stephen Diamond's examples of mass shootings, of murderously violent behavior perpetrated by pathologically angry individuals, usually men, including the 1999 Columbine High School shooting in which 12 were killed and 24 injured; the 2007 Virginia Tech shooting that killed 32 and wounded 17 others; the 2009 shooting in North Carolina at a nursing home that killed seven elderly residents and a nurse because the shooter's estranged wife once worked there; and the 2009 Binghamton, New York, shooting by a 42-year-old gunman with a high-powered rifle killed 13 victims, critically wounded four, and took at least 41 people hostage before finally shooting himself.

IED may result in job loss, school suspension, divorce, difficulties with interpersonal relationships or other impairment in social or occupational areas, accidents such as in vehicles, hospitalization because of injuries from fights or accidents, financial problems, incarcerations, or other legal problems.

Personal attacks can also cause property damage or self-injury. The disorder begins in early teens, often preceding or predisposing for later depression, anxiety, and substance abuse disorders. Almost 82 percent of people with IED also had one of the other disorders, yet only 28.8 percent ever received treatment.

Specific symptoms of IED are: several discrete episodes of failure to resist aggressive impulses that result in serious assaultive acts or destruction of property; the degree of aggressiveness expressed during the episodes is grossly out of proportion to any precipitating psychosocial stressors; and the aggressive episodes are not better accounted for by another mental disorder (e.g., antisocial personality disorder, borderline personality disorder, a psychotic disorder, a manic episode, conduct disorder, or attention deficit/hyperactivity disorder) and are not due to the direct physiological effects of a substance (e.g., a drug of abuse, a medication) or a general medical condition (e.g., head trauma, Alzheimer's disease).

Aggressive behavior can occur in the context of many other mental disorders. A diagnosis of IED should be considered only after all other disorders that are associated with aggressive impulses or behaviors have been ruled out.

Early exposure to IED violence makes it more likely for children to show the same traits as they mature. A genetic component causing this disorder to be passed from parents to children is possible.

Intermittent explosive disorder is undertreated because those who have severe anger problems may not see it as a problem or seek help. Treating anger early might prevent some of the co-occurring disorders, such as depression or anxiety. Violence prevention programs in schools might also prevent some of the associated psychopathology. Treatment may involve medications and psychotherapy to help control aggressive impulses. Other forms of treatment involve behavioral modification, group counseling, anger management sessions, and relaxation techniques.

Rosemarie Skaine

See also: Anger; Anger Management; Cycle of Abuse; Road Rage.

Further Reading

Coccaro, Emil. 2013. "Intermittent Explosive Disorder in Adults: Treatment and Prognosis." UpToDate. www.uptodate.com/contents/intermittent-explosive-disorder-in-adults-treatment-and-prognosis.

Diamond, Stephen, 2009. "Anger Disorder: What It Is and What We Can Do about It." *Evil Deeds* (blog), April 3. *Psychology Today*. http://www.psychologytoday.com/blog/evil-deeds/200904/anger-disorder-what-it-is-and-what-we-can-do-about-it.

Harvard Medical School. 2012. "Uncontrollable Anger Prevalent among U.S. Youth: Almost Two-Thirds Have History of Anger Attacks." *ScienceDaily*, July 2. http://www.sciencedaily.com/releases/2012/07/120702210048.htm.

Mayo Clinic Staff. 2012. "Definition, Intermittent Explosive Disorder." Mayo Clinic. http://www.mayoclinic.org/diseases-conditions/intermittent-explosive-disorder/basics/definition/con-20024309.

National Institute of Mental Health. 2006. "Intermittent Explosive Disorder Affects up to 16 Million Americans." http://www.nimh.nih.gov/news/science-news/2006/intermittent-explosive-disorder-affects-up-to-16-million-americans.shtml.

PsychCentral Staff. n.d. "Intermittent Explosive Disorder Symptoms." PsychCentral. http://psychcentral.com/disorders/intermittent-explosive-disorder-symptoms.

Psychology Today. 2009. "Intermittent Explosive Disorder," November 21. http://www.psychologytoday.com/conditions/intermittent-explosive-disorder.

INTERNATIONAL CULTIC STUDIES ASSOCIATION

The International Cultic Studies Association (ICSA) is a global network concerned about psychological manipulation and abuse in cultic groups, alternative movements, and other environments. Kay Barney and concerned parents of the American Family Foundation (AFF) founded ICSA in 1979 as a tax-exempt organization that supports civil liberties and is not affiliated with any religious or commercial organizations. In 2004, the name was changed to the International Cultic Studies Association. ICSA's mission is to apply research and professional perspectives to help persons who have been harmed by psychological manipulation and cultic groups, educate the public, promote and conduct research, support helping professionals interested in cults, related groups, and psychological manipulation. ICSA's president, Steve K. D. Eichel, states that the dangers presented by high demand, manipulative cults will continue as long as people exist who are able and willing to exploit and abuse others.

Daniel Shaw, CSW, a nationally certified psychoanalyst in private practice in New York City, defines a cult as "a group that is led by a person who claims, explicitly or implicitly, to have reached human perfection; or, in the case of a religious cult, who claims unity with the divine; and therefore claims to be exempt from social or moral limitations or restrictions." Shaw goes on to say that without the cult leader, there is no cult.

In 1984, the Cult Awareness Network reported over 2,000 groups had made inquiries compared to the current listing of more than 4,000 groups. Most cultic groups are small, with about a few hundred members. Some have tens of thousands and formidable financial power. Surveys reveal the number of people who may have been involved in what they perceived to be cultic groups. In the 1994 research study that led to the development of the Group Psychological Abuse Scale, the average age of joining was 24.8 and average time in their groups was 6.70 years (308 subjects from 101 groups; 60% left on their own without outside, formal assistance; 13% had been deprogrammed; 17% exit counseled; 9% were turned out by their groups). According to ISCA Executive Director Dr. Michael D. Langone, if a lifetime (30 years) incidence of 2,500,000 people having belonged to cultic groups and an average length of stay of six years, an approximate estimate is about 500,000 people belong to cultic groups at any one time and approximately 85,000 go in and out of cultic groups each year.

A 2008 study surveyed 695 psychologists found that 13.1 percent had either their own personal experience or that of a family member with cults. Thirty-three percent reported that they had treated people who were or had been members of cultic groups.

Methodological problems limit the conclusions about the destructive influence of cults on participants. Limited evidence indicates that members appear reasonably well adjusted while a cult member. ICSA found no evidence that supports that cultic involvement promotes the adjustment of individuals after they leave the cult. Most studies reported that after leaving the cult, a significant proportion experienced clinically significant psychological symptoms and/or adjustment problems.

Healing approaches include methods for psychological therapy. A therapist should help former members bear their many losses, not the least of which is the loss of belief in the cult and its leader, help them bear guilt along with intense fears about their future. As they become better able to bear the pain, they can start to regain hope and belief in their own ability to go on. To assist in reaching these goals, the focus needs to be on developing a clear picture of the abuse and exploitation. An attempt to understand the extent to which he or she has been manipulated and controlled by the cult leader is necessary as is understanding the cultural and psychological factors and her or his own vulnerabilities. Then the work begins on making sense of it all.

Rosemarie Skaine

See also: Brainwashing and Mind Control; Satanic Rituals, Abuse in.

Further Reading

Chryssides, George D., and Margaret Z. Wilkins. 2006. *A Reader in New Religious Movements: Readings in the Study of New Religious Movements.* New York: Continuum International Publishing Group. http://books.google.com/books?id=HgFlebSZKLcC&pg=PA360#v=onepage&q&f=false.

Eichel, Steve. n.d. "Welcome to the International Cultic Studies Association (ICSA)." http://www.icsahome.com.

Langone, Michael D. n.d. "Prevalence." ICSA. http://icsahome.com/view_document1.asp?ID=245.

McKibben, Jodi Aronoff, Steven Jay Lynn, and Peter Malinoski. 2000. "Are Cultic Environments Psychologically Harmful?" *Clinical Psychology Review* 20 (1): 91–111. http://icsahome.com/view_document1.asp?ID=251.

Shaw, Daniel. n.d. "Traumatic Abuse in Cults: A Psychoanalytic Perspective." ICSA. http://icsahome.com/view_document1.asp?ID=250.

INTERNATIONAL JUSTICE MISSION

To raise awareness and rescue victims of forced labor slavery, sex trafficking, sexual exploitation, and other victims who are oppressed through various means of violence, is the mission of the International Justice Mission (IJM). A 501(c)(3) nonprofit human rights organization, the International Justice Mission was established in 1997 by Gary Haugen, a former lawyer for the United States Department of Justice civil rights division and former Director in Charge of the United Nations 1994 Rwanda genocide investigations. IJM headquarters are in Washington, D.C.; however, they have established and operate worldwide through field offices located in developing countries such as Cambodia, Guatemala, India, the Philippines, Kenya, Thailand, Uganda, Rwanda, Bolivia, Zambia, and Dominican Republic. In addition, IJM has partner offices in the United Kingdom, Canada, Germany, and the Netherlands, as well as casework alliance offices in Honduras and Ecuador.

The IJM has more than 500 staff members, including lawyers, social workers, and investigators. Ninety-five percent of the staff is nationals of the countries where IJM operate their field offices. IJM has four objectives:

- Victim relief involves close coordination with foreign governments and law enforcement agencies to securely and safely rescue oppressed victims.
- Perpetrator accountability involves bringing to justice those who violate human rights. Bringing perpetrators to justice serves as a preventative measure or deterrent for any future perpetrators and demonstrates that someone cares for those being oppressed.
- Survivor aftercare partners IJM aftercare staff with trusted local aftercare partners. The rescued victims are offered the needed therapy to cope with the difficult side effects of emotional stressors associated with being victims of oppression. Ultimately, victims can successfully rebuild their lives through services that provide them direct access to shelter, education, and labor opportunities that offer fair wages, which help victims successfully reintegrate into society.
- Structural transformation means IJM stands committed to preventing future abuse to those at risk of being victims of oppression by working closely with foreign law enforcement agencies and government agencies that will ultimately lead to strengthening their judicial systems.

On a day-to-day basis, through nongovernment organizations' (NGOs) referrals and daily casework, IJM is often informed about victims who are being oppressed through violent means. Most cases involve underage victims being held captive as sex slaves who are forced into prostitution in brothels and/or streets. Some cases involve victims or families that are sold into slavery and forced to work long hours without any compensation. IJM lawyers, investigators, and other staff, in conjunction with NGOs and local law enforcement agencies, investigate these cases of abuse and ultimately facilitate the rescue of victims of oppression and bring perpetrators to justice.

IJM recognizes that prosecuting cases of abuse through the legal system is a significant indicator in identifying where the justice system is lacking resources, is denying the basic human rights protection for victims and possible future victims of oppression, and exposing the corruption that plagues the overall justice system. Through partnership with NGOs and law enforcement agencies, IJM is able to transform the justice system by strengthening laws that are intended to protect the poor and victims of oppression.

Juan Carlos Hernandez and Karunya Jayasena

See also: Child Abuse, Sexual; Child Pornography; Child Trafficking; Human Trafficking; Sex Trafficking; Sexual Slavery; Slavery, Modern-day.

Further Reading

International Justice Mission. 2013 "GuideStar Exchange Charting Impact Report." http://www.guidestar.org/CIPdf.aspx?orgId=570607730.
International Justice Mission. 2012. "Who We Are." http://www.ijm.org/who-we-are.
Miller, Dallas K. n.d. "Haugen, Gary, Just Courage: God's Great Expedition for the Restless Christian." Review. http://www.phc.edu/UserFiles/File/_Other%20Projects/Global%20Journal/7-3/DallasMiller%20REVIEW%20of%20Haugen%20bk%20for%20vol%207%20no%203.pdf.

INTERNET ABUSE

Internet abuse is improper and often damaging use of the Internet. It includes

- Installing software designed to damage or negatively affect the operation of the computer. One type of software is malware. Malware includes computer viruses, worms, Trojan horses, ransomware, spyware, adware, and scareware.
- Using computers to stalk, bully, and intimidate individuals.
- Using the Internet to excess and includes becoming addicted to programs, such as video games, or spending large amounts of time on the Internet.

Computers are intentionally affected negatively by malicious software or malware. *Malware* is any software used to disrupt computer operation, gather sensitive information, or gain access to private computer systems. It can appear in the form of executable code, scripts, active content, and other software. Malware is a general term used to refer to a variety of forms of hostile or intrusive software. It includes computer viruses, worms, Trojan horses, ransomware, spyware, adware, scareware, and other malicious programs. Malware is often disguised as, or embedded in, nonmalicious files. As of 2011, the majority of active malware threats were worms or Trojans rather than viruses. In the legal codes of several U.S. states, malware is sometimes known as a *computer contaminant*.

The Internet is abused when individuals locate others to harass, stalk, bully, or intimidate. The Internet abuser may be known to the person or may be a stranger contacted in an online chat room. Adults often stalk children via the Internet. People with low self-esteem problems frequently use the Internet to gain control over someone and to fulfill their personal needs. Often an individual befriends someone only to find him or her being stalked or obsessed over by the person.

When an individual uses the Internet to excess in a way that use interferes with that person's daily life, it is considered Internet addiction disorder (IAD). Some activities associated with this disorder involve: online gambling, online shopping, reading, playing games, and Internet videos or movies. The disorder has been subdivided into subtypes by activity, such as excessive, overwhelming, or inappropriate use of the Internet. The American Medical Association and American Psychiatric Association have refrained from adding Internet addiction disorder as a formal diagnosis. Jerald J. Block, MD, Hilarie Cash, PhD, and Kim McDaniel, MA, stated that Internet addiction should be included as a formal diagnosis.

Diagnosing IAD is complicated because 86 percent of the subjects exhibited other diagnosable mental disorders. Scientists have discovered changes in the brain and intellectual abilities when people use the Internet excessively. These changes reflect increases in learning abilities for using computers more efficiently, but they impaired short-term memory and decision-making abilities, including ones that may contribute to the desire to stay online instead of being in the real world. Professionals can diagnose people with Internet abusive behaviors, determine the causes of the excessive behavior, and recommend the appropriate treatment plan.

Web sites have been formed to combat abuse. They address areas involving cyber law enforcement investigating child pornography, cyberstalking, cyberscams, and online fraud. The Network Abuse Clearinghouse is a database of addresses for reporting Internet abuse. Pirated Sites is a portal for sites pilfered, plundered, and otherwise not original. E-zines are published to assist with teaching online users about preventing and fighting all types of fraud, misinformation, and abuse directed at consumers. To prevent becoming a victim, a person must maintain personal privacy, reveal only neutral personal information, and pay attention to the frequency with which a person makes contact.

Connie Kerns-Grams

See also: Bullying, Child and Adolescent; Cyberstalking; Internet Victimization, Child; Telephone Harassment.

Further Reading

EDinformatics: Education for the Information Age. 1999. "Internet Abuse." http://www. edinformatics.com/internet/abuse.htm.

Greenfield, David. 2013. "Internet Abuse Test." The Center for Internet and Technology Addiction. http://virtual-addiction.com/internet-abuse-test.

Hartney, Elizabeth. 2014. "Five Types of Internet Abuse Used to Cyberbully." About Health. http://addictions.about.com/od/internetaddiction/tp/Five-Types-Of-Internet-Abuse-Used-To-Cyberbully.htm.

PCSHost. n.d. "Internet Abuse." http://www.pcshost.com/legal/internet.htm.

INTERNET FRAUD

Internet fraud is a process that occurs to someone who has been harmed financially in some way using the Internet. Internet fraud is a crime that takes many forms including: auction fraud, counterfeit cashier's check, credit card fraud, debt elimination, parcel courier email scheme, and employment or business opportunities. Other forms are: escrow services fraud, identity theft, Internet extortion, investment fraud, lotteries, Nigerian Letter or "419" fraud, phishing or spoofing, Ponzi/pyramidschemes, reshipping, spam, and third-party receiver of funds.

The 2011 Internet Crime Complaint Center (IC3) Internet Crime Report reveals the scope of online crime and IC3's battle against it. The most common victim complaints included FBI-related scams, identity theft, and advance fee fraud. IC3 received and processed more than 26,000 complaints per month. Based on victim complaints, the top five states were California (34,169), Florida (20,034), Texas (18,477), New York (15,056), and Ohio (12,661). Victims in California reported the highest dollar losses, with a total of $70.5 million. For victims reporting financial losses, the average was $4,187.

In 2012, the IC3 received 289,874 consumer complaints with an adjusted dollar loss of $525,441,110, which is an 8.3 percent increase in reported losses since 2011. Complaints that reported loss were 114,908. The median dollar loss for those reporting a loss was $600, and the average dollar loss overall was $1,813. The average dollar loss for those reporting a loss was $4,573. In recognition of this increase in complaints, the IC3 expanded its efforts to inform the general public about online scams by publishing several public service announcements and providing additional tips for Internet consumers.

Preventing Internet fraud involves constant vigilance to detect unsafe e-mails, public forums, and unmonitored electronic bulletin boards. Prior to performing an online financial transaction, it is important to verify site security. In addition, questioning the site security of all professional sites used in daily financial transactions would also assist with preventing Internet fraud.

A person who believes that Internet fraud has occurred can file a complaint with the Internet Crime Complaint Center, which is a partnership between the Federal Bureau of Investigation (FBI) and the National White Collar Crime Center (NW3C). The IC3 accepts online Internet crime complaints from either the actual victim or from a third party to the complainant.

Combating Internet fraud is part of the mission of the National White Collar Crime Center. The NW3C provides training, investigative support, and research to agencies and entities involved in the prevention, investigation, and prosecution of economic and high-tech crime. While NW3C has no investigative authority itself, its job is to help law enforcement agencies better understand and utilize tools to combat economic and high-tech crime. NW3C has other sections within its organization, including training (in computer crime, financial crime, and intelligence analysis), research, and investigative support services.

Each year, Internet fraud increases. Knowing what the kinds of fraud are and the means to report it and prosecute it are effective steps in reducing it.

Connie Kerns-Grams

See also: Identity Theft; Internet Abuse.

Further Reading

Federal Bureau of Investigation. n.d. "Internet Fraud." *Common Fraud Schemes*. http://www.fbi.gov/scams-safety/fraud/internet_fraud.

Hallman-Baker, P. 2008. *Dotcrime Manifesto: How to Stop Internet Crime*. Boston: Pearson Education, Inc.

Internet Crime Complaint Center. 2013. "2011 Internet Crime Report." http://www.ic3.gov/media/annualreport/2011_IC3Report.pdf.

Internet Crime Complaint Center. 2012. "2012 Internet Crime Report." http://www.ic3.
    gov/media/annualreport/2012_IC3Report.pdf.
Internet Crime Complaint Center (IC3). n.d. "Filing a Complaint with the IC3." http://
    www.ic3.gov/default.aspx.
Internet Crime Complaint Center (IC3). n.d. "Internet Crime Schemes." http://www.ic3.
    gov/crimeschemes.aspx.
Schneir, B., R. Hasan, and W. Yurcik. 2009. *Cyber Crime*. Edited by L. Gerdes. Farmington
    Hills, MI: Greenhaven Press.

INTERNET VICTIMIZATION, CHILD

Internet victimization is abuse of a child when personal information about a child is released against his or her will or without his or her knowledge and leads to the child's being subjected to criminal behavior. Web sites and chat rooms allow the predator to expose the child to pornography, making the potential victim more comfortable with sexually explicit material and activities. The morphing of photos allows the predator to show the potential victim that the activity is common and acceptable.

Obscene material featuring children is universally condemned and is, at a minimum, an invasion of their privacy. Unlike victimless crimes such as voluntary adult pornography or smoking marijuana, online distribution and consumption of child pornography harms society as much as does its creation because it financially supports children who are being hurt.

The victim is often enticed to meet the perpetrator in person. Meetings in person set the victim up to possibly be assaulted or kidnapped or entered into the world of sex trade.

Preteens and teens are the most sought after Internet victims. Most Internet predators are pedophiles. More than 95 percent are men. They use children and teens for sex. Predators impersonate a younger person of the appropriate sex determined by their personal victim preference. The message and meetings occur in private settings and/or on public chat rooms. Information is shared through typed data and video sharing. Three organized pedophile groups have the names of Pedo University, the Wonderland Club, and the Orchid Club.

In a 2001 study, the Crimes Against Children Research Center showed that 20 percent of young people got sex messages from strangers online. About 1 young person out of 33 met a predator online, which is 725,000 out of 24 million. In 2005, the U.S. Department of Justice said that 13 percent of young people online got a message asking for sex talk or sex.

Strategies used to stop Internet victimization include stings and monitored Web sites. Stings involve setting up a meeting with the potential predator and having law enforcement at the meeting place to arrest them. Stings are commonly used to catch predators before they have a chance to interact with an actual victim. Websites have been established to fight online predators. One such site is called Perverted-Justice.com or PeeJ. People monitor the site, watching for key words that predators use frequently. TeenSpot uses a computer program that monitors chats. It also focuses on the common phrases predators use. I-Safe is a Web site for Internet education. It teaches children and their parents how to spot predators and not become their next victim. A Canadian company named LiveWires Design made a CD-ROM game called *Missing* that teaches young people how to detect predators before they fall prey to one.

Thirty-six states have Internet laws that make it a crime to be a sex predator on the Internet. The main problem with combating Internet victimization is that the age of consent varies state by state. Some states allow sexual activities as young as 14, while other states are more restrictive with higher ages of 16 to 18.

Conventions, treaties, and covenants relevant to sexual exploitation include the United Nations Convention on the Rights of the Child, and the Optional Protocol to the United Nations Convention on the Rights of the Child. The United Nations Convention on the Rights of the Child was introduced in December of 1989 at the United Nations General Assembly. Its main goal is to protect children from sexual exploitation. Optional protocols adopted by the General Assembly in the early 2000s address the sale of children, child prostitution, and child pornography. Optional Protocol to the Convention on the Rights of the Child is an attempt to expand and enhance the provisions of the convention to address Internet victimization.

Connie Kerns-Grams

See also: Abduction, Child; Child Abuse, Sexual; Child Pornography; Child Trafficking; Pedophilia.

Further Reading

Allman, T. 2007. *Internet Predators*. Yankton, SD: Erickson Press.

Holtzman, D. H. 2006. *Privacy Lost: How Technology Is Endangering Your Privacy*. San Francisco: Jossey-Bass.

United Nations, Codification Division, Office of Legal Affairs. 1989. *Convention on the Rights of the Child*. Audiovisual Library of International Law. http://legal.un.org/avl/ha/crc/crc.html.

I-SAFE FOUNDATION

The i-SAFE Foundation was established in 1998 as a nonprofit foundation whose mission is to educate and empower youth to make their Internet experiences safe and responsible. Its programs are available in all 50 states, Washington, D.C., and in Department of Defense schools located across the world. The goal is to educate students on how to avoid dangerous, inappropriate, or unlawful online behavior. i-SAFE accomplishes this through K–12 curriculum and community outreach programs to parents, law enforcement, and community leaders. It says that it is the only Internet safety foundation to combine these elements.

Since its inception, i-SAFE has revolutionized the way the world looks at Internet safety education. In a time when students can explore the world and travel to the realms of our galaxy on the Internet, many do not know that if students are not aware, they can become entrapped in the harmful realms of the human behavior. People are now aware that true safety online is not found in software filters, rather

Teri Schroeder, left, and Dena Haritos Tsamitis show an example of the game MySecure-Cyberspace during a news conference at Carnegie Mellon University on April 14, 2005, in Pittsburgh. Schroeder's i-SAFE, a foundation focused on making students safe on the Internet, partnered with Carnegie Mellon's Information Networking Institute, of which Haritos Tsamitis is director, to develop the game environment where children and their families can learn the dangers of Internet viruses and cybercriminals. (AP Photo/Keith Srakocic)

it is found in education and community support. i-SAFE provides education and community support.

i-SAFE sets the standards for Internet safety education through the i-LEARN Online program and the i-Mentor Network. i-SAFE provides students with the critical thinking and decision making skills they need in order to recognize and avoid dangerous and/or unlawful online behavior.

i-LEARN Online and the i-Mentor Network are created as an on-demand system that permits the user to learn at her or his own pace for safe and responsible use of the Internet. The i-LEARN Online program and the i-Mentor Network bring the education to the user's computer through a set of online videos on Internet safety. The videos consist of the subjects everyone needs to know to be safe and responsible on the Internet. Program users are certified to teach the lesson to others after watching each video.

One program that i-SAFE provides is on cyberbullying. In the 2003–2004 school year, i-SAFE America surveyed students from across the country on what was then a new topic: cyberbullying. It provides cyberbullying statistics and tips for how to deal with it, and i-SAFE works with law enforcement across the country to foster cyber safe communities

The i-SAFE Foundation extends education beyond the classroom with community outreach. The i-SAFE Youth Empowerment team was created to help student mentors take the message of Internet safety to their peers, their family, and their community. The i-PARENT program was designed to help parents team up and bridge the digital divide that separates them and their kids. The i-SHIELD program brings together all divisions of law enforcement for one cause, cyber safety.

Rosemarie Skaine

See also: Cyberbullying, Child and Adolescent; Cyberstalking; Internet Victimization, Child.

Further Reading

i-SAFE Foundation. n.d. "About i-SAFE." http://www.isafe.org/about.

K

KEEPING CHILDREN AND FAMILIES SAFE ACT

The Keeping Children and Families Safe Act of 2003 (KCFSA) was enacted June 25, 2003. The main purpose was to amend and improve the Child Abuse Prevention and Treatment Act (CAPTA), the Adoption Opportunities Act, the Abandoned Infants Assistance Act, and the Family Violence Prevention and Services Act. The act allows states to intervene when parents are unable, or fail, to properly care for their children.

The KCFSA reauthorized CAPTA through fiscal year 2008 and expanded the research program along with an opportunity for the public to comment on research priorities. The act emphasized communications between child protective agencies and public health, mental health, and developmental disabilities agencies.

The act made changes to state plan eligibility requirements for CAPTA state grants, and it included:

- Policies addressing the needs of infants affected by prenatal drug exposure
- Advising requirements for explaining complaints and allegations made against the abuser
- Training for the legal duties of CPA officials
- Requirements for states to disclose confidential information to any federal, state, or local government entity needing such information

KCFSA contains provisions and procedures for referral of a child under age three who is involved in a substantiated case of child abuse or neglect to early intervention services. It provided for the implementation of programs that focused on the placement of older children, including reducing barriers to placing children for adoption across jurisdictional boundaries. A key provision involved amending the Abandoned Infants Assistance grants program to prohibit grants unless the applicant agrees to give priority to infants and young children who are infected with or exposed to the human immunodeficiency virus (HIV), have a life-threatening illness, or have been prenatally exposed to a dangerous drug.

Connie Kerns-Grams

See also: Child Abandonment and Neglect; Child Abuse, Treatment for; Child Abuse Prevention and Enforcement Acts.

Further Reading

National Association of Social Workers (NASW). 2003. "Keeping Children and Families Safe Act of 2003 (S. 342 and H.R. 14)." Government Relations Update. http://www.naswdc.org/advocacy/issues/letters/070103_abuse.asp.

Public Law 108-36—Keeping Children and Families Safe Act of 2003. U.S. Government Printing Office. http://www.gpo.gov/fdsys/pkg/PLAW-108publ36/content-detail.html.

U.S. Department of Health and Human Services, Administration for Children and Families. 2003. Keeping Children and Families Safe Act of 2003. https://www.childwelfare.gov/systemwide/laws_policies/federal/index.cfm?event=federalLegislation.viewLegis&id=45.

KLAAS, POLLY

On October 1, 1993, Polly Klaas, 12 years old, of Petaluma, California, was abducted, raped, and murdered by Richard Allen Davis, who had been convicted twice for kidnapping. Armed with a knife, Davis broke into Polly's home where she was having a slumber party. While Polly's mother was asleep, he tied up the three girls, placed pillowcases over their heads, and then took Polly. The citizens of Petaluma organized a search of approximately 1,000 volunteers. T-shirts and tapes were used to ask for news of Polly. Actress Winona Ryder, a Petaluma native, began a reward fund that grew to $200,000.

On November 28, 1993, a woman who had previously reported a trespasser found pieces of white cloth on her land. Police conversations with Davis led them to Cloverdale, where on December 3, 1993, they found Polly's body in a thicket just off Highway 101, near town. In 1996, Davis was tried and convicted of first-degree murder and four special circumstances, robbery, burglary, kidnapping, and a lewd act on a child. He was sentenced to death. As of 2013, Davis remained on death row at San Quentin State Prison, Marin County, California.

A poster about Polly Klaas is displayed at the Polly Klaas Foundation in Petaluma, California on August 18, 2006. Klaas is the 12-year-old girl who was abducted from her Petaluma home and murdered by Richard Allen Davis. (AP Photo/Paul Sakuma)

Polly's father, Marc, is an advocate for children and for laws to keep violent felons off the streets. Polly's death impacted California law in 1994 when the legislature passed the Three Strikes law, which was designed to keep repeat felony offenders in prison for life. In 1994, 15 new states had adopted a sex-offender registry, bringing the total to 40.

After Polly's death, Marc Klaas founded the nonprofit KlaasKids Foundation for Children. When he announced the formation of the foundation in September 1994, he said, "We can give meaning to Polly's death and create a legacy in her name that will be protective of children for generations to come by pursuing the singular mission of stopping crimes against children." The KlaasKids Foundation works to make crimes against children a high priority on the national and personal agendas. It forms and promotes partnerships with concerned citizens, the private sector, organizations, law enforcement, and legislators to achieve its mission.

A separate organization, the Polly Klaas Foundation, is a Petaluma-based national nonprofit dedicated to the safety of all children, the recovery of missing children, and public policies that keep children safe in their communities. It began with 10 full-time and 30 part-time volunteers, undertook searches for missing children, and helped to form a school-based child safety curriculum. It makes use of the Internet to send out images of missing children across the country. By 2013, it had helped approximately 8,500 families of missing children. It has also made and distributed posters of missing children. The foundation's hotline, (800) 587-4357, has been in effect since 1993.

Rosemarie Skaine

See also: Abduction, Child; Adam Walsh Child Protection and Safety Act; AMBER Alert; Child Abuse, Sexual; Rape.

Further Reading

Beck, Melinda, and Andrew Murr. 1993. "The Sad Case of Polly Klaas." *Newsweek* 122 (24).

Egelko, Bob. 2009. "Polly Klaas Confession Illegal, Lawyer Says." *San Francisco Chronicle*, March 4.

Gleick, Elizabeth, and Maria Eftimiades. 1994. "An Angel Named Polly." *People* 42 (22).

KlaasKids Foundation. 2013. http://www.klaaskids.org.

Payne, Paul. 2013. "State Supreme Court Denies Legal Claims by Polly Klaas' Killer." *Press Democrat*, Sonoma, CA, January 23. http://www.pressdemocrat.com/article/20130123/articles/130129795.

The Polly Klaas Foundation. n.d. "Polly's Story." http://www.pollyklaas.org/about/pollys-story.html.

San Francisco Chronicle. 2012. "A More Sensible '3 Strikes' Law," September 16.

Saunders, Debra J. 2009 "Richard Allen Davis: Safe on Death Row." *TownHall Magazine*, March 12. http://townhall.com/columnists/debrajsaunders/2009/03/12/richard_allen_davis_safe_on_death_row/page/full.

Stanford Three Strikes Project. 2013. "Three Strikes Basics." Stanford University. http://www.law.stanford.edu/organizations/programs-and-centers/stanford-three-strikes-project/three-strikes-basics.

M

MALESURVIVOR

The National Organization on Male Sexual Victimization formed in 1994 as a nonprofit organization that added to its name and is known by MaleSurvivor. Its mission statement reads, "We are committed to preventing, healing and eliminating all forms of sexual victimization of boys and men through treatment, research, education, advocacy and activism." Professionals, survivors, students, individuals, and organizations that have an interest in male sexual victimization may join the group. These members benefit from MaleSurvivor's extensive agenda, as listed on their Web site, http://www.malesurvivor.org/default.html: Find Support. Survivors, Parents, Professionals, Weekends of Recovery, Dare to Dream, Myths and Facts, About Us, Contact Us, Partners in Healing, International Resource Directory, and Partners in Healing.

MaleSurvivor believes that because not many know that significant numbers of males are sexually abused, male survivors have been unseen, neglected, and therefore underserved. When understanding is needed, men must confront profound misunderstandings in a culture that values invulnerability and denial of pain as essential qualities of masculinity. MaleSurvivor states that men simply are not allowed to admit that they have been sexually exploited and abused.

Two programs MaleSuvivor offers are: Weekends of Recovery and Dare to Dream. Weekends of Recovery began in 2001 to help members make further progress in their recovery. In addition, the weekends were designed to introduce additional tools men could use when they returned home to assist in making further progress in their recovery. The weekends are highly structured and professionally facilitated. The weekends are in addition to participants' ongoing recovery work with individual and/or group psychotherapy: twelve-step programs and individual spiritual work. Dare to Dream provides male survivors with a safe and comfortable environment to lift the veil of secrecy and shame from their experiences. It has featured clips from the *Oprah Winfrey Show* that emphasized male sexual abuse and featured MaleSurvivor spokesperson Dr. Howard Fradkin.

MaleSurvivor spoke to the work of healing as only just beginning after the 2012 sentencing of Jerry Sandusky, the former Penn State assistant football coach accused of child molestation. Sandusky will spend the rest of his life behind bars, but the repercussions of his actions as well as the inactions of all those who did not intervene will continue to impact the lives of the victims for years to come. According to MaleSurvivor, it takes 20 years or more for a male sexual abuse survivor to disclose the abuse to anyone and begin the healing process. The verdict and sentence represent only a fraction of the support the abused men will need in order to be able to continue the healing process.

MaleSurvivor has a dedicated emphasis on healing. Not only does it present avenues to the survivor, but extensive attention is given to professionals serving in the field. Professionals share knowledge through posting links to articles they have written and have access to a well-researched bibliography. Other partners in healing include: other survivors, parents, and organizations. MaleSurvivor provides avenues to the survivor to: find a therapist, join a discussion or chat, and peruse a resource directory.

Rosemarie Skaine

See also: Domestic Abuse; Men as Victims of Abuse.

Further Reading

MaleSurvivor (formerly National Organization on Male Sexual Victimization). 2014. National Sexual Violence Resource Center (NSVRC). http://www.nsvrc.org.
MaleSurvivor. 2007. "What Is MaleSurvivor?" http://www.malesurvivor.org/default.html.

MANDATORY ARREST LAWS

Under mandatory arrest laws, law enforcement officers who arrived at a scene and determined that domestic violence had occurred, or was occurring, were required to arrest the offending party. These laws were enacted in much of the country and were designed to provide protection for the victim while simultaneously serving social justice.

In the 1980s, feminist groups pushed law enforcement agencies across the nation to examine alternative approaches to domestic violence that would have a more significant and lasting impact on the problem than traditional hands-off practices, such as allowing the matter to be resolved in private or suggesting a cooling-off period. One such jurisdiction was Minneapolis, Minnesota. Known as the Minneapolis Domestic Violence Experiment (1981–1982), the project was intended to determine whether mandatory arrest policies were more effective than current practices in reducing the rates of repeat offending.

The experiment was a joint venture between the National Institute of Justice, the Minneapolis Police Department, and the Police Foundation, along with procedural recommendations by the psychological community to ensure the best possible response. The random assignment, or lottery, format required responding officers to apply one of three research interventions: removing the offender from the scene for eight hours, counseling the family on strategies for deescalating the situation, or actually arresting the offender. Follow-up interviews with victims were conducted by specially trained female interviewers to determine the extent to which they were satisfied by the intervention technique as well as what, if any, impact it had on continued violence in the relationship.

Experts concluded from the Minneapolis experiment, among others, that mandatory arrest policies were the most effective strategy for handling domestic violence situations because they simultaneously lowered the likelihood of repeat offenses and served to empower the victim by being attentive to her needs and sympathetic to her concerns for her safety and the safety of her nonoffending family members.

Since this experiment, many states have adopted mandatory arrest policies. Advocates claim that mandating the arrest of perpetrators protects the victim from further injury during the time immediately following the offense. By removing the victim from the decision-making process, a great deal of emotional distress is removed. The perpetrator may be less likely to blame the victim for his arrest and perhaps be less likely to increase violence toward her at a later time. Proponents also claim that, due to the trauma and oppression they have faced at the hands of the abuser, women are unable to make an informed decision because their confidence and feeling of control over their lives has been attacked and crippled.

Mandatory prosecution policies often go hand in hand with mandatory arrest. The motivation for such legislation is similar to the rationale of law enforcement interventions: to empower the victims by proving that the justice system does indeed recognize the danger they face and will protect them from the perpetrator through any means necessary. Prosecutors in jurisdictions with hard so-called no-drop policies are required to pursue charges against all those accused of domestic violence, regardless of the victim's wishes.

Many groups, including some victims' advocates and men's rights organizations, are upset with policies requiring the arrest of all those accused of domestic violence, claiming they are easily and often manipulated. While mandatory arrest laws have minimized the effect of police discretion on the outcome of a domestic violence situation, it is not uncommon for both partners to be arrested, whether they were the aggressor, acted in self-defense, or were wrongly accused. On-sight evidence need not be found to substantiate claims of abuse in many states, and policies that require that the cases be prosecuted have dealt a handicapping blow to the legal system because time and manpower are spent on cases with little or no evidence supporting the charges.

Another criticism of mandatory arrest laws is that there are other, arguably more serious, crimes for which police are not required to make an on-the-spot arrest. Also, mandatory arrest does not allow for consideration of the victims' wishes. For some, finding a way to come up with bond money for an unwanted arrest can be as damaging as the violence itself. Conversely, many women fear having their abuser arrested because of the threat of revenge upon his return to the home. As a result, they may choose not to report these crimes at all.

Courtney Blair Thornton

See also: Domestic Abuse; Domestic Abuse, Psychological Effects of.

Further Reading

Geffner, Robert A., and Alan Rosenbaum. 2002. *Domestic Violence Offenders: Current Interventions, Research, and Implications for Policies and Standards*. Binghamton, NY: The Haworth Press, Inc.

Han, Erin L. 2003. "Mandatory Arrest and No Drop Policies: Victim Empowerment in Domestic Violence Cases." *Boston College Third World Law Journal* 23 (1): 159–192.

Roberts, Albert R. 2002. *Handbook of Domestic Violence Intervention Strategies: Policies, Programs, and Legal Remedies*. New York: Oxford University Press.

MATTHEW SHEPARD AND JAMES BYRD, JR., HATE CRIMES PREVENTION ACT

The Matthew Shepard and James Byrd, Jr., Hate Crimes Prevention Act (2009) was named after two victims of hate crimes. The killing of Matthew Shepard was motivated by his homosexual orientation. James Byrd, Jr. died after he was dragged behind a pickup truck. His death was racially motivated.

The act was signed into law by President Barack Obama and expanded on the 1969 federal hate crime law to include acts motivated by racial, sexual, gender, religious, and ethnic bias. It also created a new federal criminal law that criminalizes willfully causing bodily injury, or attempting to do so with fire, firearm, or other dangerous weapon. The act provides funding and technical assistance to state, local, and tribal jurisdictions to help them more effectively investigate and prosecute hate crimes.

Hate crimes had been a growing concern. The FBI reported 7,755 hate crimes in 1998 and 7,624 in 2007, the most current year for which the FBI has compiled hate crime data. Over 77,000 hate crime incidents have been reported to the FBI, not counting crimes committed in 2008 and 2009. In 2009, U.S. attorney general Eric H. Holder, Jr. reported that the number of hate crime incidents per year was nearly unchanged. Almost one hate crime occurred every hour of every day over a decade. Approximately half of the hate crimes were racially motivated. Religiously motivated incidents accounted for the second-highest number of hate crimes, followed closely by sexual orientation bias incidents (12,372). Hate crimes against persons of Hispanic national origin have increased four years in a row.

Section 249(a)(2) of the law for the first time allows for federal prosecution of violence committed because of the actual or perceived gender, disability, sexual orientation, or gender identity of any person. In the past, these crimes fell outside federal jurisdiction. The Department of Justice can now prosecute and deter violent acts in these categories more effectively.

The ability of federal law enforcement is strengthened to combat bias-motivated violence in two ways. First, the act eliminates the current law requirement that prosecutors prove that a violent hate crime was motivated by a victim's participation in one of six enumerated federally protected activities. Second, the law expands coverage of protected categories beyond actual or perceived race, color, religion, or national origin to include gender, disability, sexual orientation, and gender identity.

Holder testified that not only do hate crimes victimize individuals, they also victimize entire communities. Perpetrators try to deny our shared humanity, regardless of the color of our skin, the God to whom we pray, or whom we choose to love. President Obama echoed Holder's philosophy when he commemorated the passage of the Hate Crimes Prevention Act. Obama said that the basis of this issue is not just about our laws but about who we are as a people, whether we value one another, and whether we embrace our differences, rather than allowing them to become a source of strong feelings of dislike or hostility.

Rosemarie Skaine

See also: Byrd, James, Jr.; Hate Crimes; Hate Speech; Homosexuals; Racism; Shepard, Matthew; Transgender Individuals.

President Barack Obama, right, leads an applause to the parents of Matthew Shepard, Dennis Shepard, left, and Judy Shepard, center, and James Byrd Jr.'s sisters, Louvon Harris, second left, and Betty Byrd Boatner, second right, during a White House reception commemorating the enactment of the Matthew Shepard and James Byrd Jr. Hate Crimes Prevention Act on October 28, 2009, in Washington. (AP Photo/Manuel Balce Ceneta)

Further Reading

Holder, Eric H., Jr. 2009. Testimony before the Committee on the Judiciary, United States Senate, June 25. Hearing, "The Matthew Shepard Hate Crimes Prevention Act of 2009." http://www.judiciary.senate.gov/pdf/06-25-09HolderTestimony.pdf.

Matthew Shepard and James Byrd, Jr., Hate Crimes Prevention Act of 2009. 18 U.S.C. § 249, enacted as Division E of the National Defense Authorization Act for Fiscal Year 2010. Section 249 of Title 18. http://www.justice.gov/crt/about/crm/matthewshepard.php.

Obama, Barack. 2009. "Remarks by the President at Reception Commemorating the Enactment of the Matthew Shepard and James Byrd, Jr., Hate Crimes Prevention Act," October 28. Office of the Press Secretary. The White House. http://www.whitehouse.gov/the-press-office/remarks-president-reception-commemorating-enactment-matthew-shepard-and-james-byrd-.

MEGAN'S LAW

Megan's Law is named for Megan Kanka. Megan was raped and murdered by a neighbor who was a convicted pedophile. Megan's Law (H.R. 2137) was passed by the U.S. Congress and signed into law by President Bill Clinton on May 17, 1996. The passage of Megan's Law was necessary to amend the Violent Crime Control and Law Enforcement Act of 1994 and the Jacob Wetterling Crimes Against Children and Sexually Violent Offender Registration Act of 1996, which established the Sex Offender Registry (SOR) program. Under Megan's Law, two important amendments were made to SOR. First, federal, state, and local law enforcement agencies were mandated to release private and personal information pertaining to registered sex offenders deemed necessary to protect the general public. Second, any relevant information pertaining to sex offenders collected under previous or current statutes regarding the protection of children must be made public. Under stringent conditions, upon their release from prison, convicted sex offenders must register with their local police departments.

In accordance with Megan's Law, federal, state, and local law enforcement agencies must notify the public and their communities, such as schools, day care centers, and summer camps, when violent sex offenders classified under Tier II or III are likely to reoffend, reside, or relocate within these communities. Prior to public disclosure of such notifications concerning Tier II or III offenders, a preliminary notice is served to the offender as he or she has the right to contest in court as to (1) how the above mentioned notification will be made, (2) period of time the notification will be made available to the public, and (3) petition the court to lower the classification assigned to the offender. Special Agent (SA) Scholle with the Iowa, Cedar Falls Department of Public Safety mentions that the most common form of notification conducted by police agencies is "passive notification," which means that law enforcement agencies utilize the Internet by posting or updating the local SOR as an efficient and justifiable means of notifying their communities. Also, SA Scholle mentions that only concerned citizens make the effort to visit SOR to keep tabs on offenders residing within their communities.

The private and personal information of sex offenders that is made available to the public under Megan's Law include name, date of birth, current address, employment information, physical description, visible markings (i.e., scars or tattoos), type of offense, risk level (i.e., Tier I, II, or III), and a photograph. In addition, biometric information and DNA (in some states) is collected during registration; however, this information is not made available to the public.

Megan's Law differs from state to state; for instance, each state has a set of general regulations that governs their version of Megan's Law. Under these regulations, each law enforcement agency has the right to restrict the type of information made available to the public. Although Megan's Law has been adopted differently across the nation, all states provide information deemed necessary to make the public aware of convicted sex offenders residing within their communities. Megan's Law made it possible for law enforcement agencies to collect and release vital information pertaining to sex offenders to the general public, which otherwise would have been withheld in accordance to privacy mandates.

Juan Carlos Hernandez

See also: Child Abuse, Sexual; Sex Addiction; Sex Offender.

Further Reading

H.R.2137-Megan's Law. 104th Congress (1995–1996). http://beta.congress.gov/bill/104th/house-bill/2137.

Irwin, Nancy, Niki Delson, Ron Kokish, and Thomas Tobin. 2004. "Using the Internet to Provide Passive Community Notification about Registered Sex Offenders: A Resource Paper Prepared for the California Coalition on Sexual Offending." http://ccoso.org/papers/InternetNotification.pdf.

National Institute of Justice. 2009. "About Megan's Law." Office of Justice Programs. http://www.nij.gov/topics/corrections/community/sex-offenders/about-megans-law.htm.

Pennsylvania State Police. n.d. "Megan's Law Website." http://www.pameganslaw.state.pa.us/Notification.aspx?dt=.

Ramsland, Katherine. n.d. "Child Sex Offenders, Megan's Law." Crime Library. http://www.trutv.com/library/crime/criminal_mind/sexual_assault/child_sex_offenders/4.html.

Scholle, Alan D. 2000. "Sex Offender Registration, Community Notification Laws." Federal Bureau of Investigations, Bulletin. http://leb.fbi.gov/2000-pdfs/leb-july-2000.

MEN AS VICTIMS OF ABUSE

Although women are typically viewed as the victims of abuse, men can also be victims of abuse. Males can be the targets of abuse, whether physical, emotional, verbal, or sexual. The damage may be temporary or permanent and may result in the man's death. Due to societal pressures, men may be less likely than women to report incidents of abuse.

In 1999, Sweden developed the NorVold Abuse Questionnaire to measure emotional abuse, physical abuse, sexual abuse, and abuse in health care for men and women. In 2011, their study revealed a high rate of abuse reported in health care, but supposed that men's victimization may be underreported. Their study found that physical abuse was the most frequently reported type of abuse in men. Out of 1,767 men, mild or moderate severity of lifetime abuse was most often reported: mild 286 (16.5%), moderate 396 (22.8%), and severe 113 (6.5%). Of 585 men, 113 (6.5%) reported severe physical abuse that included a death threat.

In 2008, the National Violence Against Women Survey conducted a population-based survey of male abuse. Out of 8,005 men, 66.4 percent reported physical assault as a child by an adult caretaker and/or as an adult by various types of perpetrators. Of surveyed women, 51.9 percent said they were physically assaulted. An estimated 1.9 million women and 3.2 million men are physically assaulted annually in the United States. In same-sex intimate partnerships, 11 percent of lesbians reported violence by their female partners, and 15 percent of gay men who had lived with a male partner reported being victimized by a male partner.

Victimization is as much an issue for men as it is for women, according to Sabrina N. Nowinski and Erica Bowen, Department of Psychology, Coventry University, United Kingdom. Men of certain ethnicities, Hispanic and Latin, are more at risk than others. Approximately 830,000 men a year are victims of domestic violence. Every 37.8 seconds, somewhere in America, a man is battered, according to the National Violence Against Women Survey.

Men with disabilities are less likely to be abused than women with disabilities, but most research is complicated by a reliance on Adult Protective Services abuse reporting that is based on information usually provided by someone other than the victim. Adult Protective Services that have mandatory abuse reporting for people who have cognitive disabilities suggested that men and women experience similar levels of abuse. The findings of Laurie E. Powers et al., Portland State University, suggested that, despite research obstacles, men with disabilities experience abuse at a concerning rate. Powers et al. conducted a study that revealed personal assistance providers (PAS) perpetrate many types of abuse against disabled men, with 12 percent being physical in nature.

Sixty-five percent of men reported physical lifetime abuse from anyone, while 55 percent had experienced physical abuse since the onset of a disability. Abuses reported included being handled roughly during care, such as bathing, transfers, dressing, and toileting; hitting, kicking, slapping, or otherwise physically hurting; being held or restrained against the patient's will; intentionally leaving the patient in dangerous situations; neglecting or ignoring physical needs; damaging or keeping from using equipment; and withholding or giving too much medication. The least reported abuse was the provider touching sexually or forcing unwanted sexual activity.

Heterosexual intimate partner physical and emotional abuse include: kicking, shoving, slapping, and choking of the male, his children, or his pets and assaults while asleep or when previously drinking or when he is not paying attention to make up for a difference in strength. Of approximately 4,000 domestic violence programs in the United States, few offer the same services to men as they do women. The effects of physical abuse against men include: physical injuries and death as well as psychological results. Psychological effects include feelings of: stress, anger, and emotional hurt; sadness or depression; revenge; a need to protect themselves; shame or fear; and feeling unloved or helpless.

Physical abuse of men also exists in society at large. In Houston, Texas, three elderly men, 80, 74, 65, and 50-plus years, were found living in filth in a converted garage. The men reported that they were enticed with promises of beer and cigarettes but were not allowed to leave and then forced to relinquish their veterans' benefits checks. Their quarters were secured with double locks. Furniture consisted of one chair. Absent was a toilet and beds.

Male emotional abuse occurs when emotions are manipulated by game playing, verbal abuse, physical abuse, outbursts of anger, or other methods of power and control, according to Joshua M. Gold and Gabriela V. Pitariu, Counselor Education Program, The University of South Carolina. It occurs when the dominant member negates, refutes, or minimizes the legitimacy of the other member's emotional experience.

Emotional abuse is not easy to recognize because so much communication that is considered normal and acceptable is, in reality, abusive. When a woman belittles her husband's dress in public and then states that he cannot take a joke, neither she nor he recognize it as abuse, but emotional abuse has been perpetuated.

Jessica L. Stanley et al., university psychology professors, reported that studies of physical abuse in same-sex couples indicated emotional abuse occurs at rates higher than physical abuse, for example, as high as 83 percent and 95 percent. Denise A. Hines and Kathleen Malley-Morrison, psychology faculty at Boston University, reported emotional abuse reflected in studies of high school and college students. Of 736 high school students, males experienced an average of 23.41 partner emotionally abusive acts from their partners. Two other studies found that college men also experience high rates of emotional abuse (90% and 82%). Most frequent types of emotional abuse experienced included jealousy (77%), withdrawal (77%), diminishing of self-esteem (63%), verbal abuse (60%), and social and emotional control (49%).

In 2000, the Canadian Centre for Justice Statistics reported almost equal proportions of men and women had been the victims of intimate partner physical (7% and 8%) and psychological abuse (18% and 19%). These findings were consistent with several earlier studies that found equal rates of abuse by women and men in intimate relationships. Almost all studies report that abuse of men is underreported, that emotional abuse is a precursor to physical abuse, and that a correlation exists between childhood and adult abuse.

According to *Psychology Today*, male emotional abuse happens every day. The effects are more harmful than violent outbursts because they occur frequently. There is a greater likelihood that victims will blame themselves. When someone hits a victim, it is viewed as the aggressor's fault, but if someone is telling another person they are bad, it is easier for the victim to blame himself. Gold and Pitariu reported other effects, such as feelings of emotional or physical abandonment, withdrawal, a sense of fear, isolation, degradation, rigid sex-role expectations, psychological destabilization, reaction to the withholding of emotional support, and contingent expressions of love.

Treatment is challenging. Definitions of emotional abuse are sometimes unclear, and a gender bias exists in counseling. Counselors need to expand their study to include masculinity. They must also have an awareness of specific emotions in male patients because they might not consider some emotions appropriate for men. Fragility in a male patient could be overlooked by a counselor who believes men are always stoic. Gold and Pitariu point out that this failure to notice is especially harmful when men profess to be a victim of emotional abuse by their spouses. The spouse does not perceive her behavior as abusive. When the counselor also does not legitimize the man's experience, the negation creates a covert alliance between the abusive spouse and the counselor.

Sexual abuse against men represents 10 percent of crimes related to sexual assault, sexual abuse, and rape. Sexual assault includes a number of different crimes that range from unwanted sexual touching to forced penetration. The United States National Violence Against Women survey indicated that 66.4 percent of surveyed men said they were physically assaulted as a child by an adult caretaker and/or as an adult by any type of attacker. About 3.2 million men were physically assaulted per year. The survey found 7.4 percent, or 835,000 men, had been subjected to sexual victimization by an intimate partner.

The study of 248 women between ages 15 and 24 by Barbara Krahe et al. revealed the forms of sexual aggression in the different types of relationships: exploitation of a man's incapacitated state (5.6%), verbal pressure (3.2%), and physical force (2.0%). The highest prevalence of sexual aggression was against an ex-partner, followed by friends or acquaintances.

Research suggests that sexual assault of men is more likely to be violent and occur with injury. When a stranger assaults a male, weapons are more likely to be used. Male victims are not likely to seek medical attention unless injuries are significant. Most commonly, male victims suffer trauma as well as physical injuries that usually include genital or rectal trauma, soft tissue injury in the perineum and anal areas, and rectal injury.

The Krahe et al. study findings of why sexual aggression occurs among women suggest that reasons include long-term influences, such as childhood sexual abuse, and more immediate aspects of sexual interaction, such as communication strategies (saying no when yes is met and vice versa), perceived peer pressure, and a higher number of sexual partners.

The effects on a male who has survived sexual abuse can have severe psychological results because men are acculturated to believe that an assault will not happen to them. Thus, results can include: a change in his sense of self and concept of reality; experiences of anxiety, depression, and fearfulness; a concern about sexual orientation; a fear related to the assault setting; a fear of the worst happening and having a sense of a shortened future; a withdrawal from relationships and a sense of alienation; and stress that produces sleep problems, increased startle reflex, and unable to relax. Most researchers have found a common correlate on adult male sexual victimization: a high rate of the men were also subjected to sexual abuse as a child.

Factors that keep men from seeking help are:

- Society's view and male victims' view that men either are not assaulted or they can handle or should be able to handle it
- The stigma, shame, fear, and questioning of their sexuality
- Denial of victimization, especially if there is no physical injury

Kali Munro, psychotherapist, says that initial individual therapy followed with group therapy is likely to be the most effective treatment. When men are isolated in society, group therapy is the most powerful. Therapy should include: broadening men's concept of abuse, effects of abuse and that coping is not weakness; how their home and community have contributed to their concept of what it means to be male; and by giving them permission to feel and to have needs, and exploring their identity as a male.

Rosemarie Skaine

See also: Child Abuse, Physical and Emotional; Child Abuse, Sexual; Disabled Adults; Domestic Abuse; Homosexuals; Transgender Individuals.

Further Reading

Gold, Joshua M., and Gabriela V. Pitariu. 2004. "Opening the Eyes of Counselors to the Emotional Abuse of Men: An Overlooked Dynamic in Dysfunctional Families." *Journal of Humanistic Counseling, Education and Development* 43 (Fall): 178–187.

Hines, Denise A., and Kathleen Malley-Morrison. 2001. "Psychological Effects of Partner Abuse against Men: A Neglected Research Area." *Psychology of Men and Masculinity* 2 (2): 75–85.

Krahe, Barbara, Eva Waizenhofer, and Ingrid Moller. 2003. "Women's Sexual Aggression against Men: Prevalence and Predictors." *Sex Roles* 49 (5–6): 219–232.

Lupri, Eugen, and Elaine Grandin. n.d. "Intimate Partner Abuse against Men." Public Health Agency of Canada. http://www.phac-aspc.gc.ca/ncfv-cnivf/publications/mlintima-eng.php.

Mayo Clinic Staff. 2011. "Domestic Violence against Men: Know the Signs." Mayo Clinic. http://www.mayoclinic.com/health/domestic-violence-against-men/MY00557.

Munro, Kali. 2000. "Treatment Needs of Sexually Abused Men." http://kalimunro.com/wp/articles-info/sexual-emotional-abuse/the-treatment-needs-of-sexually-abused-men.

Nowinski, Sabrina N., and Erica Bowe. 2012. "Partner Violence against Heterosexual and Gay Men: Prevalence and Correlates." *Aggression and Violent Behavior* 17: 36–52.

Rape, Abuse & Incest National Network. 2009. "Male Sexual Assault." http://www.rainn.org/get-information/types-of-sexual-assault/male-sexual-assault.

Stanley, Jessica L., Kim Bartholomew, Tracy Taylor, Doug Oram, and Monica Landolt. 2006. "Intimate Violence in Male Same-sex Relationships." *Journal of Family Violence* 21 (1): 31–41.

Stosny, Steven. 2008. "Effects of Emotional Abuse: It Hurts When I Love: Love without Compassion Is Possessive, Controlling, and Dangerous." *Psychology Today*, August 26. http://www.psychologytoday.com/blog/anger-in-the-age-entitlement/200808/effects-emotional-abuse-it-hurts-when-i-love.

Tewksbury, Richard. 2007. "Effects of Sexual Assaults on Men: Physical, Mental and Sexual Consequences." *International Journal of Men's Health* 6 (1): 22–35.

Tjaden, Patricia, and Nancy Thoennes. 2000. *Full Report of the Prevalence, Incidence, and Consequences of Violence against Women: Findings from the National Violence against Women Survey*. U.S. Department of Justice. https://www.ncjrs.gov/pdffiles1/nij/183781.pdf.

N

NATIONAL ASSOCIATION OF SOCIAL WORKERS

The National Association of Social Workers (NASW) has the largest membership organization of professional social workers in the world. In 2013, it had a membership of 140,000. In 1955, seven social work organizations merged to create the National Association of Social Workers (NASW). The organizations were the American Association of Social Workers, the American Association of Medical Social Workers, the American Association of Psychiatric Social Workers, the National Association of School Social Workers, the American Association of Group Workers, the Association for the Study of Community Organization, and the Social Work Research Group.

The NASW's goals include professional growth and development, creating and maintaining professional standards, and advancing sound social policies. The *NASW Code of Ethics*, approved in 1996 and revised in 2008, is a guide to the everyday professional conduct of social workers. The organization's activities include: shaping legislation and public policy; promoting health, welfare, and education; and strengthening opportunities and social support for individuals and families. NASW provides extensive continuing education programs, including professional development conferences, through its 56 chapters.

The association offers membership in eight specialty practice sections: aging, ATOD (alcohol, tobacco, and other drugs), child welfare, health, mental health, poverty and social justice, private practice, and school social work. NASW's focus on abuse is reflected in its "Social Work Month 2012 Toolkit Topics": adolescent and youth development, aging and family caregiving, child protection and family services, health care navigation, mental and behavioral health treatment, military and veterans assistance, nonprofit management and community development, and poverty reduction.

The National Association of Social Workers Foundation (NASWF), a subsidiary of NASW, is a charitable organization whose purpose is to improve the well-being of individuals, families, and communities through the advancement of social work practice. It supports scientific, philanthropic, and educational activities that advance the social work profession; provides competitive insurance services to members; provides technical advice and financial assistance to members involved in legal proceedings; and has a Political Action for Candidate Election (PACE) that raises funds to contribute to the political campaigns of candidates.

Social workers are at the forefront in combating abuses of all types, such as child abuse and domestic violence. Their approach to child abuse is to work with the whole family and with other environmental and cultural factors. Prevention is the preferred intervention. Prevention of child maltreatment includes supporting parents with young children and expanding Early Head Start. Social workers help protect children and assist in finding safe living situations. In addressing domestic violence, the Family Violence Prevention Fund offers a domestic violence assessment and intervention approach.

In working to improve people's lives, the NASW Web site lists the following guidelines for social workers:

- Help individuals, families, and groups restore or enhance their capacity for social functioning and work to create societal conditions that support communities in need.
- Have knowledge of human development and behavior; of social, economic, and cultural institutions; and of the interaction of all these factors.
- Help people of all backgrounds address their own needs through psychosocial services and advocacy.
- Help people overcome some of life's most difficult challenges: poverty, discrimination, abuse, addiction, physical illness, divorce, loss, unemployment, educational problems, disability, and mental illness. Thus, help prevent crises and counsel individuals, families, and communities to cope more effectively with the stresses of everyday life.

Rosemarie Skaine

See also: Child Abuse, Physical and Emotional; Disabled Adults; Domestic Abuse; Elder Abuse.

Further Reading

National Association of Social Workers. 2013. http://www.naswdc.org.

National Association of Social Workers. 2013. "Domestic Violence Assessment and Intervention Provided by the Family Violence Prevention Fund." http://www.social workers.org/pressroom/events/domestic_violence/assessment.asp.

National Association of Social Workers. 2012. "Social Work Month 2012 Toolkit Topics." http://www.socialworkers.org/pressroom/swMonth/2012/default.asp.

National Association of Social Workers. 2009. "Social Work and Child Abuse and Neglect." http://www.socialworkers.org/advocacy/briefing/ChildAbuseBriefingPaper.pdf.

NATIONAL CENTER FOR MISSING AND EXPLOITED CHILDREN

The National Center for Missing and Exploited Children (NCMEC) formed in 1984 to serve as a clearinghouse for the United States on issues related to missing and sexually exploited children. Before that time, no coordinated national system for addressing missing children cases existed. Cases of affected missing children during this period of time include: Etan Patz, age 6, who disappeared in 1979 from a New York street on his way to school; 29 children and young adults were found murdered in Atlanta over the next several years; and Adam Walsh, age 6, who was abducted from a Florida shopping mall and murdered in 1981. According to the

Federal Bureau of Investigation (FBI), a child goes missing every 40 seconds or 765,000 children a year.

Due to improved public awareness, training, laws, and technology, the recovery rate of missing children in 2013 increased from 62 percent in 1990 to more than 97 percent. Advanced technology that employs sophisticated computer software to create age-progressed images of long-term missing children has led to more being recovered: Elizabeth Smart of Utah was recovered after 9 months, Shawn Hornbeck of Missouri after 4 years, Jaycee Dugard of California after 18 years, Carlina White of New York after 23 years, and Marx Barnes of Hawaii after 34 years.

In 1998, NCMEC's CyberTipline began. The tipline can be reached by dialing 1-800-THE-LOST (1-800-843-5678). Callers without access to the U.S. 800/toll-free telephone system may dial 001-703-522-9320 to reach the call center. This number is not toll-free. The tipline has processed over 1.9 million reports that include online enticement for sexual acts, sexual molestation, child pornography, and unsolicited obscene material. In addition, NCMEC has analyzed about 90 million images and videos showing apparent child pornography through the Child Victim Identification Program. It also provides assistance to law enforcement in locating noncompliant sex offenders through the Sex Offender Tracking Team as well as analytical services for their investigations of child sex trafficking through the Child Sex Trafficking Team.

NCMEC's publication section covers four areas: general information, missing children, child sexual exploitation, and child safety and prevention. Their site provides resources to families to help keep their children safer. NCMEC teaches children about safety. It outlines what to do if a child is missing:

- First, call the local law enforcement agency.
- Follow up by contacting the National Center for Missing and Exploited Children.
- If the child is missing from home, search the places where a child may crawl into or hide.
- If the child is missing in a store, notify the store manager or security officer, then call the local law enforcement agency. Many stores have a Code Adam plan of action in place.

Rosemarie Skaine

See also: Abduction, Child; Adam Walsh Child Protection and Safety Act; AMBER Alert; National Missing and Unidentified Persons System; Walsh, John Edward.

Further Reading

Girouard, Cathy. 2001. "The National Center for Missing and Exploited Children." *Office of Juvenile Justice and Delinquency Prevention Fact Sheet* 28. U.S. Department of Justice. https://www.ncjrs.gov/pdffiles1/ojjdp/fs200128.pdf.

Halpern, Mollie. 2011. "FBI and the National Center for Missing & Exploited Children." Podcasts and Radio. *Inside the FBI*. http://www.fbi.gov/news/podcasts/inside/inside_071211.mp3/view.

National Center for Missing and Exploited Children. 2013. http://www.missingkids.com/home.

National Center for Missing and Exploited Children. 2013. "Publications." http://www.missingkids.com/Publications.

NATIONAL CENTER ON ELDER ABUSE

The National Center on Elder Abuse (NCEA) is one of 27 funded resource centers directed by the U.S Administration on Aging (AoA), The center, established in 1988, is a national resource center committed to the prevention of elder mistreatment.

The NCEA provides information regarding research, training, best practices, news and resources on elder abuse, neglect and exploitation to policy makers, professionals in the elder justice field, and the public. NCEA reports that approximately 2 million elders are abused in the United States each year. The center's mission is to make certain that national, state, and local partners in the field will be fully prepared to ensure that older Americans will live with dignity, integrity, independence, and without abuse, neglect, and exploitation.

Elder abuse and neglect are intentional actions that cause harm or create a serious risk of harm, regardless of intent, to a vulnerable elder by a caregiver or other person who stands in a trust relationship to the elder. The majority of abusers are family members (about 90%), most often adult children, spouses, and partners. Women are abused at a higher rate than men, and older elders are more likely to be abused than younger ones.

Ten percent of elders had experienced abuse in the prior year, an NCEA survey of elder abuse found. The 1 in 10 elder adults who experienced abuse did not include financial abuse. The trend is for increased reporting of elder abuse, but state Adult Protective Services (APS) agencies that are accessible in all 50 states and mandatory reporting laws for elder abuse in most states, a great number of cases of abuse, neglect, and exploitation go undetected and untreated each year. One study estimated that only 1 in 14 cases of elder abuse ever comes to the attention of authorities. The New York State Elder Abuse Prevalence Study found that for every case known to programs and agencies, 24 were unknown. Major financial exploitation was self-reported at a rate of 41 per 1,000 surveyed, which was higher than self-reported rates of emotional, physical, and sexual abuse or neglect.

Even though the causes of elder abuse are not always known, individuals can detect warning signs and make a call for help if an elder needs assistance. The NCEA lists 14 awareness issues:

1. What is elder abuse?
2. What are the warning signs of elder abuse?
3. What is self-neglect and what are the signs?
4. What makes an older adult vulnerable to abuse?
5. Who are the abusers of older people?
6. Are there criminal penalties for the abusers?
7. How many people are suffering from elder abuse?
8. Who do I call if I suspect elder abuse?
9. What can I do if I am concerned about possible abuse or neglect in a nursing home?
10. What should I expect if I call someone for help?
11. What should I look for in a good nursing home or assisted living facility?
12. How can I protect against frauds and scams?
13. How can elder abuse be prevented?
14. Why Should I Care About Elder Abuse?

Getting help also means knowing intervention strategies. The laws in most states require helping professionals such as doctors and home health providers to report suspected abuse or neglect. These professionals are mandated reporters. Eight states require any person to report a suspicion of mistreatment. NCEA instructs that if an individual suspects an elder is in danger, call 911 or the police. The caller does not have to prove anything.

Rosemarie Skaine

See also: Disabled Adults; Elder Abandonment; Elder Abuse; Elder Neglect.

Further Reading

National Center on Elder Abuse. 2011. "Health Finder." http://healthfinder.gov/FindServices/Organizations/Organization.aspx?code=HR2395.

National Center on Elder Abuse. n.d. Administration on Aging, Department of Health and Human Services. http://www.ncea.aoa.gov.

NATIONAL COALITION AGAINST DOMESTIC VIOLENCE

The National Coalition Against Domestic Violence (NCADV) was founded in 1978 with the goal of supporting communities and individuals seeking to end violence around them. The organization focuses on domestic violence and child abuse as well as society-wide violence.

NCADV began at the United States Commission on Civil Rights hearing on battered women. It began with 100 individuals and expanded to thousands of members working together and sharing their experiences of domestic violence. In addition to domestic violence, NCADV members have focused on homophobia, sexism, racism, and ageism.

According to NCADV, domestic violence is one of the most chronically under-reported crimes. Only one-quarter of all physical assaults, one-fifth of all rapes, and one-half of all stalkings perpetuated against females by intimate partners are reported to the police. Domestic violence has a significant economic impact. The cost of violence by an intimate partner exceeds $5.8 billion each year, of which $4.1 billion is for direct medical and mental health services.

The NCADV's work includes building coalitions for action at the local, state, regional, and national levels; supporting the creation and maintenance of community-based services, such as safe home and shelter programs; providing public education and technical assistance; developing legislation to address pertinent issues; and working to eradicate social conditions that contribute to violence against women and children.

The coalition works to improve current public policy by collaborating with legislators on the federal level, spearheaded by the group's Washington, D.C., office. In 1994, the NCADV was involved in the passing of the seminal Violence Against Women Act, which was designed to provide funding for investigating domestic violence as well as the increased prosecution of abusers. The NCADV works to develop legislation that keeps the best interests of children in mind in cases of custody battles involving domestic abuse. The NCADV Web site (http://www.ncadv.

org) provides information on its programs, activities, events, legislative issues, and domestic violence research.

Rosemarie Skaine

See also: Domestic Abuse, Psychological Effects of; National Domestic Violence Hotline; Stalking.

Further Reading

Bureau of Justice Statistics. 2013. "Victims." http://www.bjs.gov/index.cfm?ty=tp&tid=9.

National Coalition Against Domestic Violence. 2011. "Take a Stand against Domestic Violence." http://www.ncadv.org.

PRWeb. 2012. "Every 9 Seconds in the US a Woman Is Assaulted or Beaten—Help End Domestic Violence." http://www.prweb.com/releases/2012/10/prweb9986276.htm.

NATIONAL DOMESTIC VIOLENCE HOTLINE

The National Domestic Violence Hotline (1–800–799–SAFE (7233) or TTY 1–800–787–3224) provides 24-hour support by offering advocacy, safety planning, resources, and hope to everyone affected by domestic violence. It is the only domestic violence hotline in the United States. The hotline was established as a part of the Violence Against Women Act (VAWA) in 1996. As a nonprofit organization, it makes available crisis intervention and referral information to victims, perpetrators, friends, and families.

The hotline has access to approximately 4,000 shelters and domestic violence programs in the United States, Puerto Rico, Guam, and the U.S. Virgin Islands. Calls received are about 23,500 a month. The hotline is toll-free, confidential, and anonymous. It functions 24 hours a day, 365 days a year, in about 170 languages through interpreter services and has a TTY line accessible for the deaf, deaf-blind, and hard of hearing.

The hotline's Web site has several features: current news to help identify abuse, educational materials, resources, Internet safety, and a blog, *Share Your Voice*. The current news feature reports a change in the hotline's view of the term *cycle of abuse*. Although the term is still used in courtrooms, the hotline does not use it. It maintains that if abuse were a cycle, it would be predictable, that is, a person could know what to expect and when to expect it. The hotline says it does not happen that way in cases of domestic violence. Identifiable patterns may occur in a relationship, such as knowing your partner is inclined to be more confrontational after drinking, but the violence rarely occurs in a predictable cycle.

The hotline offers downloadable awareness materials that include brochures that address the issues, including: "No Matter What I Do It's Never Right," "Is He Really Going to Change This Time?," and "Personal Safety Plans." Downloadable power and control wheels are presented to immigrant children, LGBT, and violence victims. Links are provided for two campaigns: Friends and Family and Break the Silence.

The "Internet Safety" section cautions that technology can be monitored. It provides the way to find safe computers at www.ctcnet.org.

The *Share Your Voice* blog includes such topics as "Clever Tips That May Keep You Safe," "From Your Home to the Workplace: Know Your Rights," "Pregnancy and Abuse: How to Stay Safe for Your 9 Months," and "From 'Broken' Condoms to Pill Tampering: The Realities of Reproductive Coercion."

The first menu option on the hotline site is "Get Help." Safety planning is a necessary and important step. Planning can take place while the victim is still with the abuser or after the relationship ends. Safety is of primary importance for a victim who is still in the relationship. Topics the hotline addresses are "Plan Guidelines," "Personal Safety with an Abuser," "Getting Ready to Leave," "General Guidelines for Leaving an Abusive Relationship," "After Leaving the Abusive Relationship," and a printable "Personal Safety Plan."

Rosemarie Skaine

See also: Battered Women Shelters; Domestic Abuse; Duluth Model; Violence Against Women Act.

Further Reading

National Domestic Violence Hotline. n.d. http://www.thehotline.org.

National Domestic Violence Hotline. n.d. "Get the Facts & Figures." http://www.thehotline.org/is-this-abuse/statistics.

NATIONAL MISSING AND UNIDENTIFIED PERSONS SYSTEM

The National Missing and Unidentified Persons System (NamUs) is a national centralized repository and resource center for records relating to missing individuals. The NamUs program is funded through the National Institute of Justice, Office of Justice Programs, U.S. Department of Justice.

NamUs, launched in 2009, is a free Internet-based system that can be searched by medical examiners, coroners, law enforcement officials, and the general public looking for information on missing and unidentified individuals. NamUs also provides free DNA testing and other forensic services. The system initially had two databases, Missing Persons and Unidentified Persons, and has added a third, UnClaimed Persons. The Missing Persons Database contains information about missing individuals, and entries can be entered by anyone. However, before a record appears as a case on NamUs, the information is verified with pertinent authorities.

NamUs provides a user with a variety of resources, including the ability to print missing persons posters and receive free assistance with biometric collection and testing to help solve cases of missing individuals. Other resources include links to state clearinghouses, medical examiner and coroner offices, law enforcement agencies, victim assistance groups, and pertinent legislation. The NamUs databases are available in Spanish.

The Unidentified Persons Database contains information entered by medical examiners and coroners. Unidentified persons are individuals who have died but whose bodies have not been identified. Anyone can search this database using characteristics such as sex, race, distinct body features, and dental information.

The more recently added UnClaimed Persons (UCP) Database contains information about deceased individuals who have been identified by name but for whom no next of kin or family member has been identified or located to claim the body. Like the Unidentified Persons Database, only medical examiners and corners may enter cases in this database. However, the database is searchable by the public using an individual's name and year of birth.

By 2011, the number of cases in the Missing and Unidentified Persons databases had reached a combined total of more than 15,000, and the number of registered users has grown to 10,000. More than two-thirds of the 10,000 registered NamUs users are members of the general public; the balance are death investigation professionals such as coroners, medical examiners, and law enforcement officers. The Missing Persons Database contained 7,148 entries, and the Unidentified Persons Database had 7,855 records. NamUs was credited with resolving 62 of the missing and unidentified person cases in its databases.

There are as many as 100,000 active missing persons at a given time. As of August 2012, 11,390 total missing person cases had been reported to NamUs; 3,499 cases had been resolved, 278 with direct assistance from NamUs; and 7,891 cases remained active in the Missing Person Database. In August 2012, 9,338 total unidentified person cases had been reported to NamUs; 740 cases had been resolved, 117 with direct assistance from NamUs; and 8,598 cases remained active in the Unidentified Person Database.

Nationwide, 4,400 unidentified remains are found every year, and over 1,000 of these remain unidentified after one year. There may be up to 40,000 human remains that are unidentified. Unidentified remains cases are entered by medical examiners, coroners, or their authorized registered users

Rosemarie Skaine

See also: Abduction, Adult; Abduction, Child; AMBER Alert; Child Trafficking; Human Trafficking; National Center for Missing and Exploited Children; Slavery, Modern-day.

Further Reading

National Institute of Justice. n.d. "National Missing and Unidentified Persons System." Office of Justice Programs. U.S. Department of Justice. http://www.namus.gov.

National Missing and Unidentified Persons System. 2012. "NamUs Fact Sheet." https://www.findthemissing.org/documents/NamUs_Fact_Sheet.pdf.

Office of Justice Programs. 2011. "More Than 15,000 Cases in New Database That Matches Missing Persons and Unidentified Dead Users Number 10,000." U.S. Department of Justice. https://www.findthemissing.org/documents/DOJ_RELEASE_NamUs_May_6_2011.pdf.

NURSING HOMES, ABUSE IN

Nursing home abuse is the mistreatment or neglect of nursing home residents through physical abuse, misuse of restraints, verbal or emotional abuse, physical neglect, medical neglect, verbal or emotional neglect, and personal property abuse.

Nursing home abuse is one of the most underreported forms of abuse. The statistics that exist indicate a significant problem. In 2000, states were asked to indicate the number of elder or adult reports received in the most recent year for which data were available. Based on figures gathered, the total number of reports was 472,813. Two to 10 percent of nursing home residents are abused. Over 90 percent of nursing homes in the United States are understaffed and have staffing levels too low to provide adequate care. One out of three nursing homes in the United States has been cited for nursing home abuse.

Some 1.6 million people live in nursing homes in the United States. Thirty years from now, the number is expected to increase to 5 million, suggesting that the problem is likely to grow in coming years. This increase in cases may be due to the shift from society's favoring in-home care for the elderly population to favoring nursing home care.

Abuse within nursing homes can take many forms, including physical, emotional, sexual, and even financial. Physical abuse includes physical force (such as hitting) against a nursing home resident as well as the inappropriate use of drugs (often to cause incapacitation) and the unnecessary use of physical restraints. Emotional abuse, while destructive in its own right, may also lead to physical symptoms among nursing home residents, who are often physically frail. Passive emotional abuse may include ignoring the individual or subjecting him or her to periods of extended isolation. Often categorized separately as "elder neglect," such treatment can be so extensive that nursing home employees are no longer fulfilling the legal obligations of their positions. Sexual abuse of the elderly in nursing homes consists of nonconsensual sexual contact or interaction as well as the forcible viewing of pornographic material or sexual acts or forcing the nursing home resident to undress without cause.

The most common form of abuse of the elderly in nursing homes is financial fraud and exploitation. Abusive nursing home employees can use their positions of authority and close access to a resident to steal or extort money or personal information. Or they may gain the trust of an elderly resident, particularly one who is isolated and lonely, through regular contact with the person and then use this position of trust to gain access to the individual's finances.

The reasons residents in nursing homes suffer abuse are many. Nursing home employees are often underpaid, overworked, and receive little training. This can lead to feelings of stress and job dissatisfaction, which may be taken out on residents. Nursing homes may be working to cut costs, impacting quality of care and the number of staff hired as well as the training they receive. Nursing homes may be so overwhelmed that oversight of patient care breaks down, allowing abuse to occur. Another major problem is that many nursing home residents are unwilling or unable to complain about the abusive treatment they receive.

The obvious signs of elder abuse in a nursing home include: unusual bruising or bleeding; open wounds, bed sores, or cuts; burns and abrasions; a sudden and unexplained change in weight; and soiling, poor hygiene, and torn or stained clothing or bedding. However, nonphysical abuse may be harder to detect. The less obvious signs of abuse include listlessness or unresponsiveness; infantile or other strange behaviors; physical or emotional withdrawal; the disappearance of personal items; and unusual financial transactions. It is important to note, however, that many of these changes can also be attributed to nonabusive causes, such as sickness or declining mental health. This can make identifying abuse in nursing homes particularly difficult. If nursing home staff delay or refuse a family member's access to a resident during normal business hours, this may be a sign that abuse is occurring. Another potential sign of abuse is an employee's refusal to leave the room while the visitor is interacting with the resident.

If abuse is suspected, action should be taken immediately. Depending on the nature and severity of the abuse, courses of action may range from lodging a complaint with the nursing home's administration to filing criminal charges against the nursing home and/or its employees. To minimize the chances of a loved one's experiencing abuse in a nursing home, it is important to carefully screen facilities before selecting one and to visit the individual frequently and inquire about his or her health, happiness, and the treatment he or she is receiving often.

Rosemarie Skaine

See also: Elder Abandonment; Elder Abuse; Elder Abuse Victims Act; Elder Neglect; National Center on Elder Abuse.

Further Reading

Administration on Aging. 2013. "Long-term Care Ombudsman Program." (OAA, Title VII, Chapter 2, Sections 711/712). http://www.aoa.gov/AoARoot/AoA_Programs/Elder_Rights/Ombudsman/index.aspx.

Kusserow, Richard P. 1990. "Resident Abuse in Nursing Homes: Understanding and Preventing Abuse." Office of Inspector General, U.S. Department of Health and Human Services. http://oig.hhs.gov/oei/reports/oei-06-88-00360.pdf.

Nursing Home Abuse Center. 2012. "Advocacy Groups and Government Agencies." http://www.nursinghomeabusecenter.org/resources/advocacy-groups.html.

Nursing Home Abuse Center. 2012. "Nursing Home Abuse." http://www.nursinghomeabusecenter.org.

Nursing Home Abuse Center. 2012. "Signs of Nursing Home Abuse." http://www.nursinghomeabusecenter.org/signs-of-abuse.html.

Nursing Home Abuse Center. 2012. "What to Do if You Suspect Nursing Home Abuse." http://www.nursinghomeabusecenter.org/what-to-do.html.

Silver Ribbon Project. 2013. "Statistics about Nursing Home Abuse." http://www.silverribbonproject.com/statistics-about-nursing-home-abuse.

U.S. Administration on Aging. n.d. "Frequently Asked Questions." http://www.ncea.aoa.gov/faq/index.aspx.

0

ONLINE DATING

Online dating, or Internet dating, is a dating experience that allows individuals to contact and communicate with one another over the Internet. This experience is usually with the objective of developing a personal, romantic, or sexual relationship. It is estimated that over 41 million people have tried online dating. Abuse of many kinds may occur in the context of online dating.

The ubiquity of social media and the Internet creates new avenues for nonphysical abuse by a dating partner. A new Michigan State study suggests online exhibits of controlling behavior and harassing text messages can have a serious effect on a teenager's health and well-being. The study is one of the first to examine the effects of both physical and nonphysical dating abuse—particularly relevant to today's highly connected adolescents. The study found a total of 67.4 percent of females and 57.1 percent of males reported dating violence victimization from ages 13 to 19.

Nonphysical dating violence victimization occurred more frequently than physical or sexual violence, with 64.6 percent of females and 56.4 percent of males indicating they experienced this type of dating violence. Various types of nonphysical abuse varied; for example, being yelled at, sworn at, or insulted were the most common types of nonphysical abuse for females (47.6 percent) and males (40.7 percent).

Online dating abuse can be so much more than physical. While physical violence is nothing to discount, relationship abuse can and often does include such nonphysical abuse as controlling behavior, extreme jealousy, creating isolation for one partner, codependency, and verbal harassment. Online dating is no safe haven from abuse in relationships. Threats, controlling e-mails and texts, and jealous behaviors can still make recipients feel isolated, trapped, and emotionally shackled to their partners. Online and text messaging mediums also allow for stalking behaviors to occur.

With so many different ways to connect virtually, "digital" dating abuse can develop over social media as well, for example, through Facebook. Think of it as emotional abuse perpetrated online. In digital dating abuse, one partner may tell another not to be Facebook friends or socially linked to certain people online. A partner may send negative or threatening messages and may use "checking in" applications on different sites, such as on Facebook or FourSquare, to keep tabs on a person. Status updates that insult one partner or that demand certain things be or not be posted on social media sites may also occur.

Digital abusers can make the victim feel like he or she cannot be away from the phone or computer without risking punishment. They may also make the victim feel undue guilt for spending time with friends rather than on a phone call or computer chat with the abuser. Victims may begin feeling extremely anxious about missing phone calls, texts, or e-mails to the point where it interferes with other relationships and work.

Another dimension of online dating abuse is when people purposely post inaccurate personal information pertaining to age, gender, marriage status, height, weight, or financial conditions in order to establish communication with an unsuspecting party. Through e-mails, blogs, and online environments, people are able to exchange ideas and communicate about their daily lives. Dating sites are unable to verify personal information entered by its participants. It is impossible to determine if someone has enhanced his or her statistics or if it is an accurate description of his or her profile.

Studies have proven that many people enhance their online profiles. For men, the major areas of deception are educational level, income, height, age, and marital status; at least 13 percent of online male suitors are thought to be married. For women, the major areas of deception are weight, physical appearance, and age. All of the relevant research shows the importance of physical appearance for both sexes, and online daters interpret the absence of photos negatively. According to one recent survey, men's profiles without photos draw one-fourth the response of those with photos, and women's profiles without photos draw only one-sixth the response of those with photos. The false information is misleading and may cause someone to contact a potential date they normally would have avoided in a face-to-face climate.

Blackmailing the victim by threatening to reveal personal photos or information is also a frequent abuse tactic. Many times the victim will cooperate with their abuser for fear of having the information released to their social network, peers, or work environment.

Specific topics that should not be shared online that give abusers ammunition are name, age, and birthday. Also, e-mail addresses, phone numbers, personal characteristics, logistics, and family facts are included in the list. Should you happen to be the victim of online dating abuse, refuse to respond to the e-mails or threats, record what happened, and tell someone in a position to assist you with terminating the dangerous situation. The general rule for online safety is to know with whom you are communicating and to verify plans by another means, such as a telephone call or a face-to-face discussion.

Online dating abuse is a concern of national groups. The National Coalition Against Domestic Violence (NCADV) not only focuses on domestic violence in the home but also society-wide violence and factors that perpetuate violence against women and children alike. The U.S. National Domestic Violence Hotline (1-800-799-SAFE) (TDD 800-787-3224) provides crisis intervention, education, safety planning, and referrals for counseling, shelters, and legal services nationwide.

Connie Kerns-Grams

See also: Cyberbullying, Adult; Cyberbullying, Child and Adolescent; Cyberstalking.

Further Reading

Bonomi, A. E., et al. 2013. "History of Dating Violence and the Association with Late Adolescent Health." BMC Public Health. doi:10.1186/1471-2458-13-821.

Cindrich, Sharon. 2009. *A Smart Girl's Guide to the Internet*. Middleton, WI: American Girl Publishing, Inc.

Epstein, Robert. 2007. "The Truth about Online Dating." *Scientific American*, January 30. http://www.scientificamerican.com/article.cfm?id=the-truth-about-online-da.

Hinduja, S., and J. W. Patchin. 2011. "Electronic Dating Violence: A Brief Guide for Educators and Parents." Cyberbullying Research Center (www.cyberbullying.us). http://kidsafe. com/wp-content/uploads/2011/06/electronic_dating_violence_fact_sheet.pdf.

Melton, B., and S. Shankle. 2007. *What in the World Are Your Kids Doing Online?* New York: Doubleday Broadway Publishing Group.

Nauert, Rick. 2013. "Online Dating Abuse Means Real Harm to Teens: 2 out of 3 Girls Are Victims." Psych Central. http://psychcentral.com/news/2013/09/17/online-dating-abuse-means-real-harm-to-teens-2-out-of-3-girls-are-victims/59612.html.

Therapy Twins. 2013. "The Scary Reality of Online Dating Abuse." http://joanlandinosays. com/therapy-twins/therapy-twins-blog/online-dating-abuse.

PANDORA'S PROJECT

Pandora's Project, a nonprofit organization, offers peer support to victims of rape, sexual assault, or sexual abuse through online support. Established in 2007 as Pandora's Aquarium, it changed its name in 2009 to Pandora's Project. The organization provides a message board, chat room, and blogs, which continue to be known as Pandora's Aquarium. In addition to online support, Pandora provides guest speaker chats, a lending library, healing retreat weekends, and articles and essays.

Membership is free, and survivors moderate the activities. Associating with other rape and sexual abuse survivors is an important part of healing. Specific forums are available for men and women, teens, and older survivors; LGBTQ (lesbian, gay, bisexual, transgender, and questioning); rape and sexual abuse survivors; and friends and family of survivors. Support related to relevant issues includes: healing after rape, sexual assault, sexual abuse: flashbacks, depression, posttraumatic stress disorder (PTSD); self-injury, self-harm, eating disorders, relationships, sex and intimacy, spirituality, pregnancy and parenting, and legal concerns.

Shannon Lambert of Minneapolis, the organization's president, founded Pandora's Aquarium as the first online support community for sexual assault victims. Its staff includes over 50 survivors, who are unpaid volunteers. The Web site receives more than 30,000 unique visitors and 5 million hits a month. Tori Amos, a sexual violence survivor and the founder of the Rape, Abuse & Incest National Network (RAINN), a U.S. nationwide hotline for rape and abuse survivors (1-800-656-HOPE), helped inspire Pandora's Project through her music.

Lambert was raped by a school acquaintance at age 15, but she did not tell anyone. She said, "I didn't fully understand what had happened. . . . I felt a lot of confusion and social pressures, very common with young rape victims. I just pretended it didn't happen." When she was 19 years old and starting to face her own rape, she listened repeatedly to Amos's *Little Earthquakes* album, and it brought her comfort. In her sense of isolation, Lambert founded Pandora's as a way to reach out to others. Amos's music was an important part of her healing journey.

While a freshman at the University of Minnesota's campus in Morris in 1998–1999, Lambert attended her first Take Back the Night event and realized that she had to confront her rape. To do so, she first contacted RAINN and then let friends and relatives know. That same year, she appeared on the TV news program *20/20*. Lambert went from a very secretive person to a very public figure. At the same time, she started the small online message board. At this time, she realizes the power of peer support.

Rosemarie Skaine

See also: Rape; Rape, Abuse, and Incest National Network.

Further Reading

Pandora's Project. n.d. http://www.pandorasproject.org.

Tillotson, Kristin. 2009. "Minneapolis Woman Wins Award for Pandora's Project: Shannon Lambert of Minneapolis Was Awarded $25,000 from L'Oreal's Women of Worth Program for Pandora's Project." *Star Tribune*, Minneapolis, MN, December 21.

PEDOPHILIA

Pedophilia is a psychosexual disorder when an individual fantasizes, is sexually aroused by, or experiences sexual urges for prepubescent children who are usually less than 13 years old. To be classified a pedophile, the individual must be at least 16 years old and be at least 5 years older than the child of interest. Abusers who molest because of an ongoing sex drive directed toward children have the disorder pedophilia. A child molestation prevention study reported that pedophiles were responsible for 95 percent of the sex acts committed against children.

The American Psychiatric Association (APA) has included pedophilia in its *Diagnostic and Statistical Manual of Mental Disorders* since 1968. Individuals are diagnosed as pedophiles when their attractions toward children cause them guilt, anxiety, alienation, difficulty in pursuing other personal goals, or if their urges cause them to approach children for sexual gratification. A pedophile's activities may include: observing a child undressing; touching a child; oral sex; touching of the genitals of the child; and having the child touch the genitals of the pedophile.

It is not clear whether pedophilia comes from genetics or is learned behavior. Some evidence indicates that it may run in families. Causes include:

- Abnormalities in male sexual hormones or the brain chemical serotonin
- A history of childhood sexual abuse or observation of or being victimized by inappropriate sexual behaviors (children learn to imitate and later they are reinforced for the behavior because normal social sexual contacts are not available and gratification is sought through less socially acceptable means)
- A relationship between hormones, behavior, and the central nervous system, with a focus on the role of aggression and male sexual hormones

The disorder causes significant distress or impairment in social, occupational, or other important areas of functioning. It has a high rate of presence with another compulsive sexual disorder and an equally high rate of presence with anxiety, major depression, or mood disorders and substance abuse disorders.

Compulsive sexual behavior can have many negative consequences that affect both the pedophile and others. Pedophilia may produce feelings of guilt, shame, and low self-esteem; neglect; or lying to their partner and family. It may tax or destroy meaningful relationships. The pedophile may accumulate financial debts by purchasing pornography and sexual services; contract or transmit HIV, hepatitis, or another sexually transmitted infection; engage in unhealthy substance use, such as drug or alcohol abuse; be arrested for sexual offenses; lose focus or engage in sexual activity at work, risking his or her job; or face a child's unwanted pregnancy.

Part of the solution to pedophilic behavior is to try to keep it under control. The Mayo Clinic suggests:

- Get help early to prevent it from getting worse over time or escalating into a downward spiral of shame, self-esteem problems, and harmful acts.
- Seek treatment early because it may be worsened by depression, anxiety, or obsessive-compulsive behavior.
- Identify and seek help for alcohol and drug abuse problems.
- Seek treatment for childhood sexual abuse.
- Avoid risky behaviors. Stay away from strip clubs, bars, pornographic Web sites, or other areas where it might be tempting to look for a new sexual partner. Install software that blocks pornographic Web sites.

Psychotherapy combined with medications is a treatment choice. Psychotherapy choices include: psychodynamic psychotherapy, cognitive behavioral therapy, group therapy, or family therapy or marriage counseling. These approaches can be supplemented by a self-help group of choice, such as Circles of Support and Accountability (COSA), Sex Addicts Anonymous, Sex and Love Addicts Anonymous, S-Anon International Family Groups, Sexaholics Anonymous, Sexual Compulsives Anonymous, or Sexual Recovery Anonymous.

According to *Psychology Today*, medications include antiandrogens (to lower sex drive), medroxyprogesterone acetate (Provera) and leuprolide acetate (Lupron). Selective serotonin reuptake inhibitors (SSRIs) may be prescribed to treat associated compulsive sexual disorders and/or to gain benefit from libido-lowering sexual side effects. Higher doses than are typically administered for depression are usually used of sertraline (Zoloft), fluoxetine (Prozac), fluvoxamine (Luvox), citalopram (Celexa), and paroxetine (Paxil).

Hormones, such as medroxyprogesterone acetate and cyproterone acetate, decrease the level of circulating testosterone, thus reducing sex drive and aggression. They reduce the frequency of erections, sexual fantasies, and initiations of sexual behaviors, including masturbation and intercourse. Hormones are typically used with behavioral and cognitive treatments. Antidepressants such as fluoxetine have also successfully decreased sex drive but have not effectively targeted sexual fantasies.

Not all pedophiles become sex offenders. If, however, the pedophile engages in conduct that involves molestation, child pornography, or any other illegal contact with a child, then the individual becomes a sex offender and is subject to the penalties for those crimes.

Rosemarie Skaine

See also: Child Abuse, Physical and Emotional; Child Abuse, Sexual; Sex Addiction; Sex Offender; Sex Trafficking.

Further Reading

Child Molestation Research & Prevention Institute. 2014. "An Ongoing Sex Drive Directed toward Children: What Causes Someone to Molest?" *Early Diagnosis and Effective Treatment*. http://www.childmolestationprevention.org/pages/focus_on_the_cause.html.

Cloud, John. 2003. "Pedophilia." *Time*, January 13. http://content.time.com/time/magazine/article/0,9171,232584-1,00.html.

Hall, Rayan C. W., and Richard C. W. Hall. 2007. "A Profile of Pedophilia: Definition, Characteristics of Offenders, Recidivism, Treatment Outcomes, and Forensic Issues." *Mayo Clinic Proceedings* 82 (4): 457–471. www.mayoclinicproceedings.com.

Martin, Laura J. n.d. "What Is Pedophilia?" Mental Health Center. WebMD. http://www.webmd.com/mental-health/features/explaining-pedophilia.

Mayo Clinic Staff. n.d. "Compulsive Sexual Behavior." http://www.mayoclinic.org/diseases-conditions/compulsive-sexual-behavior/basics/definition/con-20020126.

Psychology Today. n.d. "Pedophilia." http://www.psychologytoday.com/conditions/pedophilia.

PIZZEY, ERIN

Erin Patria Margaret Pizzey (nee Carney; b. February 18, 1939) began her work in domestic violence in 1971, when she opened in Chiswick, London, the first refuge (shelter) to help all victims including men. Pizzey was controversial because she contended that most domestic violence is reciprocal and that a woman is equally as capable of violence as a man.

Her organization grew to include many houses, and the organization is now known as Refuge in the UK. Soon after its founding, public protests and death threats surfaced and resulted in the killing of the family dog. Although she left England with her family, she never ceased to work for all victims of domestic violence: men, women, and children.

In 1978, her first book on domestic violence, *Scream Quietly or the Neighbors Will Hear*, was published. While she was in England, the U.S. government invited her to the United States. She assisted in establishing shelters for victims of domestic violence through a Salvation Army–sponsored 21-city tour. In 1982, she moved to the United States, opened a shelter, and gave lectures on family violence. Pizzey's work on behalf of domestic violence victims spans the globe, including Italy, England, and the United States. In March 2007, she opened the first Arab refuge for victims in Bahrain.

The awards she received reflect her international presence. They include: the International Order of Volunteers for Peace, Diploma of Honor (Italy) in 1981, the Nancy Astor Award for Journalism in 1983, the World Congress of Victimology (San Francisco) in 1987, the Distinguished Leadership Award, and the St. Valentino Palm d'Oro International Award for Literature (Italy) in 1994.

Pizzey and Jeff Shapiro's 1982 book, *Prone to Violence*, suggests that many of the women who took refuge sought abusive relationships. This tendency is similar to addiction. Adults are violent with intimate partners due to high levels of hormones and neurochemicals associated with pervasive childhood trauma and are unaware that the violence is an attempt to simulate the emotional impact of traumatic childhood experiences. The authors also address reasons why the modern state's caretaking agencies are, for the most part, ineffective.

Rosemarie Skaine

See also: Battered Women Shelters; Domestic Abuse; Men as Victims of Abuse.

Further Reading

Corry, Charles E. 2002. "Erin Pizzey." Equal Justice Foundation. http://www.ejfi.org/DV/dv-63.htm.

Esmay, Dean. 2012. "Exclusive Interview with Domestic Violence and Women's Shelter/Women's Refuge Pioneer." YouTube. http://www.youtube.com/watch?v=pyfwJ55hKgE. Transcript with references available at http://www.avoiceformen.com/mens-righ.

Pizzey, Erin. 2011. *This Way to the Revolution: A Memoir*. London: Peter Owen Publishers.

Pizzey, Erin. 2009. "Timeline." http://www.erinpizzey.com/time.html.

Pizzey, Erin. 1978. *Scream Quietly or the Neighbors Will Hear*. Berkeley Heights, NJ: Enslow Publishers Inc.

Pizzey, Erin, and Jeff Shapiro. 1982. *Prone to Violence*. London: Hamlyn Publishing.

POLICE, ABUSE BY

Police abuse or police brutality is the abuse of authority by the unwarranted infliction of excessive force by personnel involved in various aspects of law enforcement while in performance of their official duties. The excessive force is usually physical, but potentially, it is in the form of verbal attacks and psychological intimidation. The term is also applied to abuses by corrections personnel in municipal, state, and federal penal facilities, including military prisons.

While the number of cases involving police brutality each year is significant, high-profile cases of police brutality get the public's attention. These cases include:

- The beating of Rodney King in Los Angeles in March 1991 that was videotaped. The officers charged in the beating were acquitted, and the acquittals sparked riots in the Los Angeles area in 1992.
- The killing of an unarmed teenager, Trayvon Martin, by a Neighborhood Watch captain, George Zimmerman, in February 2012. Zimmerman was tried and found not guilty, in part, on the basis of the Florida's stand your ground law.
- The killing of a homeless man in Phoenix, Arizona, in March 2014. Even before this shooting, the U.S. Department of Justice had been reviewing the Phoenix police department since 2012, the police department's record of shooting 25 suspects, of which 17 were fatal.
- The killing of an unarmed teenager, Michael Brown, by a police officer in Ferguson, Missouri.

Police officers kill hundreds of people each year. In 2011, according Jim Fisher, police officers in the United States shot 1,146 people, killing 607. These figures only include instances in which a person was either killed or wounded by police gunfire. The total of people shot and killed is a small fraction of the total number of cases each year in which police use of force is reported. A 2001 U.S. Department of Justice report indicated that, in 1999, approximately 422,000 people 16 years old and older were estimated to have had contact with police in which force or the threat of force was used.

Violence used by police can be excessive despite being lawful, especially in the context of political repression. Indeed "police brutality" is often used to refer

Protestors on Pennsylvania Avenue in downtown Washington, D.C., on December 13, 2014. The sign the man is holding says stop unjust police brutality against black people. The protest was led by Reverend Al Sharpton. (Richard Gunion/Dreamstime.com)

to violence used by the police to achieve politically desirable ends and, therefore, when none should be used at all, according to widely held values and cultural norms in the society (rather than to refer to excessive violence used where at least some may be considered justifiable).

Studies show that there are officers who believe the legal system they serve is failing and that it is their duty to pick up the slack. This is known as "vigilantism," where the officer involved may think the suspect deserves more punishment than what he or she may have to serve under the court system.

The reasons why police abuse occurs include the passage of stand your ground laws and the increased number of individuals authorized to legally carry concealed firearms. As a result, there has been an increase in the number of police officers that are killed every year in the line of duty. In 2010, 59 officers were shot to death among 122 killed while on the job. This marked a 20 percent jump from 2009, when 49 officers were killed by gunfire. In 2011, 173 officers died from all causes in the line of duty. The fact police officers feel they are increasingly under attack from the public may help explain, in part, why they are shooting so many citizens.

There are, however, other reasons why police officers are excessively aggressive to civilians. Some personality traits make some officers more susceptible to the use of excessive force than others. In one study, police psychologists were surveyed on officers who had used excessive force. The information obtained allowed the researchers to develop five unique types of officers, only one of which was similar to the bad apple stereotype. These include:

- Personality disorders
- Previous traumatic job-related experience
- Young, inexperienced, or macho officers
- Officers who learn inappropriate patrol styles
- Officers with personal problems
- Systemic factors also are causes of misconduct in policing. These factors include:

- Pressures to conform to certain aspects of police culture, which can sustain an oppositional criminal subculture protecting the interests of police who violate the law and a "we-they" perspective in which outsiders are viewed with suspicion or distrust.
- Command and control structures with a rigid hierarchical foundation. The results indicate that the more rigid the hierarchy, the lower the scores on a measure of ethical decision making.
- Deficiencies in internal accountability mechanisms (including internal investigation processes).

Most police brutality goes unreported. In 1982, the federal government funded a Police Services Study, in which over 12,000 randomly selected citizens were interviewed in three metropolitan areas. The study found that 13.6 percent of those surveyed claimed to have had cause to complain about police service (including verbal abuse, discourtesy, and physical abuse) in the previous year. Yet only 30 percent of those who acknowledged such brutality filed formal complaints.

Another concern is that almost all police-involved shootings, while investigated by special units, prosecutors' offices, or outside police agencies, were investigated by governmental law enforcement personnel. More than 95 percent of all police-involved shootings were ruled administratively and legally justified. A handful of cases led to wrongful death lawsuits. Even fewer resulted in the criminal prosecution of officers.

The investigation process explains why a low number of cases investigated by law enforcement agencies are found to have merit. A 2006 Department of Justice report showed that, of the 26,556 citizen complaints that were made in 2002 about excessive use of police force among large U.S. agencies, only about 2,000 were found to have merit.

Efforts are being made to reduce police abuse. The police's use of force is kept in check in many jurisdictions by the issuance of a use-of-force continuum. A use-of-force continuum sets levels of force considered appropriate in direct response to a subject's behavior. This power is granted by the civil government, with limits set out in statutory law as well as common law.

The system needs to establish completely independent investigative agencies in cases of police-involved shootings. The evidence shows that administrative investigations do not work to curb police abuse.

Rosemarie Skaine

See also: Gun Violence; Prisoner Abuse, Adult; Prisoner Abuse, Juvenile; Stand Your Ground Law.

Further Reading

Fisher, Jim. 2013. "Police Involved Shooting Statistics: A National One-year Summary." *Jim Fisher True Crime* (blog), December 25. http://jimfishertruecrime.blogspot.com/2012/01/police-involved-shootings-2011-annual.html.

Lynch, Tim. 2014. "National Police Misconduct NewsFeed Daily Recap 04-29-14." The Cato Institute's National Police Misconduct Reporting Project. http://www.policemisconduct.net.

Murdock, Sebastian. 2014. "Police Shoot Homeless Man during Camping Arrest." *Huffington Post*, March 24. http://www.huffingtonpost.com/2014/03/24/james-boyd-killed-by-cops_n_5021117.html.

National Law Enforcement Officers Memorial Fund. 2012. "2011 Law Enforcement Fatalities." http://www.nleomf.org/facts/officer-fatalities-data/2011-law-enforcement-fatalities.html.

Robles, Frances, and Julie Bosman. 2014. "Autopsy Shows Michael Brown Was Struck at Least 6 Times." *New York Times*, August 17. http://www.nytimes.com/2014/08/18/us/michael-brown-autopsy-shows-he-was-shot-at-least-6-times.html?_r=0.

POSTTRAUMATIC STRESS DISORDER

Posttraumatic stress disorder (PTSD) is a mental health condition set off by a traumatic event. PTSD can result from a variety of traumatic incidents, such as mugging, rape, torture, being kidnapped or held captive, child abuse, car accidents, train wrecks, plane crashes, bombings, or natural disasters such as floods or earthquakes. Its symptoms may include flashbacks, nightmares, severe anxiety, and uncontrollable thoughts about the event, even when there is no longer any danger. The individual with PTSD may be the person harmed, a loved one of the person harmed, or a witness to the traumatic event.

A significant number of military personnel who returned from the wars in Vietnam, Afghanistan, and Iraq have been diagnosed with PTSD. About 19 percent of Vietnam veterans experienced PTSD at some point after the war. In 2008, nearly 20 percent (300,000) of military service members who returned from Iraq and Afghanistan reported symptoms of PTSD or major depression. Although 71 percent of female military personnel who experienced sexual assault within the ranks developed PTSD, only a little more than half of those with symptoms sought treatment.

Private contractors who worked in Iraq, Afghanistan, or other conflict environments during 2012 and 2013 reported suffering from PTSD (25%) and depression (18%), but only a few sought help.

According to the National Institutes of Health, approximately 7.7 million (3.5%) American adults age 18 and older have PTSD. It can develop at any age, including childhood, but the median age of onset is 23 years. Of teens and children, 3 percent to 15 percent of girls and 1 percent to 6 percent of boys will develop PTSD.

Events that are considered risk factors that may predispose a person to developing PTSD are:

- Living through dangerous events and traumas
- Having a history of mental illness
- Getting hurt
- Seeing people hurt or killed
- Feeling horror, helplessness, or extreme fear
- Having little or no social support after the traumatic event
- Dealing with extra stress after the event, such as loss of a loved one, pain and injury, or loss of a job or home

Children and youths who have had traumatic experiences were diagnosed with PTSD with these percentages of causes:

- 77 percent of children exposed to a school shooting, according the National Center for PTSD

- Up to 100 percent of children who witness a parental homicide or sexual assault
- 90 percent of sexually abused children
- 3 percent to 6 percent of high school students in the United States who survive a specific disaster

Posttraumatic stress disorder can disrupt all aspects of a person's life, specifically, employment, relationships, and enjoyment of everyday activities. It may place individuals at a higher risk of other mental health problems, including: depression, drug abuse, alcohol abuse, eating disorders, or suicidal thoughts and actions. It may also increase risk of developing certain medical illnesses, including: cardiovascular disease, chronic pain, autoimmune diseases (such as rheumatoid arthritis and thyroid disease), and musculoskeletal conditions.

An adult with PTSD may be affected by reexperiencing the event, avoiding anything related to the event, or being hyperaroused. The effect on older children is similar to that of adults. They may feel responsible, seek revenge, or become disruptive. Young children may experience bedwetting, forgetting how or being unable to talk, acting out the scary event during playtime, or being unusually clingy.

The major treatments for PTSD, according to the Mayo Clinic, are:

- Cognitive therapy. A type of talk therapy that helps recognize the ways of thinking (cognitive patterns) that are keeping the patient stuck, for example, negative or inaccurate ways of perceiving normal situations. Cognitive therapy often is used with a behavioral therapy called exposure therapy.
- Exposure therapy. This behavioral therapy technique helps safely face the very thing that found frightening, so that the patient can learn to cope with it effectively. A new approach to exposure therapy uses virtual reality programs that allow the sufferer to reenter the setting in which the trauma was experienced, for example, a Virtual Iraq program.
- Eye movement desensitization and reprocessing (EMDR). This type of therapy combines exposure therapy with a series of guided eye movements that help process traumatic memories.

The U.S. Food and Drug Administration (FDA) has approved two medications, sertraline (Zoloft) and paroxetine (Paxil), for treating adults with PTSD. Both are antidepressants. They may help control PTSD symptoms, such as sadness, worry, anger, and feeling numb inside. In addition, other types of medications that may prove helpful are:

- Antipsychotics for severe anxiety and related problems, such as difficulty sleeping or emotional outbursts
- Antianxiety medications to improve feelings of anxiety and stress
- Prazosin (Minipress) for symptoms that include insomnia or recurrent nightmares

Regardless of the treatment choice, early management increases success for recovery.

Rosemarie Skaine

See also: Anger Management; Child Abuse, Sexual; Gun Violence; Rape; Torture; Women in the Military, Abuse of.

Further Reading

Dunigan, Molly, et al. 2013. "Out of the Shadows: The Health and Well-being of Private Contractors Working in Conflict Environments." RAND Corporation. http://www.rand.org/pubs/research_reports/RR420.html.

Heal My PTSD. 2014. "PTSD Statistics." http://healmyptsd.com/education/post-traumatic-stress-disorder-statistics.

Mayo Clinic Staff. 2011. "Post-traumatic Stress Disorder (PTSD)." *Diseases and Conditions.* Mayo Clinic. http://www.mayoclinic.org/diseases-conditions/post-traumatic-stress-disorder/basics/definition/con-20022540.

Tanielian, Terri, and Lisa H. Jaycox, eds. 2008. "Invisible Wounds of War: Psychological and Cognitive Injuries, Their Consequences, and Services to Assist Recovery." RAND Corporation. http://www.rand.org/pubs/monographs/MG720.html.

Taylor, Marisa. 2013. "Study Downplaying Military Suicide-PTSD Link Questioned." Aljazeera America, August 18. http://america.aljazeera.com/articles/2013/8/13/military-suicidescausedbymentalillnessnotptsdresearcherssay.html.

U.S. Department of Health and Human Services. n.d. "Post-Traumatic Stress Disorder." National Institutes of Health. http://www.nimh.nih.gov/health/topics/post-traumatic-stress-disorder-ptsd/index.shtml.

U.S. Department of Veteran Affairs. n.d. "PTSD Overview." PTSD: National Center for PTSD. Professional Section. http://www.ptsd.va.gov/professional/PTSD-overview/index.asp.

PRIESTS, SEXUAL ABUSE BY

Sexual activity by a priest involving a child is a severe abuse that harms the children as victims, the priests as perpetrators, and the religious institution itself. Although abuse by members of the clergy may happen within any religion or denomination, in the United States, sexual misconduct by priests is most closely associated with the Catholic Church. As of May 9, 2013, the U.S. Conference of Catholic Bishops (USCCB) released data on accused priests and persons making allegations. There were 6,275 accused priests and 16,795 survivors.

The children that Roman Catholic priests abuse are 78 percent males and 22 percent females. Some priests abuse both girls and boys (3.6%). Most reported victims were at or approaching the age of puberty; 60 percent of male victims were first abused between the ages of 10 and 14.

A 2004 national survey of victimization conducted for the 2004 American Catholic Bishops' Conference found that, in the United States, only 4 percent of priests and deacons were involved in the abuse. Outside of the Catholic Church, most juvenile victims of sexual abuse were female. Within the church, four out of five of their victims were male. Most were adolescents aged 14 or over; 15 percent were under 10.

The causes of priest abuse of youth include:

- Improper screening for candidates for the priesthood, with few requirements.
- Poor informing or training of candidates about sexuality, celibacy, and appropriate boundary setting between a priest and others.
- Poor response by church leaders to the problem of sexually abusive priests. Bishops were uninformed on the consequences of the abuse, and their need to protect the

institution above the needs of the people added to the secrecy. Bishops held conflicting opinions about the treatability of pedophilia and other forms of sexual offenses and placed the image of the priests above the rights and welfare of the victims.

- Institutionally based causes were the discomfort of bishops with sexual topics due to generational norms, and family and cultural values, and fear that the scandal would bring about great changes in the Church.

Priest sexual abuse produced a wide range of consequences. The strength of the authority of the Church caused victims of both genders to experience trauma and disillusionment with the church and a loss of religious faith. Twenty percent of children considered suicide. Adult survivors testified to having feelings of extreme anger and resentment and a psychological inability to confide in anyone about the abuse. Some women experienced a loss of faith, felt forced into secrecy, faced accusations of having been seductive with an innocent priest, repressed the memory, and/or blamed themselves.

Court testimony revealed additional consequences of abuse by priests that are severe and long term, such as sexual dysfunction. The failure to function properly may include impotence, sexual aversion, hypersexuality, the development of paraphilias (the need for an extreme or dangerous stimulus such as a sadistic or masochistic practice in order to achieve sexual arousal or orgasm) that may include pornography, voyeurism, fetishes, or continuance of the abuse into a new generation.

On January 17, 2014, a first of its kind internal Vatican document revealed the number of priests forcibly removed for sex abuse by the Vatican's in-house procedures In two years, Pope Benedict XVI defrocked almost 400 priests for raping and molesting children, more than twice as many as the two years that preceded a 2010 explosion of sex abuse cases in Europe and beyond. In 2011, 260 priests were defrocked, and in 2012, 124: a total of 384. The number reflected a dramatic increase over the 171 priests defrocked in 2008 and 2009. The increase began a year after the Vatican decided to double the statute of limitations on the crime, enabling victims in their late 30s to report abuse committed against them when they

Cardinal Bernard Law explains the priest sexual abuse policy. (AP/Wide World Photos)

were children. A canon lawyer reported that the real figure is probably much higher, since the numbers do not include sentences given by diocesan courts.

In January 2014, the UN Committee on the Rights of the Child meeting in Geneva, Switzerland, questioned Vatican officials about sexual abuse of children by members of the clergy. The committee criticized the officials for their handling of the cases. The Vatican responded that changes were taking place, but, around the world, action against abusive priests is taken by local law enforcement officials.

Legal prosecutions and settlements are another indicator of solutions being implemented. According to the U.S. Conference of Catholic Bishops, as of 2012, there were: $2.5 billion in settlements, therapy bills for victims, attorneys' fees, and costs to care for priests removed from the ministry from 2004 to 2011. Legal action, rehabilitative efforts, institutional changes, and/or personal therapy are all solutions in process for abuser and victim alike.

Prevention is a good option for the individual pastor and begins at the level of seminary training. Pastors need to understand the nature of their power, the authority of their role, and the responsibility that goes along with it. They need to learn how to maintain boundaries in relationships. They need to learn how to care for their own emotional and sexual needs. Prevention in the church should focus on unequivocal policies and procedural safeguards to help churches avoid hiring an offending pastor. The best way to prevent inappropriate hiring is to discuss, in the open, a pastor's violation of professional ethics.

Rosemarie Skaine

See also: Child Abuse, Sexual; Pedophilia.

Further Reading

Associated Press. 2014. "Vatican Defrocked Nearly 400 Priests for Sex Abuse in 2 Years." Al Jazeera America, January 17. http://america.aljazeera.com/articles/2014/1/17/vatican-defrockedover400priestsforsexabusein2years.html.

BishopAccountability.org. 2013. "Number of Priests Accused of Sexually Abusing Children as Reported by the U.S. Conference of Catholic Bishops with Numbers of Persons Alleging Abuse." Compiled from reports commissioned by the USCCB. http://www.bishop-accountability.org/AtAGlance/USCCB_Yearly_Data_on_Accused_Priests.htm.

Frawley-O'Dea, Mary G., and Virginia Goldner, eds. 2007. *Predatory Priests, Silenced Victims: The Sexual Abuse Crisis and the Catholic Church*. Mahwah, NJ: The Analytic Press.

Grossman, Cathy Lynn. 2013. "Clergy Sex Abuse Settlements Top $2.5 Billion Nationwide." *USA Today*, March 13. http://www.usatoday.com/story/news/nation/2013/03/13/sex-abuse-settlement-cardinal-roger-mahony/1984217.

Howie, Michael. 2014. "UN Hearing Confronts Vatican for Protecting Child Sex Abuse Priests." *Evening Standard*, January 16.

Kington, Tom. 2014. "U.N. Panel Grills Vatican Officials about Abuse of Children." *Los Angeles Times*, January 16. http://www.latimes.com/world/worldnow/la-fg-wn-vatican-united-nations-abuse-children-20140116,0,5561107.story#ixzz2rX7C9p2j.

Sipe, A. W. Richard. 2006. "Unspeakable Damage: The Effects of Clergy Sexual Abuse." *Gould v. Soens*, Appendix B. http://www.bishop-accountability.org/docs/davenport/2006_09_05_Gould_v_Soens_Statement_Disputed_Facts/2006_09_05_Gould_v_Soens_Exhibit_21_B.pdf.

Skaine, Rosemarie. 1996. *Power and Gender: Issues in Sexual Dominance and Harassment.* Jefferson, NC: McFarland.

United States Conference of Catholic Bishops. 2004. "A Report on the Crisis in the Catholic Church in the United States." National Review Board for the Protection of Children and Young People. http://old.usccb.org/nrb/nrbstudy/nrbreport.htm.

van Wormer, Katherine S. 2010. "Priest Abuse: Male Compared to Female Victimization Impact." *Crimes of Violence.* http://www.psychologytoday.com/blog/crimes-violence/201005/priest-abuse-male-compared-female-victimization-impact.

PRISONER ABUSE, ADULT

Adults in the criminal justice system in the United States are subjected to abuse by the system, prison inmates, and prison employees. Overcrowding in the prisons contributes to prisoner abuse. In the 1981 case, *Rhodes v. Chapman*, the U.S. Supreme Court ruled that prison overcrowding is not unconstitutional, per se, but that overcrowding can lead to other conditions that violate the Eighth Amendment, which prohibits cruel and unusual punishment. The court defined those conditions as "the wanton and unnecessary infliction of pain," "pain without any penological purpose," "serious deprivation of basic human needs," or deprivation of "the minimal civilized measure of life's necessities."

The State of California has been ordered to reduce the overcrowding in its prison system, which is deemed so severe it has deprived inmates of adequate medical and mental health care. The state was ordered to reduce its prison population by 30,000, to 110,000, by April 2014.

In some overcrowded, understaffed institutions, the authorities sometimes use racial conflict as a means to divide and conquer the inmate population. They allow one or more violent cliques to dominate the rest of the prison population and maintain internal order and discipline. Some prisons are run by gangs, and prisoners must join one group or the other to survive. According to the "Convict Code," convicts can beat, rape, even kill their fellow inmates, but one must not snitch on them.

Abuse by inmates against other inmates is a common occurrence. The corrections industry itself estimates that there are 12,000 rapes per year. The number one fear of those going to prison is being raped, and getting killed is second. It is common in prison for an inmate or group of inmates to coerce other prisoners into sexual activity.

Amnesty International reports that, in 2004, a total of 2,298 allegations of staff sexual misconduct against both male and female inmates were made, and more than half of these cases involved women as victims. Allegations against prison staff involved 822 cases total from 2000 to 2004. Of the cases, 322 cases were investigated by the Office of the Inspector General. Of those cases, 186 cases resulted in administrative penalties, and 65 cases resulted in criminal penalties.

Violent assault on inmates is the most common type of abuse committed by correctional officers. This is the needless beating, hitting, kicking, or striking of a prisoner. An officer's unnecessary or excessive use of a weapon upon a defenseless inmate is a typical example. These attacks can cause lacerations, broken bones, internal injuries, disfigurement, brain or spinal cord damage, and even death. At

New York City's Rikers Island Jail, a former corrections officer was sentenced to six years in prison for a series of assaults that occurred while he worked as a guard. He had orchestrated severe beatings of teenage inmates in an organized scheme called "The Program."

Abuse by guards is more subtle than violence inflicted by the inmates on each other. They may tear up an inmate's mail, refuse to turn up the heat, deny privileges, or search the cell. Strip searches are another form of intimidation or abuse. They may occur multiple times a day, in various areas. It may also involve a cavity search.

Sexual assault from guards is more common in detention facilities than one would think. The National Inmate Survey reveals that 4.4 percent of prison and jail inmates report being sexually victimized in the past 12 months. Sexual abuse can occur verbally or through physical contact, although verbal sexual abuse is extremely difficult to prove and rarely leads to recovery of damages. Sexual abuse can also result in severe physical injury.

In order to prevent prison rape, Congress passed the Prison Rape Elimination Act (PREA) in 2003. PREA aims to establish zero-tolerance standards of sexual assaults, to increase data and information on the occurrence of prison sexual assault, and to develop and implement national standards for the detection, prevention, reduction, and punishment of prison sexual assault.

Although inmates know that officer misconduct is unlawful, they tolerate the assault as a simple fact of prison life. Prisoners do have the power to bring personal injury suits to protect their rights, obtain compensation for their injuries, and punish the misbehaving guards. Abused inmates have multiple causes of actions including: assault; deprivation of civil rights; negligence in ownership, operation, maintenance, supervision, and security of the correctional facility; negligent hiring of personnel; and negligent retention of personnel.

When an inmate brings a lawsuit against New York City for prison guard abuse, the court will make the ultimate determination on whether the guard was acting unlawfully. In determining whether the city is legally liable for inmate injuries, the court will base its decision upon the particular facts and circumstances involved in each case. It is crucial for victims to seek an experienced legal advocate to give themselves a powerful voice. New York law has a time-sensitive process that inmates must follow to bring claims against the city. Inmates must file a notice of claim with the city within 90 days after the harm occurred, although, in rare circumstances, there can be valid excuses for a delay. Any procedural error or delay in filing the notice of claim or subsequent lawsuit may forfeit the victim's right to recover.

Connie Kerns-Grams

See also: Prisoner Abuse, Juvenile.

Further Reading

Beam, Christopher. 2009. "Roommates for Life: How Do Prisons Deal with Overcrowding?" Slate.com, June 30. http://www.slate.com/articles/news_and_politics/explainer/2009/06/roommates_for_life.html.

CA.Gov. 2014. "Prison Overcrowding State of Emergency Proclamation." Office of Governor Edmund G. Brown Jr. http://gov.ca.gov/news.php?id=4278.

Fogel, Nussin S. 2014. "Inmate Abuse by Corrections Officers and the Legal Recourse Available." Law Offices of Nussin S. Fogel. http://www.nsfogel.com/Articles/Inmate-Abuse-by-Corrections-Officers-and-the-Legal-Recourse-Available.shtml.

Mintz, Howard. 2014. "California Prison Overcrowding: Governor Asks Court for More Time to Shed Inmates." *San Jose Mercury News*, January 24. http://www.mercurynews.com/crime-courts/ci_24980457/california-prison-overcrowding-governor-asks-court-more-time.

Ross, Jeffrey Ian, and Stephen C. Richards. 2002. *Behind Bars*. Indianapolis: Alpha Books.

Summer, Nicole, and Daniel Brook. 2010. "Women in Prison Are Sexually Vulnerable" and "Men in Prison Are Sexually Vulnerable." In *Crime and Criminals: Opposing Viewpoints*, edited by Christina Fisanick and Elizabeth Des Chenes, 35–49. Farmington Hills, MI: Greenhaven Press.

PRISONER ABUSE, JUVENILE

Abuse of juvenile prisoners occurs when they are emotionally or physically harmed or harassed into thinking or behaving against their will. Abuse of juvenile inmates occurs from prison officials and other inmates. Juvenile prisoners experience the same abuses adults face when incarcerated.

Over the years, some juvenile prisons or reformatories have been the scene of brutal and deadly treatment of the juvenile inmates. One of these was the Dozier School for Boys, a shuttered Florida juvenile detention facility formerly known as the Florida State Reform School and the Florida Industrial School for Boys. Dozier garnered a lasting reputation for brutality: 96 boys died while incarcerated there, and 45 are believed to be buried at the site. In August 2013, state legislators approved a plan to let researchers excavate for human skeletal remains at the school. Researchers will use DNA testing to determine the identities of the bones of boys.

The case of Thomas Varnadoe demonstrates the nature of the concern. Varnadoe was 13 years old when he was sent to the Florida Industrial School for Boys, as it was then called. On September 21, 1934, he and his 15-year-old brother, Hubert, were accused of stealing a typewriter from the back porch of a woman's house. They said they were innocent, but the local sheriff sent both boys immediately to the reform school nearly 300 miles away. Today, the only evidence that remains of the boys' alleged crime is their names written in the school's inmate logbook along with their ages, parents' names, and crime, "malicious trespass."

Abuse of juveniles by prison staff is common. The Justice Department reported in 2014 that 12 percent of incarcerated juveniles, or more than 3,200 young people, had been raped or sexually abused in the past year by fellow inmates or prison staff. The study by the department's Bureau of Justice Statistics reported a "very high rate of staff sexual misconduct" against juvenile inmates. The report, based on surveys from 195 facilities in all 50 states and Washington, D.C., is the first of its kind. Rates varied among the institutions, but at 13 detention facilities, nearly one out of three juveniles said they had been victims of some type of sexual abuse.

Data presented is from the 2012 National Survey of Youth in Custody (NSYC), conducted in 326 juvenile confinement facilities between February and September 2012, with a sample of 8,707 adjudicated youth. The report ranks facilities according to the prevalence of sexual victimization, as required under the Prison Rape Elimination Act of 2003 (P.L. 108-79). The prevalence of victimization, as reported by youth during a personal interview, is based on sexual activity in the 12 months prior to the interview or since admission to the facility, if less than 12 months. This report provides state and national estimates of juvenile sexual victimization by type of activity, including estimates of youth-on-youth nonconsensual sexual contact, staff sexual misconduct, and level of coercion.

An estimated 9.5 percent of adjudicated youth in state juvenile facilities and state contract facilities (representing 1,720 youth nationwide) reported experiencing one or more incidents of sexual victimization by another youth or staff in the past 12 months or since admission. About 2.5 percent of youth (450 nationwide) reported an incident involving another youth, and 7.7 percent (1,390) reported an incident involving facility staff. An estimated 3.5 percent of youth reported having sex or other youth-reported sexual contact with staff without any force, threat, or explicit form of coercion.

Thirteen facilities were identified as having a high rate based on the prevalence of sexual victimization by youth or staff. Rates in each of these facilities had a 95 percent confidence interval with a lower bound that was at least 35 percent higher than the average rate of sexual victimization among facilities nationwide. About 67.7 percent of youth victimized by another youth reported experiencing physical force or threat of force, 25.2 percent were offered favors or protection, and 18.1 percent were given drugs or alcohol to engage in sexual contact.

Legislation has been created and implemented to assist with eliminating juvenile abuse in prisons. Congress enacted the Juvenile Justice and Delinquency Prevention (JJDP) Act (Pub. L. No. 93-415, 42 U.S.C. § 5601 et seq.) in 1974. This landmark legislation established OJJDP to support local and state efforts to prevent delinquency and improve the juvenile justice system. On November 2, 2002, Congress reauthorized the JJDP Act. The reauthorization (the 21st Century Department of Justice Appropriations Authorization Act, Pub. L. No. 107-273, 116 Stat. 1758) supports OJJDP's established mission while introducing important changes that streamline the office's operations and bring a sharper focus to its role. The provisions of the reauthorization took effect in fiscal year 2004 (October 2003).

The Juvenile Justice and Delinquency Prevention Act is the single most important piece of federal legislation affecting youth in juvenile justice systems across the country. It is the primary vehicle through which the federal government sets standards for state and local juvenile justice systems and provides direct funding for states, research, training and technical assistance, and evaluation. Since the original enactment of the JJDPA, in 1974, the periodic reauthorizations have been very contentious, as the act's opponents have sought to weaken its protections for youth, reduce prevention resources, and encourage the transfer of youth to the adult criminal justice system.

Connie Kerns-Grams

See also: Child Abuse Prevention and Enforcement Acts; Prisoner Abuse, Adult.

Further Reading

Beck, A., D. J. Cantor, J. Hartge, and T. Smith. 2013. *Sexual Victimization in Juvenile Facilities Reported by Youth, 2012*. Bureau of Justice Statistics. Office of Justice Programs. (NCJ241708). http://www.bjs.gov/index.cfm?ty=pbdetail&iid=4656.

Center for Children's Law and Policy. n.d. *Juvenile Justice and Delinquency Prevention Act (jjdpa)*. Center for Children's Law and Policy. http://www.cclp.org/contact.php.

Fogel, Nussin S. 2014. "Inmate Abuse by Corrections Officers and the Legal Recourse Available." Law Offices of Nussin S. Fogel. http://www.nsfogel.com/Articles/Inmate-Abuse-by-Corrections-Officers-and-the-Legal-Recourse-Available.shtml.

Johnson, C. 2010. "Justice Study Tracks Rape, Sexual Abuse of Juvenile Inmates." *Washington Post*, January 8. http://www.washingtonpost.com/wp-dyn/content/article/2010/01/07/AR2010010703849.html.

Office of Justice, Office of Juvenile Justice and Delinquency Prevention. n.d. *Legislation*. http://www.ojjdp.gov/about/legislation.html.

Towey, Megan. 2013. "The Search for The Dead: Families of Boys Who Died at Shuttered Dozier Juvenile Detention Facility Seek Answers." *CBS News*. August 8. http://www.cbsnews.com/news/the-search-for-the-dead-families-of-boys-who-died-at-shuttered-dozier-juvenile-detention-facility-seek-answers.

R

RACISM

Racism is a powerfully negative phenomenon that can lead to hate speech, hate crimes, sexual harassment, rape, and other forms of physical, emotional, and verbal abuse. One definition of racism is power plus prejudice. Color prejudice is an unquestioned emotional attachment to a falsehood about someone who has a different appearance. Racism believes in the superiority of one group over another, an attitude of arrogance and ignorance. It goes further than personal values and beliefs to broader societal systems that support the idea of white superiority and nonwhite inferiority.

Systemic racism disadvantages people of color and advantages whites, whether or not whites are aware of or want these privileges. Examples of racial groups classified according to obvious physical characteristics such as skin color include: Blacks, Native Americans, Asian Americans, Hawaiians, and Hispanics.

The Changing Face of America, 1950–2050, presented by PEW Institute, demonstrated the racial representations of Asians, Hispanics, Blacks, and Whites. Respectively, for example, these groups represented the following percentage of the total population:

- In 1950: 0, 3, 10, 87
- In 2010: 5, 16, 13, 65
- Projected for 2050: 9, 29, 13, 47

In 2013, the Pew Research Center reported that fewer than half (45%) of all Americans say the country has made substantial progress toward racial equality, and about the same share (49%) say that "a lot more" remains to be done.

Since racism preserves domination, power, and control, it provides rationale and justification for debasing, degrading, and acts of violence to people of color. According to Kenneth T. Ponds in *Reclaiming Children & Youth*, this thinking is the basis of trauma because trauma leaves a person feeling hopeless, helpless, and fearing for safety or survival. Racial trauma is the physiological, psychological, and emotional damage resulting from the stressors of racial harassment or discrimination.

In the racism that exists in the United States today, attitudes are more subtle than the strong and blatant expressions in the past. In racism today, there is the belief that racial minorities are overly aggressive and forceful in attaining societal resources, that they receive unfair opportunities, and are undeserving of the positions or status they have achieved. Those who hold racist views contend that racial discrimination no longer happens. One position that racists hold is that there should be color blindness and that race should not be used in making education or employment decisions. These attitudes have been displayed in the way that President Obama is depicted in much of the media. The media campaign has been successful because 84 percent of the Republicans in one poll said they disapproved of Obama.

Racist attitudes communicate that racial minorities push themselves where they are not wanted or have gotten more economically than they deserve. These attitudes are found in the stated positions of racial resentment expressed by Tea Party members and in discussions of the ban on ethnic studies in Arizona. Attitudes and beliefs that contribute to racism attitudes among white individuals include social dominance orientation and right-wing authoritarianism and are among the strongest predictors of racial prejudice.

The killing of 17-year-old African American Trayvon Martin, in February 2012, by a white Neighborhood Watch captain, George Zimmerman, who used a stand your ground law as his defense, is an example of how the law has been changed to enable racially based attacks. Zimmerman was acquitted of murder in July 2013. The polls showed a racial divide in public opinion surrounding the case, with disparities on issues ranging from reaction to the verdict to the need for a national discussion on race. According to a Pew Research Center poll, 86 percent of African Americans expressed dissatisfaction with the verdict, compared with 30 percent of whites. A *Washington Post/ABC News* poll reported a similar finding: 9 percent of blacks approved of acquitting George Zimmerman of criminal charges in Martin's death, compared with 51 percent of whites who approved. The *Post/ABC News* data reported that 87 percent of blacks say the shooting was unjustified, compared to 33 percent of whites.

Individual and systemic forms of racism have social, economic, and personal consequences. Racism Free Edmonton believes that long-standing racism can result in trauma that can impact for generations in the following ways:

- Prevents members from feeling like equal and valued members of society
- Isolates and excludes people, creating resentment and mistrust
- Creates ongoing psychological stress and anxiety, which can have an impact on work, family life, and overall health and well-being
- Prevents equal opportunities to better their lives and is the primary reason for higher levels of unemployment and underemployment among Aboriginal people and other racialized groups
- Prevents groups and communities from interacting with each other and can increase discomfort, fear, and resentment
- Causes negative effects on an individual's physical and mental health

Scholar Kenneth T. Ponds suggests that one race, the human race, is a concept that is part of racial healing and the lessening of trauma. Racial healing of youth must become an important component in education and treatment. First, an atmosphere of safety must be created as well as one of valuing youth. Education of including rethinking the entire concept of race and gaining a historical view of racism.

President Obama outlined solutions to racism in 2008 by responding in a speech titled "Not This Time":

- This time we want to talk about the crumbling schools that are stealing the future of black children and white children and Asian children and Hispanic children and Native American children.
- This time we want to reject the cynicism that tells us that these kids can't learn; that those kids who don't look like us are somebody else's problem. The children of America are not those kids, they are our kids, and we will not let them fall behind in a 21st century economy. Not this time.
- This time we want to talk about how the lines in the emergency room are filled with whites and blacks and Hispanics who do not have health care; who don't have the power on their own to overcome the special interests in Washington, but who can take them on if we do it together.
- This time we want to talk about the shuttered mills that once provided a decent life for men and women of every race, and the homes for sale that once belonged to Americans from every religion, every region, every walk of life.
- This time we want to talk about the fact that the real problem is not that someone who doesn't look like you might take your job; it's that the corporation you work for will ship it overseas for nothing more than a profit.
- This time we want to talk about the men and women of every color and creed who serve together, and fight together, and bleed together under the same proud flag. We want to talk about how to bring them home from a war that never should've been authorized and never should've been waged, and we want to talk about how we'll show our patriotism by caring for them, and their families, and giving them the benefits they have earned.

The events in Ferguson, Missouri, where the unarmed teenager, Michael Brown, was killed by a police officer, have led to a civil rights investigation by U.S. Attorney General Eric Holder. On September 4, 2014, Holder stated that the investigation will focus on the Ferguson police department.

Having the United States be free of racism will require the good faith cooperation of the American society and the people. Progress has been made, but more is needed.

Rosemarie Skaine

See also: Hate Crimes; Homosexuals; Matthew Shepard and James Byrd, Jr., Hate Crimes Prevention Act; Stand Your Ground Law; Transgender Individuals.

Further Reading

CNN Library. 2014. "Trayvon Martin Shooting Fast Facts." http://www.cnn.com/2013/06/05/us/trayvon-martin-shooting-fast-facts.

Levinson, Alana. 2013. "Polls Show Wide Racial Gap on Trayvon Martin Case." *NPR*. http://www.npr.org/blogs/itsallpolitics/2013/07/22/204595068/polls-show-wide-racial-gap-on-trayvon-martin-case.

McClam, Erin, and Aaron Mermelstein. 2014. "Eric Holder Opens Broad Probe into Ferguson Police." *Nightly News*, September 4. NBC News. http://www.nbcnews.com/storyline/michael-brown-shooting/eric-holder-opens-broad-probe-ferguson-police-n195886.

Obama, Barack. 2008. "A More Perfect Union." National Constitution Center, March 18. http://constitutioncenter.org/amoreperfectunion.

Pew Research Center. 2013. "King's Dream Remains an Elusive Goal; Many Americans See Racial Disparities." http://www.pewsocialtrends.org/2013/08/22/kings-dream-remains-an-elusive-goal-many-americans-see-racial-disparities.

Pew Research Center. 2013. "PowerPoint Presentation: State of Race." Aspen Institute Symposium, April 22. http://www.pewresearch.org/2013/05/03/the-state-of-race-in-america.

Ponds, Kenneth T. 2013. "The Trauma of Racism: America's Original Sin." *Reclaiming Children & Youth* 22 (2). Reclaiming Youth International. www.reclaimingjournal.com.

Poteat, V. Paul, and Lisa B. Spanierman. 2012. "Modern Racism Attitudes among White Students: The Role of Dominance and Authoritarianism and the Mediating Effects of Racial Color-Blindness." *Journal of Social Psychology* 152 (6): 758–774.

Racism Free Edmonton. n.d. "What Is the Impact of Racism?" http://racismfreeedmonton.ca/site/what_is_the_impact_of_racism.

Schaefer, Richard T. n.d. "What Is a Minority Group?" Race, Racism and the Law. http://www.racism.org/index.php?option=com_content&view=article&id=280:minor0101&catid=15:understanding-minority-group-status&Itemid=118.

RAPE

The traditional definition of rape is the unlawful compelling of a woman through physical force or duress to have sexual intercourse. Defining rape as "the carnal knowledge of a female, forcibly and against her will," addresses only forcible penetration of a woman's vagina by a penis. The definition now has been expanded to include males, and the types of sexual assault that will be counted include forcible anal or oral penetration, the penetration of the vagina or anus with an object or other body part, the rape of a man, or the rape of a woman by another woman, or nonconsensual sex that does not involve physical force including the rape of victims who are unable to grant consent because they are under the influence of alcohol or younger than the age of statutory consent in their state. The definition specifically covers "penetration, no matter how slight, of the vagina or anus with any body part or object, or oral penetration by a sex organ of another person, without the consent of the victim."

Each year, there is an average of 207,754 rape and sexual assault victims age 12 or older, according to the U.S. Department of Justice's National Crime Victimization Survey. Every two minutes, someone in the United States is sexually assaulted. Men and women are victims of rape. About 9 out of 10 victims are female. Three percent of American men have been victims of an attempted or completed rape in his lifetime. Two-thirds of rapes are committed by someone known to the victim, and 73 percent of sexual assaults were perpetrated by a nonstranger. Of these, 38 percent were by a friend or acquaintance, 28 percent by an intimate, and 7 percent by a relative.

The majority of sexual assaults are not reported to the police. In the 2006 to 2010 period, 54 percent of assaults, on average, were not reported. Of the 46 out of 100 rapes that get reported to the police, 12 lead to an arrest, 9 get prosecuted, 5 lead to a felony conviction, and 3 receive a prison sentence.

A University of Virginia student looks over postings on the door of Peabody Hall related to the Phi Kappa Psi gang rape allegations at the school in Charlottesville, Virginia, on November 24, 2014. The university suspended activities at all campus fraternal organizations amid an investigation into a published report in which a student described being sexually assaulted by seven men in 2012 at the Phi Kappa Psi house. (AP Photo/Steve Helber)

The culture of the American society contributes to the low percentages of reporting and the number of prison sentences. The victim is often blamed for the attack. The reasons given are the victim was (1) dressed provocatively, (2) participated willingly, (3) had been sexually active, or (4) was drunk or on drugs. In one case, the victim's volition and sexuality were presented as mitigating factors that somehow "invited" the sexual assault. The victim was accused of being older than her chronological age and of being "in control of the situation." She was 14, and the perpetrator was a 48-year-old man in a position of authority over her. The victim took her own life before justice could be served—an act her mother believes was connected to her sexual assault and its aftermath.

The causes of rape are not clear in all cases, but the most dominant motives include power, anger, sadism, and sexual gratification. Power rape is the desire to control and dominate rather than hurt the survivor. Anger rape is resentment toward others, usually women. The offender believes that something should be done to punish the victim and achieve some type of revenge. Anger rape is more violent than power rape and usually occurs between total strangers.

Sadistic rapes are the least common and are usually preplanned and are the most brutal, using torture, bondage, and sexual abuse. The offender derives pleasure and sexual gratification from hurting and degrading the victim. Rape seeking sexual gratification is the most common type and is committed most in acquaintance and date rapes. Just enough force is used to make the victim cooperate, and violence occurs only if there is resistance.

The effects of rape can be long lasting and include: shock and disbelief, painful remembering of what happened, intense emotions, physical symptoms, fears about safety, self-blame, and shame. Effects include: posttraumatic stress disorder (PTSD), substance abuse, self-harm or self-injury, Stockholm syndrome (bonding with rapist), depression, sexually transmitted infections, pregnancy, flashbacks, borderline personality disorder, sleep and/or eating disorders, body memories, dissociative identity disorder, suicide, and military sexual trauma.

When the sexual assault is not immediately reported, Carol K. Bates suggests the following steps be taken:

- Find a safe environment away from the assailant.
- Call a close friend or relative—someone who will offer unconditional support.
- Seek medical care. Do not change clothes, bathe, douche, or brush teeth until evidence is collected. A complete medical evaluation includes evidence collection, a physical examination, treatment, and/or counseling. You do not have to do any part of this evaluation that you do not want to do.
- Discuss filing a police report with a crisis counselor, experienced social worker, sexual assault nurse examiner, or health care provider.
- Follow up with a health care provider one to two weeks later.
- Seek counseling services.
- Inquire about victim compensation services.

Rape and sexual assault are significant crimes, and yet the criminal justice statistics on prosecution, conviction, and sentencing do not reflect the seriousness. The culture of blaming the victim contributes to the reluctance to prosecute. The criminal justice system should decide rape and sexual assault cases on the evidence, as it would any other crime.

Rosemarie Skaine

See also: Rape, Abuse, and Incest National Network; Rape, Date; Rape, Gender Stereotypes and; Rape, Marital; Rape, Statutory.

Further Reading

Bates, Carol K. 2013. "Patient Information: Care after Sexual Assault (Beyond the Basics)." UpToDate. http://www.uptodate.com/contents/care-after-sexual-assault-beyond-the-basics.

Bronner, Ethan. 2012. "A Candidate's Stumble on a Distressing Crime." *New York Times*, August 23. http://www.nytimes.com/2012/08/24/us/definition-of-rape-is-shifting-rapidly.html?_r=0.

FindLaw. 2013. "Rape." http://criminal.findlaw.com/criminal-charges/rape.html.

Horvath, Miranda, Angel Helena, and Liz Kelly. 2009. "Multiple Perpetrator Rape: Naming an Offence and Initial Research Findings." *Journal of Sexual Aggression*: 83–96.

911rape. n.d. "Impact of Rape." Rape Treatment Center (RTC), Santa Monica–UCLA Medical Center. http://www.911rape.org/impact-of-rape/common-reactions.

One in Four. n.d. "Sexual Assault Statistics." http://www.oneinfourusa.org/statistics.php.

Rape, Abuse, and Incest National Network (RAINN). 2009. "Effects of Sexual Assault." http://www.rainn.org/get-information/effects-of-sexual-assault.

Rape, Abuse, and Incest National Network (RAINN). 2009. "The Offenders." http://www.rainn.org/get-information/statistics/sexual-assault-offenders.

Rape Crisis Center of Medina and Summit Counties. 2013. "Get the Facts." 2013. http://www.rccmsc.org/resources/get-the-facts.aspx.

Savage, Charlie. 2012. "U.S. to Expand Its Definition of Rape in Statistics." *New York Times*, January 6. http://www.nytimes.com/2012/01/07/us/politics/federal-crime-statistics-to-expand-rape-.definition.html.

SexInfo Online. 2013. "Rape." http://www.soc.ucsb.edu/sexinfo/article/rape.

Shea, Rachel Hartigan. 2013. "UN Study Looks at High Rate of Rape." *National Geographic*, September 14. http://news.nationalgeographic.com/news/2013/09/130914-rape-asia-pacific-un-men-violence-women.

Skjelsbæk, Inger. 2006. "Victim and Survivor: Narrated Social Identities of Women Who Experienced Rape during the War in Bosnia-Herzegovina." *Feminism and Psychology* 16 (4): 373–403. http://www.usip.org/sites/default/files/missing-peace/Inger-Skjelsbaek.pdf.

Truman, Jennifer L. 2011. "National Crime Victimization Survey: Criminal Victimization, 2010." U.S. Department of Justice, Office of Justice Programs, Bureau of Justice Statistics. http://www.bjs.gov/content/pub/pdf/cv10.pdf.

RAPE, ABUSE & INCEST NATIONAL NETWORK

Working to reduce rape and sexual violence and to help the victims of rape and sexual violence is the mission of the Rape, Abuse & Incest National Network (RAINN). RAINN works with 1,100 local rape crisis centers throughout the United States. Since 1994, RAINN has helped over 1.5 million through its Web-based crisis hotline, 1-800-656-HOPE, by providing live and anonymous support. It also operates the DoD Safe Helpline for the Department of Defense. In 2007, hotline services were expanded to include the National Sexual Assault Online Hotline, the nation's first secure Web-based hotline. In November 2007, RAINN won the NPower Greater DC Region Technology Innovation Award for its online hotline.

RAINN assists policy makers and the media in issues related to rape and sexual violence. RAINN works to educate Americans to prevent sexual violence through its extensive entertainment industry relationships and community partnerships. The result is that more than 120 million Americans are educated each year about sexual assault. In August 2007, movie actress Christina Ricci joined RAINN as a national spokesperson. In addition to entertainers, athletes, and media networks, tens of thousands across the United States comprise two support groups: the RAINNMakers raise money to support RAINN's programs, and the RAINN Day volunteers work to end sexual violence on over 1,000 campuses.

Scott Berkowitz, president and founder of RAINN, reported that the rapist does not often pay a price for the crime because out of every 100 rapes, only 46 are reported to police, and only three rapists will spend a day in jail. Since rapists tend to be serial criminals, each one that is left on the streets is likely to commit more attacks.

In 2010, Berkowitz testified before the U.S. Senate Subcommittee on Crime and Drugs on the failure to report and investigate rape cases. In spite of progress, 15 out of every 16 rapists in America will walk free, and as long as they have a 94 percent chance of escaping punishment, they are not likely to be deterred. In 2013, he submitted a commentary on the U.S. Supreme Court ruling in *Maryland v. King* that police can take a DNA swab when there is a serious crime. Berkowitz said that if the ruling had not favored police taking the DNA, it would have hurt the fight against rape. Instead, the court preserved a valuable tool in the fight. The issue before the court involved a man convicted of a six-year-old rape after his DNA was taken after an arrest. In 2009, Alonzo King was arrested on assault charges and had his cheek swabbed. The resulting DNA was linked to the six-year-old crime scene, and King was then convicted for the rape of a 53-year-old woman at gunpoint.

RAINN emphasizes the importance of the victim reporting the rape. On its Web site, it has an entire section called "Get Help." In addition to the hotlines, help is available through the ability to search for a local crisis center. The centers offer assistance in individual or group counseling or support groups, legal/criminal justice system and crime victim assistance advocacy, community and professional education, casework/practical assistance, emergency shelter, and hospital accompaniment.

Because victims are reluctant to report rape and thus take advantage of help, police officers and doctors misjudge the impact they have on rape victims and the extent to which their statements or actions affect victims. Victims have reported more "post-system-contact" distress than service providers thought they were experiencing, such as left feeling responsible, distressed, depressed, disappointed, and reluctant to seek further help. This post-system-contact distress is significant because the quality of the initial contact that a victim has with law enforcement and medical personnel has the potential to strongly affect whether or not that victim goes forward through the criminal justice system. RAINN works to eliminate the post-system-contact distress.

Rosemarie Skaine

See also: Rape; Rape, Date; Rape, Statutory.

Further Reading

Berkowitz, Scott. 2013. "High Court's DNA Ruling Will Help Catch Rapists." Opinion, June 3, *CNN*. http://www.cnn.com/2013/05/29/opinion/berkowitz-dna-rape-cases.

Berkowitz, Scott. 2010. Testimony. "Rape in the United States: The Chronic Failure to Report and Investigate Rape Cases." Hearing, September 14. Senate Judiciary Committee. Subcommittee on Crime and Drugs. 111th Congress. 2nd session. http://www.judiciary.senate.gov/pdf/10-09-14BerkowitzTestimony.pdf. View a Webcast of the hearing: http://www.judiciary.senate.gov/hearings/hearing.cfm?id=e655f9e2809e5476862f735da16234b.

Rape, Abuse, and Incest National Network (RAINN). 2009. "Mission Statement." About. http://www.rainn.org/about-rainn/mission-statement.

Ricci, Christina, and Scott Berkowitz. 2011. "Presenting the Television Academy Honors Award to Candi Carter for the *Oprah Winfrey Show*." Uploaded on May 5, 2011. http://www.youtube.com/watch?v=Ys1ceL8wT00&noredirect=1.

RAPE, DATE

Date rape refers to forcible sexual intercourse committed against an individual during or after a social engagement by a person who could be a friend, acquaintance, or stranger. The person is usually the individual's date or escort. Date rape is commonly called *acquaintance rape*. A form of date rape is a drug-facilitated sexual assault and involves the individual raped, knowingly or unknowingly, consuming alcohol or taking drugs. In 1994, a national survey found that 15 percent of women students on college campuses reported being victims of rape, and 12 percent reported attempted rape. Fifty-seven percent of the incidents occurred during dates, and 75 percent of the assailants and 55 percent of the victims had used alcohol or other drugs prior to the assault.

Under the law, a person has to get a clear verbal or nonverbal "yes" to have sex. Just because consent is given for one sexual activity (sexual contact, even with few clothes on) in one instance, does not mean permission is given for any other. Silence does not mean consent. Being under the influence of alcohol does not mean the individual gives consent.

Drugs facilitate rape because rapists do not have to overcome resistance by the individual being raped. Since drug-facilitated rape is often initiated in social settings, the action appears to bystanders to be voluntary substance consumption. The targeted individual does not sense any threat. The overpowering and disabling drug is placed in a drink. Afterward, the victim does not recall events.

Alcohol usage is more common than drugs in drug-facilitated rape. The most commonly used drugs are Rohypnol (flunitrazepam) and GHB (gamma-hydroxybutyrate). Rohypnol, is a central nervous system depressant in the benzodiazepines class of drugs. Rohypnol incapacitates an individual, mentally and physically, especially when used in combination with alcohol. It is capable of producing anterograde amnesia, a condition in which events that occur during the time the drug was in effect are forgotten.

Gamma hydroxybutyrate (GHB) is a powerful, rapidly acting central nervous system depressant. GHB is abused for its ability to produce euphoric and hallucinogenic states. Coma and seizures can occur following abuse of GHB and, when combined with methamphetamine, there appears to be an increased risk of seizure. Combining use with other drugs such as alcohol can result in nausea and difficulty breathing. GHB may also produce withdrawal effects, including insomnia, anxiety, tremors, and sweating.

Club drugs that include Ecstasy (MDMA), Special-K, methamphetamines (meth, speed, crystal, ice, or crank), GHB, and roofies, increasingly are the illegal drugs of choice, especially at all-night dance parties or raves. Club drugs are sometimes coupled with abuse of prescribed drugs. Some are stimulants, others are depressants or hallucinogenic. Ecstasy is also known as the "hug drug." It has a quick high, allowing the user to engage in activities all night. The heart rate and body temperature are accelerated, and judgment is impaired. Methamphetamines can cause anxiety, paranoia, and cardiovascular problems.

In 2007, the National Crime Victims Research and Treatment Center of the Medical University of South Carolina conducted a national study that revealed out of the 112 million women surveyed, nearly 3 million women experienced drug-facilitated rape. Victims of drug-facilitated or incapacitated rape were to some extent less likely to report than victims of forcible rape. They were less likely to report for fear of disclosure and retaliation, and uncertainty how to report or of evidence or whether the rape was a crime or whether harm was intended. Injury was reported in 30 percent of drug-facilitated or incapacitated rape incidents, and medical care was received following 21 percent of drug-facilitated or incapacitated rape incidents.

Victims of forcible versus drug-facilitated and incapacitated rape were comparable with regard to risk for posttraumatic stress disorder (PTSD) (23% and 34% national and college samples) and depression (9.1% and 13.1%). Notably, victims of drug-facilitated or incapacitated rape were nearly twice as likely as victims of forcible rape to have in the past year substance abuse problems. This was true both in the national and college student samples. Drug-facilitated or incapacitated rape victims were almost twice as likely as forcible rape victims to have past-year substance abuse problems; 6.7% and 19.8% of women in the national and college samples. The National Crime Victims Research and Treatment Center found the most common rape risk situation was not being rendered intoxicated, but being taken advantage of by a sexual predator after becoming intoxicated voluntarily.

Treatment of drug-induced rape is multifaceted. Drugging should be recognized as a separate and distinct act of victimization in addition to any other acts of abuse and degradation. The message needs to be very clear that club drugs are deadly and to stay away from them. Date rape, especially when facilitated with drugs, may lead to feelings of confusion afterward. Victims may not even be sure if they were raped.

The stress, shame, fear, and self-blame that may arise after date rape can lead to intense emotional trauma. Such trauma may take months or even years to heal, although professional treatment and support from loved ones can speed the victim's recovery. Although counseling and other forms of professional treatment can have enormous value, even many years after a rape has occurred, they are most effective when sought soon after an incident has occurred. In such cases, services can prevent damaging and negative long-term changes in emotional functioning and life choices from emerging.

The Drug Induced Rape Prevention Act in 1996 provided harsh penalties for the distribution of controlled substances without the individual's consent and with the intent to commit a crime of violence, including sexual assault. Under this act, the punishment for the importation and distribution of Rohypnol includes up to 20 years in prison and a fine; possession is punishable by three years and a fine. Under the Date-Rape Drug Prohibition Act of 2000, regulation tightened. GHB was classified as a Schedule I controlled substance, like heroin. It is now illegal for Americans to produce, sell, or possess GHB, except for medical use. Prevention strategies should reach new audiences in low-risk environments, such as bartenders, party hosts, cab drivers, and others who might frequent places where drug-facilitated rapes are initiated or who might see the victim prior to rape.

Rosemarie Skaine

See also: Rape; Rape, Abuse, and Incest National Network; Rape, Gender Stereotypes and; Rape, Marital; Rape, Statutory.

Further Reading

Casa Palmera Staff. 2010. "Healing from Date Rape and Trauma." Casa Palmera. http://casapalmera.com/healing-from-date-rape-and-trauma.

Fitzgerald Nora, and K. Jack Riley. 2000. "Drug-facilitated Rape: Looking for the Missing Pieces." *National Institute of Justice Journal* (April).

Hickman, Laura J., Lisa H. Jaycox, and Jessica Aronoff. 2005. *Dating Violence among Adolescents: Prevalence, Gender Distribution, and Prevention Program Effectiveness.* RAND Corporation. http://www.rand.org/content/dam/rand/pubs/reprints/2005/RAND_RP1176.pdf.

Kilpatrick, Dean G., Heidi S. Resnick, Kenneth J. Ruggiero, Lauren M. Conoscenti, and Jenna McCauley. 2007. "Drug-facilitated, Incapacitated, and Forcible Rape: A National Study." National Crime Victims Research & Treatment Center. Medical University, SC. https://www.ncjrs.gov/pdffiles1/nij/grants/219181.pdf.

National Institution on Drug Abuse. 2013. "Rohypnol and GHB." *Alcoholism.* About.com. http://alcoholism.about.com/cs/date/l/blnida12.htm.

Stepp, L. 2007. "A New Kind of Date Rape." *Cosmopolitan* 243 (3): 198.

U.S. Congress. House. 2000. "Methamphetamine and Date Rape Drugs: A New Generation of Killers." Hearing before the Subcommittee on Criminal Justice, Drug Policy, and Human Resources of the Committee on Government Reform, September 18. 106th Congress. 2nd sess.

Warsaw, Robin. 1994. *I Never Called It Rape: The Ms. Report on Recognizing, Fighting, and Surviving Date and Acquaintance Rape.* New York: Harper Collins Publishers.

RAPE, GENDER STEREOTYPES AND

According to the Bureau of Justice Statistics, 203,830 Americans became victims of rape or first-degree sexual assault in 2008. The crime of first-degree sexual assault is defined as "non-consensual sexual intercourse that is committed by physical force, threat of injury, or other duress." A lack of consent could include the inability of one party to reject sex because of the effect of alcohol or drugs. The victim can be a date or even the offender's spouse. A second kind of rape is called *statutory rape.* This type includes sexual intercourse between an adult and a consenting child. This generally means that the child is someone not yet age 18.

Because the victims of this crime are often embarrassed to report the assault to the police, rape is sometimes described as the "hidden crime." Although there has been a rise in the number of rapes reported to the police since the 1970s, most such crimes remain unreported. In fact, it has been estimated that even in the early 21st century, only 31 percent of rapes are ever reported to the police.

These circumstances make prosecution for rape difficult. Among the difficulties are the attitudes of the police toward the rape victims and the perpetrators. Police are as much the product of their socialization as any other member of a society, so the attitude that police personnel have toward rape victims and women in general affects the outcome of complaints against rape perpetrators. Undoubtedly, the patriarchy that has until recently dominated life in the United States has led to the failure of many female rape victims to report this crime.

The attitudes of both victims and police, as well as others, with reference to rape are, of course, socially constructed. Thus, gender determines the manner in which each sex responds to the other, the term "gender" being defined as the social outcome and interpretation of sex in various cultures. There are those critics who hold that "gender performance" contributes greatly to sex stereotypes that are difficult to overcome and appear to be self-perpetuating. Gender performance refers to aggressive male behavior, docility among women, and a neat fit between sex and emotional and social characteristics exhibited by either sex.

The gender performance model is, of course, gradually disappearing as more and more women become heads of households, earn advanced degrees, become professionals, and raise their income and their social standing higher than their mothers could have imagined. As a result, traditional patriarchy is no longer as effective as it was a generation ago, although it still exists and must be accounted for with reference to police attitudes concerning rape victims.

Therefore, police treat women who adhere closely to the gender stereotypes expected of them differently than they do complainants who deviate from such gender-driven beliefs. Indeed, the sexual history of a female complainant is often used to decide whether or not the victim should be given credibility.

A number of beliefs about the victims of rape have been current for some years and continue to plague the prosecution of this crime. The first of these beliefs is that only "bad" girls get raped. "Bad" here refers to the sexual conduct of the victim, although smoking, drinking, using prohibited substances, being divorced, and other prejudicial categories are also factors in how victims are judged by the police and by society in general. This belief is augmented by the view that "women ask for it" and the further rapist defense that women use the rape tactic only to cover up that they have been rejected by the alleged offender.

A further myth relates to the view that sexually active women are more likely to be raped, particularly if they wear "provocative" clothing. Women are advised by some believers in these myths not to walk alone at night but assure themselves the company of a man; further, women should also not enter a bar alone nor be visibly inebriated or otherwise impaired. All these behaviors are viewed by American men as unacceptable for women but perfectly fine for men, and thus such behaviors have been used to "blame the victim" of rape.

Gerhard Falk

See also: Rape; Rape, Date; Rape, Marital; Rape, Statutory; Victim Blaming.

Further Reading

Falk, Gerhard. 2010. *The American Criminal Justice System: How It Works, How It Doesn't, and How to Fix It*. Santa Barbara, CA: Praeger.

Fortier, Laura. 1975. "Women, Sex and Patriarchy." *Family Planning Perspectives* 7 (6): 278–81.

U.S. Department of Justice, Bureau of Justice Statistics. *Criminal Victimization, Number and Rates, 2008*. http://bjs.ojp.usdoj.gov.

Wesely, J. K., and Edward Gaarder. 2004. "The Gendered Nature of the Urban Outdoors: Women Negotiating Fear of Violence." *Gender and Society* 18 (5): 645–663.

RAPE, MARITAL

First legally recognized in 1975, the concept of marital rape remains difficult to define. Many cultural elements and conflicting definitions affect the approach a state or government takes toward the act of marital rape. Generally defined as nonconsensual sexual activity perpetrated by the victim's spouse, marital rape frequently occurs throughout the United States. Despite its legal recognition, many people view marital rape not as a form of rape but rather as a small conflict resulting from differing opinions of sexual frequency in a marriage.

The concept of marital rape did not take form until the 1970s, when the state of South Dakota first recognized rape by a spouse as a form of rape. With the precedent set by South Dakota, the remaining states changed their rape laws to include spousal rape, with the last state doing so in 1993. However, a majority of states in the United States continue to prosecute marital rape as a lesser crime than other forms of rape.

General society stigmatizes marital rape in the United States as a minimal marital conflict. Many people view the act as not "real" rape, but rather a disagreement as to how frequently sex should occur in a marriage. In actuality, victims of marital rape often experience worse long-term psychological effects than victims of nonmarital rape. In addition to the feelings of violation, loss of control, and violence, victims of marital rape feel betrayed by their spouse. Following the rape, the victim also continues living with their rapist at home, forcing them to relive their experience frequently.

Studies of occurrences and types of rape among female populations indicate that marital rape may be the most common type of rape in the United States. Studies of occurrences of rape indicate that millions of women state that their spouse or ex-spouse has raped them. Reports also suggest that the highest percentage of marital rapes occur in relationships in which the husband batters the wife. These studies have also suggested that marital rape victims come largely from lower socioeconomic classes, with high school dropouts four times more likely to be raped than graduates.

While motivations for marital rape vary, the act frequently occurs near the end of a relationship, resulting from a spouse's anger, desperation regarding the end of the relationship, or marital problems. The National Clearinghouse on Marital and Date Rape was founded in 1978 to address the lack of marital rape laws in the United States. Providing educational information, counseling, and litigation, the organization has helped thousands of women to resolve their marital rape problems.

Rosemarie Skaine

See also: Domestic Abuse; Rape; Reproductive Coercion.

Further Reading

Finley, Laura L., ed. 2013. *Encyclopedia of Domestic Violence*. Santa Barbara, CA: Greenwood.
McNulty, Faith. 1980. *The Burning Bed*. New York: Harcourt.

RAPE, STATUTORY

Statutory rape occurs when a person, regardless of age, has consensual sexual relations with an individual not old enough to legally consent. The FBI's definition characterizes statutory rape as nonforcible sexual intercourse with a person who is younger than the statutory age of consent. Although every state has laws that make sex with a minor illegal, the age of consent differs from state to state as does the label of and the punishment for the crime. The offender may be an adult or a juvenile.

In the most states (34), the age of consent is 16 years of age. In the remaining states, the age of consent is either 17 or 18 (6 and 11 states, respectively). Only 12 states have a single age of consent below which a person cannot consent to sexual intercourse under any circumstances, and above which it is legal to engage in sexual intercourse with another person above the age of consent. In Massachusetts, the age of consent is 16. In 39 states, other factors are considered, such as age differentials, minimum age of the victim, and minimum age of the defendant.

From 1996 to 2000, the FBI's National Incident-Based Reporting System (NIBRS) analyzed statutory rape in 21 states. Out of 28,098 victims, 7,557 aged 7 to 17 (27%) involved statutory rape. Victims were primarily female (95%), but about three of every five victims were age 14 or 15, regardless of gender. Offenders were mainly male (99%), except in cases of male statutory rape; victims were chiefly female (94%). Of male offenders of female victims, 18 percent were younger than age 18. Of all offenders of male victims, 70 percent were age 21 and older, compared to 45 percent of offenders of female victims being 21 and older. Age difference between female offenders of male victims was nine years compared to the difference between male offenders and female victims of six years. Three out of 10 offenders were boyfriends or girlfriends, and 6 in 10 were acquaintances. Arrests were made in 42 percent of the cases, with the likelihood of arrest declining as the victim's age increased.

Common causes of statutory rape include: ignorance of or disregard for the law, unthinking state of mind, or the younger party's untruthfulness about his or her age. Regardless of stated reasons for the rape, consequences, especially for the offender, are great. Statutory rape is a strict liability crime, administering the offender punishment whether or not the victim consented. Strict liability crimes significantly diminish or eliminate the defenses allowed.

Devastating human and social consequences result when adults prey sexually upon children, according to the Massachusetts Family Institute. These effects include: increased rates of fatherlessness and teenage pregnancy, higher levels of welfare dependency, higher rates of child poverty, and sexual coercion and abuse of children.

Since defense of statutory rape is difficult, seeking advice from a lawyer experienced in criminal defense law is an optimal solution. A conviction can lead to prison, fines, or registration as a sex offender. A lawyer can advise on laws in particular states. Some states have Romeo and Juliet laws. This law provides a defense to a person who is less than a specified number of years older than the victim at the time of the sexual contact. If both participants are close in age (usually within three years), they can take advantage of the Romeo and Juliet law.

To reduce statutory rape, the Massachusetts Family Institute suggested legislative reform, strong enforcement of the law, and education campaigns. Legislative reforms would include: increasing the criminal penalties, creating a new child abuse felony, enacting civil penalties for offenders, and consider raising the age of sexual consent to 18 to reflect the age of marriage laws. Enforcement of laws include: allocating funds to allow district attorneys to target prosecution, creating special crime fighting units to investigate and prosecute, prosecuting regardless of pregnancy, and expanding statutory rape education for law enforcement personnel.

Rosemarie Skaine

See also: Adult Sexual Attraction to Adolescents; Child Abuse, Sexual; Pedophilia; Rape; Rape, Abuse, and Incest National Network; Rape, Date.

Further Reading

Daniels, Matthew, and Dan Englund. 1998. "Statutory Rape: When Adults Prey Sexually upon Children." Newton Upper Falls, MA: Massachusetts Family Institute. http://www.hawaii.edu/hivandaids/Statutory%20Rape%20%20%20When%20Adults%20Prey%20Sexually%20Upon%20Children%20MA.pdf.

England, Deborah C. n.d. "Do Statutory Rape Laws Apply When the Adult Is an Older Woman and the Minor Is Male?" Criminal Defense Lawyer.com. http://www.criminaldefenselawyer.com/resources/do-statutory-rape-laws-apply-when-adult-older-woman-a.

Glosser, Asaph, Karen Gardiner, and Mike Fishman. 2004. "Statutory Rape: A Guide to State Laws and Reporting Requirements." Office of the Assistant Secretary for Planning and Evaluation, U.S. Department of Health and Human Services. http://aspe.hhs.gov/hsp/08/sr/statelaws/index.shtml.

Parsons, David Joseph. "Statutory Rape: A General Overview." *AVVO*. http://www.avvo.com/legal-guides/ugc/statutory-rape-a-general-overview.

Troup-Leasure, Karyl, and Howard N. Snyder. 2005. "Statutory Rape Known to Law Enforcement." *OJJDP*. Office of Justice Programs, U.S. Department of Justice. https://www.ncjrs.gov/pdffiles1/ojjdp/208803.pdf.

REPRODUCTIVE COERCION

Sexual coercion is defined as unwanted sexual penetration after being pressured in a nonphysical way. Sexual coercion affects both women and men. In 2010, the Centers for Disease Control and Prevention estimated 13 percent of women and 6 percent of men have experienced sexual coercion in their lifetime. Twenty-seven percent of women and 11.7 percent of men have experienced unwanted sexual contact.

Reproductive coercion is defined as behaviors used to have power and control over the reproductive health of a woman. When a woman is forced to engage in sexual activity, to get pregnant or maintain a pregnancy against her will, she is subjected to reproductive coercion. The coercion can come from a male or from governmental agencies. Rape is sexual coercion. If the rape results in pregnancy and the woman is forced to carry the fetus full term, it is reproductive coercion.

Reproductive control exists in violent and nonviolent relationships. Violence used by an intimate partner to enforce the coercion makes the woman less likely to make independent decisions about contraception and family planning. Male reproductive control not only includes pregnancy-promoting behaviors but also control and abuse during pregnancy in an effort to control the pregnancy outcome, wrote scholars Ann

M. Moore et al. Pregnancy promotion involves male partner attempts to impregnate a woman, including verbal threats about getting her pregnant, unprotected forced sex, and contraceptive sabotage. Once a woman is pregnant, coercion includes threatening a woman if she does not do what the male wants with the pregnancy.

Some women engage in reproductive coercion. When differences arise over whether to stay together or get married or have children, some evidence suggests that the most common way women "trap" a man is to become pregnant. The question of whether they would have chosen pregnancy could undermine the relationship, cause insecurities, or affect attitudes toward the child once it is born. "It would be more useful to learn new ways to communicate with your partner," according to the Professor's House Web site.

Reproductive coercion on the part of males undermines women's ability to prevent an unwanted pregnancy and sometimes leaves her unable to act independently. These inabilities make reproductive coercion a public health problem.

Poor reproductive health outcomes include unplanned pregnancies that contribute to unsafe abortions and mortality, add to the abortion rate, or result in mistimed or unwanted births. Adolescents especially face the additional result of missed opportunities, including the adverse consequence of contracting HIV.

For adolescents, Michael Takura Mbizvo and Shahida Zaidi recommend dissemination "of information on sexual and reproductive health issues, such as safe sexual practices, contraception, risks related to early childbearing; unsafe abortion and its adverse consequences; and inadequate linkages between sexual and reproductive health and HIV interventions that result in missed opportunities for addressing both."

Health care providers may be able to provide education by assessing for male reproductive control among women looking for reproductive health services, including antenatal care. In addition, providers can employ counseling to help women protect their reproductive health and physical safety. When education is ineffective, family planning clinics' intervention may reduce the risk for reproductive coercion from abusive male partners and support such women to leave unsafe relationships. Counseling women and men is also recommended.

Rosemarie Skaine

See also: National Coalition Against Domestic Violence; Rape, Marital.

Further Reading

Black, M. C., K. C. Basile, M. J. Breiding, S. G. Smith, M. L Walters, M. T. Merrick, J. Chen, and M. R. Stevens. 2011. "The National Intimate Partner and Sexual Violence Survey (NISVS): 2010 Summary Report." Atlanta, GA: National Center for Injury Prevention and Control, Centers for Disease Control and Prevention. http://www.cdc.gov/violenceprevention/nisvs.

Cantor, Julie D. 2012. "Court-ordered Care—A Complication of Pregnancy to Avoid." *New England Journal of Medicine* 366 (June 14): 24.

Mbizvo, Michael Takura, and Shahida Zaidi. 2010. "Addressing Critical Gaps in Achieving Universal Access to Sexual and Reproductive Health (SRH): The Case for Improving Adolescent SRH, Preventing Unsafe Abortion, and Enhancing Linkages between SRH and HIV Interventions." *International Journal of Gynecology and Obstetrics* 110: S3–S6.

Miller, Elizabeth, Michele R. Deckerb, Heather L. McCauleyc, Daniel J. Tancredia, Rebecca R. Levensond, Jeffrey Waldmane, Phyllis Schoenwalde, and Jay G. Silverman. 2011. "A Family Planning Clinic Partner Violence Intervention to Reduce Risk Associated with Reproductive Coercion." *Contraception* 83: 274–280.

Moore, Ann M., Lori Frohwirth, and Elizabeth Mille. 2010. "Male Reproductive Control of Women Who Have Experienced Intimate Partner Violence in the United States." *Social Science and Medicine* 70: 1737–1744.

Planned Parenthood Federation of America. 2012. "Fact Sheet." www.plannedparenthood .org.

Professor's House. 2013. "Trapping a Man." http://www.professorshouse.com/Relationships/ Dating/Articles/Trapping-a-Man.

ROAD RAGE

Road rage is a motorist's uncontrolled anger that is usually provoked by another motorist's irritating act and is expressed in aggressive or violent behavior. The National Highway Traffic Safety Administration (NHTSA) defines aggressive driving as: when individuals commit a combination of moving traffic offenses so as to endanger other persons or property. Some other communities define aggressive driving as: the operation of a motor vehicle involving three or more moving violations as part of a single continuous sequence of driving acts, which is likely to endanger any person or property.

Some behaviors typically associated with aggressive driving include exceeding the posted speed limit, following too closely, erratic or unsafe lane changes, improperly signaling lane changes, failure to obey traffic control devices (stop signs, yield signs, traffic signals, railroad grade cross signals, etc.), and red-light running. NHTSA calls the act of red-light running one of the most dangerous forms of aggressive driving.

In the past, young men have been the most prone to road rage. In a 2002 Rage-Depression Survey, the most competitive, aggressive population of those polled were men under the age of 19. Men reported feeling a sense of rage more frequently than women. Fifty-six percent of the men surveyed said they experienced rage on a daily basis versus 44 percent of the women. More men also admitted to retaliating against others when they felt angry or provoked.

A recent poll showed that women are more likely to feel road rage. A new study finds women are more likely to act out when stressed behind the wheel. Of the nearly 4,000 drivers polled nationwide, 58 percent said they experience rage while commuting. Women are more likely to fly off the handle. The study found 61 percent of women admit feeling road rage, compared to only 56 percent of men. Age is another factor. It found that about 68 percent of respondents between 25 and 34 were the most likely to get angry behind the wheel.

Drivers who engage in road rage tend to vent their stress or frustration on other motorists who share the road. The AAA Foundation for Traffic Safety reported that an average of at least 1,500 men, women, and children are injured or killed each year in the United States as a result of aggressive driving. Road rage gives impatient or aggressive drivers an avenue to vent their frustrations and anger on other drivers who share the road. Unfortunately, innocent passengers, bystanders,

U.S. Department of Defense poster (1999) issued during the 1988–2000 campaign against road rage. (Department of Defense)

and pedestrians get caught up in road rage. A report from the AAA Foundation for Traffic Safety states that at least 218 men, women, and children are known to have been killed and 12,610 people injured as a result 10,037 road rage incidents it examined. The 12,610 injuries included cases in which people suffered paralysis, brain damage, amputation, and other seriously disabling injuries. Victims are usually considered accidental deaths, and found themselves unable to avoid the onslaught of an aggressive driver.

Road rage can lead to an angry motorist driving into a building to seek revenge on the establishment or its owners. Some drivers may wish to wage a vendetta against the owner of the property or attempt to gain attention. Drivers use their vehicles as weapons to cause damage to properties, such as government buildings, schools, or a place of residence.

The response to road rage ranges from anger management for the motorist to outlawing talking on a cell phone while driving to increasing police presence on the roads. Public awareness campaigns and extensive driver's education courses beginning at grade school level are necessary to decrease road-rage incidents. Criminal penalties for road rage are being increased. In New Jersey, the penalties for road rage were increased to as much as five years in jail and fined $15,000, the same penalties for those who cause injuries while driving drunk.

Rosemarie Skaine

See also: Anger; Anger Management; Intermittent Explosive Disorder (IED).

Further Reading

CBS New York. 2012. "Women More Prone to Road Rage, New Study Finds." http://newyork. cbslocal.com/2012/07/31/women-more-prone-to-road-rage-new-study-finds.

National Highway Traffic Safety Administration. n.d. "Define Aggressive Driving." *Aggressive Driving Enforcement.* http://www.nhtsa.gov/people/injury/enforce/aggressdrivers/ aggenforce/define.html.

Shure, Olivea. n.d. "The Effects of Road Rage." eHow. http://www.ehow.com/info_8375862_ effects-road-rage.html.

SAFE HAVEN LAWS

Safe haven laws provide safe places for parents to relinquish their newborn infant when they want to abandon the child at birth. The purpose of these laws is to prevent babies from being abandoned at places that might bring them harm. The first Baby Moses law, or infant safe haven law, was enacted in Texas in 1999 as an incentive for mothers in crisis to safely give up their babies at designated locations where the babies are protected and provided with medical care until a permanent home is found for them. The laws usually allow parents anonymity and to be shielded from prosecution. Providers who accept the infants have responsibility, but are immune from liability for anything that might happen to the infant while in their care, unless evidence demonstrates major negligence on the part of the provider.

As of 2013, all 50 states, the District of Columbia, and Puerto Rico have enacted safe haven legislation to protect newborns. In 12 states and Puerto Rico, infants who are 72 hours old or younger may be given to a designated safe haven. Nineteen states accept infants up to one month old. Other states specify varying age limits in their statutes.

In most states, either parent may surrender the baby to a safe haven. In four states and Puerto Rico, only the mother may do so. Idaho and the District of Columbia allow only a custodial parent, and the District also requires that the custodial parent be a resident. In 11 states, an agent approved by the parent may take a baby to a safe haven. In California, Kansas, and New York, if the person relinquishing the infant is someone other than a parent, he or she must have legal custody of the child. Eight states do not specify the person who may relinquish an infant.

The provider must be able to administer the immediate care needed for the baby's safety and well-being. To ensure this care, 16 states and Puerto Rico require parents to relinquish their infants only to a hospital, emergency medical services provider, or health care facility. In 27 states, fire stations also are designated as safe haven providers. Personnel at police stations or other law enforcement agencies may accept infants in 25 states. In 5 states, emergency medical personnel responding to 911 calls may accept an infant, and 4 states allow churches to act as safe havens as long as the parent has assurance that church personnel are present at the time the infant is relinquished.

Requirements for the safe haven provider vary from state to state. Requirements include:

- Being able to accept emergency protective custody and to provide any needed immediate medical care

- When the provider that receives the baby is not a hospital, the baby must be transferred to a hospital as soon as possible, and to notify the local child welfare department that an infant has been relinquished.
- Asking the parent for family and medical history information
- Giving the parent or parents information about the legal repercussions of leaving the infant and information about referral services
- Offering the parent a copy of the infant's numbered identification bracelet to help link the parent to the child in case of future reunification

Parents have protections when they relinquish an infant. These safeguards include a guarantee of anonymity and protection from criminal liability. Evidence of child abuse or neglect forfeits the protections.

The child welfare department assumes custody of the infant as an abandoned child when the provider notifies them. The department then places the infant and petitions the court to terminate the birth parents' rights. Twenty states and the District of Columbia allow a parent to reclaim the infant.

Rosemarie Skaine

See also: Child Abandonment and Neglect; Domestic Abuse; Safe House.

Further Reading

Child Welfare Information Gateway. 2013. "Infant Safe Haven Laws." *State Statutes*. Washington, D.C.: U.S. Department of Health and Human Services, Children's Bureau. https://www.childwelfare.gov/systemwide/laws_policies/statutes/safehaven.cfm.

Child Welfare Information Gateway. 2013. "State Statutes Search." Washington, D.C.: U.S. Department of Health and Human Services, Children's Bureau. https://www.childwelfare.gov/systemwide/laws_policies/state.

National Safe Haven Alliance (NSHA). n.d. Confidential Toll-free Crisis Hotline: 1-888-510-BABY (2229). http://www.nationalsafehavenalliance.org/about.php.

Sanger, Carol. 2006. "Infant Safe Haven Laws: Legislating in the Culture of Life." *Columbia Law Review* 106 (4): 753–829. http://www.jstor.org/stable/4099469.

SAFE HOUSE

A safe house is a premise established by an organization for the purpose of conducting clandestine or covert activity in relative security. Safe houses serve a wide range of purposes:

- To provide a secure location, suitable for hiding witnesses, agents, or other persons perceived as being in danger
- To be a place where people may go to avoid prosecution of their activities by authorities
- To be a place where undercover operatives may conduct clandestine observations or meet other operatives surreptitiously
- To be a location where a trusted adult or family or charity organization provides for victims of domestic abuse
- To provide a home of a trusted person, family, or organization where victims of war and/or persecution may take refuge or be given asylum, receive protection and/or live in secret

The safe house for witnesses whose testimony is under threat provides protection until the threat subsides. Witness protection safe houses are expensive to maintain over a long period, so law enforcement has moved to using the relocation method instead. The problem with relocation is that it can be too harsh a solution for innocent witnesses, some of whom do not want to permanently leave their neighborhoods and families.

State and national child advocates were not in favor of proposed state legislation that would authorize child sex trafficking victims to be "locked up" in treatment centers for up to 10 months. An amendment to the Safe Harbor Act of January 2013 provided for a secure safe house" pilot program for sexually exploited children with the greatest needs.

Safe houses are used in intervention, including to encourage members to disengage from gangs. The Rossbrook House in Winnipeg, Canada, offers intervention within a safe house, providing young people a safe haven and opportunities for socialization, recreation, crisis intervention, and personal development through encouraging education and job training.

Victims of domestic violence and sexual assault benefit from access to safe houses. The United Way Safe House Center in Ann Arbor, Michigan, provides free and confidential services for any victimized person that lives or works in Washtenaw County. Services include emergency shelter for those in danger of being hurt or killed, counseling, legal advocacy, and support groups.

Rosemarie Skaine

See also: Child Abuse, Sexual; Child Trafficking; Domestic Abuse, Physical; YWCA Abuse Services.

Further Reading

Cetin, Hakan Cem. 2010. "The Effectiveness of the Witness Security Program in the Fight against Organized Crime and Terrorism: A Case Study of the United States and Turkey." PhD diss., Rutgers, State University of New Jersey. ProQuest.

Chu, Chi Meng, Michael Daffern, Stuart D. M. Thomas, and Jia Ying Lim. 2011. "Elucidating the Treatment Needs of Gang-affiliated Youth Offenders." *Journal of Aggression, Conflict and Peace Research* 3 (3): 129–140. doi:10.1108/17596591111154167 E.

Cravey, Beth Reese. 2014. "'Secure Safe House' Program to Lock Up Victims; Opponents of Amendment to Safe Harbor Act Say It's Bad Public Policy." *Florida Times Union*, B-4, March 19.

SafeHouse Center. 2014. Washtenaw County, MI. http://www.safehousecenter.org.

SAME-SEX RELATIONSHIPS, VIOLENCE IN

Men rape men, and women rape women. Such violence may take the form of date or marital rape. Lesbian, gay, bisexual, and transgendered (LGBT) victims of same-sex domestic violence often feel very isolated because of a lack of support from both the wider community and the LGBT community. Many lesbian, gay, bisexual, and transgendered people believe that if domestic violence exists within the LGBT community, it takes the form of mutual fighting and does not reflect the same power and control as heterosexual domestic abuse. Just like many straight men, many gay men believe that men are supposed to be able to defend themselves from other men's violence. Men are "not supposed to be victims." Harkening back to a distant past when many people believed that two women could not have sex with each other because no penis was present, some people believe that one woman lacks the ability to rape another.

Sexual violence within same-sex relationships has been particularly difficult to acknowledge. Gay culture often holds that men are supposed to want and enjoy sex pretty much whenever it is available from someone that they are attracted to. Patrick Letellier, a rape survivor, related his story in *Same-sex Domestic Violence: Strategies for Change*: "I called it rough sex," he wrote, before adding, "forcing himself on me. Being selfish and inconsiderate, a beast, a monster. He called it getting what he wanted. What he was entitled to. . . . [I] occasionally tell a sexual partner that sex can be difficult for me because I was . . . raped. They almost always furrow their eyebrows. Gay men don't use that word when they talk about themselves."

Among women, attitudes toward butch and femme roles can lead to unintended support for the attackers. Batterers can play on the misassumption, both within and outside of the lesbian community, that butch is the same as male. A femme can abuse her butch partner by forcing sexual activity that her partner does not want. The abuser can deflect responsibility by claiming that the victim is just not butch enough. A butch woman may have her bad behavior excused as just being a part of being butch.

Caryn E. Neumann

See also: Domestic Abuse; Homosexuals: Transgender Individuals.

Further Reading

Hawley, John C., ed. 2009. *LGBT America Today: An Encyclopedia*. Westport, CT: Greenwood.
Neumann, Caryn E. 2009. *Sexual Crime: A Reference Handbook*. Santa Barbara, CA: ABC-CLIO.

SANDUSKY, JERRY

Gerald Arthur "Jerry" Sandusky (born January 26, 1944) was involved in a child sexual abuse scandal that involved minor boys. The scandal had serious consequences for Sandusky and Pennsylvania State University.

Sandusky was a starter as a defensive end in the Penn State football program from 1963 to 1965. He returned to Penn State in 1969 as an assistant coach and remained there until his retirement at the end of the 1999 season. After he retired, Sandusky hosted many summer football camps and was active in the Second Mile, a children's charity he founded in State College, Pennsylvania, in 1977.

Sandusky had a strategy to cull vulnerable boys (whom he would first approach when they were 8 to 12 years old) through the Second Mile organization, targeting his potential victims at will (boys tended to be from homes without a father present), at which point Sandusky employed classic child-grooming strategies (offering trips to football games, gifts, leading to incremental touching). This form of manipulation, generally the modus operandi of pedophiles, Sandusky used as a ploy to build trust while invading personal boundaries, all part of instilling confusion, leading up to and part of the sexual abuse. (Sandusky often initiated overtly sexual behavior in the locker room showers.) One victim testified that he was forced to put his hand on Sandusky's erection when he was 8 to 10 years old. One investigator said that the poor kid was too young to even understand what an erection was.

In 2002, Sandusky was observed sexually assaulting a 10-year-old boy in the shower of the football locker room. Mike McQueary, a graduate assistant assigned to the football program, observed the assault and reported it to the football coach, Joe Paterno. Paterno then informed Penn State athletic director Tim Curley. Curley and the senior vice president for finance and business, Gary Schultz (who oversaw the Penn State police department), called McQueary to a meeting a week and a half later. During the meeting, McQueary said that he relayed in graphic detail what he had witnessed in the locker room showers at the Lasch Building. No action was taken against Sandusky at that time.

An investigation was initiated by the Pennsylvania attorney general's office into sexual abuse allegations against Sandusky in 2008. The charges were initiated at Central Mountain High School, where a student made allegations of abuse against Sandusky. The investigation reached a new level of urgency when it became apparent that the allegations were not an isolated set of incidents, but that Sandusky had a strategy to involve vulnerable boys sexually through the Second Mile organization.

On November 4, 2011, a grand jury, that had been convened over two years earlier, indicted Sandusky on 40 counts of sex crimes against young boys. The indictment came after a three-year investigation that explored allegations of Sandusky's having inappropriate contact with an underage boy over the course of four years, beginning when the boy was 10 years old. The boy's parents had reported the incident to police in 2009. The grand jury identified eight boys that had been singled out for sexual advances or sexual assaults by Sandusky, taking place from 1994 through 2009. At least 20 of the incidents allegedly took place while Sandusky was still employed at Penn State. The indictment also accused Curley and Schultz not only of failing to tell the police but also of falsely telling the grand jury that McQueary never informed them of the alleged sexual activity.

On November 5, 2011, Sandusky was arrested and charged with seven counts of involuntary deviate sexual intercourse, eight counts of corruption of minors, eight counts of endangering the welfare of a child, seven counts of indecent assault, and other offenses. Curley and Schultz were charged with perjury and failure to report suspected child abuse by Sandusky. On November 6, 2011, Penn State banned Sandusky from campus. His bail conditions did not include restrictions on his travel.

In December 2011, Sandusky was charged with an additional 12 counts of sexual crimes against children. The grand jury's second presentment charged Sandusky with an additional count of involuntary deviate sexual intercourse and two additional counts of unlawful contact with a minor. The additional victims, known only as "Victim 9" and "Victim 10," were participants in Sandusky's youth program and were between the ages of 10 and 12 at the time of the sexual assaults.

On December 7, 2011, Sandusky was arrested for a second time based on the additional sexual abuse charges. Sandusky was released on $250,000 and placed on monitored house arrest while he awaited trial.

At the trial, Sandusky was charged with 52 counts of sexual abuse of young boys over a 15-year period. Four of the charges were subsequently dropped. On June 22, 2012, Sandusky was found guilty on 45 of the 48 remaining charges. He was sentenced on October 9, 2012, to 30 to 60 years in prison. He remains in prison.

The consequences for Joe Paterno, Penn State administrators, and the university were swift and severe. On November 10, 2011, Penn State trustees fired Paterno and university president Graham Spanier for how the school handled the sex abuse allegations. The action came hours after Paterno announced that he planned to retire at the end of his 46th season, but the outcry following the arrest of Sandusky on molestation charges proved too much for the board to ignore. The ouster of the man affectionately known as "JoePa" brought to an end one of the most storied coaching careers, not just in college football but in all of sports. Paterno has 409 victories, a record for major college football; won two national titles; and guided five teams to unbeaten, untied seasons. He reached 300 wins faster than any coach.

The Sandusky scandal proved to be the undoing of the legacy of Paterno. The NCAA fined Penn State $60 million, vacated from the record its 112 wins from 1998–2011, and banned it from bowl games until 2016. Paterno died on January 22, 2012, at the age of 85.

On July 12, 2012, a special investigative group headed by former FBI director Louis Freeh that had been commissioned by the Penn State Board of Trustees issued its report. After interviewing over 400 people and reviewing over 3.5 million documents, the report's main finding was that, in order to avoid the consequences of bad publicity, the most powerful leaders at the university, President Graham Spanier, Schultz, Paterno, and Curley, repeatedly concealed critical facts relating to Sandusky's child abuse from authorities, the university's Board of Trustees, the Penn State community, and the public at large.

The avoidance of the consequences of bad publicity was the main driver in failing to protect child abuse victims and failing to report to authorities. The report found that there was (1) a striking lack of empathy for child abuse victims by the most senior leaders of the university; (2) a failure of oversight by the Board of Trustees and a university president who discouraged discussion and dissent; (3) a lack of awareness of child abuse issues; and (4) a culture of reverence for the football program that is ingrained at all levels of the campus community.

Jerry Sandusky caused great harm to the boys he molested and to Penn State University. Those who knew but did not report it were also penalized.

Rosemarie Skaine

See also: Child Abuse, Sexual; Pedophilia; Sex Offender.

Further Reading

Neumaier, Joe, Christian Red, and Joe Belock. 2014. "New Documentary Looks at How Jerry Sandusky's Child Sex Scandal at Penn State Rocked the Identity of 'Happy Valley.'" *New York Daily News*, April 19. http://www.nydailynews.com/sports/college/score-hears-back-valley-article-1.1762008.

News Services. 2011. "Joe Paterno, Graham Spanier Removed." ESPN.com. http://espn.go
.com/college-football/story/_/id/7214380/joe-paterno-president-graham-spanier-
penn-state.
PennLive. "Jerry Sandusky Scandal." 2014. VIRB. http://www.pennlive.com/jerry-sandusky.

SATANIC RITUALS, ABUSE IN

Satanic ritual uses the Christian concept of Satan as the personification of evil as the basis for its ritual. Satanic and nonreligious rituals abuse affects children, adolescents, and adults. The rituals are used to inflict physical, sexual, and psychological harm. Although satanic ritual does not necessarily promote harm, most survivors state that they were ritually abused for the purpose of indoctrinating them into satanic beliefs and practices. The abuse occurred over an extended period of time.

In ritualized abuse, repeated physical, emotional, mental, and spiritual assaults are combined with the well-organized use of symbols and secret ceremonies to turn children or adults against themselves, their families, society, and God. Sexual assault is ritualistic in that it is not performed for sexual gratification. It is performed in a painful, humiliating way as a means of gaining dominance. The physical assault is severe and, at times, includes torture and results in the death of the individual. Psychological abuse results from indoctrination through methodical mind control techniques that cause the victim to have a feeling of intense fear of the cult members.

Extensive evidence supports the existence of ritual abuse crimes as a worldwide phenomenon. A 1993 study found that in 2,292 alleged ritual abuse cases, 15 percent of the perpetrators in adult cases and 30 percent of the perpetrators in child cases confessed to the abuse. In 1991, the American Psychological Association found out of 2,709 members, 30 percent had seen cases of ritual or religion-related abuse. Of those psychologists who have seen cases of ritual abuse, 93 percent believed that the reported harm took place, and 93 percent believed that the alleged ritualism occurred. In 1992, a national survey of therapists found that 88 percent of the 1,185 respondents said that they believed in ritual abuse involving mind control and programming.

From 1983 to 1991, more than 100 American day care centers were investigated for satanic ritual abuse (SRA) of children. From these centers, 650 children, from ages two to six, were identified as victims and 200 adults as perpetrators, some of whom were connected to the centers. Twenty-eight people were criminally indicted; 26 were teachers, aides, or administrators; 17 were female; and 11 were male. Two were African American, 4 were Latino, and the remaining 22 were white. They ranged in age at the time of arrest from 14 to 61.

An FBI report lists groups and practices that allegedly are involved in SRA. The list includes the Church of Satan, demonology, witchcraft, the occult, paganism, Santeria, voodoo, Freemasonry, the Knights Templar, heavy metal music, rock music, the KKK, Nazis, skinheads, Scientology, the Unification Church, religious cults, New Age, astrology, transcendental meditation, and holistic medicine.

Abuse cases sometimes have little to do with the perpetrators' belief systems. SRA is fraught with controversy and credibility issues. Adult victims seeking help are often dismissed or prescribed medication for a resulting problem, such as migraines. Children are sometimes not believed. In the American day care study, the most commonly reported features of SRA were animal sacrifice, death threats, and pornography. Other features were infant sacrifice, sexual orgies, and blood use in rituals. Reported to a lesser extent were forced drug ingestion, murder, drinking urine or blood, cannibalism, torture, and eating feces.

Ritual abuse can lead to secondary crimes, such as crossing state boundaries or using the mail to commit a crime; money laundering; prostitution, pimping and pandering; creating, distributing, and possessing child pornography; selling and possession of illegal drugs; and conspiracy to commit crimes

In all states, there are criminal laws against particular physical acts that are committed during ritual abuse. These acts include murder, rape, sexual contact with children, kidnapping, assault and battery, cruelty to animals, vandalism, and defilement of corpses. In some states, additional penalties can be imposed if it can be proved that the criminal act was motivated by the hate advocated by a particular group.

Rosemarie Skaine

See also: Brainwashing and Mind Control; Child Abuse, Psychological and Behavioral Effects of; International Cultic Studies Association; Torture.

Further Reading

Brown, Rebecca. 1987. *Prepare for War*. Chino, CA: Chick Publications.

Catfangz.com. n.d. "Ritual Abuse." http://catfangz.com/ra.html.

Childabuseinfo. n.d. "Ritual Abuse Information." *Reader Diaries*. http://my.firedoglake.com/childabuseinfo/tag/satanic-ritual-abuse.

Coleman, Joan. 1994. "Presenting Features in Adult Victims of Satanist Ritual Abuse." *Child Abuse Review* 3: 83–92.

de Young, Mary. 1997. "Satanic Ritual Abuse in Day Care: An Analysis of 12 American Cases." *Child Abuse Review* 6: 84–93.

Lanning, Kenneth V. n.d. "1992 FBI Report—Satanic Ritual Abuse." *Cultwatch*. http://www.cultwatch.com/satanicabuse.html.

Oksana, Chrystine. 2001. *Safe Passage to Healing: A Guide for Survivors of Ritual Abuse*. Bloomington, IN: iUniverse.

Ritual Abuse, Ritual Crime and Healing. 2013. "What Is Ritual Abuse?" http://ra-info.org/faqs.

Ritual Abuse Website. 2008. http://stopritualabuse.webs.com.

S.M.A.R.T. Ritual Abuse Pages. n.d. http://ritualabuse.us.

SEX ADDICTION

Sexual addiction is a progressive intimacy disorder characterized by compulsive sexual thoughts and acts. It negatively impacts the addict, family members, and, in some cases, others, such as children, who become victims. Sexual desire increases as the disorder progresses. Over time, the addict usually has to intensify the sexual behaviors in order to achieve the same results as before. In some cases, sexual addiction may lead to abusive acts such as rape.

The addiction becomes abuse if it involves illegal activities, such as exhibitionism, voyeurism, obscene phone calls, child molestation, or rape. The addict's illegal activity may include fetishism, sexual fantasies involving the use of objects;

frotteurism, touching and rubbing against a nonconsenting person; sexual masochism or sadism; transvestic fetishism; necrophilia, an obsession with dead bodies; partialism, a focus on a body part; zoophilia, animals; coprophilia, feces; klismaphilia, enemas; and urophilia, urine,. The behavior of the sex addict may not progress beyond compulsive masturbation or the extensive use of pornography or the use of phone or computer sex services.

Twelve million people suffer from sexual addiction. The accessibility of sexual material on the Internet, cable television, and videos has enabled the number of addicts to increase. Seventy-one percent of child molesters are sex addicts. All sex addicts do not become sex offenders, and not all sex offenders are sex addicts. About 55 percent of convicted sex offenders are sex addicts.

Causes of compulsive sexual behavior remain unclear, according to the Mayo Clinic. Causes may include: an imbalance of natural brain chemicals that assist in regulating mood, for example, high levels of certain chemicals in the brain (neurotransmitters), such as serotonin, dopamine, and norepinephrine; sex hormone levels of androgens that have a vital role in sexual desire; conditions that affect the brain, such as diseases or health problems, that may cause damage to parts of the brain that affect sexual behavior. Multiple sclerosis, epilepsy, Huntington's disease, dementia, and the treatment of Parkinson's disease with some dopamine agonist medications may cause compulsive sexual behavior. Changes in brain pathways over time can cause changes in the brain's neural circuits that comprise the network of nerves that permits brain cells to communicate with one another. The changes may cause pleasant reactions when engaging in sexual behavior and unpleasant reactions when the behavior ceases.

Sex addicts often come from dysfunctional families and are products of abuse. One study found that 82 percent of sex addicts reported being sexually abused as children. Some sex addicts described their parents as rigid, distant, and uncaring. These families and the addicts are more likely to be substance abusers. One study found that 80 percent of recovering sex addicts reported some type of addiction in their families of origin.

Many negative consequences affect the addict and others involved. These consequences include: feelings of guilt, shame, and low self-esteem; mental health conditions, such as depression, extreme stress, and anxiety; neglecting or lying to partners and family, taxing or destroying meaningful relationships; accumulating financial debts by purchasing pornography and sexual services; contracting or infecting someone else with HIV, hepatitis, or another STD; engaging in unhealthy substance use, such as drug or alcohol abuse; being arrested for sexual offenses; losing focus or engage in sexual activity at work, risking their job; and face an unwanted pregnancy.

Intimate partners have feelings of invalidation and that, compared to others, they are not good enough, according to *Intimate Treason*. The partners also say their feelings are not listened to, and honesty and respect are absent. Guilt is common because, although the relationship is painful, the problem does not seem as serious as other types of problems. Partners also experienced: mental intrusions, such as images, nightmares, or flashbacks. Partners report feeling numb, detached; on guard; easily startled; and experiencing lower functioning, not able to perform at usual levels at work, in relationships, and in other major life areas.

If the addict's behavior involves others, the effect on his or her victim has the potential to be severe or life altering. Engaging sexually with a child, depending on the seriousness, the duration, and type of abuse, may cause the child to have psychological, social, sexual, or physical problems.

Treatment for the addict is usually psychotherapy, medications, and self-help groups. Self-help and support groups are often modeled after the 12-step program of Alcoholics Anonymous (AA). Groups include: COSA (codependent of sexual addiction, as a co-sex addict), Sex Addicts Anonymous, Sex and Love Addicts Anonymous, S-Anon International Family Groups, Sexaholics Anonymous. Sexual Compulsives Anonymous, and Sexual Recovery Anonymous. The goal of treatment is to help the addict manage urges and reduce excessive behaviors while maintaining healthy sexual activities. Sex addicts often have alcohol or drug abuse problems or other mental health problems that need treatment, especially obsessive-compulsive behaviors, and anxiety or a mood disorder such as depression. The addict's problems may be so severe that imprisonment is the only solution.

Partners and children also have emotional issues that need to be addressed. There are three, sometimes four, recoveries involved: the addict, the partner, the children, and the relationship. Both partners can take part in the 12-step recovery program, for example. Child welfare authorities must be contacted and treatment initiated immediately in cases where a child has been the focus of the addict.

Rosemarie Skaine

See also: Child Abuse, Sexual; Child Abuse, Treatment for; Sex Offender.

Further Reading

Bailey, C. Everett, and Brian Case. n.d. "Sexual Addiction." American Association for Marriage and Family Therapy. http://www.aamft.org/imis15/content/Consumer_Updates/Sexual_Addiction.aspx.

Black, Claudia, and Cara Tripodi. 2012. *Intimate Treason: Healing the Trauma for Partners Confronting Sex Addiction*. Las Vegas: Central Recovery Press.

Herkov, Michael. 2006. "What Is Sexual Addiction?" Psych Central. http://psychcentral.com/lib/what-is-sexual-addiction/000748.

James, Susan Donaldson. 2011. "Wives of Sex Addicts Seek Support after Suffering in Silence." *ABC News*, September 27. http://abcnews.go.com/Health/wives-sex-addicts-seek-support-suffering-silence/story?id=14609889.

Mayo Clinic Staff. 2011. "Compulsive Sexual Behavior." *Health Information*. Mayo Clinic. http://www.mayoclinic.com/health/compulsive-sexual-behavior/DS00144.

SEX OFFENDER

Sex offenders commit abusive sex offenses that are crimes, and their management is under the control of the justice system. Sex crimes can involve physical contact, such as unwanted sexual touching, or no physical contact, such as Internet crimes. Sexual abuse by an offender includes: unwanted sexual contact between two or more adults or two or more minors, any sexual contact between an adult and a minor, any unwanted sexual contact initiated by a youth toward an adult, and sexual contact between two minors with a significant age difference.

Registered sex offenders in the United States number 747,408, and 265,000 are under the supervision of corrections agencies. Anyone can become a victim of a sex offense, but women and girls are especially vulnerable, with women six times more likely to be than men. In 2010, over 63,000 cases of child sexual abuse were reported, according to the U.S. Department of Justice.

One in three girls and one in seven boys are sexually abused in childhood, usually by an acquaintance, 47 percent by family or extended family. In 93 percent of child sexual abuse cases, the child knows the abuser. About 1.8 million adolescents have been the victims of sexual assault; 82 percent are female, and 33 percent occur between the ages of 12 and 17.5. Sixty-nine percent of teen assaults occurred in the residence of the victim, the offender, or another individual. About 20 million out of 112 million women (18%) have been raped during their lifetime.

Predators seek youth through technology and face-to-face. One in 25 youths received an online sexual solicitation, and in 27 percent of incidents, solicitors asked youths for sexual photographs. Fifteen percent of teens who owned cell phones received sexually suggestive, nude, or seminude images of someone they knew via text. The results of the survey describe characteristics of interactions between Internet predators and their juvenile victims and found that: the majority of victims were girls who had met the predator willingly, and 93 percent of the meetings included sexual contact. The first contact usually came from an online chat room (76%).

Most offenders said that they were older males seeking sexual relations. Youths are vulnerable and in need of further education regarding the negative effects of such relationships. Sex offenses represent under 1 percent of all arrests because many victims do not report it because they: fear their abuser will harm them again; do not want to make the matter public; are concerned that they will be blamed or that not be believed; and feel ashamed, guilty, or embarrassed.

Teaching personal safety awareness is part of the solution for all ages. In the case of a child, some offenders will test a child's personal safety awareness and decide whether a risk exists that the child will tell an adult. If offenders believe that the child will tell, victimization is less likely. The child needs to be aware of online and offline grooming techniques. Grooming means building trust with a child and adults around the child to gain access to and time alone with a child. Grooming tactics include:

- Posing as someone needing help or in distress
- Keeping part, if not all, of the relationship secret
- Having conversations that focus on the meaning of true love, sexual issues, requests for photos, and Webcam sex
- Securing more online meetings
- Handling the confusion that comes when the groomer who they had begun to trust starts to do things that make them feel uncomfortable

Most convicted sex offenders live in our communities and have a period of community supervision (probation or parole) following their release. If offenders are at risk for reoffending or do not comply with their release conditions, they may be returned to confinement. During the supervision, restrictions may include: no contact with victims; no or limited contact with minors; attending sex offender–specific treatment; limited or no Internet access; no use of alcohol or drugs; restrictions on where they can live and work; restricted movement within the community and within and across state lines; and reporting to probation/parole officers as required. In some cases, electronic technologies such as electronic monitoring or GPS devices are used in surveillance.

The most effective treatment assists offenders in developing healthy thinking patterns, understand factors connected to their offending, and develop effective coping skills. For some, medications, such as those that reduce testosterone, are prescribed.

To assist the general population, the Department of Justice has made available the Dru Sjodin National Sex Offender Public Website (NSOPW), a public safety resource that provides the public with access to sex offender data nationwide. NSOPW is a partnership between the U.S. Department of Justice and state, territorial, and tribal governments. Parents, employers, and concerned residents can search for location information on sex offenders residing, working, and attending school in their own neighborhoods or in other nearby states and communities.

Rosemarie Skaine

See also: Adults Sexual Attraction to Adolescents; Child Abuse, Sexual; Incest; Internet Victimization, Child; Online Dating; Pedophilia; Rape; Sex Addiction.

Further Reading

Center for Sex Offender Management (CSOM). 2013. "Fact Sheet: What You Need to Know about Sex Offenders." http://www.csom.org/pubs/needtoknow_fs.pdf.

National Sex Offender Public Website (NSOPW). n.d. "Education and Prevention." U.S. Department of Justice. http://www.nsopr.gov/en/Education.

Statistic Brain. 2013. "Sex Offender Statistics." NCMEC, Prevent Abuse Now, Criminal Justice Agency. http://www.statisticbrain.com/sex-offender-statistics.

SEX TRAFFICKING

The U.S. Department of State defines sex trafficking as when an adult (including persons under the age of 18) is coerced, forced, or deceived into prostitution or maintained in prostitution through coercion. Sex trafficking is a human rights abuse that many nations recognize as a growing global social problem. It is a critical social issue and a form of modern-day slavery. It is no longer an isolated problem unique to European and Southeast Asian countries. Sex trafficking has become an increasingly domestic social issue in the United States. This lucrative underground business is estimated to be worth between $7 billion to $10 billion each year.

The majority of the victims of sex trafficking are primarily underage, mostly female, and under the age of 25. Sex traffickers persist in exploiting women because of the unequal status of women and girls. Women are seen as sexual objects, servants, and marketable items. Most sex traffickers are male and represent every social, racial, and ethnic group, but there are women who run and operate well-established criminal enterprise rings. For instance, in October 2012, Sacramento residents Tynisha Marie Hornbuckle, 24, and Tamrell Rena Hornbuckle, 26, were sentenced to 15 years and 8 months in prison and 12 years and 7 months in prison, respectively, for sex trafficking of minors.

Perpetrators take advantage of and capitalize on the misogyny and negative images of women and girls. Sex traffickers can be seen as smart businessmen who understand that, unlike a bag of narcotics, a woman's body can be sold and resold many times as a profitable business. In the United States, women and children are at high risk for sexual exploitation by sex traffickers, also known as "pimps."

According to the Federal Bureau of Investigation, pimps use Web sites such as www.craigslist.com and www.backpage.com to lure vulnerable women with fake employment advertisements. Those who respond to the advertisements are mostly women who live in poverty. They are lured with promises of financial stability and employment opportunities that appear to be legitimate. Pimps also target women who appear to be lonely and are looking for romance or male attraction through popular social networking sites, such as Facebook. Young persons who appear to be naïve or weak-minded or who come from broken homes or who seem to be unhappy with their lives are easily victimized. Teenage runaways, women who come from abusive families, victims of child molestation, and drug addicts who turn to prostitution in order to support their addictions become prey for the pimps.

Most sex traffickers in the United States are part of smaller crime organizations, such as motorcycle gangs and street gangs, that are often are associated with criminal networks. Tactics used by pimps to target and victimize vulnerable individuals include taking away personal processions, such as wallets and identification cards; psychological manipulation; physical violence; and forcing dependency on illicit substances. According to National Center for Missing and Exploited Children (NCMEC), these tactics lead victims who are forced to prostitute themselves to believe they are useless, trapped, and powerless to escape or seek outside help. Sex traffickers transport victims throughout the United States by means that are least likely to attract suspicion, mostly to nightclubs, brothels, massage parlors, and bars located in and around metropolitan cities, such as San Francisco, Los Angeles, Las Vegas, and New York.

Sex trafficking has become much more organized and widespread and is a violent crime. It is a homegrown problem and a form of emotional and physical abuse that damages individuals across the country. According to the U.S. Department of Justice, the United States is not only facing an increasing number of victims from around the world who are smuggled into the country but also a homegrown dilemma of cross-country sex trafficking of underage girls. NCMEC emphasizes that sex traffickers can be anyone, such as immediate family members, friends, boyfriends, or close acquaintances of the family, and minors are at greater risk of being coerced into sex trafficking.

Governments have enacted laws and created programs to combat commercial sexual exploitation of individuals. Nonprofit organizations, including the National Center for Missing and Exploited Children (NCMEC), FAIR Girls, and the Polaris Project have programs to address sex trafficking. The U.S. government enacted the Victims of Trafficking and Violence Protection Act of 2000 (TVPA) to combat the trafficking of individuals.

Juan Carlos Hernandez

See also: Human Rights; Sexual Slavery; Slavery, Modern-day.

Further Reading

Federal Bureau of Investigation. 2012. "Man Who Operated Sex Trafficking Rings Sentenced to Life in Federal Prison." http://www.fbi.gov/atlanta/press-releases/2012/man-who-operated-sex-trafficking-ring-sentenced-to-life-in-federal-prison.

Federal Bureau of Investigation. 2012. "Sacramento Sisters Sentenced for Child Sex Trafficking." http://www.fbi.gov/sacramento/press-releases/2012/sacramento-sisters-sentenced-for-child-sex-trafficking.

Fink, Erica, and Laurie Segall. 2013. "Pimps Hit Social Networks to Recruit Underage Sex Workers. *CNNMoney*, February 27. http://money.cnn.com/2013/02/27/technology/social/pimps-social-networks/index.html.

National Center for Missing and Exploited Children. 2010. "The Prostitution of Children in America: A Guide for Parents and Guardians." http://www.missingkids.com/en_US/documents/Fact_Sheet_Parents_Guardians.pdf.

Rieger, April. 2007. "Missing the Mark: Why the Trafficking Victims Protection Act Fails to Protect Sex Trafficking Victims in the United States," *Harvard Journal of Law & Gender* 30: 232, 233, 235. http://www.law.harvard.edu/students/orgs/jlg/vol301/rieger.pdf.

U.S. Department of State. n.d. "What Is Modern Slavery?" http://www.state.gov/j/tip/what/index.htm.

SEXTING

Sexting is sharing sexually suggestive photos, videos, or messages using cell phones and other mobile media. Although sexting can be a harmless activity among consenting individuals, it can also become predatory or abusive.

In 2012, a national telephone survey of youth who used the Internet (ages 10–17 years), 2.5 percent appeared in or created sexually provocative images and 7.1 percent had received provocative images. Older teens, young adults, and adults do more sexting than the youths. In a 2012 study of 760 young adults aged 18–24 years, more than half (57%) of the respondents were nonsexters, 28.2 percent were two-way sexters, 12.6 percent were receivers, and 2 percent were senders. Men were more likely to receive than women. Sexually active respondents were more likely to participate in two-way sexting. Adults also engage in sexting. In 2011, U.S. Congressman Anthony Weiner resigned from Congress after he admitted that he had sent explicit text messages.

Sexting occurs because of the rapid spread and use of ever-present cell phones and other technologies. In 2013, the PEW Research Center found that the percent of 802 teens 12 to 17 who owned technology to be high: cell phone (78%), smartphone

(37%), desktop or laptop computer (80%), and tablet (23%). The primary reasons that young adults might engage in sexting include that it is: a standalone and safer sex practice, a risky and risqué sexual behavior, and part of the repertoire of sexually active young adults in a relationship. Causes of teen sexting include: impulsivity, raging hormones, peer or partner pressure, and inability to effectively predict potential negative harmful consequences. Adults aged 50 and older engage in sexting to add flare to their sex lives because it is convenient, fast, fun, and easy to work into their busy lives.

The consequences of sexting are varied. Most images appear to be exchanged between individuals who are in a relationship. In one study, 44 percent of the participants said they had sex with a new partner for the first time after sexting with

Anthony D. Weiner, a Democratic Congressman from New York, was forced to resign from Congress in 2011 after he was found to have engaged in sexting on social media. (U.S. House of Representatives)

that person. Sexting may be a technology-mediated flirtation strategy, but it can also be considered high-risk behavior such as multiple sexual partners, unprotected sex, and higher rates of sexually transmitted infections. Sexting is also associated with substance use and cyberbullying, sexual harassment, and stalking.

Suicide can be a consequence of sexting. In July 2008, 18-year-old Jessica Logan e-mailed a nude photo of herself to a boyfriend. He sent it to four high school girls, who sent it to other students. In the following weeks, Jessica's picture was viewed by hundreds of teenagers in local high schools. Jessica was overwhelmed with humiliating taunts that caused her to take her own life.

Legal issues present a range of consequences for the sender. A 2009 Iowa case, *State v. Canal*, resulted in a civil conviction for an 18-year-old who sent a picture of his genitals to a 14-year-old minor with the message, "I love you." His act was ruled obscene; he was fined $250, with a one-year probation period with the State Department of Corrections, and was required to register as a sex offender. Cases can also result in criminal or felony charges for distributing child pornography. In 2006, in the Alabama case *S.B. v. St. James School*, four female ninth grade students were expelled for taking nude photographs of themselves and e-mailing them to a male friend.

Part of the treatment for teens who participate in inappropriate sexting rests in balancing the negative consequences with the sexter's First Amendment rights. Teens who have been convicted under child pornography laws, sent to prison, and required to register as sex offenders are penalized for developmentally typical behavior. Child pornography laws were designed to deter and punish serious offenses. Julia Halloran McLaughlin of the Florida Coastal School of Law states that teen sexting images are communication and should be considered forms of protected teen sexual speech. Any legislation related to teen sexual speech must be narrowly tailored to protect the minor from harm or further another compelling state interest creating a zone of protected teen sexual speech.

Treatment of abusive sexting lies in prevention and intervention. School policies that focus on professional development sessions for educators will help prevent some abuse. Policies related to criminal investigations should include reporting and investigation protocol. Education of students about the consequences and providing counseling are treatment options. Educating parents on how to manage their child's time on cell phones, text messaging, and computer use technology are necessary components in prevention.

Rosemarie Skaine

See also: Bullying, Child and Adolescent; Child Abuse, Psychological and Behavioral Effects of; Cyberstalking; Sexual Harassment in Education; Stalking.

Further Reading

Benotsch, Eric G., Daniel J. Snipesa, Aaron M. Martin, and Sheana S. Bull. 2013. "Sexting, Substance Use, and Sexual Risk Behavior in Young Adults." *Journal of Adolescent Health* 52: 307–313.

CNN. 2013. 2013. "Sydney Leathers Said She Had 'No Choice' But to Come Forward." *CNN Politics*, August 8. http://politicalticker.blogs.cnn.com/2013/08/08/sydney-leathers-said-she-had-no-choice-but-to-come-forward/?iref=allsearch.

Gordon-Messer, Deborah, Jose Arturo Bauermeister, Alison Grodzinski, and Marc Zimmerman. 2013. "Sexting among Young Adults." *Journal of Adolescent Health* 52: 301–306.

Levine, Deb. 2013. "Sexting: A Terrifying Health Risk . . . or the New Normal for Young Adults?" Editorial. *Journal of Adolescent Health* 52: 257–258.

McLaughlin, Julia Halloran. 2012. "Article: Exploring the First Amendment Rights of Teens in Relationship to Sexting and Censorship." *University of Michigan Journal of Law Reform* 45 (Winter): 315.

Mitchell, K. J., D. Finkelhor, L. M. Jones, and J. Wolak. 2012. "Prevalence and Characteristics of Youth Sexting: A National Study." *Pediatrics* 129: 13–20.

Pew Research Center's Internet and American Life Project. 2012. "Teen Gadget Ownership." http://pewinternet.org/Static-Pages/Trend-Data-%28Teens%29/Teen-Gadget-Ownership.aspx.

Russo, Charles J., and Kelli Jo Arndt. 2010. "Technology and the Law: The Dangers of Sexting in Schools." *School Business Affairs* (May): 36–38.

Willard, Nancy E. 2010. "Sexting and Youth: Achieving a Rational Response." *Journal of Social Sciences* 6 (4): 542–562.

SEXUAL HARASSMENT

Sexual harassment is unwelcome sexual behavior by one person(s) against another person(s); if it is unwelcome, it is sexual harassment. The definition is straightforward, but it is not simple because it can involve behaviors that in other contexts are considered positive and reaffirming. Sexual harassment, a form of sex discrimination, is against the law. The Equal Employment Opportunity Commission's definition is the most widely accepted and has the greatest force. Sexual harassment is: "Unwelcome sexual advances, requests for sexual favors, and other verbal or physical conduct of a sexual nature constitute sexual harassment when submission or rejection of this conduct explicitly or implicitly affects an individual's employment, unreasonably interferes with an individual's work performance or creates an intimidating, hostile or offensive work environment." Federal and state courts have applied this definition to work and educational settings.

The two types of sexual harassment are quid pro quo and hostile environment. Quid pro quo harassment exists when an employee's supervisor or a person of higher employment rank demands sexual favors from a subordinate in exchange for tangible job benefits. The U.S. Supreme Court affirmed quid pro quo as harassment in 1986, in the *Meritor Savings Bank v. Vinson* case. Hostile environment or environmental harassment is a pattern of intimidating, hostile, or offensive behaviors that affect the person being harassed. The criteria for this kind of harassment were set down in 1982 by the United States 11th Circuit Court of Appeals in the *Henson v. City of Dundee* case.

A 2011 *ABC News/Washington Post* poll found that 1 in 4 women and 1 in 10 men had experienced workplace sexual harassment. Twenty-five percent of men said they worried about being falsely accused. Middle and high school students who experience sexual harassment range from 50 percent to 80 percent. In 2011, the American Association of University Women reported that 62 percent of female college students and 61 percent of male college students report having been sexually harassed at their universities.

Although the victim is usually a woman, sexual harassment victims are both women and men. Neither is it about love and romance, but rather social control. Frequently, it is a power bid. It is much more than a man telling a dirty joke or making a comment about appearance. On the contrary, "It is an abuse of power in which a worker who depends for her livelihood and professional survival on the goodwill of a supervisor is made to feel vulnerable." Or in the case of education, it is an abuse of power in which a student, who depends on a teacher for grades, on the goodwill of a teacher is made to feel vulnerable. In the case of peer harassment, the balance of power may be fragile in that the victim depends on a teacher or school official to believe his or her accusation should he or she go forward with a complaint.

So what exactly constitutes unwelcome behavior? The forms range from easy to identify sexual behaviors to subtle and not so subtle nonsexual behaviors. Easy to identify sexual forms are: an open invitation for sexual intercourse in exchange for a favor, stroking, squeezing, assaultive hugs, pinching, grabbing, offensive sexual comments, rape, and attempted rape. Subtle nonsexual forms are: staring, intimidating through silence, and innuendo. Not so subtle nonsexual forms are: isolating, altering a person's job responsibility, and terminating a person's job or the giving of a failing grade. The prevalent form of harassment varies with the type of occupation; for example, women in menial jobs are most often the target of physical violence. The unequal power position is a basic cause of sexual harassment, with sometimes life-altering consequences for the victim, such as job termination or alteration, grade alteration in school, or physical and/or mental suffering. Ultimately, a victim's life chances could be negatively altered as well as his or her personal well-being.

Psychological distress is not necessary to a legal cause of action, but it is common following sexual harassment. Emotional reactions include anger, fear, depression, anxiety, irritability, lowered self-esteem, humiliation, alienation, helplessness, and vulnerability. On the job or in the classroom, some harassed individuals show: lowered satisfaction with coworkers and supervision, increased work withdrawal, decreased psychological well-being, and symptoms of posttraumatic stress disorder (PTSD). Sexual harassment has been associated with negative health conditions and psychological stress, such as lowered self-confidence and self-esteem, alcohol and drug abuse, nervousness, and eating disorders.

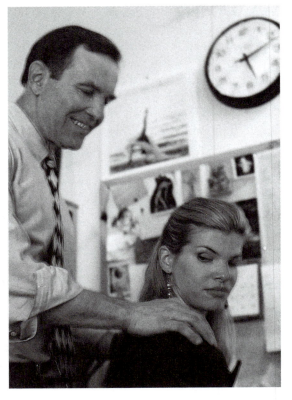

Victims of sexual harassment in the workplace can be either male or female, and the harasser does not have to be of the opposite sex. (PhotoDisc, Inc.)

Ideally, treatment for perpetrators and victims alike lies in prevention. While sexual harassment is sometimes complex, being able to recognize it is very important. To be able to identify it involves recognizing accepted human sexual responses that are a genuine recognition of our maleness and femaleness. Examples include: honest attraction between two people and/or genuine reaffirmation of one's sexuality, such as a touch or look appropriate to the time and place. Another genuine human response is an opportunity for closeness or emotional intimacy. Recognition is prevention.

Even with effective recognition, prevention can fail. Effective treatment will have to be considered. It includes informal and formal steps. Informal steps include

1. Performing assigned duties well (often attempts are made to shift attention away from the sexual harassment to the victim's performance)
2. Avoiding self-blame
3. Keeping a diary of occurrences for evidence
4. Confronting the harasser
5. Reporting the harasser

When informal steps do not work, the formal recourses of institutional grievance and/or legal procedures are necessary. Formal steps include:

1. Acquainting himself or herself with the processes and policies that apply to his or her work or educational setting. It is wise to know the law previous to proceedings. Be well informed. Seek information and advice from an expert, such as the appropriate internal institutional officer, the Civil Rights Commission, the Equal Employment Opportunity Commission (EEOC), or a private attorney.
2. Filing a grievance against the harasser. If the institution does not support the harassed, he or she should file a grievance against the school or workplace.
3. Being aware of the timeline required for filing a lawsuit or filing with external agencies.
4. Filing a civil suit requires that the harassed be sure that the conduct: (a) meets the definition of sexual harassment, (b) is the result of a sexual requirement imposed on the academic endeavor or employment, and (c) has interfered with academic or work performance.
5. Filing criminal charges requires that the harassment includes actual or attempted rape or assault.

Victims and perpetrators require coping mechanisms and healing. Healing should focus on five aspects: understanding sexual harassment, healing the victim, healing the perpetrator, healing relationships, and healing society. If the victim, the perpetrator, or society does not understand what sexual harassment is, it will be very difficult to help each heal. The healing dimensions include taking control. Too often sexual harassment, as are other forms of sexual abuse, is closed, secret, devious, and whitewashed. Healing requires that personal experiences be brought into the open. Confronting is strength producing; being a victim is inaction. During confrontation and litigation, the focus of health professionals for recovery might be presenting coping strategies and encouraging the development of a sense of control over the recovery process. As all empowering steps of possible action are explored, a better feeling about themselves and their environment should exist.

Rosemarie Skaine

See also: Sexual Harassment in Education; Sexual Harassment in Employment; Sexual Harassment, Legal Ramifications of.

Further Reading

Bass, Ellen, and Laura Davis. 2008. *The Courage to Heal 4e: A Guide for Women Survivors of Child Sexual Abuse 20th Anniversary Edition*. New York: William Morrow Paperbacks.
Collinsworth, Linda L., Louise F. Fitzgerald, and Fritz Drasgow. 2009. "In Harm's Way: Factors Related to Psychological Distress Following Sexual Harassment." *Psychology of Women Quarterly* 33: 475–490.

Lichty, Lauren F., and Rebecca Campbell. 2012. "Targets and Witnesses: Middle School Students' Sexual Harassment Experiences." *Journal of Early Adolescence* 32 (3): 414–430.

Skaine, Rosemarie. 1996. *Power and Gender: Issues in Sexual Dominance and Harassment.* Jefferson, SC: McFarland Publishers.

SEXUAL HARASSMENT, LEGAL RAMIFICATIONS OF

Three acts of Congress govern sexual harassment: Title VII of the 1964 Civil Rights Act, Title IX of the 1972 Education Amendments, and the 1991 Civil Rights Act. Title VII focused on sexual harassment in the workplace and, with the enforcement mechanism of the Equal Employment Opportunity Commission (EEOC), began the process of definition and resolution of the issue. Title IX prohibited sex discrimination, including sexual harassment, in education.

Title VII is federal legislation prohibiting sex discrimination in employment. A complainant alleging sexual harassment should file with a state agency and appeal through the Equal Employment Opportunity Commission. It is possible for a victim to be awarded monetary compensation for back pay, lost benefits, damages, and possible job reinstatement. The statute of limitations is six months to one year on the state level and two to three years federally. One of the problems of this act is it applies to workplaces with at least 15 employees. The victim must also prove harassment as a form of sex discrimination.

Title IX is federal legislation prohibiting sex discrimination in education. The victim must file with the Office for Civil Rights of the U.S. Department of Education. Possibly there is also a private right of action, for example, tort law. The most drastic result is a discontinuance of federal funding to the educational institution. Letters of Finding have revealed that the Office for Civil Rights expends great effort to allow the educational institution in question to rectify any policy and come into compliance with the law. The statute of limitations varies regionally, but if taken to court, it can take one to two years.

The 1991 Civil Rights Act, passed shortly after the Anita Hill–Clarence Thomas hearings, contains three titles that impact on sexual harassment. Title I made legal for the first time that a victim may receive compensatory damages for sexual harassment, although those damages are limited according to the size of the employer. Title II, or the Glass Ceiling Act of 1991, addresses the underutilization of females and minorities in certain positions in employment and the elimination of barriers preventing advancement. Title III extends fair employment practices to government employees, including the House, Senate, and Office of the President. It extends protection to some state and local employees not covered by current federal laws, such as political appointees. Since high governmental work environments are predominately controlled by men, it addresses male dominance in power positions.

Many court cases represented evolving case law during the 1980s and clarified the scope of sexual harassment. Two important cases were among those many. *Henson v. City of Dundee* and *Meritor Savings Bank, FSB v. Vinson* ruled that a hostile environment is against the law, thus resulting in sexual harassment being divided into two categories: quid pro quo and hostile environment. *Meritor* ruled in part that in quid pro quo cases, the employer is liable whether the employer knows about the sexual harassment incident or not.

In 1993, *Harris v. Forklift Systems* freed women from having to say sexual conduct on the job caused "severe psychological injury." No single factor is required, and the totality of circumstances is to be considered.

In 2003 and 2004, the Supreme Court strengthened title VII protection for same-sex harassment cases by accepting both types of harassment and associated employer liabilities and distinguishing between hostile harassment and constructive discharge.

Students who are subjected to sexual harassment had their rights expanded in *Franklin v Gwinnett County* in 1992. For the first time, students had the right to win monetary damages from schools that receive federal funds. A Georgia high school student, Christine Franklin, had unwelcomed sexual intercourse with a teacher. The law at issue was Title IX, which prohibits schools that receive federal funds from discrimination but does not explicitly give alleged victims the right to file lawsuits. This decision motivates schools to engage in a proactive strategy of prevention.

Rosemarie Skaine

See also: Sexual Harassment; Sexual Harassment in Education; Sexual Harassment in Employment.

Further Reading

Civil Rights Act of 1991 (S.1745). "Title I—Federal Civil Rights Remedies," § 102, § 1977a, (b).

Civil Rights Act of 1991 (S.1745) "Title II—Glass Ceiling," § 201–204.

Civil Rights Act of 1991 (S.1745). "Title III—Government Employee Rights," § 301 (b), 303–319.

Civil Rights Act of 1964 (Pub. L. 88-352). 78 Stat. 241, Title VII, 2, 28, and 42 U.S.C. § 2000e-2[35]).

Education Amendments of 1972 (Pub. L. 92-318). 86 Stat. 235, Title IX, 20 U.S.C. § 1681–688.

Franklin v. Gwinnett County and William Prescott. 1992. (503 U.S. 60 (112 S.Ct. 1028), 117 L.Ed.2d 208). No. 90-918.

Gutman, Arthur, and Eric M. Dunleavy. 2013. "Contemporary Title VII Enforcement: The Song Remains the Same?" *Journal of Business Psychology* 28 (4): 487–503.

Henson v. City of Dundee. 1982. (U.S. Court of Appeals, 11th Circuit) Cited 26 EPD Article 32, 993.

Meritor Savings Bank, FSB v. Vinson, 106 Ct., 1986, 2399, 2405.

Skaine, Rosemarie. 1996. *Power and Gender: Issues in Sexual Dominance and Harassment*. Jefferson, SC: McFarland Publishers.

SEXUAL HARASSMENT IN EDUCATION

Sexual harassment in education is illegal under the provisions of Title IX of the 1972 Education Amendments to the 1964 Civil Rights Act. The Office for Civil Rights (OCR) of the U.S. Department of Education (USDE) has the responsibility for enforcing Title XI that prohibits sex discrimination, including sexual harassment in educational settings. Title IX prohibits sexual harassment and sexual violence, a form of sexual harassment, at institutions that receive federal funding.

The Office for Civil Rights defines sexual harassment two ways: quid pro quo and hostile environment. Quid pro quo means "this for that." If a student's grade depends on whether she or he submits to unwelcome sexual advances, it is quid pro quo sexual harassment. Hostile environment occurs when the unwelcome conduct of a sexual nature is so severe, persistent, or pervasive that it affects a student's ability to participate in or benefit from an educational program or activity or creates an intimidating, threatening, or abusive educational environment. The law recognizes that sexual harassment may occur between individuals of the opposite sex or of the same sex.

The courts recognize that sexual harassment occurs in three situations in education: employer/employee, employee/student, and student/student (or peer to peer). Students' experiences with sexual harassment include being harassed, harassing someone else, or witnessing harassment.

In 1992, the U.S. Supreme Court significantly expanded protection for the student in *Christine Franklin, Petitioner v. Gwinnett County Public Schools and William Prescott*. For the first time, students had the right to win monetary damages from schools that receive federal funds. This decision provided strong motivation for schools to engage in a proactive strategy to prevent sexual harassment.

Sexual harassment has negative consequences. Middle school students reported negative psychological effects, including: feeling upset, worthless, and hopeless, and increased shame about their bodies. Other effects include talking less in class, difficulty paying attention at school, skipping school, and dropping out of activities or classes.

Sexual harassment is pervasive: 75 percent to 80 percent of students experience direct sexual harassment before graduating from high school. Fifty percent of high school students experience harassment. For both groups, peer-to-peer verbal sexual harassment was the most common form. In 2011, the American Association of University Women reported that 62 percent of female college students and 61 percent of male college students report having been sexually harassed at their universities.

When sexual harassment is perpetrated by a teacher, most students adopt avoidance as a coping mechanism, which keeps them from forming mentor relationships. But a more obvious and severe resulting abuse is the denial of a benefit, such as a course, grade, or activity. Worse yet are the long-term negative effects on the student's attachment and enthusiasm for academic programs designed to prepare him or her for life's work.

An area of ongoing societal concern is the presence of sexual harassment in the problem of bullying in American society.

Rosemarie Skaine

See also: Bullying, Child and Adolescent; Sexual Harassment; Sexual Harassment in Employment; Sexual Harassment, Legal Ramifications of.

Further Reading

Association of American Colleges and Universities. 2011. "Department of Education Issues New Guidance on Sexual Violence and Title IX." *On Campus with Women* 40 (1): In Brief.

Hall, Richard F., Richard D. Graham, and Gail A. Hoover. March 2004 "Sexual Harassment in Higher Education: A Victim's Remedies and a Private University's Liability." *Education and the Law* 16 (1): 33–45.

Lichty, Lauren F., and Rebecca Campbell. 2012. "Targets and Witnesses: Middle School Students' Sexual Harassment Experiences." *Journal of Early Adolescence* 32 (3): 414–430.

Skaine, Rosemarie. 2012. "Sexual Harassment." *St. James Encyclopedia of Popular Culture.* 5 Vols. Edited by Tom Pendergast and Sara Pendergast. Farmington Hills, MI: St. James Press.

Skaine, Rosemarie. 1996. *Power and Gender: Issues in Sexual Dominance and Harassment.* Jefferson, SC: McFarland Publishers.

University of Miami. 2013. "Harassment FAQs." http://www.miami.edu/index.php/equality_administration/sexual_harassment-1/sexual_harassment_faqs/#top.

SEXUAL HARASSMENT IN EMPLOYMENT

Sexual harassment in employment is illegal behavior. Sexual harassment differs from harassment and bullying in that it has an explicit sexual dimension. It has a range of abusive behaviors, but at its core is the unequal power dimension. These behaviors include general bullying; mobbing; racial harassment; sex-based harassment, such as verbal put-downs; abusive remarks; and marginalizing or exclusionary behaviors on the basis of gender. It can include rape and/or assault. In these cases, criminal charges are filed. All other behaviors are civil offenses with legality set down in Title VII of the Civil Rights Act of 1964, succeeding EEOC guidelines, and case law. Civil law makes clear: sexual harassment is against the law.

In 1986, in a landmark employment case, *Meritor Savings Bank, FSB v Vinson*, the U.S. Supreme Court ruled that in quid pro quo cases, the employer is liable whether the employer knows about the sexual harassment incident or not. Quid pro quo exists when a person of higher employment rank demands sexual favors from a subordinate in exchange for tangible job benefits. In the 1997 New Hampshire federal court case *McGuinn-Rowe v. Foster's Daily Democrat*, the court ruled that sexual harassment can occur after hours and away from the place of work.

Sexual harassment exists in all levels of employment, including the government, the military, religious institutions, and sports. In 2012, Paula McDonald reported that American estimates indicate that 40 percent to 75 percent of women and 13 percent to 31 percent of men have experienced sexual harassment in employment. Women file approximately 85 percent of complaints and men 15 percent. Female-perpetrated harassment is filed in only a small portion of cases.

Effects on victims are often devastating. In 1982, in *Henson v. City of Dundee*, the U.S. Court of Appeals ruled,

> Sexual harassment which creates a hostile or offensive environment for members of one sex is every bit the arbitrary barrier to sexual equality at the work place that racial harassment is to racial equality. Surely, a requirement that a man or woman run a gauntlet of sexual abuse in return for the privilege of being allowed to work and make a living can be as demeaning and disconcerting as the harshest of racial epithets.

Specific effects include mental and physical health setbacks, ranging from irritation and anxiety to anger, powerlessness, humiliation, and depression to posttraumatic stress disorder. Effects are more severe when the harasser is a supervisor who used coercion; occurs cross-racially; takes place over a long period of time; or happens in male-dominated workplaces. These effects manifest in absenteeism; lower job satisfaction, commitment, and productivity; and employment withdrawal.

Sexual harassment in employment usually happens to women by men, but it happens when men are harassed by women and when same-gender persons harass or are harassed. When a woman, usually a woman of lower organizational status, is harassed, it is usually because of unequal power. Often, because the male harasser has a sexual desire for the woman, he does not view his behavior as sexual harassment.

Victims include divorced or separated women, young women, women in nontraditional jobs, women in temporary positions, women with disabilities, lesbian women and women from ethnic minorities, gay men, and young men. Some male harassers lack social conscience. Some are naïve about heterosexual relationships and perform immature, irresponsible, manipulative, and exploitative behaviors. He draws erroneous conclusions about the woman's criticism and rejection, and he exhibits aggressive behaviors that are sexually harassing rather than what he considers to be seductive overtures.

Psychological distress that follows sexual harassment adds to the abuse. The severity of the harassment and the victim's thoughts and opinions about why the experiences occurred are the most powerful predictors of the level of the psychological distress, according to a study by Linda L. Collinsworth et al. Severity affected the posttraumatic stress disorder (PTSD) symptoms and the overall distress level. The more the victim blamed herself, the more psychological disruption she experienced. Kathleen M. Rospenda et al. suggest that enduring negative effects of harassment over time are hazardous to the victim's health as well as the cause of workplace illness, injury, and assault.

Rosemarie Skaine

See also: Bullying, Adults; Sexual Harassment; Sexual Harassment in Education; Sexual Harassment, Legal Ramifications of; Rape.

Further Reading

Collinsworth, Linda L., Louise F. Fitzgerald, and Fritz Drasgow. 2009. "In Harm's Way: Factors Related to Psychological Distress Following Sexual Harassment." *Psychology of Women Quarterly* 33: 475–490.

McDonald, Paula. 2012. "Workplace Sexual Harassment 30 Years On: A Review of the Literature." *International Journal of Management Reviews* 14: 1–17.

Meritor Savings Bank, FSB v. Vinson, 477 U.S. 57, 106 S.Ct. 2399 (1986).

Rospenda, Kathleen M., Judith A. Richman, Jennifer L. Z. Ehmke, and Kenneth W. Zatoper. 2005. "Is Workplace Harassment Hazardous to Your Health?" *Journal of Business and Psychology* 20 (1): 95–110.

Skaine, Rosemarie. 1996. *Power and Gender: Issues in Sexual Dominance and Harassment.* Jefferson, SC: McFarland Publishers.

SEXUAL SLAVERY

Sexual slavery is the unwanted, coerced, and/or forced enslavement of women and girls for sexual purposes. It includes the conditions that create this servitude. Five forms of sexual enslavement are: sex trafficking, war-induced sexual slavery, ritual sexual slavery, forced marriage, and sexual servitude. Sex trafficking is a form of human trafficking and is defined by U.S. federal law when a commercial sex act is induced by force, fraud, or coercion or in which the person induced to perform such an act has not attained 18 years of age. Sexual trafficking involves the recruitment, transportation (within national or across international borders), transfer, harboring, or receipt of persons for the purposes of commercial sexual exploitation.

In the United States, estimates of trafficking that involve exploitation are approximately 80 percent sexual and 19 percent labor. Between 700,000 and 4 million women, children, and men worldwide are trafficked each year. Reports of trafficking originate from 20 states, including New York, California, and Florida. Immigration and Naturalization Service (INS) and Labor Department officials discovered 250 brothels in 26 different cities, which probably involved trafficking victims. California has three of the FBI's 13 highest child sex trafficking areas: Los Angeles, San Francisco, and San Diego. A teen enters the sex trade in the United States between 12 and 14 years of age. Many are runaway girls who were sexually abused. Foreign nationals are also brought into the United States as slaves for labor or commercial sex through force or fraud.

According to UNICEF, over 1 million children worldwide enter the sex trade every year, and that about 30 million children have done so over the past 30 years. The U.S. Department of State reported that each year about 600,000 to 800,000 people, mostly women and children, are trafficked from outside national borders. Eleven countries of origin for trafficking victims are: Belarus, the Republic of Moldova, the Russian Federation and Ukraine (Commonwealth of Independent States), Albania, Bulgaria, Lithuania, Romania, China, Thailand, and Nigeria.

Sexual slavery is a result of patriarchal systems that institutionalize women's diminished worth. This system is characterized by a mistrust and hatred of women and that views women as less worthy than men. Because many women lack economic wherewithal and face illiteracy, cultural expectations, family obligations, war and civil strife, and domestic abuse, they are forced to seek a better life or escape from a torturous one. Sex traffickers seemingly offer a better life, and they also play to the fear of deportation that a woman has who is in the country illegally. The accessibility and anonymity of the Internet has aided the rapid growth of sex trafficking and makes the trading in women and children easier than ever before.

Women have been trafficked to the United States mainly for the sex industry, such as, prostitution, stripping, peep and touch shows, and massage parlors. Police records reveal that young women can be sold to brothel owners in North America for up to $16,000 each. Once sold, women are forced to work off debts to traffickers of up to $40,000 by sexually servicing large numbers of men daily. In 2001, Interpol reported that the sex industry generates $19 billion a year.

The effects on sexually enslaved girls and women include: lifelong physical and psychological trauma; exposure to diseases, including HIV; malnutrition; unsanitary and inhumane living conditions; and rejection and alienation from their families, country, and culture. A leading health risk of prostitution is premature death. The Institute Against Sexual Trafficking reported in a 2004 U.S. study involving 2,000 prostitutes followed over a 30-year period that found the most common causes of death were homicide, suicide, drug- and alcohol-related problems, HIV infection, and accidents. The homicide rate among active female prostitutes was 17 times higher than those in the general population. A total of 785 (89%) people in prostitution from nine countries wanted to escape prostitution, and 75 percent had been homeless at some point in their lives. Overall, 827 (68%) suffered post-traumatic stress disorder (PTSD).

Laws are in place on the state and federal level designed to prevent prostitution and protect the victim. The 2000 Trafficking Victims Protection Act (TVPA) created the first comprehensive federal law to address trafficking. Its focus on the international level includes

- An approach of prevention through overseas public awareness programs and a State Department monitoring and sanctions program
- Protection through a new T visa and services for foreign national victims
- Prosecution through new federal crimes and severe penalties
- Enforcing all applicable laws within the Thirteenth Amendment to the U.S. Constitution.

In 2003, the U.S. Immigration and Customs Enforcement (ICE), the FBI, the Department of Justice Child Exploitation and Obscenity Section, and the National Center for Missing and Exploited Children launched the Innocence Lost National Initiative. The groups have rescued approximately 900 children and convicted more than 500 pimps, madams, and their associates. These convictions have resulted in lengthy sentences, in some cases multiple 25 years to life, and the seizure of real property, vehicles, and monetary assets.

Sexual slavery has been banned and criminalized under international laws, including the 1949 UN Convention for the Suppression of the Traffic in Persons and of the Exploitation of the Prostitution of Others and the International Agreement for the Suppression of the "White Slave Traffic." Law enforcement agencies are providing training of their officers in recognizing sexual slavery. The FBI lists indicators for patrol officers and investigators to observe including: suspicious calls or complaints; Web sites that advertise dating or hookups; businesses, especially massage parlors; physical abnormalities, such as injuries, torture bands, or scars and malnutrion; unusual financial or legal situations, such as someone else having possession of an individual's legal or travel documents or a third party who insists on interpreting; and brothel evidence, such as large amounts of cash and condoms and places where men come and go frequently.

Rosemarie Skaine

See also: Abduction, Adult; Abduction, Child; Child Abuse, Sexual; Human Rights; Human Trafficking; Slavery, Modern-day.

Further Reading

DoSomething.org. n.d. "11 Facts about Human Trafficking." http://www.dosomething.org/tipsandtools/11-facts-about-human-trafficking.

Initiative Against Sexual Trafficking. 2013. "Facts." http://s147851.gridserver.com/facts.

Initiative Against Sexual Trafficking. 2013. "U.S. Laws." http://s147851.gridserver.com/u-s-laws.

International Agreement for the Suppression of the "White Slave Traffic." 1904. 35 Stat. 1979, 1 L.N.T.S. 83, entered into force July 18, 1905. http://www1.umn.edu/humanrts/instree/whiteslavetraffic1904.html.

National Institute of Justice. 2012. "Human Trafficking." Office of Justice Programs. http://www.nij.gov/topics/crime/human-trafficking/Pages/welcome.aspx.

Parrot, Andrea, and Nina Cummings. 2008. *Sexual Enslavement of Girls and Women Worldwide*. Westport, CT: Praeger.

Prop 35 is Law: Use It. 2012. "What Is Human Trafficking?" http://www.caseact.org/learn/humantrafficking.

Shared Hope International. 2009. *National Report on Domestic Minor Sex Trafficking: America's Prostituted Children*. http://sharedhope.org.gravitatehosting.com/Resources/TheNationalReport.aspx.

Sidun, Nancy M. 2009. "Modern Day Slavery: The Hidden and Unspoken Horror for Girls and Women." *Psychology of Women Quarterly* 33: 491–497.

UN Convention for the Suppression of the Traffic in Persons and of the Exploitation of the Prostitution of Others. 1949. UN General Assembly. http://www2.ohchr.org/english/law/trafficpersons.htm.

U.S. Department of Justice. 2009. *The Federal Bureau of Investigation's Efforts to Combat Crimes against Children*. Audit Report. 09-08. Office of the Inspector General, Audit Division. http://www.justice.gov/oig/reports/FBI/a0908/final.pdf.

U.S. Department of State. 2011. *Trafficking in Persons Report*. http://www.state.gov/j/tip/rls/tiprpt/2011/index.htm.

Walker-Rodriguez, Amanda, and Rodney Hill. 2011. "Human Sex Trafficking." *FBI Law Enforcement Bulletin*. http://www.fbi.gov/stats-services/publications/law-enforcement-bulletin/march_2011/human_sex_trafficking.

SHEPARD, MATTHEW

On October 7, 1998, 21-year-old Matthew Shepard was murdered. Shepard had attended a meeting of the University of Wyoming Lesbian, Gay, Bisexual, Transgendered Association (LGBTA). After the meeting, Shepard went to the Fireside Bar in Laramie, where he met Aaron McKinney, 22, and Russell Henderson, 21. They gave the impression that they were gay. Matthew left the bar with them. Shortly after midnight, McKinney and Henderson robbed Shepard and then led him to a remote area east of Laramie, Wyoming. They pistol whipped him and tied him in the pose of a crucifix to a split-rail fence. They left him to die in temperatures below freezing. A cyclist found him 18 hours later.

Shepard never regained consciousness and died on October 12. The killers were caught and tried. Each was given two consecutive life sentences. In 2004, the killers claimed it was not a gay hate crime but rather a robbery. When asked why then the extensive beating of Shepard, McKinney was said to have been on methamphetamines.

Documentaries, television movies, and a play, *The Laramie Project*, have told Shepard's story. They are used in schools as lessons on the workings of hate and prejudice. Shepard's mother created the Matthew Shepard Foundation, dedicated to promoting tolerance and diversity, lobbying for hate crime legislation.

The deaths of Shepard and James Byrd led to the passage of the Matthew Shepard and James Byrd, Jr., Hate Crimes Prevention Act of 2009. The act provides funding and technical assistance to state, local, and tribal jurisdictions to help them to more effectively investigate and prosecute hate crimes.

Rosemarie Skaine

See also: Hate Crimes; Homosexuals; Matthew Shepard and James Byrd, Jr., Hate Crimes Prevention Act; Racism.

Further Reading

ABC News. 2004. "New Details Emerge in Matthew Shepard Murder," November 26. http://abcnews.go.com/2020/story?id=277685&page=1.

Hurst, James C. 1999. "The Matthew Shepard Tragedy: Management of a Crisis." *About Campus* 4 (3): 5–11.

Matthew Shepard and James Byrd, Jr., Hate Crimes Prevention Act of 2009. 18 U.S.C. § 249, enacted as Division E of the National Defense Authorization Act for Fiscal Year 2010. Section 249 of Title 18. http://www.justice.gov/crt/about/crm/matthewshepard.php.

Matthew Shepard Foundation. 2013. http://www.matthewshepard.org.

Matthew's Place. 2013. "Matthew's Story." http://www.matthewsplace.com/matthews-story.

Shepard, Judy. 2009. *The Meaning of Matthew: My Son's Murder in Laramie, and a World Transformed*. New York: Hudson Street Press.

SIBLING VIOLENCE AND ABUSE

Sibling violence or abuse occurs when one sibling intentionally causes psychological or physical harm, injury, or death to a brother or sister. Repeated patterns of abuse define the behavior as sibling abuse. Evidence of maltreatment can include:

- Physical abuse, including repeated hitting, biting, slapping, shoving, tickling excessively, and choking
- Emotional abuse, including repeated teasing, ridiculing, name calling, destroying personal possessions, and abusing pets
- Sexual abuse, including repeated unwanted touching, indecent exposure, an attempt to penetrate, intercourse, rape, and sodomy

Data reported from 1980 to 2004 suggest that sibling abuse is widespread and can have fatal outcomes. In 1980, 40 percent of children in the United States engaged in physical aggression against siblings, and 85 percent regularly took part in verbal aggression. In 1990, 60 percent of 272 high school students reported being either a victim or a perpetrator. Also in 1990, national surveys of 8,145 families reported that 80 percent of children ages 3 to 17 years commit some form of violence against a sibling.

Estimates in 1998 revealed that 53 out of every 100 children perpetrated sibling abuse. In 2002, FBI data indicated that siblings perpetrated 6.1 percent of all murders committed by family members. A 2005 study found that about 35 out of 100 children abuse a sibling. The same study found the rate to be similar across income levels and racial and ethnic groups. In 2012, estimates are that 3 children in 100 are dangerously violent toward a brother or sister.

Maladaptive parental behavior and dysfunctional family structures contribute to sibling abuse. Parental treatment has a strong effect on the siblings' relationship. For example, in an effort to follow the model of a parent who abuses a child, another child may also abuse a sibling. In addition, when parents do not identify the difference between normal rivalry and abuse, risk factors, such as inappropriate expression of anger, can develop. If parents allow the display, aggression is likely to increase. Family structures that support power imbalances, rigid gender roles, different treatment of siblings, and lack of parental supervision also increase the risk for sibling abuse.

When sibling interactions are strained, the following problems can arise: difficulty with relationships, mistrust, suspiciousness, fearfulness, hateful feelings, aversion to nonsexual physical contact, revictimization in subsequent relationships, self-blame, depression, anxiety, anger, low self-esteem, sexual dysfunction, and posttraumatic stress symptoms of intrusive thoughts and flashbacks. The victim may also exhibit the following specific behaviors: screaming and crying; avoidance of the abusive sibling; behavior changes or changes in sleep patterns, including nightmares or eating habits; abusing a younger sibling; telling their parents; fighting back; and believing they deserve the abuse.

The National Association of Social Workers suggests that solutions include parenting intervention groups to provide parents with information and resources to identify and manage sibling abuse. Social work practitioners can help parents by designing and implementing interventions, especially those designed to deal with tension and violent behaviors between children and assist parents in learning to tell apart sibling rivalry and sibling violence.

Interventions open to parents include: not ignoring constant, obvious victimization; make and enforce rules and boundaries about privacy and possessions; create and consistently enforce consequences; have appropriate parental behavior; observe what the children watch on television; praise children when their behavior is appropriate; consult a family therapist if behaviors remain out of control.

Rosemarie Skaine

See also: Bullying, Child and Adolescent; Child Abuse, Psychological and Behavioral Effects of; Incest.

Further Reading

Boyse, Kyla. 2012. "Sibling Abuse." *YourChild Topics*. University of Michigan Health System. http://www.med.umich.edu/yourchild/topics/sibabuse.htm#top.

Kiselica, Mark S., and Mandy Morrill-Richards. 2007. "Sibling Maltreatment: The Forgotten Abuse." *Journal of Counseling and Development* 85 (Spring): 148–160.

Lourdes. 2013. "When Sibling Rivalry Crosses the Line into Abuse." http://www.elourdes.com/wo_emagazines_show.asp?article_id=1229.

Shadik, Jennifer A., Nathan H. Perkins, and Pamela J. Kovacs. 2013. "Practice Forum: Incorporating Discussion of Sibling Violence in the Curriculum of Parent Intervention Programs for Child Abuse and Neglect." *Health and Social Work* 38 (1): 53–57.

USF Health. 2013. "Sibling Violence." Harrell Center, University of South Florida. http://health.usf.edu/publichealth/cfh/harrellcenter/sibling.html.

SLAVERY, MODERN-DAY

Slavery is a relationship in which one person is controlled by violence, the threat of violence, or psychological coercion by another person(s). A person who is a slave has lost free will and free movement, is exploited economically, and paid nothing beyond subsistence. Modern-day slavery is a growing problem. It is not only demeaning to the person held as a slave; it demeans society. It is often associated with organized crime. Slavery exploits millions of women, men, and children across the world. Common characteristics that distinguish slavery from other forms of human rights violations are that the individual who is subjected to slavery is forced to work for little or no pay, is owned or controlled mentally or physically by an employer, is treated as a commodity, and is physically constrained.

The United States abolished "involuntary servitude" when President Abraham Lincoln issued the Emancipation Proclamation on January 1, 1863. The Thirteenth Amendment added the abolition to the U.S. Constitution: "Neither slavery nor involuntary servitude, except as a punishment for crime whereof the party shall have been duly convicted, shall exist within the United States, or any place subject to their jurisdiction." Despite being made illegal, slavery exists in the United States. Although slavery is legal in some countries, it is banned by international convention, such as the 1948 Universal Declaration of Human Rights and the 1956 UN Supplementary Convention on the Abolition of Slavery, the Slave Trade, and Institutions and Practices Similar to Slavery.

Statistics on slavery are limited due to the crime's hidden nature, limited awareness, the victims' fear of retaliation, and lack of comprehensive study. The CNN Freedom Project estimates that approximately 14,500 to 17,500 people are trafficked into the United States each year. The International Labor Organization (ILO) puts the global number of people who are slaves at a minimum of 10 million to 30 million. The most vulnerable populations that are likely to become victims to slavery are minorities and the socially excluded groups.

Modern slavery is a criminal industry that thrives and transforms itself into new forms year after year, according to Gulnara Shahinian, the UN special rapporteur on contemporary forms of slavery. Shahinian states that slavery is not just a word that explains violence and ruthless exploitation; it is a word that describes people who have been beaten mercilessly, shut indoors, made to work without pay, sexually abused, poorly fed, and threatened with more abuse against themselves and their families if they attempt to leave.

Slavery can be in the form of forced labor, slavery by descent, trafficking, child labor, early and forced marriage, and bonded labor. The Polaris Project, a national anti-human trafficking group, has found various types of forced labor in the United States. Approximately 100,000 children become victims in the sex trade in the United States every year. Many victims have also been forced to work in factories, the agricultural industry, strip clubs, hostess clubs, residential brothels, fake massage businesses, traveling carnivals, forced begging and street peddling rings, and as domestic workers.

The Trafficking Victims Protection Act (TVPA) of 2000, the Fair Labor Standards Act (FLSA), the Occupational Safety and Health Act (OSHA), and the National Labor Relations Act (NLRA) protect the rights of domestic workers and help combat human trafficking in the United States. According to the United Nations Trafficking in Persons 2012 report, a significant number of Mexican, Central American, Thai, Filipino, Haitian, and other East Asian victims were detected in the United States. Most confirmed labor trafficking victims were identified as undocumented aliens.

According to National Human Trafficking Resource Center (NHTRC) 2011 annual report, they have received reports of potential human trafficking in every U.S. state. The top 10 states for potential trafficking locations are California, Texas, Florida, New York, the District of Columbia, Illinois, Virginia, Ohio, and North Carolina. Building partnerships to eradicate modern-day slavery has been one of the main goals of our country, especially for modern-day abolitionists and leaders of the anti-trafficking movement. U.S.-based organizations such as Courtney's House, Girls Educational & Mentoring Services (GEMS), Humanity United, International Justice Mission, Made In A Free World, and Polaris Project are among the nation's leading organizations dedicated to serve the victims and help counter modern-day slavery at all levels.

A holistic approach is required to eradicate slavery. Governments, businesses, international aid organizations, and consumers all have a role to play. Cooperative efforts of our law enforcement partners domestically and internationally have been instrumental in bringing justice to victims of all forms of modern-day slavery and to dismantling trafficking organizations. Every individual has the right to a better life, a life of dignity, and the right to be free from any form of modern-day slavery.

Karunya Jayasena

See also: Human Rights; Human Trafficking; Sex Trafficking; Sexual Slavery; Torture.

Further Reading

Anti-human Trafficking Task Force Initiative. n.d. Bureau of Justice Assistance, U.S. Department of Justice. https://www.bja.gov/ProgramDetails.aspx?Program_ID=51.

Anti-slavery. n.d. "What Is Modern Slavery?" http://www.antislavery.org/english/slavery_today/what_is_modern_slavery.aspx.

Bales, Kevin. 2007. "Defining and Measuring Modern Slavery." http://www.freetheslaves.net/Document.Doc?id=21.

Children at Risk. 2014. "Child Trafficking." http://childrenatrisk.org/research/child-trafficking.

Free the Slaves. 2014. https://www.freetheslaves.net/SSLPage.aspx?pid=285.

Polaris Project. 2014. "Labor Trafficking in the US." http://www.polarisproject.org/human-trafficking/labor-trafficking-in-the-us.

Polaris Project. 2014. "Sex Trafficking." http://www.polarisproject.org/resources/resources-by-topic/sex-trafficking.

Polaris Project. 2011. "Increasing Awareness and Engagement: Strengthening the National Response to Human Trafficking in the U.S." https://na4.salesforce.com/sfc/p/300000006E4S11Sv6mFa.D_CBl0UueofejFjNL0=.

President's Advisory Council on Faith-based and Neighborhood Partnerships. 2013. "Building Partnerships to Eradicate Modern-day Slavery: Report of Recommendations to the President." http://www.whitehouse.gov/sites/default/files/docs/advisory_council_humantrafficking_report.pdf.

Shahinian, Gulnara. 2013. "Slavery Must Be Recognize in All Its Guises." *Guardian*, April 26. http://www.guardian.co.uk/global-development/poverty-matters/2013/apr/26/slavery-recognised-all-guises.

United Nations Office on Drugs and Crime. 2012. "Global Report on Trafficking in Persons 2012." http://www.unodc.org/documents/data-and-analysis/glotip/Trafficking_in_Persons_2012_web.pdf.

U.S. Department of State. 2005 "Trafficking in Persons Report." http://www.state.gov/documents/organization/47255.pdf.

SOUTHERN POVERTY LAW CENTER

The Southern Poverty Law Center (SPLC) in Montgomery, Alabama, is a nonprofit civil rights organization committed to fighting hate and bigotry and to seeking justice for the most vulnerable members of society. The organization has offices in Atlanta, Georgia; New Orleans, Louisiana; Miami, Florida; and Jackson, Mississippi. In 1971, civil rights lawyers Morris Dees and Joseph Levin Jr. founded the SPLC. The center has an international reputation for tracking and exposing the activities of hate groups. Its Teaching Tolerance program produces and distributes, free of charge, documentary films, books, lesson plans, and other materials that promote tolerance and respect in schools in the United States.

SPLC's agenda addresses five areas: children at risk, hate and extremism, immigrant justice, LGBT rights, and teaching tolerance. Its strategy to combat racial and social injustice involves three parts:

- Tracking the activities of U.S. hate groups and domestic terrorists and initiating lawsuits to destroy networks of radical extremists
- Court action and other advocacy to gain reforms
- Providing educators with free resources that teach schoolchildren to reject hate, embrace diversity, and respect differences

A large section of the SPLC Web site is devoted to "Get Informed." This category includes "News," "Case Docket," "Teaching Tolerance," "Hatewatch Blog," "Hate Map," "Intelligence Files," "Intelligence Report," and "Hate Incidents." The SPLC's searchable "Case Docket" can be examined for all cases, landmark cases, or by agenda area. Although the agenda area "Children at Risk" primarily addresses vulnerable children who are disproportionately black, frequently have learning

Tania Galloni, behind podium, Managing Attorney for the Southern Poverty Law Center's Florida office, gestures as she speaks during a news conference on March 21, 2012, in Tampa, Florida. The group has filed a lawsuit on behalf of seven children imprisoned with adults in the Polk County Jail. (AP Photo/Chris O'Meara)

disabilities, and who are pushed out of schools and into the juvenile justice system, SPLC also addresses other types of vulnerabilities that affect children.

"M. C." was born with an intersex condition, a difference in reproductive or sexual anatomy that does not fit the typical definition of male or female, When M. C. was 16 months old, the South Carolina Department of Social Services, doctors, and department officials decided M. C. should have sex-assignment surgery to a girl. When he was 8 years old, M. C. had all the mannerisms of a boy but the genitalia of a girl. SPLC held that there was no medical reason to perform this surgery and that M. C. was denied the opportunity to decide what should happen to his body. On May 14, 2013, SPLC filed the landmark case *M.C. v. Aaronson*. The case is still pending in the courts and has moved forward because the courts have rejected the efforts to dismiss it.

Under the agenda area "Hate and Extremism," SPLC filed a notable 1996 landmark case, *Macedonia v. Christian Knights of the Ku Klux Klan*. In 1995, members of the Christian Knights of the KKK set fire to and destroyed a 100-year-old black Baptist church in South Carolina. The SPLC sued the Klan and won the largest judgment ever awarded against a hate group.

In 2012, the center reported that 1,007 active hate groups existed in the United States. SPLC continues its effort to expose and take action against hate groups.

Rosemarie Skaine

See also: Child Abuse, Physical and Emotional; Hate Crimes; Hate Speech; Homosexuals; Prisoner Abuse, Adult; Racism; Transgender Individuals.

Further Reading

Dees, Morris, and Steve Fiffer. 1991. *A Season for Justice*. New York: Charles Scribner's Sons.

Southern Poverty Law Center. 2013. http://www.splcenter.org.

Southern Poverty Law Center. 2013. *The Intelligence Report*, quarterly. http://www.splcenter.org/get-informed/intelligence-report.

Southern Poverty Law Center. 2013. "Publications." http://www.splcenter.org/get-informed/publications.

STALKING

When individuals find themselves to be the unsolicited focus of another's attention, they are being stalked. The Stalking Resource Center defines stalking as the course of conduct directed at a specific person that would cause a reasonable person to feel fear. Stalking behaviors include repeated following, surveillance, and communication that would lead a person to fear that he or she will be harmed. A stalker is identified as any person who harasses another person or willfully, maliciously, and repeatedly follows another person with the intent to place that person in reasonable fear of bodily injury. Technological advances enable stalkers to track their victims with the Global Positioning System (GPS) or engage in stalking using the Internet, known as cyberstalking.

Six million people are stalked each year. In the United States, 1 in 6 women (16.2%) and 1 in 19 men (5.2%) have experienced stalking victimization at some point during their lifetime in which they felt very fearful or believed that they or someone close to them would be harmed or killed. Forty-six percent of stalking victims experience at least one unwanted contact per week, and 11 percent of victims have been stalked for five years or more.

The majority of stalking victims are stalked by someone they know, according to the Stalking Resource Center. A current or former intimate partner stalked 66 percent of females and 41 percent of males. More than half of female victims and more than one-third of male victims said they were stalked before the age of 25, and 1 in five females and 1 in 14 males experience stalking between the ages of 11 and 17.

Women who make threats and who stalk their prior sexually intimate partners are more likely to be violent. Women who write letters are less likely to be violent. Men and women celebrities are stalked. Celebrity men include: Leonardo DiCaprio, Michael Douglas, Mel Gibson, Richard Gere, Jerry Lewis, and David Letterman. Letterman has been a target several times. According to the NBC Bay Area, the most recent stalker of Letterman was a woman who was charged with plotting to kidnap his 18-month-old son and nanny. In the late 1990s, a woman stalker committed suicide after a longtime obsession with him.

There is a relationship between stalking and domestic violence and the woman being killed. Seventy-six percent of intimate partner victims who were killed were stalked by their intimate partner, and 67 percent had been physically abused by their intimate partner. Eighty nine percent of the victims killed who had been physically assaulted were also stalked in the 12 months before their murder. In their efforts to take action against their stalkers, 79 percent of abuse victims who were later killed reported they were stalked during the same period that they were abused, and 54 percent of them had reported the stalking to police before they were killed by their stalkers.

Women who were stalked:

- Fear the stalking will never stop
- Have lost work time
- Relocate their residences
- Experience anxiety, insomnia, social dysfunction, and severe depression, especially if the stalking involves being followed or having property destroyed
- Experience health consequences, such as poor health, depression, injury, and substance use

All 50 states, the District of Columbia, the U.S. Territories, and the federal government have laws that make stalking a crime. Less than one-third of states classify stalking as a felony upon first offense. Approximately half do so upon second or subsequent offense or when the crime involves aggravating factors.

The Violence Against Women Act of 2013 has added provisions associated with stalking and cyberstalking. Intimidate is defined as intended action with intent to kill, injure, harass, intimidate, or place under surveillance. Emotional distress was changed to causes, attempts to cause, or would be reasonably expected to cause substantial emotional distress. In education, the Clery provisions of the Higher Education Act were amended to require that stalking be included in campus crime statistics reports and the word *stalking* was added to issues related to grants.

Stalking victims require education, counseling, and possibly medications. They also need to understand practical safety issues. Abrams and Robinson state that, when treating a victim, the therapist needs to

- Provide a supportive and empathic environment
- Avoid revictimizing the patient
- Be aware that sometimes repressed emotions in the therapist that are awakened by identification with the experiences and feelings of the patient might interfere with therapy

Despite legal advances, civil or criminal legal sanctions are often ineffective in preventing stalking because the problems that motivate the stalker are unresolved. Treatment of stalkers includes pharmacological therapy when mental illness is evident. Psychological intervention is the treatment of choice for nonpsychotic stalkers. Intervention will depend on accurate assessment of the risks of continued stalking, the identification of psychological deficits and needs, and the positive response factors of the stalker. Tailoring treatment to the stalker aids therapeutic effectiveness.

Rosemarie Skaine

See also: Cyberstalking; Men as Victims of Abuse; Violence Against Women Act.

Further Reading

Abrams, Karen M., and Gail Erlick Robinson. 2008. *Psychiatric Times* 25 (10): 43.
Davis, K. E., A. L. Coker, and M. Sanderson. 2002. "Physical and Mental Health Effects of Being Stalked for Men and Women." *Violence and Victims* 4 (August 17): 429–443.

Hines, Denise A., Jan Brown, and Edward Dunning. 2007. "Characteristics of Callers to the Domestic Abuse Helpline for Men." *Journal of Family Violence* 22: 63–72.

Logan, T. K., Jennifer Cole, Lisa Shannon, and Robert Walker. 2006. *Partner Stalking: How Women Respond, Cope, and Survive.* New York: Springer Publishing Company.

MacKenzie, Rachel D., and David V. James. 2011. *Behavioral Sciences and the Law* 29: 220–239.

National Center for Victims of Crime. 2012. Stalking Resource Center. http://www.victimsofcrime.org/our-programs/stalking-resource-center.

NBC Bay Area. 2013. "Celebrities Who've Been Stalked." http://www.nbcbayarea.com/entertainment/celebrity/Celebrities_Whove_Been_Stalked.html.

Skaine, Rosemarie. 1996. *Power and Gender: Issues in Sexual Dominance and Harassment.* Jefferson, SC: McFarland Publishers.

STAND YOUR GROUND LAW

A stand your ground law is a self-defense law that gives individuals the right to use deadly force to defend themselves without any requirement to evade or retreat from a dangerous situation. The law differs from the self-defense laws based on the Castle Doctrine that say a person has no duty to retreat whatsoever when attacked in their homes (their castles). The regular self-defense law requires people to show that they are in reasonable fear of serious bodily injury or imminent death.

The model stand your ground law was drafted by the American Legislative Exchange Council (ALEC) and was first enacted in Florida in 2005. Laws in at least 22 states allow that there is no duty to retreat from an attacker in any place in which one is lawfully present: Alabama, Arizona, Florida, Georgia, Indiana, Kansas, Kentucky, Louisiana, Michigan, Mississippi, Montana, Nevada, New Hampshire, North Carolina, Oklahoma, Pennsylvania, South Carolina, South Dakota, Tennessee, Texas, Utah, and West Virginia. At least nine of those states include language stating one may "stand his or her ground": Alabama, Florida, Georgia, Kansas, Kentucky, Louisiana, Oklahoma, Pennsylvania, and South Carolina.

Stand your ground laws have been controversial since they were passed, and the shooting death in Florida of Trayvon Martin by George Zimmerman gave the law national attention. Trayvon Martin was a 17-year-old black teenager who was followed, shot, and killed by George Zimmerman, a Neighborhood Watch coordinator. Zimmerman was subsequently charged with the killing but was found not guilty by a Florida jury. Judge Debra Nelson's instructions to the jury in the case included the statement that he had no duty to retreat as per Florida's stand your ground law.

In Florida, over 200 incidents have occurred under the stand your ground law. Of those cases, the verdicts were that 75 were justified and the perpetrator was not convicted, and 44 were not justified. In states with stand your ground laws, 17 percent of incidents in which a white person fatally shot a black person have been ruled "justified" homicides, but when a black person fatally shot a white person in those states, it was deemed "justified" less than 2 percent of the time.

Stand your ground laws are frequently criticized and called "shoot first" laws by critics, which includes the Brady Campaign to Prevent Gun Violence. In Florida, self-defense claims tripled in the years following enactment. The law's critics argue that Florida's law makes it very difficult to prosecute cases against people who shoot others and then claim self-defense. The shooter can argue that he felt threatened, and, in most cases, the only witness who could have argued otherwise is the deceased.

John Roman's analysis of murders that were justified in non-stand your ground states and stand your ground states reveals an increase in justified murders in stand your ground states.

Roman found a significant difference in the number of white on black murders that were justified (11.41%) and in those justified in non-stand your ground states (9.51%) and in stand your ground states (16.85%). The black on white murders that were justified were significantly lower (1.2%) and with no significant difference in whether the state had a stand your ground law (1.13% and 1.4%).

The future of stand your ground laws is uncertain. After the jury verdict that acquitted George Zimmerman of charges originating from the shooting death of Trayvon Martin, Attorney General Eric Holder, in a

A memorial to Trayvon Martin stands outside The Retreat at Twin Lakes community where Trayvon was shot and killed by George Michael Zimmerman, a neighborhood watch volunteer, on April 12, 2012, in Sanford, Florida. Second degree murder charges were brought against defendant George Zimmerman who initially was not charged with any crime due to Florida's "Stand Your Ground" self-defense law. Zimmerman was arrested, tried, and found not guilty by a Florida jury. (Getty Images)

July 16, 2013, speech criticized stand your ground laws, saying that they senselessly

Percentage of Homicides Ruled Justified, 2005–2010

	Total	Non-Stand Your Ground States	Stand Your Ground States
White on white	2.21	1.68	3.51
White on black	11.41	9.51	16.85
Black on white	1.20	1.13	1.40
Black on black	2.43	2.15	3.16
Total	2.57	2.15	3.67

Source: FBI Uniform Crime Statistics Supplementary Homicide Reports, 2005–2010.

expand the concept of self-defense and sow dangerous conflict in our neighbor-hoods. The Department of Justice has launched a civil rights investigation into the Trayvon Martin case. A civil rights lawsuit may be filed by Trayvon Martin's parents against George Zimmerman. The NAACP is also considering a civil rights lawsuit.

The controversy over stand your ground laws continues. States that have them have not yet begun to repeal them, despite public pressure to do so.

Rosemarie Skaine

See also: Gun Violence; Racism.

Further Reading

Cameron, Darla, and William M. Higgins. 2013. "Florida's Stand Your Ground Law." *Tampa Bay Times*, August 13. http://www.tampabay.com/stand-your-ground-law/fatal-cases.

Chuck, Elizabeth. 2013. "Florida Had First Stand Your Ground Law, Other States Followed in 'Rapid Succession.'" NBCNEWS.com. http://usnews.nbcnews.com/_news/2013/07/18/19522874-florida-had-first-stand-your-ground-law-other-states-followed-in-rapid-succession?lite.

FindLaw. 2014. "States That Have Stand Your Ground Laws." 2014. http://criminal.findlaw.com/criminal-law-basics/states-that-have-stand-your-ground-laws.html.

Investigative Reporters & Editors. 2012. "Uniform Crime Reports." http://www.ire.org/nicar/database-library/databases/fbi-uniform-crime-reports.

Lum, Lydia. 2013. "American Bar Association Examines Stand Your Ground Laws." *Diverse Issues in Higher Education*. http://diverseeducation.com/article/55179/#.

National Conference of State Legislatures (NCSL). 2013. "Self Defense and 'Stand Your Ground.'" http://www.ncsl.org/issues-research/justice/self-defense-and-stand-your-ground.aspx.

Roman, John K. 2013. "Race, Justifiable Homicide, and Stand Your Ground Laws: Analysis of FBI Supplementary Homicide Report Data." Urban Institute. http://www.urban.org/UploadedPDF/412873-stand-your-ground.pdf.

STOP THE SILENCE

Stop the Silence: Stop Child Sexual Abuse is a 501(c)3 nonprofit organization that was founded in 2002. Its mission is to collectively address and raise awareness of the social problem of child sexual abuse. Stop the Silence brings attention not only to child sexual abuse but also to preventing and treating what it calls the "silent epidemic."

According to the Stop the Silence Web site, child abuse is possible because of the differences in power and control between the offender and the victim. Its founder and CEO, Dr. Pamela Pine, is a global health and development specialist who has worked and continues to work globally on social problems, such as child survival in the Congo, use of children in coca farming in Ecuador, HIV/AIDS, Hansen's disease (leprosy) treatment and control in Yemen and Ethiopia, and tuberculosis control.

The Stop the Silence Web site provides toll-free numbers and Web sites of specific agencies within the United States that are designated to obtain and investigate reports of suspected child abuse and neglect. It also provides a "Get Help" link for victims, family, and friends who have to deal with the aftermath of child sexual abuse. Stop the Silence currently has an all-volunteer board of directors that supports the organization's mission and work.

The objectives of Stop the Silence are to (1) promote healing of victims and survivors and (2) to celebrate the lives of those healed. The organization addresses the connection between child sexual abuse and the collective issue of family and violence within and between communities. It explains (1) what child sexual abuse is; (2) how common it is; and (3) what its consequences are. The organization states that, based on long-term research, adults who were sexually victimized in their childhood are more apt to become negatively impacted in their adulthood by numerous types of psychological and physiological ailments and sociological pathologies, including posttraumatic stress disorder (PTSD) and self-destructive and violent behaviors. The consequences of child sexual abuse include depression; anxiety; PTSD; behavior problems, such as delinquency; decreased performance at school; substance abuse; promiscuity; teen pregnancy; sexually transmitted diseases, including HIV; prostitution; suicide; and incarceration. The organization further states that most child sexual abuse incidents are never reported and that most victims do not disclose their experiences for social reasons, such as stigma, shame, fear, and manipulation.

Stop the Silence holds annual events to educate communities across the United States about child sexual abuse, to give voice to the voiceless, and to help survivors heal and thrive. Over the years, the movement has sponsored an annual event that receives attention across the globe. The Road to Change, is a 10,000-mile walk that visits 31 of the major cities in the European Union (EU). The walk helps to raise awareness, to build commonality among organizations and local communities, and to positively influence social and political change.

Stop the Silence is continuing to partner with other agencies and organizations to help educate the public about child sexual abuse, how to prevent it, and how to minimize its consequence through appropriate intervention on the psychological, medical, and policy (legal and judicial) fronts.

Juan Carlos Hernandez

See also: Child Abuse, Psychological and Behavioral Effects of; Child Abuse, Sexual; Child Abuse, Treatment for.

Further Reading

Lee, Carter. 2011. "Dr. Pamela Pine, Stop the Silence, Discusses Pedophilia Awareness." *The Washington Times*, December 21. http://communities.washingtontimes.com/neighborhood/moment-space/2011/dec/21/stop-silence-dr-pamela-pine-discusses-pedophilia-a.

McVarish, Matthew. n.d. "Walk to Stop the Silence: Stop Child Sexual Abuse." Road to Change. http://roadtochange.eu.

Stop the Silence: Stop Child Sexual Abuse. 2013. "Road to Change: A 10,000 Mile Walk across Europe." http://stopthesilence.org/road-to-change.

SUBSTANCE ABUSE

Substance abuse means dependency on a drug considered dangerous to a person's health and well-being. Substances are ingested, inhaled, or injected.

Substances include tobacco, alcohol, over-the-counter (OTC) medications, prescription painkillers such as oxycodone and codeine, or illegal stimulants such as cocaine, marijuana, methamphetamines, and heroin. Other substances include hallucinogens, inhalants, solvents, and anabolic steroids. Substance abuse is often a factor that can lead an individual to engage in abusive behaviors, such as domestic violence.

Illicit drug use in America is increasing. In 2012, about 23.9 million (9.2 % of the population) aged 12 or older had used an illicit drug or abused a psycho-therapeutic medication (such as a pain reliever, stimulant, or tranquilizer) in the past month. This figure shows an 8.3 percent increase from 2002. The increase primarily reflects a recent rise in the use of marijuana, the most commonly used illicit drug. In 2012, users numbered 18.9 million (7.3 percent) of people aged 12 or older, an increase from 14.4 million (5.8 percent) in 2007. Use of most drugs other than marijuana has not changed substantially over the past decade or has declined.

High-profile cases of substance abuse by movie stars offer insights. Some died abusing a substance. On February 2, 2014, Oscar-winning actor Philip Seymour Hoffman, age 46, was found dead with a hypodermic needle stuck in his left arm and bags of heroin scattered about his home. Hoffman struggled with addiction and had participated in a 10-day rehab period in May 2013. In 2006, Hoffman won the Best Actor Academy Award for playing the title role in *Capote*. Hoffman is a case that combined heroin with prescription drugs. The combination has become increasingly deadly.

On January 22, 2008, another screen star, Heath Ledger, age 28, died from an accidental overdose of prescription medications, including painkillers, anti-anxiety drugs, and sleeping pills. The combined effects of the drugs found in his body led to his death: Oxycodone, narcotic/painkiller, trade names: OxyContin and Percodan; Hydrocodone, narcotic/painkiller, trade name (combined with acetaminophen): Vicodin; Diazepam, anti-anxiety drug, trade name: Valium; Alprazolam, anti-anxiety drug, trade name: Xanax; Doxylamine, sleep medication, trade name: Unisom; and Temazepam, sleep medication, trade name: Restoril. Ledger was well-known for his portrayal of Ennis Del Mar in Ang Lee's film *Brokeback Mountain*.

Prescription medications include central nervous system (CNS) depressants, stimulants, and opioid pain relievers. Commonly abused classes of prescription drugs include opioids (for pain), CNS depressants (for anxiety and sleep disorders), and stimulants (for ADHD and narcolepsy). Opioids include: Fentanyl (Durage-sic), Hydrocodone (Vicodin), Oxycodone (OxyContin), Oxymorphone (Opana), Propoxyphene (Darvon), Hydromorphone (Dilaudid), Meperidine (Demerol), and Diphenoxylate (Lomotil). CNS depressants include: Pentobarbital sodium (Nembutal), Diazepam (Valium), and Alprazolam (Xanax). Stimulants include: Dextroamphetamine (Dexedrine), Methylphenidate (Ritalin and Concerta), and Amphetamines (Adderall).

The most commonly abused drugs as identified by the National Institute on Drug Abuse are the following:

- Nicotine is found in tobacco products: cigarettes, cigars, bidis, and smokeless tobacco (snuff, spit tobacco, chew). It is administered by smoking, snorting, and chewing. Acute effects are an increase in blood pressure and heart rate. Health risks include chronic lung disease; cardiovascular disease; stroke; cancers of the mouth, pharynx, larynx, esophagus, stomach, pancreas, cervix, kidney, bladder, and acute myeloid leukemia; adverse pregnancy outcomes; and addiction.
- Alcohol (ethyl alcohol) is found in liquor, beer, and wine. It is administered by swallowing. Acute effects in low doses include euphoria, mild stimulation, relaxation, and lowered inhibitions. Effects of higher doses are drowsiness, slurred speech, nausea, emotional volatility, loss of coordination, visual distortions, impaired memory, sexual dysfunction, and loss of consciousness. Health risks include increased risk of injuries, violence, and fetal damage; depression; neurologic deficits; hypertension; liver and heart disease; addiction; and fatal overdose.
- Cannabinoids include marijuana and hashish. Marijuana is also known as blunt, dope, ganja, grass, herb, joint, bud, Mary Jane, pot, reefer, green, trees, smoke, sinsemilla, skunk, and weed. It is smoked or swallowed. Hashish is also known as boom, gangster, hash, hash oil, and hemp. It is smoked or swallowed. The acute effects for both drugs include euphoria, relaxation, slowed reaction time, distorted sensory perception, impaired balance and coordination, increased heart rate and appetite, impaired learning and memory, anxiety, panic attacks, and psychosis. Health risks include cough, frequent respiratory infections, possible mental health decline, and addiction.
- Opioids include heroin and opium. Heroin is known as diacetylmorphine, smack, horse, brown sugar, dope, H, junk, skag, skunk, white horse, China white, and cheese (with OTC cold medicine and antihistamine). Heroin is injected, smoked, or snorted. Opium is known as laudanum, paregoric, big O, black stuff, block, gum, and hop. It is swallowed or smoked. Acute effects of both drugs include euphoria, drowsiness, impaired coordination, dizziness, confusion, nausea, sedation, feeling of heaviness in the body, and slowed or arrested breathing. Health risks include constipation, endocarditis, hepatitis, HIV, addiction, and fatal overdose.
- Stimulants include cocaine, amphetamines, and methamphetamines. Cocaine is known by cocaine hydrochloride, blow, bump, C, candy, Charlie, coke, crack, flake, rock, snow, and toot. It is snorted, smoked, and injected. Amphetamines are known as Biphetamine, Dexedrine, bennies, black beauties, crosses, hearts, LA turnaround, speed, truck drivers, and uppers. They are swallowed, snorted, smoked, and injected. Methamphetamines are known as Desoxyn, meth, ice, crank, chalk, crystal, fire, glass, go fast, and speed. They are also swallowed, snorted, smoked, and injected. Acute effects of these drugs are increased heart rate, blood pressure, body temperature, and metabolism; feelings of exhilaration; increased energy and mental alertness; tremors; reduced appetite; irritability; anxiety; panic; paranoia; violent behavior; and psychosis. Health risks include weight loss; insomnia; cardiac or cardiovascular complications; stroke; seizures; and addiction. Cocaine produces the added risk of nasal damage from snorting, and methamphetamines cause severe dental problems.
- Club drugs include MDMA (methylene-dioxy-methamph-etamine), Flunitrazepam, and GHB (Gamma-hydroxybutyrate). MDMA is known as Ecstasy, Adam, clarity, Eve, lover's speed, peace, and uppers. It is swallowed, snorted, and injected. Flunitrazepam is known as Rohypnol, forget-me pill, Mexican Valium, R2, roach, Roche, roofies, roofinol, rope, and rophies. It is swallowed and snorted. GHB is known as G, Georgia home boy, grievous bodily harm, liquid ecstasy, soap, scoop, goop, and

liquid. It is swallowed. Acute effects of MDMA include mild hallucinogenic effects, increased tactile sensitivity, empathic feelings, lowered inhibition, anxiety, chills, sweating, teeth clenching, and muscle cramping. Flunitrazepam's effects include sedation, muscle relaxation, confusion, memory loss, dizziness, and impaired coordination. GHB effects include drowsiness, nausea, headache, disorientation, loss of coordination, and memory loss. Health risks for MDMA include sleep disturbances, depression, impaired memory, hyperthermia, and addiction. Flunitrazepam's health risks include addiction. GHB's health risks include unconsciousness, seizures, and coma.

- Dissociative drugs include Ketamine Ketalar SV, PCP and analogs Phencyclidine, Salvia divinorum, and Dextrometh-orphan (DXM). Ketamine Ketalar SV is known as cat Valium, K, Special K, and vitamin K. It is injected, snorted, and smoked. PCP and analogs Phencyclidine are known as angel dust, boat, hog, love boat, and peace pill. It is swallowed, smoked, and injected. Salvia divinorum is known as Salvia, Shepherdess's Herb, Maria Pastora, magic mint, and Sally-D. It is chewed, swallowed, and smoked. DXM is found in some cough and cold medications and known as Robotripping, Robo, and Triple C. It is swallowed.

- Hallucinogens include LSD Lysergic acid diethylamide, Mescaline, and Psilocybin. LSD is known as acid, blotter, cubes, microdot yellow sunshine, and blue heaven. It is swallowed and absorbed through mouth tissues. Mescaline is known as buttons, cactus, mesc, and peyote. It is swallowed and smoked. Psilocybin is known as magic mushrooms, purple passion, shrooms, and little smoke. It is swallowed. Acute effects of these three drugs include altered states of perception and feeling, hallucinations, and nausea. Additional effects for LSD include increased body temperature, heart rate, and blood pressure; loss of appetite; sweating; sleeplessness; numbness, dizziness, weakness, and tremors; impulsive behavior; and rapid shifts in emotion. For Mescaline, additional effects include increased body temperature, heart rate, and blood pressure; loss of appetite; sweating; sleeplessness; numbness, dizziness, weakness, and tremors; impulsive behavior; and rapid shifts in emotion. For Psilocybin, effects include nervousness, paranoia, and panic. Health risks for LSD include flashbacks and Hallucinogen Persisting Perception Disorder. Acute effects also include feelings of being separated from one's body and environment and impaired motor function. For ketamine, acute effects include analgesia, impaired memory, delirium, respiratory depression and arrest, and death. For PCP and analogs, effects are analgesia, psychosis, aggression, violence, slurred speech, loss of coordination, and hallucinations. For DXM, effects are euphoria, slurred speech, confusion, dizziness, and distorted visual perceptions. For all drugs, health risks are anxiety, tremors, numbness, memory loss, and nausea.

- Other compounds include Anabolic steroids and inhalants. Anabolic steroids are known as Anadrol, Oxandrin, Durabolin, Depo-Testosterone, Equipoise, roids, juice, gym candy, and pumpers. They are injected, swallowed, and applied to the skin. Inhalants include solvents (paint thinners, gasoline, glues); gases (butane, propane, aerosol propellants, nitrous oxide); and nitrites (isoamyl, isobutyl, cyclohexyl). They are known as laughing gas, poppers, snappers, and whippets. They are inhaled through the nose or mouth. Anabolic steroids have no intoxication effects. Inhalants vary by chemical, but effects include stimulation, loss of inhibition, headache, nausea or vomiting, slurred speech, loss of motor coordination, and wheezing. Health risks for Anabolic steroids include hypertension; blood clotting and cholesterol changes;

liver cysts; hostility and aggression; acne; in adolescents, premature stoppage of growth; in males, prostate cancer, reduced sperm production, shrunken testicles, and breast enlargement; and in females, menstrual irregularities, development of a beard, and other masculine characteristics. In addition, inhalants can cause cramps, muscle weakness, depression, memory impairment, damage to cardiovascular and nervous systems, unconsciousness, and sudden death.

Withdrawal of CNS depressants can produce a rebound effect, resulting in seizures or other harmful consequences. Withdrawal symptoms associated with discontinuing stimulant use include fatigue, depression, and disturbance of sleep patterns. Repeated abuse of some stimulants includes feelings of hostility or paranoia and psychosis. High doses of a stimulant may result in dangerously high body temperature, an irregular heartbeat, and cardiovascular failure or seizures. Opioids can be used to manage pain safely and effectively, but when abused, a single large dose can cause severe respiratory depression and death.

The National Institute on Drug Abuse addresses substance abuse for all ages in the population. For the adolescent, the institute recommends four treatment approaches: behavioral, family based, addiction medications, and recovery support services. Interventions as well as medications are emphasized. The clinician needs to be trained and well supervised to ensure that he or she adheres to the instructions and guidance described in the institute's treatment manuals. Most treatments have been tested over 12–16 weeks, but for some adolescents, longer treatments may be warranted; decisions are made on a case-by-case basis.

The institute's Principles of Adolescent Substance Use Disorder Treatment include

1. Early identification
2. Intervention, even when the adolescent is not addicted
3. Routine annual medical visits
4. Legal interventions and sanctions or family pressure to get adolescents to enter, stay in, and complete treatment
5. Substance use disorder treatment tailored to the unique needs of the adolescent
6. Treatment that addresses the needs of the whole person, rather than just focusing on his or her drug use
7. Behavioral therapies that are effective in addressing adolescent drug use
8. Families and the community as important aspects of treatment
9. Effectively treating substance use disorders in adolescents by also identifying and treating any other mental health conditions they may have
10. Identifying and addressing sensitive issues such as violence, child abuse, or risk of suicide
11. Monitoring drug use during treatment
12. Staying in treatment for an adequate period of time and continuity of care afterward
13. Testing for sexually transmitted diseases, such as HIV and hepatitis B and C, as an important part of drug treatment

Rosemarie Skaine

Further Reading

CNN. 2008. "Ledger's Death Caused by Accidental Overdose," February 6. http://www.cnn.com/2008/SHOWBIZ/Movies/02/06/heath.ledger/index.html?_s=PM%253Cimg%2520class=.

Marcius, Chelsia Rose, Lachlan Cartwright, and Tina Moore. n.d. "Philip Seymour Hoffman Dead at 46: Actor Found in His New York City Apartment with Needle in Arm after Using Heroin, Sources Say." *New York Daily News*, updated February 3, 2014. http://www.nydailynews.com/new-york/philip-seymour-hoffman-found-dead-new-york-city-apartment-report-article-1.1599537#ixzz30UHl5KUF.

McGill, Natalie. 2013. "How to Recognize the Signs of Substance Abuse." *Nation's Health* 43 (8): 28.

National Institutes of Health. 2014. "Drug Facts: Nationwide Trends." National Institute on Drug Abuse. http://www.drugabuse.gov/publications/drugfacts/nationwide-trends.

National Institutes of Health. 2014. "Principles of Adolescent Substance Use Disorder Treatment: A Research-based Guide." National Institute on Drug Abuse. http://www.drugabuse.gov/publications/principles-adolescent-substance-use-disorder-treatment-research-based-guide.

National Institutes of Health. n.d. "Drugs of Abuse." National Institute on Drug Abuse. http://www.drugabuse.gov/drugs-abuse.

SUICIDE

Suicide is the taking of one's own life. Suicide is a problem for people of all ages. Suicide is the third-leading cause of death among persons aged 15–24 years, the second from 25–34 years, the fourth from 35–54 years, and the eighth from 55–64 years. Abuse, particularly bullying, may lead some individuals, particularly adolescents, to attempt suicide.

Between 1990 and 2000, the suicide rate decreased from 12.5 suicide deaths to 10.4 per 100,000, but by 2010 the rate increased to 12.1 deaths per 100,000. The Centers for Disease Control and Prevention (CDC) found that, in 2010, there were 38,364 suicides (one every 13.7 minutes) reported, making suicide the 10th leading cause of death. In 2010, the most common method for committing suicide was firearms (50.6%). The second- and third-most common methods were suffocation (including hangings) (24.8%) and poisoning (17.3%).

Suicide is a significant health problem, with high costs to not only the deceased but also to survivors and to society. The estimated economic impact of completed suicides is $34 billion a year. Since the burden of suicide falls most heavily on adults of working age, the cost to the economy results almost entirely from lost wages and work productivity. Suicide attempts are mixed in with reports of self-harm, making it more difficult to measure the economic impact of suicide attempts. Nonfatal injuries due to self-harm cost an estimated $3 billion a year for medical care. Another $5 billion is spent for indirect costs, such as lost wages and productivity.

Many suicide attempts are unreported or, if reported, untreated. It is estimated that at least 1 million persons a year engage in intentionally inflicted self-harm. Males are four times more likely than females to die by suicide, but females attempt suicide three times as often as males. The ratio of suicide attempts to suicide death in youth is about 25:1. The ratio in the elderly is about 4:1.

Teen on bridge contemplates suicide. Suicide is the third leading cause of death among young people, resulting in about 4,400 deaths per year, according to the Centers for Disease Control and Prevention. For every suicide among young people, there are at least 100 suicide attempts. (Ken Tannenbaum/Dreamstime.com)

CNN reported that the suicide rate for military veterans increased an average of 2.6 percent a year from 2005 to 2011, more than double the rate for civilian suicide. Veterans represent about one in five suicides, even though they comprise about 10 percent of the population. The annual suicide rate among veterans is about 30 for every 100,000, compared with the civilian rate of 14 per 100,000. Every day, 22 veterans (one every 65 minutes) take their own lives.

The act of suicide differs from person to person, from one time to another, from one circumstance to another, and motivations vary. Emile Durkheim, in his classic study, *Le Suicide*, published in 1897, identified the types of suicide as egoistic, altruistic, anomic, and fatalistic. Additional types identified by others include dutiful, existential, revengeful, and political or ideological. Egoistic results from lack of integration of a person into society. Egoistic suicide occurs less in ordered institutions than in less regulated ones. Altruistic suicide occurs in social groups where there is a greater degree of integration; for example, a person may take his or her own life for reasons of religious sacrifice or political allegiance. Altruistic is the type of suicide takes place in the military, where obedience is predominant. In anomic suicide, society regulates needs and satisfaction. Common beliefs and practices learned make the individual the personification of the collective consciousness. Fatalistic suicide derives from excessive regulation to the point of oppression. The motives of individuals likely to commit suicide are interrelated with the social conditions wherein it occurs.

Certain risk factors may provoke suicide. The presence of a firearm in the home has been found to be an independent, additional risk factor. At least 90 percent who died by suicide were suffering from a mental illness at the time, most often depression. Depressed people who experience intense emotional states, such as desperation, hopelessness, anxiety, or rage, increase the risk of suicide. People who are impulsive, or who use alcohol or drugs are also at higher risk. The most common risk factors include: mental disorder, previous suicide attempt, family history of attempted or completed suicide, and/or serious medical condition and/or pain. Additionally, environmental factors play a role, such as a highly stressful life event; prolonged stress due to adversities such as unemployment, serious relationship conflict, harassment, or bullying; exposure to another person's suicide or to graphic or sensationalized accounts of suicide; and access to lethal methods of suicide during a time of increased risk.

Other factors noted include: men and the elderly are more likely to have fatal attempts than are women and youth. Risk factors for attempted suicide by youth include depression, alcohol or other drug use disorder, physical or sexual abuse, and disruptive behavior. Factors for nonfatal suicide attempts by adults include depression and other mental disorders, alcohol and other substance abuse, and separation or divorce.

Abuse of social media is sometimes the cause of teen suicide. In 2009, two cases of suicide were attributed to sextings gone viral. For example, in 2008, a teen, Jessica Logan, and some friends took nude photos of themselves. She sent hers to her boyfriend who forwarded the photo, and it spread throughout her school. Sexual harassment from her peers followed, and she started skipping school. She graduated, but a month later, she hanged herself in her room. Her parents sued her school for not taking action against the students responsible for the harassment.

Suicide is a significant public health problem. The number of suicides can be reduced with an effective prevention program. One strategy is to learn the warning signs, which include: talking about wanting to hurt themselves, increasing substance use, and having changes in mood, diet, or sleeping patterns. When these warning signs appear, quickly connecting the person to supportive services is critical. Prevention should concentrate on all levels of influence: individual, relationship, community, and societal. Effective prevention strategies are needed to promote awareness of suicide and encourage a commitment to social change.

Cognitive therapy reduced the rate of repeated suicide attempts by 50 percent in the following year. A previous suicide attempt is among the strongest predictors of subsequent suicide, and cognitive therapy helps consider alternative actions when thoughts of self-harm surface. Certain kinds of psychotherapy may be helpful for certain groups of people. For example, dialectical behavior therapy reduced suicide attempts by one-half in people with borderline personality disorder, a serious disorder of emotion regulation.

Rosemarie Skaine

See also: Bullying, Child and Adolescent; Gun Violence; Homosexuals; Suicide

Further Reading

American Foundation for Suicide Prevention. 2014. "Facts and Figures." http://www.afsp.org/understanding-suicide/facts-and-figures.

Basu, Moni. 2013. "Why Suicide Rate among Veterans May Be More Than 22 a Day." CNN, November 14. http://www.cnn.com/2013/09/21/us/22-veteran-suicides-a-day.

Centers for Disease Control Suicide Prevention Website. 2013. "Suicide Prevention." http://www.cdc.gov/violenceprevention/suicide.

Durkheim, Emile. 1951. *Suicide: A Study in Sociology*. Translated by John A. Spaulding and George Simpson. Edited by George Simpson. New York: Free Press.

MedicineNet. n.d. "Suicide." http://www.medicinenet.com/script/main/art.asp?articlekey=84760.

Meyer, Elizabeth J. 2009. "'Sexting' and Suicide." *Psychology Today*, December 16. http://www.psychologytoday.com/blog/gender-and-schooling/200912/sexting-and-suicide.

National Institutes of Health. n.d. "Suicide in the U.S.: Statistics and Prevention." http://www.nimh.nih.gov/health/publications/suicide-in-the-us-statistics-and-prevention/index.shtml.

Skaine, Rosemarie. 2013. *Suicide Warfare: Culture, the Military, and the Individual as a Weapon*. Santa Barbara, CA: Praeger Security International.

TARA TENG INITIATIVE

The Tara Teng Initiative was developed by Canadian beauty pageant winner Tara Teng in 2011. Its mission is to end modern-day slavery. During the summer of 2011, Teng and her father, Terry, went to Thailand and Cambodia, where they stayed in some red-light districts. Teng wanted them to get a sense of the situation and returned to share their stories.

Teng conducted her initiative, in part, through a Freedom Week tour during the week of March 6 to 13, 2011. Freedom Week had three main goals:

1. To raise awareness to the general public to understand the issues of modern-day slavery and human trafficking
2. To introduce the general public to partnership with various organizations that are working on the front lines of fighting human trafficking, such as the International Justice Mission
3. To provide the general public of Greater Vancouver and the Fraser Valley with ways to take action for this cause, such as walking during the Freedom March on Saturday, March 12, 2011.

The Freedom Week tour reached 10 Canadian cities, from Greater Vancouver to the Fraser Valley of British Columbia. The tour was called Ignite the Road to Justice, and its objective was to create a powerful, unified grassroots movement that supports the oppressed. Teng circulated a petition stating, "The demand for commercial sex with women and children is the root cause for prostitution and trafficking for sexual purposes."

The initiative called for criminalization of buying and decriminalization of selling sex as the solution to end trafficking. During the tour, Teng focused on the labor trafficking incident of the Mumtaz Ladha case. Ladha was a 55-year-old West Vancouver woman who was charged with human trafficking and human smuggling. Allegedly, Ladha had hired a 21-year-old African woman in 2008. Ladha promised her a work visa and a job but took her passport and forced her to work long hours with no pay.

Teng used her beauty titles to raise awareness in Canada of the problem of human trafficking. She was crowned Miss World Canada in 2012, Miss Canada in 2011, and Miss British Columbia in 2010. She received awards, including Woman of Excellence—Rotary Club of the Langleys (2012); Catalyst "Young Influencers" list, March (2012); and International Freedom Award—Joy Smith Foundation (October 2012). In 2012, she was nominated for three additional awards, YWCA Women of Distinction, Vancouver Women of Worth, and Diamond Jubilee Medal.

Rosemarie Skaine

See also: Human Trafficking; Sexual Slavery; Slavery, Modern-day.

Further Reading

Berger, Stephanie M. 2012. "No End in Sight: Why the 'End Demand' Movement Is the Wrong Focus for Efforts to Eliminate Human Trafficking." *Harvard Journal of Law & Gender* 35 (2) 523–570.

Colpitts, Heather. 2011. "Beauty Battles Beastly Trade: A Langley Woman Will Lead a National Tour." LangleyAdvance. http://www.langleyadvance.com/news/Beauty+battles+beastly+trade/5226193/story.html.

Radia, Andy. 2011. "Domestic 'Slavery'—A Growing Problem in Canada." Canada. Yahoo News, August 15. http://ca.news.yahoo.com/blogs/canada-politics/domestic-slavery-growing-problem-canada-184202383.html.

Teng, Tara. 2013. LinkedIn. http://www.linkedin.com/pub/tara-teng/41/6b9/465.

Teng, Tara. n.d. "Completed: Freedom Week—March 6–13, 2011." TWU Impact. http://impact.twu.ca/project.aspx?asset=637.

Watton, Jennifer. 2011. "TWU's Tara Teng Takes the Fight for Justice across Canada." Trinity Western University News. http://twu.ca/news/2011/037-ignite-the-road-to-justice.html.

TELEPHONE HARASSMENT

Telephone harassment as an abuse is any phone communication where the offender knowingly makes a call, causes a call to be made, or allows a phone call from a phone controlled by the offender to someone with the intent of annoying, alarming, or causing substantial emotional distress in that person, serves no legitimate purpose, and is an unwarranted invasion of privacy. The offender may be an acquaintance, a stalker, a telemarketer, or a debt collector. The calls may be malicious, harassing, crank, threatening, obscene, or nuisance.

Telephone harassment may occur at any time of the day or night. In addition, the offender may call the victim's cell phone and use text messaging to harass. Text harassing uses the same tactics as telephone harassing but with the message assured to reach the victim. Sexting, sending sexually suggestive text messages to someone or about someone, is a common type of text harassment. Telephone officials report that over a million people each year receive phone calls that could be categorized as harassing.

The Communications Act of 2003 makes it a criminal offense to purposely place offensive phone calls or leave offensive messages with the intent to harass. The courts may treat offensive phone calls as an assault if it causes the victim to fear future assault or grievous bodily harm or if the victim suffers from psychological problems as a result of the call. If the telephone harassment continues, the victim has the right to have the telephone company trace the calls to identify the perpetrator. The victim may then obtain an injunction against the harasser. Forty-four states now have laws that explicitly include electronic forms of communication within stalking or harassment laws.

To end harassing telephone calls, it is important to document the incidents. The victim should also note the time of the call, the number of calls, length of calls, gender of the caller, and the content of the call. It is important to refrain from responding to anything the perpetrator says and to refuse to release personal information. Call the police immediately if the caller makes any threats.

When persons receive harassing telephone solicitation calls, they should clearly state that they want to be added to the caller's Do-Not-Call list. The caller will be added to the Do-Not-Call list for five years. Keep a list of persons or businesses that have been asked not to call. Whether or not the home phone number is registered on the national Do-Not-Call list, the FCC requires a person or entity placing voice telephone solicitations to the home to maintain a record of the direct request to that caller that he or she is not to receive future telephone solicitations from that person or entity.

The calling company must honor a Do-Not-Call request for five years. To prevent calls after five years, the person will need to repeat the request to the company, and it must honor it for another five years. The Do-Not-Call request should also stop calls from affiliated entities, if it is reasonable to expect them to be included, given the identification of the caller and the product being advertised. Unless a phone number is registered on the national Do-Not-Call list, it will be necessary to make a separate Do-Not-Call request to each telemarketer from whom calls are not to be received.

Harassing creditor phone calls are often the first step used in pursuing an outstanding debt. Whether the money in question is actually owed, it is important to understand what to do to put a stop to aggressive collection practices. In the United States, the Fair Debt Collection Practices Act (FDCPA) outlines what debt collectors can and cannot do to collect a debt.

If a state does not have specific legislation to address telephone harassment, federal regulations should assist with addressing the issue. The Protection of Harassment Act of 1997 (PHA) makes it a criminal offense to pursue a course of conduct that amounts to harassment of a person. In addition to the criminal offense, the PHA also creates a civil statutory tort of harassment, which enables a person to obtain a civil court injunction to stop harassment occurring and to claim damages where appropriate.

A person who is the victim of telephone harassment may file a complaint with the FCC by e-mail (fccinfo@fcc.gov); phone (1-888-225-5322 or TTY 1-888-835-5322); or mail (Federal Communications Commission, Consumer & Governmental Affairs Bureau, Consumer Inquiries and Complaint Division, 445 12th Street, SW, Washington, DC 20554).

Connie Kerns-Grams

See also: Cyberbullying, Child and Adolescent; Sexting; Sexual Harassment.

Further Reading

Bullying Statistics. 2013. "Text Bullying." http://www.bullyingstatistics.org/content/text-bullying.html.

Crisis Connection, Inc. n.d. "Harassing and Obscene Phone Calls." http://www.crisisconnectioninc.org/domesticviolence/cell_phone_harassment.htm.

Fairmont Police Department. n.d. "Ending Malicious and Harassing Telephone Calls." http://www.fairmontpolice.org/stats/phone.

Federal Communications Commission. n.d. "Unwanted Telephone Marketing Calls Guide." http://transition.fcc.gov/cgb/consumerfacts/tcpa.pdf.

FindLaw. 2013. "Harassment." http://criminal.findlaw.com/criminal-charges/harassment. html?DCMP=GOO-CRIM_Harassment-Gen&HBX_PK=phone+harassment+laws.

Holtzman, D. H. 2006. *Privacy Lost: How Technology Is Endangering Your Privacy*. San Francisco: Jossey-Bass.

Liberty80. 2009. "Offensive Telephone Calls 1997." http://www.yourrights.org.uk/about.

Liberty80. 2009. "Protection from Harassment Act 1997." 2009. http://www.yourrights. org.uk/about.

San Jose Police Department. 2013. "Online Crime/Incident Reports." http://www.sjpd.org/ ReportingCrime/OnlineReport.

TORTURE

Torture (Latin *torquere*, "to twist") involves the infliction of severe physical or mental pain in an attempt to punish or to compel a person to confess to a crime or to extract information for legal proceedings. Torturing slaves for securing confession or for obtaining evidence was a legal practice in ancient Greece and Rome. With the development of legal practice and law enforcement, the rationale for the idea of torture became unjustifiable, and by the 19th century, much of Europe abandoned the practice of torture. However, extensive use of torture as a political tool revived during the 20th century in Fascist, National Socialist, and Communist regimes of Europe.

After the bitter experience of the Second World War, the 1948 Universal Declaration of Human Rights and the 1949 Geneva Conventions became the foremost legal response against torture. The International Covenant on Civil and Political Rights (ICCPR), adopted in 1966 and entered into force later in 1976, also prohibited torture. However, the most important breakthrough came in 1984, with the signing of the Convention against Torture and Other Cruel, Inhuman or Degrading Treatment or Punishment, which criminalized the practice of torture, obliged states to investigate and act against allegations of torture, and proposed to provide reparations for the victims. The convention's widely accepted definition of torture appears in Article 1:

> Any act by which severe pain or suffering, whether physical or mental, is intentionally inflicted on a person for such purposes as obtaining from him or a third person information or a confession, punishing him for an act he or a third person has committed or is suspected of having committed, or intimidating or coercing him or a third person, or for any reason based on discrimination of any kind, when such pain or suffering is inflicted by or at the instigation of or with the consent or acquiescence of a public official or other person acting in an official capacity. It does not include pain or suffering arising only from, inherent in or incidental to lawful sanctions.

The definition clearly indicates that the responsibility lies with public officialdom, even when the guilty party of torture is not the office holder. Moreover, the convention also made it clear that no exceptional circumstances, such as war, terrorism, or a similar public emergency that threatens the life of the nation, can be invoked as a justification of torture. The Committee Against Torture monitors the implementation of the torture convention by its state parties. In 2006, this committee recommended to the United States to implement a definition of torture in federal law in line with Article 1 of the torture convention.

Police brutality and sexual abuse in prison in the United States have remained a major concern for human rights activists who are advocating for ending torture by public officials. The 1978 UN Code of Conduct for Law Enforcement Officials, later augmented by the 1990 Basic Principles on the Use of Force and Firearms by Law Enforcement Officials, unambiguously prohibited torture and similar ill-treatment. These documents also provide that there should be no penalty against law enforcement officials who decline to take part in the practice of torture or who report others for so doing.

It has also been recognized by the international community that the medical profession is also vulnerable to involvement of torture since in many countries, doctors often certify persons as "fit" for interrogation involving torture and ill-treatment. In 1990, the Eighth UN Congress on the Prevention of Crime and the Treatment of Offenders adopted the Guidelines on the Role of Prosecutors, which set a requirement that prosecutors must refuse to use evidence obtained by torture or ill-treatment. Besides, various human rights bodies have set standards to prevent torture during any form of imprisonment or detention. Under international humanitarian law, torture and cruel or inhuman treatment are considered as war crimes.

Despite global concerns and various legal initiatives, torture is still widely practiced through state machineries. A range of methods and techniques of torture and ill-treatment have been developed. After the September 11, 2001, attack on New York's World Trade Center, it was revealed that, while dealing with the terrorists, a number of countries, particularly the United States, had been exercising torture, often with judicially issued torture warrants. The interrogation practices of U.S. officials in various detention centers located in Iraq, Afghanistan, and Cuba have been severely criticized by human rights organizations.

Mohammad Sajjadur Rahman

See also: Police, Abuse by; Prisoner Abuse, Adult.

Further Reading

Khan, Paul W. 2008. *Sacred Violence: Torture, Terror and Sovereignty.* Ann Arbor, MI: University of Michigan Press.
Rejali, Darius. 2007. *Torture and Democracy.* Princeton, NJ: Princeton University Press.

TRANSGENDER INDIVIDUALS

A transgender individual is a person who appears as the gender she or he wishes to be or has undergone surgery to become a member of the opposite sex. *Transgender* is an umbrella term that includes people who are transsexual, cross-dressers, or otherwise gender nonconforming. A transsexual is a person who has changed, or is in the process of changing his or her physical sex to conform to his or her internal sense of gender identity. The term also describes people who, without undergoing medical treatment, identify and live their lives full-time as a member of the gender opposite their birth sex. Transsexuals transitioning from male to female are often referred to as Male to Females (MTFs). Female-to-male transsexuals are called Female to Males (FTMs).

The cause of abuse of transgender and transsexuals has been rooted in the religious beliefs within society. Religious abuse occurs when the tenets of a religion are used to condemn, reject, or shame the individual for behaving a particular way. The condemnation results in confusion, incongruence, and hopelessness that causes psychological distress among transgender individuals and feelings of lessened self-worth.

Transgender individuals are subjected to abuse on a regular basis that includes jokes, innuendo, verbal harassment, discrimination, and assault. Serious assault leads to injury or death in some cases. According to the FBI, transgenders are high among the groups targeted for hate crimes. Fear of abuse or discrimination is one factor that leads transgender individuals to hide their relationships and life choices from family, friends, and coworkers. Abuse of individuals identifying themselves as transgender occurs not just among the individual's peers but at the hand of those charged with protecting them.

According to Amnesty International, across the globe a person's sexuality may lead to a person's being regularly subjected to verbal abuse, denial of employment, housing, or health services and in some countries, subject to being executed by the state. These abuses are carried out frequently at the hand of state authorities and governments, with or without a legal right to do so. In these situations, it is often difficult for transgender individuals who are the victims of crime to receive the assistance they need from authorities who may further abuse, torture, or exploit them.

In the workplace, transgender individuals experience the most discrimination and abuse. Coworkers and supervisors alike may feel having a transgender employee in the office is bad for company morale and business. Transgender individuals encounter workplace discrimination and harassment at even higher rates than gays and lesbians. In early 2013, the National Center for Transgender Equality and the National Gay and Lesbian Task Force released a comprehensive study on transgender discrimination that revealed near universal problems at the workplace. Ninety percent of transgender individuals have encountered some form of harassment or mistreatment on the job. Forty-seven percent of workers have experienced an adverse job outcome because they are transgender, including 44 percent who were passed over for a job, 23 percent who were denied a promotion, and 26 percent who were fired because they were transgender.

Abuse can also happen between transgender and homosexual individuals in same-sex relationships. Though the term *domestic violence* is most often used to describe violence in male/female relationships, the concept of partner-against-partner violence is not absent in transgender relationships. Physical, sexual, and emotional abuse all occur in transgender relationships, with the added dimension of specific abuse behaviors that play on some of the common threats felt by transgender individuals, such as the threat to "out" one to coworkers, employers, family members, or friends. The fear of losing custody of one's children's because of gender orientation or sexuality can be used as a controlling or manipulative behavior by the abuser. The magnitude of such abuse is difficult to ascertain due to low reporting rates. Those involved in such abuse have a multitude of reasons for not reporting the abuse to mainstream agencies that deal with such issues. It is a widely held belief that abuse in same-sex partnerships is the same as or slightly more prevalent than in male/female "traditional" partnerships.

Transgenders are beginning to be protected from hate crimes. In 2009, transgender abuse was included in the Matthew Shepard and James Byrd, Jr., Hate Crimes Prevention Act. State and local laws are also including language banning discrimination against transgenders. They have been extended health care and other benefits that traditionally have been available to heterosexuals. The cost of the hormone therapy and sex-reassignment surgery is an ongoing problem for transgender individuals. Pfc. Bradley Manning, who was convicted in the Wikileaks documents case, has revealed that he is a woman and is seeking treatment while in prison.

Carolyn Martin

See also: Hate Crimes; Matthew Shepard and James Byrd, Jr., Hate Crimes Prevention Act; Sexual Harassment; Sexual Harassment in Employment; Torture.

Further Reading

Amnesty International. 2013. "About LGBT Human Rights." http://www.amnestyusa.org/our-work/issues/lgbt-rights/about-lgbt-human-rights.

Burns, Crosby, and Jeff Krehely. 2011. "Gay and Transgender People Face High Rates of Workplace Discrimination and Harassment." Center for American Progress. http://www.americanprogress.org/issues/lgbt/news/2011/06/02/9872/gay-and-transgender-people-face-high-rates-of-workplace-discrimination-and-harassment.

Civilrights.org. 2013. "Hate Crimes against Lesbian, Gay, Bisexual, and Transgender Individuals." http://www.civilrights.org/publications/hatecrimes/lgbt.html.

Human Rights Watch. 2013. "Tanzania: Police Abuse, Torture, Impede HIV Services." http://www.hrw.org/news/2013/06/18/tanzania-police-abuse-torture-impede-hiv-services.

Moulton, Brian, and Liz Seaton. 2007. *Transgender Americans: A Handbook for Understanding*. Human Rights Campaign Foundation. http://www.hrc.org/files/assets/resources/hrcTGguide.pdf.

Pan American Health Organization and World Health Organization. 2013. "PAHO/WHO Calls for Equitable Access to Care and Respectful Treatment for LGBTs in Health Services." http://www.paho.org/hq/index.php?option=com_content&view=article&id=8670%3Astigma-and-discrimination-jeopardize-the-health-of-lesbians-gays-bisexuals-and-transgender-people&catid=740%3Anews-press-releases&Itemid=1926&lang=en.

Super, John, and Almeria Jacobson. 2011. "Religious Abuse: Implications for Counseling Lesbian, Gay, Bisexual, and Transgender Individuals." *Journal of LGBT Issues in Counseling* 5 (3–4): 180–196.

U

U.S.C. TITLES IV-B AND IV-E OF THE SOCIAL SECURITY ACT

The Child Welfare Services Program, Title IV-B, subpart 1, 42 U.S.C. 620 et seq. (2000) of the Social Security Act, is a federally funded grant program that provides funds to states and tribes for child welfare services. Children receiving services from the child welfare system through these funds do not have to meet any federal income requirements. Title IV-B, subpart 2, 42 U.S.C. 629 et seq. (2000), a supplemental funding program, provides funding for family preservation, community -based family support, time-limited family reunification and adoption promotion, and support services for states and tribes. The Child and Family Services Improvement Acts of 2006 and 2011 reauthorizes and renews portions of Title IV-B.

The Adoption Assistance and Child Welfare Act of 1980, Title IV-E, 42 U.S.C. 670 et seq. (2000) is an entitlement program for the states. It reimburses states for payments to foster and adoptive families when the children come from a family below a certain income and the child meets other eligibility criteria. It funds administrative and training costs connected with administering the foster care and adoptive assistance program. The federal funds are known as foster care maintenance payments to states to help cover the costs of providing food, clothing, shelter, daily supervision, school supplies, personal incidentals, liability insurance, reasonable travel to the child's home for visitation, and reasonable travel for the child to remain in the school in which the child was enrolled at the time of placement in foster care. During fiscal years 2002–2004, expenditures for the IV-E program ranged from $6.4 billion to $6.8 billion.

Title IV-E requires child welfare agencies to make reasonable efforts to keep families together and to return children in foster care to their original homes. Originally Title IV-E was intended to: prevent unnecessary separation of children from their families, reduce the length of a child's stay in foster care, protect the autonomy of the family, encourage adoption, improve the quality of care and services, reduce the number of children in foster care, and encourage the return of children to their families.

In addition, since the family court plays a major role in meeting IV-E eligibility requirements for foster care maintenance payments, findings are to ensure family courts hear and weigh the facts and circumstances of each case at each stage of the case. This federal requirement that the family court judges make specific findings is a safeguard against the inappropriate removal of children from their homes and/or the inappropriate retention of children in foster care.

Rosemarie Skaine

See also: Adopted Children; Child Abandonment and Neglect; Child and Family Services Improvement Acts.

Further Reading

Children's Law Center. 2012. "Guide to Title IV-E Requirements: An Overview the Title IV-E Foster Care Maintenance Payments Program and Requirements for Specific Judicial Findings to Establish Eligibility." University of South Carolina School of Law. http://childlaw.sc.edu/frmPublications/Title%20IV-E%20Guide%20Final.pdf.

McCarthy, Jan, Anita Marshall, Julie Collins, Girlyn Arganza, Kathy Deserly, and Juanita Milon. 2003. "Relevant Federal Laws/Policies." *A Family's Guide to the Child Welfare System*, 111–118. http://www.nicwa.org/indian_child_welfare_act/familyguide.pdf.

Native American Rights Fund. n.d. "What Is Title IV-B of the Social Security Act?" and "What Is Title IV-E of the Social Security Act?" *A Practical Guide to the Indian Child Welfare Act*. http://www.narf.org/icwa/faq/application2.htm.

Social Security. n.d. "Title IV—Grants to States for Aid and Services to Needy Families with Children and for Child-Welfare Services." *Compilation of the Social Security Laws*. http://www.ssa.gov/OP_Home/ssact/title04/0400.htm.

V

VICTIM BLAMING

People who blame victims for their hardships rather than the perpetrator are engaging in victim blaming. Blaming the victim has been demonstrated in cases of rape, robbery, domestic abuse, and bullying. When cases end up in court, a second victimization can take place. Psychologists Steffen Bieneck and Barbara Krahé found more blame was attributed to the victim rather than the perpetrator in cases of rape than occurred in cases of robbery. Knowledge of a previous relationship between the victim and perpetrator increased victim blaming in the rape cases but not in robbery cases. The findings of Bieneck and Krahé support that there is a special leniency bias for the perpetrator in sexual assault cases.

Bullying often involves blaming the victim. In October 2013, Jonathan Martin, a National Football League (NFL) player on the Miami Dolphins, left the team because he had received harsh and harassing treatment from another player. The player who bullied Martin had been told to toughen Martin up, but the player went beyond that boundary. Even so, some suggested that Martin bears at least part of the responsibility. One NFL player stated that Martin was just as much to blame because he allowed it to happen and should have behaved like a man. Others believed that Martin was overly sensitive and made himself an easy target. The NFL did not find Martin responsible. As a result of the Martin case, concerns about bullying came to the forefront within the NFL

The reasons people blame victims include:

- The need for control
- The need to make sense of the event
- Stereotypical thinking
- Hostile sexism
- Attribution errors
- The Just World concept
- Culpability and vulnerability avoidance

People blame victims to establish control and to make sense of otherwise uncomfortable events, such as domestic violence. It is a way to make sense of a husband beating his wife by assuming that the wife did something to cause the abuse. In stereotypical thinking, people blame the victim. If the abused wife is said to lack warmth, the perpetrator is justified in abusing her. If this social climate of tolerance of abuse is maintained, the woman receives no help. Psychologists Nicole M. Capezza and Ximena B. Arriaga state that a victim's lack of warmth offers a reason why nontraditional women are perceived more negatively and blamed more frequently because they are perceived in a stereotypical way.

Hostile sexism is associated with perceptions of the victim. Victim blaming is also caused by attribution errors. Personal characteristics are overemphasized and environmental characteristics devalued. Individuals who make this error view the victim as partially responsible. Victim blaming occurs when the events that have happened cannot be changed. It is concluded that victims deserve what they experienced and are to be blamed for what happened to them. In other words, the world is just and the victim deserved it.

Victim blaming is a way to avoid culpability and vulnerability. The more innocent a victim, the more threatening they are. *Psychology Today* stated that victims threaten the sense that the world is a safe and moral place where good things happen to good people and bad things happen to bad people. When bad things happen to good people, no one is safe; no matter how good we are, we too could be vulnerable. Misfortune can be random, striking anyone at any time, and we are faced every day with evidence that this may be true.

A consequence of victim blaming is that it is more difficult for the victim to come forward and report the abuse. The person becomes marginalized and knows that society blames her or him for being abused. Another consequence is that it reinforces what the abuser has been saying all along: that the victim is at fault and caused the abuse to happen. Victim blaming attitudes allow the abuser to perpetrate a relational abuse or commit sexual assault while avoiding accountability for her or his actions. The Center for Relationship Abuse Awareness stresses that it is not the fault or responsibility of the victim to fix the situation; it is the abuser who has the responsibility.

The victims of crime are negatively affected by victim blaming in the media. The media is often insensitive when discussing what happened to the victim. They present the victim in a negative light and create the impression that she or he deserved what happened, or depict her or him not really as the victim, but the perpetrator.

It is vital to shift the focus of our blame from the victim of the crime to the perpetrator in order to ensure that the perpetrator is held responsible. One way of assuring that offenders are held accountable is to have a community response through the police, courts, schools, clergy, health care providers, and social service agencies. The justice system and social agencies need to work together in order to promote offender accountability while simultaneously helping individuals recover from being blamed.

Rosemarie Skaine

See also: Bullying, Adult; Bullying, Child and Adolescent; Domestic Abuse; Rape; Rape, Gender Stereotypes and.

Further Reading

Bieneck, Steffen, and Barbara Krahe. 2011. "Blaming the Victim and Exonerating the Perpetrator in Cases of Rape and Robbery: Is There a Double Standard?" *Journal of Interpersonal Violence* 26 (9): 1785–1797. (EJ924207). Database: ERIC.

Bos, Kees van den, and Marjolein Maas. 2009. "On the Psychology of the Belief in a Just World: Exploring Experiential and Rationalistic Paths to Victim Blaming." *Social Psychology Bulletin* 35: 1567.

Breines, Juliana. 2013. "Why Do We Blame Victims? When Others' Misfortune Feels Like a Threat." *Psychology Today*, November 24. http://www.psychologytoday.com/blog/in-love-and-war/201311/why-do-we-blame-victims.

Canadian Resource Centre for Victims of Crime. 2009. "Victim Blaming." http://www.crcvc.ca/docs/victim_blaming.pdf.

Capezza, Nicole M., and Ximena B. Arriaga. 2008. "Why Do People Blame Victims of Abuse? The Role of Stereotypes of Women on Perceptions of Blame." *Sex Roles* 59: 839–850.

Center for Relationship Abuse Awareness. 2014. "Avoiding Victim Blaming." http://stoprelationshipabuse.org/educated/avoiding-victim-blaming.

Skaine, Rosemarie. 1996. *Power and Gender: Issues in Sexual Dominance and Harassment.* Jefferson, NC: McFarland.

VICTIM EMPOWERMENT MODELS

Victim empowerment models are becoming an increasingly popular form of domestic violence intervention being considered and implemented in many jurisdictions. The foundation of these strategies rests on making the victim feel as if he or she is in charge of the outcome of the situation, a position that often is entirely opposite of the deeply engrained victim mentality of someone who has been abused.

The cycle of violence that often traps generations of families can be broken only through the determination of the victim(s) to learn from their experiences and prevent similar circumstances from surfacing in the future. Victim empowerment models respond to this sentiment. Often combined with soft-drop or victim-decided prosecution policies, the abused is encouraged to exercise control over many parts of her life, which she may not have been able to do for quite some time. This can easily become overwhelming, and it is common for women to be unable to follow through with charges and a trial the first time they attempt to do so. If the abuser violates her again, she is able to start the process anew with the knowledge that she was able to stand up for herself before. This leads to increased levels of confidence and a greater likelihood that she will seek restitution.

Victim empowerment intervention strategies have also been found to increase the public's confidence in the justice system by demonstrating empathy for the victim and determination in deterring future crimes. Researchers found in a 2003 study that victims who were allowed to drop charges against their offender were significantly less likely to suffer additional violence six months after the arrest than were victims who were forced to follow through with charges. These techniques, much like mandatory arrest laws, have come under intense criticism. It is argued that women, frozen in the role of victim, are incapable of making an appropriate decision in regard to their safety and the consequences of their action or inaction. They may blame themselves or fear reprisal from the abuser and decline to have him arrested even if encouraged to do so by police. This often places officers in a delicate position where they must balance satisfying the wishes of an individual complainant and protecting the public.

Courtney Blair Thornton

See also: Battered Person Syndrome; Cycle of Abuse; Domestic Abuse; Duluth Model.

Further Reading

Geffner, Robert A., and Alan Rosenbaum. 2002. *Domestic Violence Offenders: Current Interventions, Research, and Implications for Policies and Standards*. Binghamton, NY: The Haworth Press, Inc.

Han, Erin L. 2003. "Mandatory Arrest and No Drop Policies: Victim Empowerment in Domestic Violence Cases." *Boston College Third World Law Journal* 23 (1): 159–192.

Roberts, Albert R. 2002. *Handbook of Domestic Violence Intervention Strategies: Policies, Programs, and Legal Remedies*. New York: Oxford University Press.

VIOLENCE AGAINST WOMEN ACT

The Violence Against Women Reauthorization Act of 2013 (VAWA) expanded protections for domestic violence victims into law, renewing a measure that had expired in 2011. This act is credited for reducing attacks against women. The White House reported that from 1993 to 2010, intimate partner violence declined 67 percent, and from 1993 to 2007, intimate partner homicides of females decreased 35 percent and the rate for males decreased 46 percent.

The law authorizes funding to strengthen transitional housing, legal assistance, law enforcement training, and hotlines. One focus is on ways to reduce sexual assault on college campuses. In addition, it reauthorizes the Trafficking Victims Protection Act, adds stalking to the list of crimes that make immigrants eligible for protection, and authorizes programs to reduce the backlog in rape investigations. The law expands to protect homosexuals, bisexuals, and transgender Americans and gives tribal authorities power to prosecute individuals who are not Native Americans for abuse committed on tribal lands.

The White House states more specifically that VAWA has improved the criminal justice response to violence against women by:

- Holding rapists accountable for their crimes by strengthening federal penalties for repeat sex offenders and creating a federal "rape shield law," which is intended to prevent offenders from using victims' past sexual conduct against them during a rape trial
- Mandating that victims, no matter their income levels, are not forced to bear the expense of their own rape exams or for service of a protection order
- Keeping victims safe by requiring that a victim's protection order will be recognized and enforced in all state, tribal, and territorial jurisdictions within the United States
- Increasing rates of prosecution, conviction, and sentencing of offenders by helping communities develop dedicated law enforcement and prosecution units and domestic violence dockets
- Ensuring that police respond to crisis calls and judges understand the realities of domestic and sexual violence by training law enforcement officers, prosecutors,

victim advocates, and judges; VAWA funds train over 500,000 law enforcement officers, prosecutors, judges, and other personnel every year

- Providing additional tools for protecting women in tribal lands by creating a new federal habitual offender crime and authorizing warrantless arrest authority for federal law enforcement officers who determine there is probable cause when responding to domestic violence cases

Further, VAWA achieves safety and rebuilds lives by: establishing the National Domestic Violence Hotline, which has answered over 3 million calls and receives over 22,000 calls every month; 92 percent of callers report that it's their first call for help; developing coordinated community responses, and focusing on the needs of underserved communities such as creating legal relief for battered immigrants so that abusers cannot use the victims' immigration status to prevent victims from calling the police or seeking safety.

According to the White House, all states have taken the following actions: reformed laws that previously treated date or spousal rape as a lesser crime than stranger rape; passed laws making stalking a crime; authorized warrantless arrests in misdemeanor domestic violence cases where the responding officer determines that probable cause exists; and provided for criminal sanctions for the violation of a civil protection order. Many states have passed laws prohibiting administering polygraphs to rape victims, and over 35 states, the District of Columbia, and the U.S. Virgin Islands have adopted laws addressing domestic and sexual violence

House Minority Leader Nancy Pelosi (D-CA), center, accompanied by House Democrats, leads a news conference to discuss the Violence Against Women Act on Capitol Hill in Washington, D.C. on January 23, 2013. On March 7, 2013, President Obama signed the Violence Against Women Reauthorization Act. (AP Photo/Jacquelyn Martin)

and stalking in the workplace. Some laws offer a victim time off from work to address the violence in their lives, protect victims from employment discrimination related to the violence, and/or provide unemployment insurance to survivors who must leave their jobs because of the abuse.

Rosemarie Skaine

See also: Domestic Abuse; Homosexuals; Men as Victims of Abuse; Stalking; Transgender Individuals.

Further Reading

Lederman, Josh. 2013. "Obama Signs Violence Against Women Act." *Huffington Post*, March 7. http://www.huffingtonpost.com/2013/03/07/obama-violence-against-women-act_n_2830158.html.

Violence Against Women Reauthorization Act of 2013 (VAWA). 2013. Public Law 113–4. 127 Stat. 54. http://www.gpo.gov/fdsys/pkg/PLAW-113publ4/pdf/PLAW-113publ4.pdf.

White House. 2012. "Factsheet: The Violence Against Women Act." http://www.whitehouse.gov/sites/default/files/docs/vawa_factsheet.pdf.

W

WALSH, JOHN EDWARD

After his son, Adam, was kidnapped and murdered, John Walsh became involved in not only capturing and convicting his son's killer, he also worked to help other children from meeting the same fate as Adam. The murder of Adam led Walsh to a new purpose in life: to fight for victim's rights through advocacy.

John Edward Walsh was born in Auburn, New York, on December 26, 1945. He married Reve Drew in 1971. They had their first son, Adam, in 1974. What happened to Adam changed the Walshes' lives when their six-year-old son Adam was abducted from a Sears department store in Florida by serial killer Ottis Elwood Toole in 1981. Two weeks later, Adam's decapitated head was found floating in a canal by a fisherman; his body was never found. After the death of Adam, Walsh and his wife, Reve, had three more children: Meghan, Callahan, and Hayden.

Walsh and Reve lobbied the U.S. Congress and helped in the passage of the Missing Children's Act of 1982 and the Missing Children's Assistance Act of 1984, which established the National Center for Missing and Exploited Children. To further strengthen and close existing loopholes in previous laws protecting children, he advocated for the passage of the Adam Walsh Child Protection and Safety Act of 2006, in honor of his son Adam.

Walsh is credited with creating and hosting the hit television show *America's Most Wanted (AMW)*, which first aired in 1988. As a result of taking his crime-fighting spirit and new purpose in life on national television, over 1,000 criminals wanted by U.S. local and federal authorities have been apprehended, and 50 missing children have been reunited with their families. He has also published three books: *Tears of Rage: From Grieving Father to Crusader for Justice the Untold Story of the Adam Walsh Case* (1997), *No Mercy* (1998), and *Public Enemies: The Host of America's Most Wanted Targets the Nation's Most Notorious Criminals* (2001).

For over 25 years, Walsh has been tirelessly advocating for victims rights and tougher legislation to protect children from predators and pedophiles, and he has received numerous awards and recognitions from various law enforcement agencies across the United States for his commitment, hard work, and sacrifices to bring justice to victims of crimes. In 1988 and 1990, Walsh was awarded the U.S. Marshals' Man of the Year award by the Federal Bureau of Investigations (FBI). In 2003, Walsh was honored with the Honorary US Marshal award by the FBI.

Walsh's most important honors and recognitions have been from four U.S. presidents on various occasions at the White House Rose Garden by Ronald Reagan, on two occasions, George H. W. Bush, Bill Clinton, and George W. Bush. In 2011, the Academy of Television Arts & Sciences Board of Governors awarded Walsh the

Governor's Award. Walsh has appeared before Congress and state legislatures more than 50 times and petitioned the U.S. Congress for amendments to the Constitution to further protect victims' rights. Through the creation of *AMW*, John Walsh has brought closure to many victims and their families.

Juan Carlos Hernandez

See also: Abduction, Child; AMBER Alert; Child Abuse, Physical and Emotional; Pedophilia; Sex Trafficking.

Further Reading

Bio. 2013. "John Walsh Biography." 2013. A&E Television Networks. http://www.biography.com/people/john-walsh-9542164?page=1.

CNN.com. 2005. "Then & Now: John Walsh," June 19. http://www.cnn.com/2005/US/03/17/cnn25.tan.walsh.

Grant, Meg. 2013. "What I Know Now, John Walsh, Host of 'America's Most Wanted,' on What He's Learned from Life and Loss." *AARP the Magazine* (August–September). http://www.aarp.org/entertainment/television/info-08-2013/john-walsh-americas-most-wanted.html.

National Center for Missing and Exploited Children. n.d. "John Walsh Co-founder Host of 'America's Most Wanted.'" http://www.missingkids.com/en_US/documents/PressKit_JohnWalsh.pdf.

Television Academy. 2011. "John Walsh of 'America's Most Wanted' to receive Governors Awards." http://www.emmys.com/articles/john-walsh-americas-most-wanted-receive-governors-awards-emmys.

WOMEN IN THE MILITARY, ABUSE OF

Abuse of servicewomen in the U.S. military has been and continues to be a major problem. Military women are abused sexually and occupationally. The sexual abuse comes from sexual assaults, including rape, that deny a woman her right to control her body and exposes her to the risks of infection, the danger and discomfort of abortion or pregnancy, and damage in childbirth.

In fiscal year 2012, of the 3,374 sexual assaults reported by service members, 88 percent were against women. According to Sexual Assault Prevention and Response, of these assaults, 2,558 were unrestricted and 816 restricted. Unrestricted reporting results in a referral to a military criminal investigation organization, and restricted reporting allows the victim to receive confidential care. This represents an estimated 11 percent reporting rate, lower than the estimated 11.5 percent reporting rate of civilian college-aged women and much lower than the estimated 16.5 percent reporting rate of U.S. civilian women estimated to have suffered nonconsensual vaginal, oral, or anal penetration in 2005. Of the unrestricted cases, 11 percent of the victims refused to participate in the military justice process, probably wisely. Of the 6.1 percent of military women and 1.2 percent of military men who experienced unwanted sexual contact in 2012, 33 percent of the women and 19 percent of the men reported to either a military authority or military *and* civilian authorities.

Only 38 percent of the active-duty women who reported did not experience retaliation. The women and men who report are subjected to the military's established record of being far more willing to separate, without benefits, those who report sexual assault and harassment than the men who commit these crimes and engage in these threats. One estimate is that 90 percent of service members who report sexual assault are involuntarily discharged from the military: women are discharged for mental disorders, which often eliminates their eligibility for benefits, at more than twice the rate of men. Even a conviction for sexual assault does not guarantee a dishonorable discharge in the military, K. King reported.

As with other serious violent crime, most nonstranger rapes and sexual assaults are committed by repeat offenders—regardless of victim behavior and relationship to the suspect—according to M. C. Harwell. Just as focusing on the suspect is the norm in investigations of other serious offenses, it should be the norm in nonstranger sexual assault cases. Approximately 94 percent to 95 percent of rape allegations are true, even when the evidence or the victim's character are not considered good enough to win at trial, reported D. L. Lisak.

The military's tolerance of the crime and protection of the perpetrators costs the nation the human talents and energy of the victims, just as surely as if they had been wounded or killed by the enemy. And as horrible as the human cost is, worse is the military's betrayal of the nation, the military's ultimate client. Its ultimate purpose is to protect the citizens of the nation. To retain, train, and arm those who prey on their fellow citizens is a direct violation of the military's mission. To say that the military cannot do better because it is the product of a society in which 1 in 6 American women and 1 in 33 men have been victims of attempted or completed rape is to say two things: that duty, honor, and country are nonsense words and that women will never be anything more than chattel, inside or outside the military.

The military has not yet accepted that tolerating sexual assault and sexual predators mocks the very idea of military discipline and betrays the trust service members must have in each other. But sexual assault produces thousands of horribly hurt servicewomen and servicemen every year. The Associated Press reported that a 2012 accounting by the Department of Veterans Affairs found that, in that year alone, more than 85,000 veterans were treated for illness and injuries linked to sexual abuse and more than 4,000 of them sought disability benefits; nearly 40 percent of these veterans were men.

Women are also abused occupationally. Servicewomen have been assigned to a second-class support status. In the military, first-class status is reserved for the combat troops, especially in the infantry specialties. Although the great majority of servicemen choose noncombat specialties, these specialties do not stigmatize them as innately second class as servicewomen's segregation to noncombat specialties. The inferior occupational status of servicewomen is reinforced by physical standards that ask so little of servicewomen that they are insulting and dangerous, both to the servicewomen and to any serviceman inclined to take them seriously as comrades. The low physical standards are legal and are widely touted as being protective and respectful of women and their biological differences from men.

Their second-class status exposes military women to abusive and prejudicial language. In the privacy of his skull, a serviceman may think women do not deserve to be in combat or in the Marine Corps. But calling a servicewoman "WM," which is slang not for "Woman Marine" but "Walking Mattress"; discussing whether she is "attractive enough" to urinate on or rape with a piece of equipment; or calling cadences and singing jodies that celebrate rape, reported J. Hlad, is entirely different. This kind of speech is prejudicial to good order and discipline.

Ending abuse of military women require ending their second-class status. Progress is being made by ending the restrictions on women in combat.

Ending abuse also requires that sexual assault and related crimes be justly prosecuted by removing them from the Uniform Code of Military Justice (UCMJ). As the military is and will remain for the foreseeable future overwhelmingly male by demographic and masculine by ethos, to ask senior officers and NCOs to choose to believe and support a female over a male is to ask them to engage in a cultural conflict of interest. It is also to ask them to risk the retaliation of their seniors, such as Lieutenant Generals Craig Franklin and Susan J. Helms did when they respectively overturned the convictions of Lieutenant Colonel James Wilkerson and Captain Matthew S. Herrera for sexual assault.

They are also part of an organization where some assigned to protect victims are predators themselves: as of May 2013, Lieutenant Colonel Jeffrey Krusinski of the Air Force, and an unnamed Sergeant First Class at Ft. Hood are two. It remains to be determined whether they were knowingly placed in those positions by other predators or deliberately sought positions where they could protect predators and persecute their victims.

The number of prosecutions, convictions, and dishonorable discharges for both sexual assault and those who retaliate against and persecute victims must dramatically increase: cruelty toward and maltreatment of subordinates is an offense under the UCMJ. In addition, the Feres Doctrine exempting the U.S. military from suing the U.S. government for personal injuries experienced in the performance of their duties should no longer apply to sexual assault and related crimes, such as persecution of and retaliation against either victims or those who support them.

Erin Solaro

See also: Rape; Sexual Harassment.

Further Reading

Harwell, M. C. 2010. "Why Rapists Run Free." *Sexual Assault Report* (November–December): 17–32.

Hlad, J. 2013. "Does Military Culture Foster Sex Abuse?" *Stars and Stripes*, May 24.

King, K. 2013. "Systematic Injustice: Part Two of Three." *San Antonio Express-News*, May 20.

King, K. 2013. "Twice Betrayed: Part One of Three." *San Antonio Express-News*, May 19.

Lisak, D. L. 2010. "False Allegations of Sexual Assault: An Analysis of Ten Years of Reported Cases." *Violence against Women* 16 (12): 1318–1334.

Rape, Abuse and Incest National Network (RAINN). n.d. "Reporting Rates." http://www.rainn.org/get-information/statistics/reporting-rates.

Rape, Abuse and Incest National Network (RAINN). n.d. "Who Are the Victims?" http://www.rainn.org/get-information/statistics/sexual-assault-victims.

Sexual Assault Prevention and Response. 2013. *Department of Defense Annual Report on Sexual Assault in the Military: Fiscal Year 2012.* Vol. 1. Washington, D.C.: Department of Defense, 57, 81.

Sexual Assault Prevention and Response. 2013. *Department of Defense Annual Report on Sexual Assault in the Military, Fiscal Year 2012.* Vol. 2. Washington, D.C.: Department of Defense.

WORKPLACE VIOLENCE

The U.S. Department of Labor defines workplace violence as: an action (verbal, written, or physical aggression) that is intended to control or cause, or is capable of causing, death or serious bodily injury to oneself or others or damage to property. Every year, 2 million people are victims of nonfatal violence at the workplace.

The Department of Justice found violence a leading cause of fatal injuries at work, with about 1,000 workplace homicides each year. Violence against employees occurs in a variety of circumstances and situations, including: robberies and other crimes, actions by frustrated or dissatisfied clients and customers, acts by disgruntled coworkers or former coworkers, and domestic incidents that extend into the workplace. In 2006, the International Labor Organization (ILO) reported increases in all types of workplace violence, from active shooters to bullying.

Workplace violence includes abusive behavior toward authority, intimidating or harassing behavior, and threats. The violence includes: assault; possession of a dangerous weapon capable of causing death or serious bodily injury, such as guns, knives, clubs, chemicals, and explosive devices; and intimidating or harassing behavior, such as threats or other conduct that creates a hostile environment, impairs agency operations, or frightens, alarms, or inhibits others. Psychological intimidation or harassment includes making statements that are false, malicious, disparaging, derogatory, rude, disrespectful, abusive, obnoxious, insubordinate, or which have the intent to hurt others' reputations. Physical intimidation or harassment may include holding, impeding, or blocking movement; following; touching; or any other inappropriate physical contact or advances.

The violence may be sabotage, which is to destroy, damage, incapacitate, or contaminate property, equipment, supplies, or data (e.g., hard copy files and records, computerized information), to cause injury, illness, or death to humans or to interfere with, disrupt, cripple, disable, or hinder the normal operations of the workplace. Stalking is approaching or pursuing another person with intent to place that person in reasonable fear of serious bodily injury or death to himself or herself or to a third party and threats, oral or written expressions, or gestures that could be interpreted by a reasonable person as conveying an intent to cause physical harm to persons or property, such as "I'll get him" or "She won't get away with this."

Workplace violence can occur at or outside the workplace. Although no one is immune, some workers are at greater risk. According to Occupational Safety and Health Administration (OSHA), these workers exchange money with the public;

deliver passengers, goods, or services; or work alone or in small groups during late night or early morning hours, in high crime areas, or in community settings and homes. This group includes health care and social service workers, such as visiting nurses, psychiatric evaluators, and probation officers; community workers, such as gas and water utility employees, phone and cable TV installers, and letter carriers; retail workers; and taxi drivers.

For this group, OSHA suggests that employers establish a zero-tolerance policy complete with a prevention program and policy education. In addition, employers should secure the workplace such as installing video surveillance, extra lighting, and alarm systems; provide drop safes to limit the amount of cash on hand; equip field staff with cellular phones and handheld alarms or noise devices; instruct employees not to enter any location where they feel unsafe; and develop policies and procedures covering visits by home health care providers.

Although nothing can guarantee that an employee will not become a victim of workplace violence, OSHA suggests that employees:

- Learn how to recognize, avoid, or diffuse potentially violent situations by attending personal safety training programs
- Alert supervisors to any concerns about safety or security and report all incidents immediately in writing
- Avoid traveling alone into unfamiliar locations or situations whenever possible
- Carry only minimal money and required identification into community settings

A primary cause of workplace violence centers on access to guns. Guns are becoming easier to get, even when extensive controls exist over gun purchases. The active shooter events in recent years attest to this reality, including the 2012 Newtown, Connecticut, school shooting in which 20 children, 7 adults, and the shooter perished. The increase in incidents is directly related to the expiration of the assault weapons ban in 2005, which permitted assault weapons to be purchased again.

The FBI offers suggestions for workplace violence prevention. Workplace violence does not happen at random or "out of the blue." Perpetrators usually exhibit some behaviors of concern. An awareness of them and the subsequent implementation of an action plan form essential parts of workplace violence prevention. Specific behaviors of concern that should increase vigilance include: sadness, depression, threats, menacing or erratic behavior, aggressive outbursts, references to weaponry, verbal abuse, inability to handle criticism, hypersensitivity to perceived slights, and offensive commentary or jokes referring to violence. These behaviors, when observed in clusters and coupled with diminished work performance (such as shown by increased tardiness or absences, poor coworker relations, and decreased productivity), may suggest a heightened violence potential.

Intervention strategies consider two aspects of the range of workplace violence: action and flash points. An action point is when a coworker recognizes that an employee may be considering committing some type of violent act and takes action to prevent it. Action points offer an opportunity for coworkers to intervene before a situation becomes dangerous.

Intervention can take place in a number of ways: talking with the person and "checking in" to see if everything is all right; relay information regarding questionable behaviors to human resources or security department, ombudsman, or employee assistance program; and communicate their concerns via an e-mail, text message, drop boxes, 24-7 tip lines, and ethics hotlines which permit employees to report suspicious behavior while maintaining their anonymity.

A flash point, the moment when workplace violence occurs, is too late for preventive strategy. Workers must be trained so that when behaviors of concern occur, a red flag is raised and appropriate action taken. In this strategy, "awareness + action = prevention" constitutes the key to prevention.

Although OSHA is responsible for workplace safety, states have laws that apply to employers and violence in the workplace. The laws cover two of main areas: the carrying of concealed weapons and the duty to retreat from deadly force. Most of the states that have laws allow employers to prohibit the possession of certain weapons on their private property if notice is posted or if consent is obtained. Some state laws have an exception for weapons in vehicles in parking lots whether they are public lots or private property owned by the employer.

Rosemarie Skaine

See also: Bullying, Adult; Domestic Abuse; Gun Violence; Sexual Harassment in Employment; Stalking.

Further Reading

BizFilings. 2012. "Workplace Violence Laws by State." *Managing the Workplace*. http://www.bizfilings.com/toolkit/sbg/office-hr/managing-the-workplace/workplace-violence.aspx.

Hamilton, Caroline Ramsey. 2014. "Active Shooters and Workplace Violence Incidents around the World." *Security* (April). SecurityMagazine.com.

International Labor Organization (ILO). 2006. "New Forms of Violence at Work on the Rise Worldwide, Says the ILO." http://www.ilo.org/global/about-the-ilo/newsroom/news/WCMS_070505/lang--en/index.htm#1.

Occupational Safety and Health Administration (OSHA). 2002. "Fact Sheet Workplace Violence." U.S. Department of Labor. https://www.osha.gov/OshDoc/data_General_Facts/factsheet-workplace-violence.pdf.

Romano, Stephen J., Micòl E. Levi-Minzi, Eugene A. Rugala, and Vincent B. Van Hasselt. 2011. "Workplace Violence Prevention Readiness and Response." *FBI Law Enforcement Bulletin*. http://www.fbi.gov/stats-services/publications/law-enforcement-bulletin/january2011/workplace_violence_prevention.

U.S. Department of Labor. n.d. "Workplace Violence Program." http://www.dol.gov/oasam/hrc/policies/dol-workplace-violence-program.htm.

Wilder, Steve. 2014. "Minimizing Workplace Violence." *Long-Term Living: For the Continuing Care Professional* (January–February). www.ltlmagazine.com long-term living.

YWCA ABUSE SERVICES

The YWCA is the oldest and largest multicultural women's organization in the world. It is a worldwide organization founded in London in 1855 by Mary Jane Kinnaird and Christian Emma Roberts. They were concerned about the safety of young women who moved to London, often alone, to work or serve in the Crimean War. Because of the expansiveness of the British Empire, the YWCA spread rapidly to Western and Eastern Europe, India, and the United States.

The YWCA made its first appearance in the United States in 1858, when New York and Boston opened women's residences. There are currently nearly 250 associations in the United States, with 2,000 locations in all 50 states serving 2 million women and girls and their families. The YWCA in the United States is dedicated to eliminating racism, empowering women, and promoting peace, justice, freedom, and dignity for all. This mission drives all its programming and services.

The YWCA has long advocated for the health and safety of women and girls. The YWCA is the largest provider of battered women's shelters and domestic violence services in the country, serving over 500,000 women and children annually. Violence against women takes many forms, including domestic violence, sexual assault, dating violence, and stalking. These crimes impact millions of individuals and families in every community in our nation.

The YWCA supports antiviolence policies and programs that protect survivors, hold perpetrators accountable, and work to eradicate sexual assault and domestic violence, trafficking of women and girls, and dating violence. Specifically, it advocates for the continuance and full funding for the Victims of Crime Act (VOCA) and Violence Against Women Act (VAWA) and legislation that ensures employment stability and economic security for survivors of violence against women. YWCAs around the country provide a variety of services and programs to address violence against women, ranging from emergency shelters, support groups, and crisis hotlines.

Among the innovative and effective YWCA programs that are helping women to regain safety and strength are:

- YWCA Wichita, Kansas, Women's Crisis Center, founded in 1976, is located in a confidential location and provides women and children fleeing violent homes with safe shelter and the supportive services needed to establish and maintain a violence-free life
- YWCA Central Alabama's SOAR (Survivors Overcoming Abuse Relationships) Program has a volunteer group of domestic violence survivors whose mission is to

promote, advocate, and work for the elimination of domestic violence and to provide a voice to battered women everywhere. SOAR provides a way for women to work together to change the systems that perpetuate domestic violence. This is accomplished through participation in local public education efforts, speaking engagements, and working with the media to spread the message that violence against women is not acceptable.

• YWCA Pueblo's (Colorado) Teresa's Place Visitation and Safe Exchange Program provides a safe and secure place for parents to visit or exchange their children when domestic violence, sexual assault, child abuse, or stalking has occurred within the family. The unique setup is designed to assure that children affected by an abusive relationship can have safe contact with the absent parent without having to be put in the middle of their parents' conflicts or problems. This setup allows children to maintain a relationship with both of their parents—an important factor in having a positive adjustment during family dissolution.

Jane Teaford

See also: Battered Women Shelters; Domestic Abuse, Psychological Effects of; Violence Against Women Act.

Further Reading

Agosto, Denise E. 2013. "The Big Picture of YA Services." *Young Adult Library Services* 11 (3): 13–18.

Bogue, Ellie. 2012. "YWCA Provides a Haven from Domestic Violence." *News-Sentinel*, Fort Wayne, IN, October 25.

YWCA. n.d. "YWCA Domestic Violence and Violence Against Women Programs." http://www.ywca.org/atf/cf/%7bbf8ea0ec-d765-4988-acd0-e6f97718cc89%7d/ywca-domestic-violence-and-violence-against-women-programs-042213.pdf.

Index

Page references to main articles are indicated by **bold type.** Page references to photographs are in *italics.*

About the Editor

Rosemarie Skaine, MA, has published 13 books and numerous articles. Her published works include ABC-CLIO's *Suicide Warfare: Culture, the Military, and the Individual as a Weapon*, and *Women in Combat: A Reference Handbook*, as well as *Paternity and American Law*. She was keynote speaker on "Suicide Warfare and Violence Against Women" at the Interactive Dialogue panel "Dying to Kill: The Allure of Female Suicide Bombers," United Nations Commission on the Status of Women 57: Elimination and Prevention of All Forms of Violence Against Women and Girls, March 2013.

Her special awards include the Gustavus Myers Center Award for the Study of Human Rights in North America for her outstanding work on intolerance in North America for *Power and Gender: Issues in Sexual Dominance and Harassment*. She is included in Marquis's *Who's Who in the World*, *Who's Who in America*, and *Who's Who of American Women*.

Skaine holds a master's degree in sociology from the University of Northern Iowa.

Contributors

Lauren Krohn Arnest
Independent Writer

Henry Frank Carey
Georgia State University

Gerhard Falk
Buffalo State College

Juan Carlos Hernandez
Independent Writer

Karunya Jayasena
Independent Writer

Connie Kerns-Grams
Independent Writer

Shawna Lee
University of Michigan, Ann Arbor

Mary Little
University of Central Florida

Carolyn Martin
Independent Writer

Caryn E. Neumann
Miami University

Jacqueline K. Payne
Planned Parenthood Federation of America

Mohammad Sajjadur Rahman
University of Chittagong (Bangladesh)

Erin Solaro
Independent Writer

Jyotsna Sreenivasan
Independent Writer

Randal W. Summers, PhD
Independent Writer

Jane Teaford
Independent Writer

Courtney Blair Thornton
Independent Writer

Judith Ann Warner
Texas A&M International University